TABLE OF INDEX

TABLE OF INDEX

INSTRUCTIONS

The answers to each problem is in the back of this book, section 100.0. I think it is best for the parents to remove this part of the book.

Calculators are allowed only on question that start with the number 4, or the Geometry section

The problems might not be in sequential order. Don't worry its correct.

If you don't get the correct answer, and want an explanation on how to work the problem, go to YouTube and type in "MMT" then the problem number. An example would be, MMT 3.9.w12,. The video will show you how to work problem 3.9.w12.

For one on one tutoring via skype at $35.00/Hr.; contact me at marksmathtutoring@yahoo.com

REFERENCES

LENGTH

ENGLISH

1 mile (mi) = 1,760 yards (yds)
1 yard (yd) = 3 feet (ft)
1 foot (ft) = 12 inches (in)

METRIC

1 kilometer (km) = 1,000 meters (m)
1 meter (m) = 100 centimeters (cm)
1 centimeters (cm) = 10 millimeters (mm)

VOLUME AND CAPACITY

ENGLISH

1 gallon (gal) = 4 quarts (gt)
1 quart (qt) = 2 pints (pt)
1 pint (pt) = 2 cups (c)
1 cup © = 8 fluid ounces (fl oz)

METRIC

1 liter = 1,000 millimeters (ml)

WEIGHT AND MASS

ENGLISH

1 ton (T) = 2,000 pounds (lb)
1 pound (lb) = 16 ounces (oz)

METRIC

1 kilogram (kg) = 1,000 grams (g)
1 gram (g) = 1,000 milligrams (mg)

TIME

1 year = 12 months
1 year = 52 weeks
1 week = 7 days
1 day = 24 hours
1 hour = 60 minutes
1 minute = 60 seconds

REFERENCES

PERIMETER

Square 4 X SIDE = PERIMETER

Rectangle LENGTH + LENGTH + SIDE + SIDE = PERIMETER

Circle $C=2\Pi R$ or $C=\Pi D$

AREA

Square SIDE X SIDE = AREA

Rectangle or parallelogram LENGTH X SIDE = AREA

Triangle (1/2)BH or (1/2) Base X Height

Trapezoid $(1/2)(b_1+b_2)H$

Circle $A=\Pi R^2$

VOLUME

Rectangle prism or Cylinder V=BHW

Pyramid or Cone $V={}^1/_3BH$

Sphere $V={}^4/_3\Pi R^3$

LINEAR EQUATIONS

Slope-Intercept Form	Y=MX+B
Slope of a Line	m= $^{(y2-y1)}$ / $_{(x2-x1)}$

SURFACE AREA

	Lateral	Total
Prism	S=PL	S=PH+2B
Cylinder	S=2ΠRH	$S=2\Pi RH+2\Pi R^2$

EXTRA INFO

Pythagorean Theorem	$a^2+b^2=c^2$
Simple Interest	I=PRT
Compound Interest	$A=P(1+R)^T$

If you don't get the correct answer, and want an explanation on how to work the problem, go to YouTube and type in "MMT" then the problem number. An example would be, MMT 3.9.w12,. The video will show you how to work problem 3.9.w12.

DEFINITIONS

Sum is the answer after adding the numbers

Product is the answer after dividing the numbers

Difference is the answer after subtracting the numbers

Congruent means if two shapes have the same shape and size of each other. They don't need two have the same orientation. In other words one can be up side down from the other.

Lines of symmetry is a line that divides a shape into two equal size and shape. Two examples are shown below

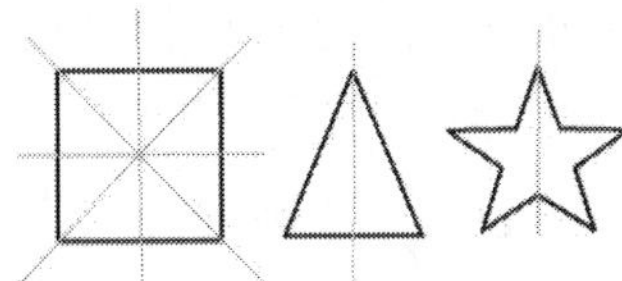

Vertical Line of Symmetry the shape can be divided into two equal sizes and shapes about a vertical line

Horizontal Line of Symmetry the shape can be divided into two equal sizes and shapes about a horizontal line

Transition The object remains the same size and shape but is slide or moved up down or to the side

Rotational Transition The object remains the same size and shape but is rotated or spun around

Reflection Transition The object remains the same size and shape but is flipped over and would have the image a mirror would give

Right Angle: The measure of the angle is 90 degrees

Serza is a 7 sided figure. It is also called a heptagon. Example is below.

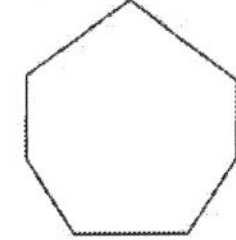

Rhombus is a figure with four side all of equal length. All Rhombuses are parallelograms and kites. A square is a Rhombus with all 90 degree angle. A diamond, or kite shape is also a Rhombus. Two example are below.

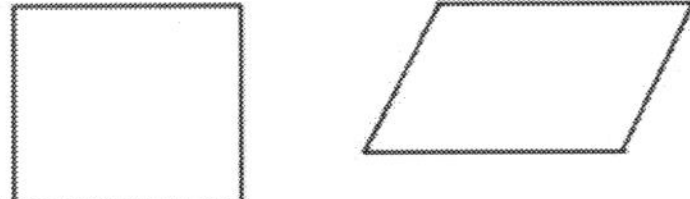

Square is a parallelogram with 4 right angle (90 degrees), or a Quadrilaterals with 4 right angles with four sides of equal length

Kite: Is a Rhombus with angles that are not right angles (90 degrees)

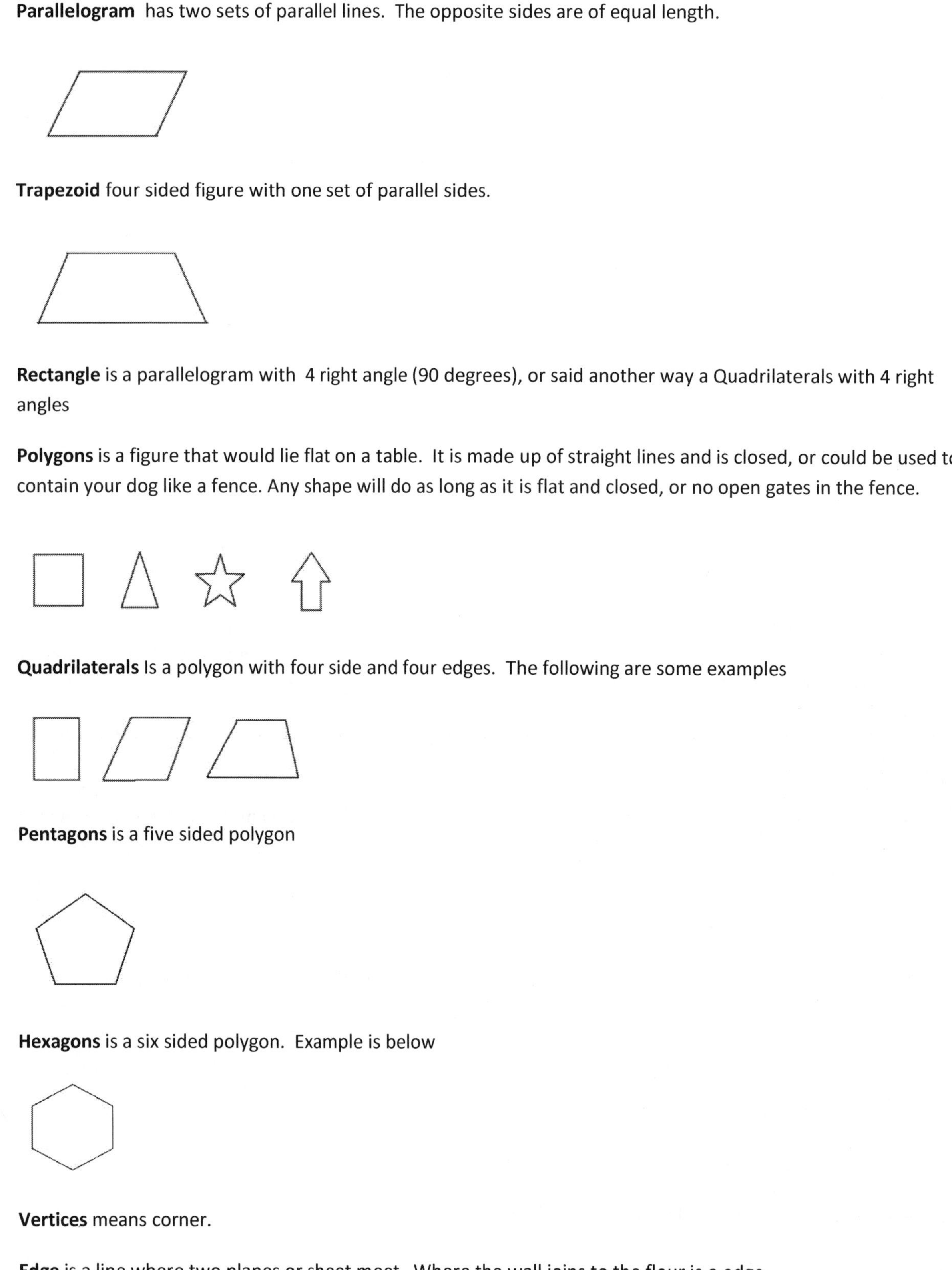

Parallelogram has two sets of parallel lines. The opposite sides are of equal length.

Trapezoid four sided figure with one set of parallel sides.

Rectangle is a parallelogram with 4 right angle (90 degrees), or said another way a Quadrilaterals with 4 right angles

Polygons is a figure that would lie flat on a table. It is made up of straight lines and is closed, or could be used to contain your dog like a fence. Any shape will do as long as it is flat and closed, or no open gates in the fence.

Quadrilaterals Is a polygon with four side and four edges. The following are some examples

Pentagons is a five sided polygon

Hexagons is a six sided polygon. Example is below

Vertices means corner.

Edge is a line where two planes or sheet meet. Where the wall joins to the flour is a edge.

Parallel lines: Two lines in the same plane that never change the distance between them

Acute Angle: An angle that is less than 90 degrees

Obtuse Angle: An angle that is more than 90 degrees

Right Angle: An angle that is exactly 90 degrees

Complementary Angle: Two angle that add up to 90 degrees

Supplementary Angle: Two angle that add up to 180 degrees

Similar: If the measure of a angel is the same as the measure of another angle that is corresponding

Isosceles triangle: Triangle with two side of equal length.

Equilateral Triangle: triangle with three side of equal length

Congruent: Two geometric shapes that have the size and shape

NUMBERS

Even is a whole number that is divisible by two. The best way at your age to determine this is start with 2 and count up by 2s. Ex 2, 4, 6, 8, 10, etc. If you say the number it is even.

Odd whole number that is not even. The last digit of the number is a 1,3,5,7,or a 9. Examples of add number would ne 221, 683, 66889, or 7.

ONES PLACE: is the place holding the smallest value. The underlined bold number is in the ones place in these examples: 2**4**, 34**6**, 48**6**, 126**7**, 32**5**, 67**9**,1125**8**

TENS PLACE: IS the smallest value that can divided by 10 evenly. The underlined bold number is in the tens place in these examples: 2**3**6, **4**5, 57**7**8, 825**7**8, **5**4, 1**2**8, 7**7**8

HUNDREDS PLACE: TENS PLACE: IS the smallest value that can divided by 100 evenly. The underlined bold number is in the hundreds place in these examples: **1**27, 3**4**67, 5**7**88, 3**2**75, **3**46

THOUSANDS PLACE: IS the smallest value that can divided by 1000 evenly. The underlined bold number is in the THOUSANDS place in these examples: **3**276, 4**5**887, **2**457, 1**1**278, 1**2**895

Interest Is the extra money you pay back. If you borrow $200 and pay back $210, the interest is $10.

Rational Number: Any number that can be expressed as a fraction of two integers

Integer: A number that can be written without a fraction

Whole number: The numbers we use to count plus the number 0

Irrational number: A number that is not rational is a repeating decimal without a pattern, such as Π

UNITS

Units of weight: pounds, grams, ounces, tones

Units of volume: Gallons, quarts, pints

Units of Length: Centimeter (cm), Millimeter (mm), Meter (m), Kilometer, Inch (in), Foot (ft), Mile

SYMBOLS

GREATER THAN: Uses the symbol **>** It mean the item on the left is greater than the item on the right. An example would be 8>3. In words this is eight is greater than 3. Remember the bird always eats the bigger worm.

LESS THAN: Uses the symbol **<** It mean the item on the left is less than the item on the right. An example would be 8<3. In words this is eight is greater than 3. Remember the bird always eats the bigger worm.

GREATER THAN OR EQUAL TO: Uses the symbol ≥ It mean the item on the left is greater than or equal to the item on the right. An example would be 8≥8. In words this is eight is greater than or equal to 8. Remember the bird always eats the bigger worm.

LESS THAN OR EQUAL TO: Uses the symbol ≤ It mean the item on the left is less than or equal to the item on the right. An example would be 8≤8. In words this is eight is greater than or equal to 8. Remember the bird always eats the bigger worm.

Mean: average means the same. Add all the number up and then divide by the total number of numbers you added

Median: Put the number is order of least to greatest. The number is the middle is the median. If there is two numbers in the middle then add them together and divide the sum by 2

Mode: The number that occurs most frequently in the data.

Range: The difference between the high and the low of a set of numbers

Interquartile Range. In a set of numbers ordered from low to high, the Q1 is the middle between the first value and the mean. The Q3 is the middle between the mean and the last value. If there are a even number of values take the average of the two middle ones. The interquartile is the difference between Q1 and Q3.

Dependent Variable: The number you get out of an equation, usually the Y value

Independent Variable: The number you put into the equation, usually the X value

2.0 LOGIC

2.1) What would be the best unit of measurement for the size of your dog?
a) Gallons, b) pounds, c) pints, d) Quart

2.2) You parents borrowed $5,000.00 from the bank to buy a car. They repaid $6,500.00. Which statement best explains why they paid the extra $1,500.00
a) They wanted to donate $1,500.00 to the bank to be nice
b) They repaid the loan on a week day and the bank charges money for these days
c) They had extra money and nothing to do with it.
d) The bank charged $1,500.00 in interest for a $6,000.00 loan

2.3) I'm thinking of a number. It has a 3 in the thousands place and a 4 in the hundreds place Which of the following could be the number I am think about?
a) 1,356
b) 3,247
c) 3,456
d) 4,389

2.4) I'm thinking of a number. It has a 4 in the thousands place and a 5 in the tens place. Which of the following could be the number I am think about?
a) 2,557
b) 1376
c) 4,157
d) 6578

2.5) I'm thinking of a number. It has a 2 in the tens place and a 7 in the ones place. Which of the following could be the number I am thinking about?
a) 137
b) 27
c) 331
d) 72

2.6) I'm thinking of a number. It has a 6 in the thousands place and a 8 in the ones place. Which of the following could be the number I am thinking about?
a) 8,236
b) 4,468
c) 4,648
d) 6,458

2.7) What number is in the hundreds palace of 137

2.8) What number is in the thousands place of 7,689

2.9) Which of the following has the same value of 6,315,256
a)6,000,000+300,000+5,000,+200+50+6
b)6,000,000+300,000+10,000+200+50+6
c)6,000,000+300,000+10,000+5,000,+200
d)6,000,000+300,000+10,000+5,000,+200+50+6

2.10) Which of the following has the same value of 140,312
a)100,000+140,000+3000+10+2
b) 1,400,000+40,000+300+10+2
c) 100,000+40,000+10+2
d) 100,000+40,000+300+10+2

2.11) The number 65.03 can be expressed as
a) (6X10)+(5X1)+(3X0.10)
b) (6X10)+(50X1)+(3X0.01)
c) (6X10)+(50X1)+(3X0.10)
d) (6X10)+(5X1)+(3X0.01)

2.12) The number 142.18 can be expressed as
a) (1X100)+(40X10)+(2X1)+(1X0.1)X(8X0.01)
b) (1X100)+(4X10)+(2X1)+(1X0.01)X(8X0.01)
c) (1X100)+(4X10)+(2X1)+(1X0.1)X(8X0.001)
d) (1X100)+(4X10)+(2X1)+(1X0.1)X(8X0.01)

2.13) What is the relationship between the hundreds place and the tens place in the number 4,221
a) The hundreds place is 2 times larger than the tens place
b) The hundreds place is 1 more than the tens place
c) The hundreds place is 10 times the tens place
d) There is no relationship between them.

2.14) What is the relationship between the thousands place and the hundreds place in the number 4,411
a) The hundreds place is 2 times larger than the tens place
b) The hundreds place is 1 more than the tens place
c) The thousands place is 10 times the hundreds place
d) There is no relationship between them.

2.15) Which statement about the number 48 is true
a) It is odd, because it can be divided by 3
b) It is even, because it can be divided by 2
c) It is even because 8+4=12 is even
d) It is even because 4 and 8 are both even

2.16) Which of the following numbers is even
a) 27, b) 32, c) 81, d) 127

2.17) Which of the following numbers is even
a) 236, b) 137, c) 5179, d) 331

2.18) Which of the following numbers is odd
a) 24, b) 377, c) 6428, d) 46

2.19) Which of the following numbers is odd
a) 45, b) 224, c) 56, d) 2246

2.20) Which of the following numbers is even
a) 2278, b) 321, c) 56797, d) 33

2.21) Which of the following numbers is odd
a) 3357, b) 324, a) 32, d) 124

4.22) Loren has six football jerseys hanging on the wall. Which ones are even numbered?

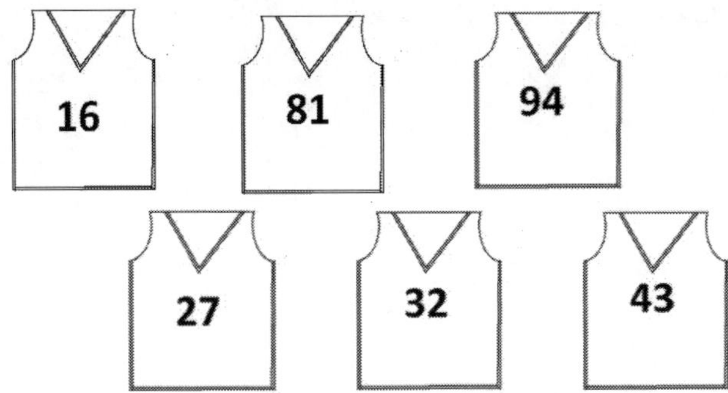

2.23) There are four glass of milk in the refrigerator. Glass A is 4 days older than glass B. Glass B is 6 days older than glass C. Glass C is twice the age as glass D. D is 3 days old. What is the combined age in days of all four glasses?

2.24) If you roll a dice and spin the spinner. How many combination with an odd number can occur?

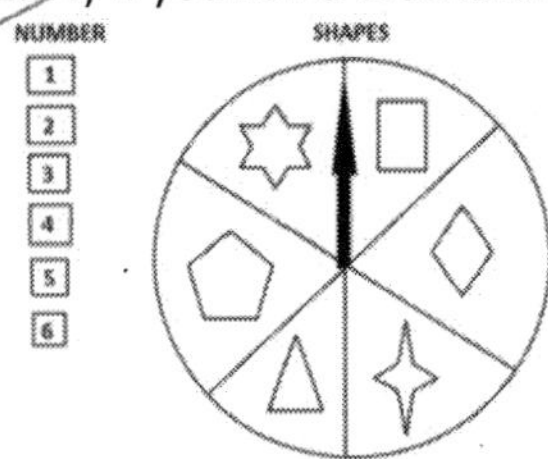

2.25) Given the combinations of types of music at a party and snakes how many combination are possible?

MUSIC

ROCK
JAZZ
CLASSICAL
POP
OPERA

SNACKS

CANDY
POPCORN
CAKE
PIE

2.26) Given the options of clothing how many possible options are available?

SHIRTS

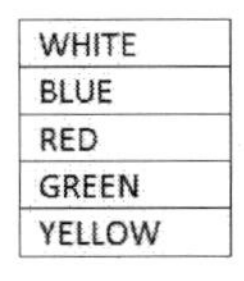

WHITE
BLUE
RED
GREEN
YELLOW

PANTS

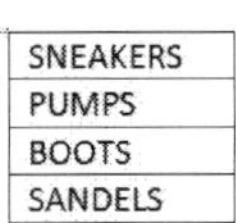

SHORTS
JEANS
SLACKS

SHOES

SNEAKERS
PUMPS
BOOTS
SANDELS

Croquis of a Deliberate Crime

For one on one tutoring via skype at $35.00/Hr.; contact me at marksmathtutoring@yahoo.com

2.27) I am thinking of a number. There are three clues below.

The value of the digit 7 is (7X100)
The value of the digit 6 is (6X10)
The value of the digit 3 is (3X1)

Which of the following number could be the number I am thinking about

a) 367
b) 673
c) 763
d) 736

2.28) I am thinking of a number. There are three clues below.

The value of the digit 5 is (5X1000)
The value of the digit 5 is (5X10)
The value of the digit 4 is (4X1)

Which of the following number could be the number I am thinking about

a) 5054
b) 5145
c) 4154
d) 5545

2.29) A book has the weight of 3 kilograms. Which of the following could have the same mass.

a) a car
b) airplane
c) peanut
d) small cat

2.30) There four times as many birds as dogs in my neighborhood. There are three times as many cats as dogs. Which combination below could be the population of this neighborhood.

A) 12 dogs, 4 cats, 24 birds
B) 12 dogs, 4 cats, 3 birds
C) 12 dogs, 48 birds, 36 cats
D) 12 dogs, 4 cats, 4 cats

2.31) If I make cookies with the following rations

64 chocolate
23 mores oatmeal than chocolate
17 more peanut butter than oatmeal

What is the total number of cookies I made

2.32) I caught 124.6 pounds of fish. My friend caught 3 times this. What was the weight of the fish he caught.

2.33) On my fishing trip I caught the following fish.

236 mediums
29 less then mediums were large
69 more than mediums were small

How many small fish did I catch

2.34) What is the relationship between the number pairs below
(12, 168), (8,112), (16,224), (18,252)
A) The first number is the quotient of the second divided by 14
B) The first number is the sum of the second plus 146
C) The first number is the product of the first multiplied by 8
D) The first number is the result of the first minus 146

2.35) My dog is 3 ½ years older than mikes dog. Sarah's dog is 5 ¼ year older than mike's dog. Mikes dog is 12 years old. What is the age of my dog?

2.36) If I start washing cars at 10:45 and wash for 2 hours and 54 minutes, and wash 7 cars how long does each car take me.

2.37) My dogs weights 10 pounds. One day he drinks three times his weight in water and ate half his weight in food. What is his final weight.

2.38) There are two taxi cabs services in my town. They charge a fixed price for the pickup and a variable price for each mile as shown below.

COMPANY	PICK UP COST	COST PER MILE
A	$5.00	$0.50
B	$8.00	$1.00

Based on this information if I am going 12 miles which company would be cheaper to hire?

2.39) There are two cell phone services in my town. They charge a fixed price for each month and a variable price for each hour of use as shown below.

COMPANY	MONTHLY	HOURLY
A	$15.00	$0.25
B	$20.00	$0.36

Based on this information if I am going to use the phone for 150 hours a month which company would be cheaper to hire?

2.40) There are two pizza delivery services in my town. They charge a fixed price for the drop off and a variable price for each pizza as shown below.

COMPANY	DROP OFF COST	EACH PIZZA
A	$15.00	$12.00
B	$18.00	$11.00

Based on this information if I am going to buy 5 pizzas which company would be cheaper to hire?

2.41) An text book is divided into two parts, history and math, in a ratio of 2:3. If the book is 450 pages long how many pages does the math section have

2.42) If there are 90 dogs in the neighborhood. They are in the ration of 6 small for every 3 big. How many big dogs are there.

2.43) 64 kids are going to the movies. The ratio of girls to boys is 3:5. How many girls are in this group.

2.44) If I buy 5 pies for 60 dollars how much would 7 pies cost

2.45) If admission to a theme park cost $125 for 5 kids, what would be the cost of 8 kids.

2.46) If movie tickets cost $49 for 7 kids, how much 9 kids cost

2.47) 8 books cost $96, how much would 9 books cost

2.48) 12 bowls of soap cost $144, how much does 8 bowls of soap cost

2.49) Are the ratios 2:3 and 24:36 the same

2.50) Are the rations 4:5 and 16:20 the same

2.51) Are the rations 6:8 and 42: 64 the same

2.52) Are the ratios 3:5 and 21:45 the same

2.53) Are the rations 4:7 and 24:42 the same

2.54) Given the drawing below what is the length of the segment labeled A

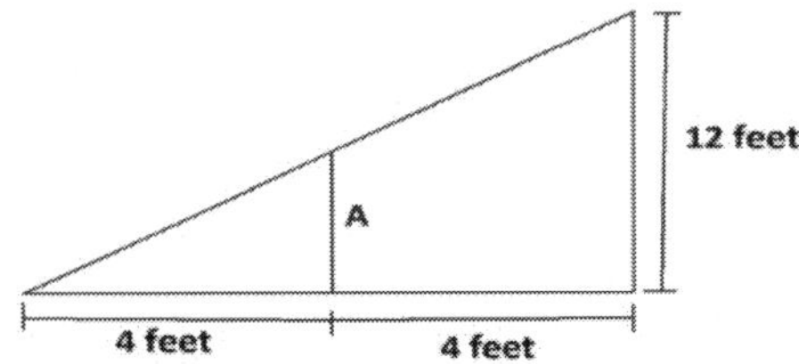

2.55) Given the drawing below what is the length of A

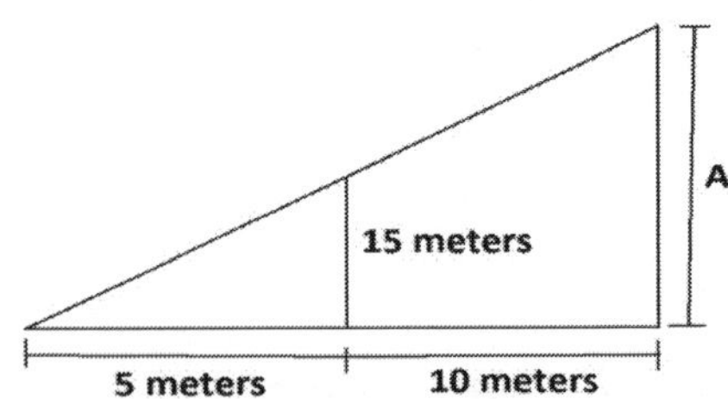

2.56) If I use 350 chocolate chips to make 50 cookies how many chips will I used for 65 cookies

2.57) My 2 dogs eats 12 pounds of food per day. How much food would 3 dogs eat per day

2.58) There are 32 slices of pizza in 4 pizza pies. How many slices would there be in 7 pizza pies.

2.59) A dolphin eats 120 fish in 4 hours. How many fish will it eat in 7 hours.

2.60) The following is a list of ingredients used to make 12 cookies.

6 eggs
12 tablespoons butter
4 chocolate chips
2 cups flour

Based on this information which statement below is **NOT** true to make 18 cookies

A) 9 eggs
B) 18 tablespoons of butter
C) 5 chocolate chips
D) 3 cups flour

2.61) If my car burns 6 gallons of gas to drive 72 miles, how much gas will it use for 132 mile trip

2.62) If I use 3 cups butter for 4 pounds sugar to make pies. Which table below show this relationship.

A)

BUTTER	3	6	9	15
SUGAR	4	8	12	20

B)

BUTTER	3	6	9	15
SUGAR	4	10	12	20

C)

BUTTER	3	6	9	15
SUGAR	4	8	12	18

D)

BUTTER	3	6	9	15
SUGAR	4	8	16	20

2.63) 8 goats eat 24 pounds of food in 1 days. At this rate how much will 10 goats eat per day.

2.64) I bought three toys. The most expensive was $8.40 and the least was $4.51. which of the following could be the total cost of the toys.

A)$16.32

B) $34.39

C) $19.41

D)$21.41

2.65) Which description best described the relationship between X and Y as shown below

Y = 2X

#Y = 2 + X

A) In the equation Y = 2X, Y is two times X and in the equation Y = 2 + X, Y is twice X

B) In the equation Y = 2X, Y is two more than X and in the equation Y = 2 + X, Y is twice X

C) In the equation Y = 2X, Y is two times X and in the equation Y = 2 + X, Y is two more than X

D) In the equation Y = 2X, and the equation Y = 2 + X, Y is more than X

2.66) Which statement cannot be represented by the equation X + 10 = 34

A) I bought fishing equipment for $45.00. The real cost $10.00, and the pole cost X

B) I ran for 34 miles last week. Monday I ran 10 miles and the rest of the week I ran x miles

C) I caught two fish. The first weighted 10 pounds and the second weighted x pounds. The total weight was 34 pounds

D) I gave 10 friends X cupcakes. The total cupcakes was 34.

2.67) At a school of 800 kids 3 out of 5 ate a hamburger for lunch. What was the total number that ate a burger

2.68) If I catch 3 bass for every 5 trout, and I catch a total of 168 fish, how many are trout

2.69) two dogs weigth in proportion of 2:5. If their weights in total are 840 what is the weight of the smaller one

2.70) 400 kids are interviewed and asked what is their favorite food. For every 2 that said hamburger 3 said pizza. How many of the 400 picked pizza

2.71) I make 12 more chocolate chip cookies than oatmeal. I make 8 less peanut butter than oatmeal. If make 100 chocolate chip cookies how many peanut butter cookies did I make

Croquis of a Deliberate Crime

2.72) If cookies cost $3.00 for 12 cookies, and I spend $8.00 which equation below could help me determine how many cookies I will get

A) $^{3}/_{12}={}^{X}/_{12}$

B) $^{8}/_{3}={}^{x}/_{12}$

C) $^{X}/_{12}={}^{3}/_{12}$

D) $X={}^{3}/_{12X12}$

2.73) I started fishing at 7:26 a.m.

I stopped fishing at 10:16

#I caught 5 fish

What was the average time to catch each fish

2.74) If I am making dinner and the recipe for 6 people is given below

4 cups butter

#2 pounds rice

3 pounds meat

6 tomatoes

Which of the following would be true if I make dinner for 10 people

A) 6 cups butter

B) 5 pounds meat

C) 3 pounds rice

D) 10 tomatoes

2.75) If I go to a theme park and the price is $10.00 for an adult, and $6.00 for a child. Which equation below best describes the total amount, t, for a adults and k kids

A) t = 6a+10k

B) t= (10+6)x(a+k)

C) t= 10k+6a

D) t= 10a+6K

2.76) A school comprises 100% of boys and girls. If the girls make up 53% of the population which equation below could be used to find the percentage of boys, B.

A) 100+53=B

B) 53-100=B

C) 100-53=B

D) 53+100=B

2.77) Two different phone companies charge the following fees for service

COMPANY	CHARGES
X	$5.00 + $0.01 per minute
Y	$10.00

Based on the information in the table which of the following is true

A) Company X will always be cheaper

B) Company Y will always be cheaper

C) At 510 minutes company X becomes less expensive

D) At 500 minutes both companies charge the same

2.78) If 1.5 gallons is 12 pints how many pints is 4 gallons

2.79) If I charge $155 for the first hour and $125 for the following hours and I earned 530 how many hours did I work

2.80) If I eat 4 cupcakes in 32 minutes, how many would I eat in 24 minutes

2.81) If I buy 2.5 ounces of silver for $42.5 what is the price for one ounce

2.82) If I use 24 chocolate chips to make 6 cookies how many chips will I use to make 300 cookies.

2.83) If I make a model of a town using 1 inch equals 2 miles and the town is 4.5 miles wide how wide is my model

2.84) If I draw a map of a state and one inch is equal to 85 miles and the state is 425 miles wide how many inches is the state in my map

2.85) Given the table below, about the number of cookies I eat each day for 3 weeks

	Mon	Tue	Wed	Thur	Fri	Sat	Sun
Wk 1	25	12	25	14	10	20	10
Wk 2	20	15	30	20	15	25	15
Wk 3	15	10	20	15	15	25	13

Which of the following statements is **NOT** true
A) I ate three more cookies in the first week than the third week
B) I ate the most cookies in the second week
C) I ate the most cookies on the Wednesdays
D) I ate the least number of cookies of Sunday

2.86) When I interviewed the kids at a school I asked them which deserts they ate in the last week I got the following data

9 cake only
10 Pie only
#12 Cookies only
5 Cake and Pie
7 Cake and Cookies
3 Pie and Cookies
2 ate all three

Based on this information which of the following Venn diagrams describes this data

A)

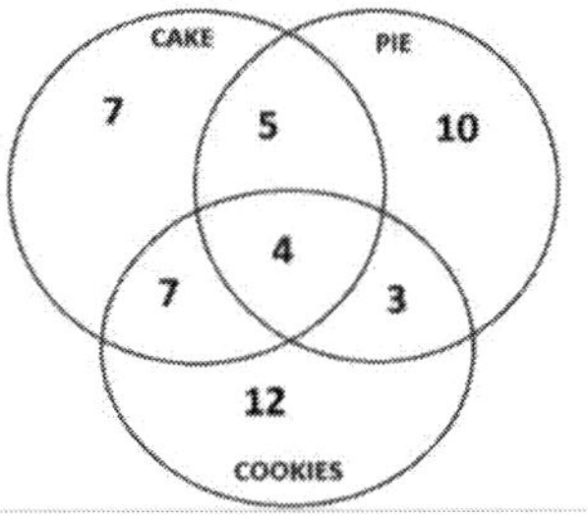

CAKE
PIE
7
5
10
4
7
3
12
COOKIES

B)

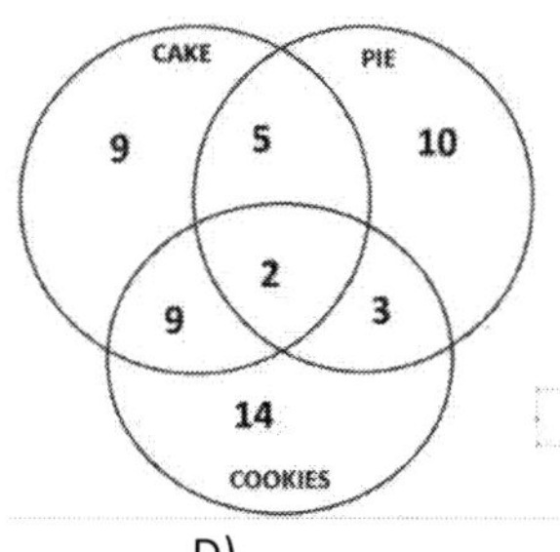

C)

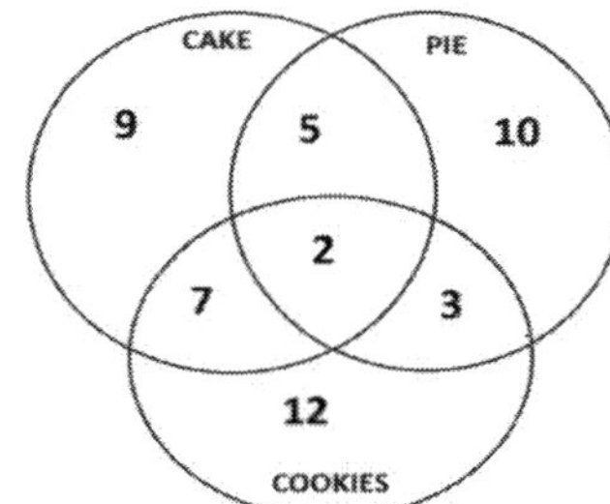

D)

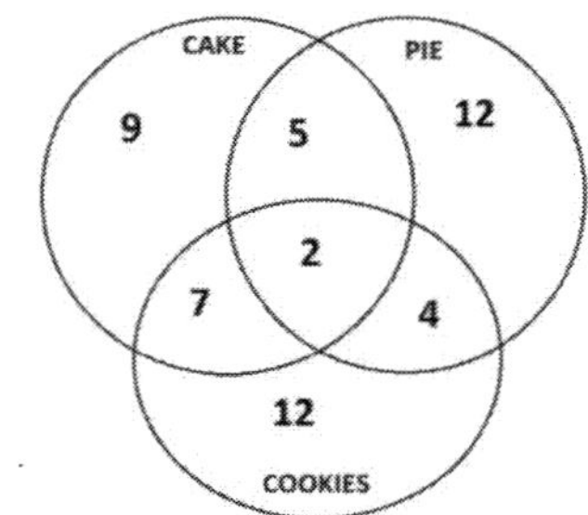

2.87) If I caught 200 fish while on vacation in the proportions show in the diagram below

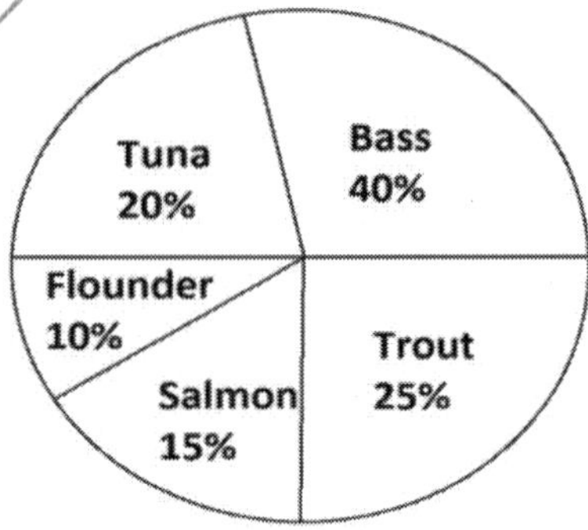

Which of the following statements is **NOT** true
A) I caught 40 Tuna
B) I caught 120 Bass and Tuna
C) I caught 10 Flounder
D) I caught 80 Salmon and Trout

2.88) If I spin the two spinners shown below how many outcomes are possible

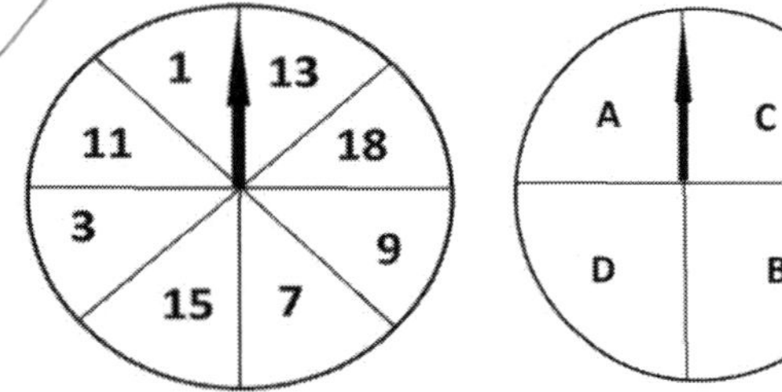

2.89) If in 4 days I spend 1 hour and 45 minutes on Math homework and 1 hour on History homework how much time will spend on Math in 7 days.

2.90) If I loss ¾ of a pound per day which of the following equation could help me determine the amount of weight I have lost by the 7 day.
A) Add ¾ to the product of 7 and $^3/_4$
B) The product of seven and three fourths
C) The sum of ¾ six times
D) The product of six times three fourths

2.91) If I run 30 miles in two hours. How far will I run in 4.5 hours.

2.92) At a school football game 2 out of 7 students attending were in the band. If 2170 students were there how many were band members.

2.93) If I buy 6 boxes of cupcakes and each has 24 cakes in them of which 8 are chocolate. How many chocolate cakes did I get.

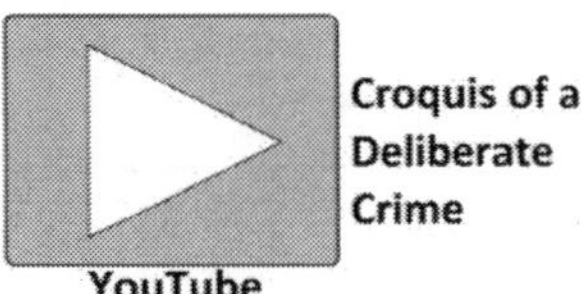

2.94) I surveyed the dog owners in my neighborhood to see if they like hamburgers or pizza better. Which of the following could best describe the problem with this approach
A) I should have interviewed the cat owners
B) I should have interviewed half the dog owners
C) The interview strategy was perfect
D) I should have interviewed everyone in the neighborhood to get a true cross section of the population

2.95) If the circle drawn below is rotated about the origin for 180 degrees clockwise what expression below best describe the new coordinates

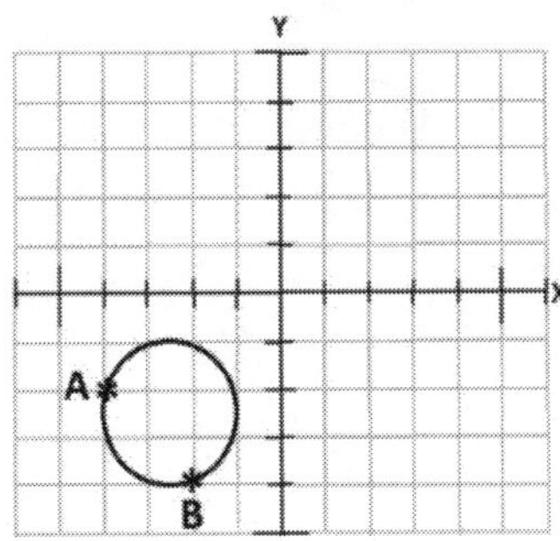

A) (X,Y)→(Y,X)
B) (X,Y)→(X,-Y)
C) (X,Y)→(-X,Y)
D) (X,Y)→(-X,-Y)

2.96) I placed food out for the squires to eat. I plotted the amount of food and the number of squirrels that showed up. The results are shown below

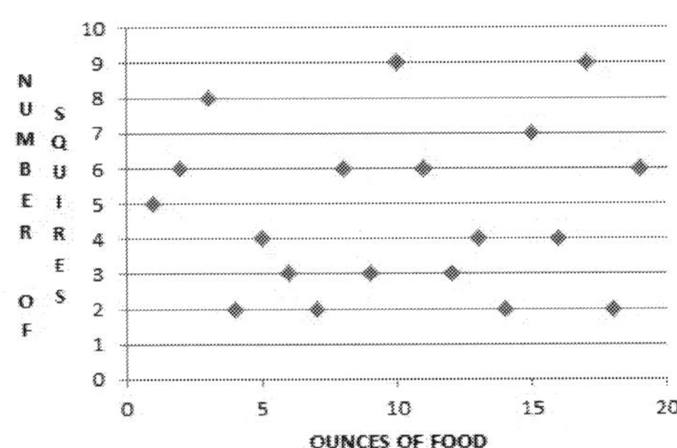

Which of the following conclusions is supported by the data shown above
A) The more food I put out the more squires showed up
B) There is no relationship between the number of squires and the amount of food
C) The more squires that showed up the more food I put out
D) The more food I put out the fewer squires showed up

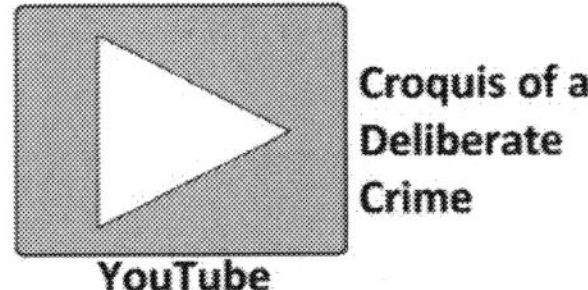

For one on one tutoring via skype at $35.00/Hr.; contact me at marksmathtutoring@yahoo.com

2.97) If the following diagram is reflected across the Y axis which of the following would describe the transformation

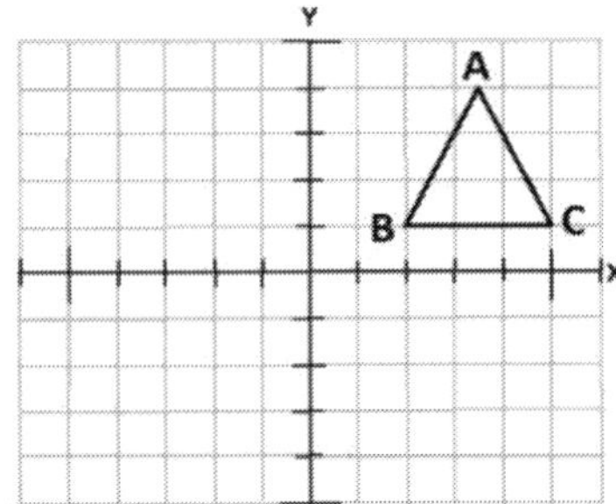

A) (X,Y)→(Y,X)
B) (X,Y)→(X,-Y)
C) (X,Y)→(-X,Y)
D) (X,Y)→(-X,-Y)

Conversions

2.1.1) If I have 12 gallons of ice cream how many cups do I have

2.1.2) If my dogs weights 34 kilograms how many milligrams is this

2.1.3) How many ounces are in 9.5 pounds

2.1.4) If a fish is 1 meter and 23 centimeters long is it in millimeters.

2.1.5) If a garden has a perimeter of 762 ft how many yards long is it.

2.1.6) If a fish weight 2.36 kilograms which of the following is the same value in grams
A)2360 milligrams
B) 236 milligrams
C) 2 $^{36}/_{100}$ Milligrams
D) 2360 grams

2.1.7) If I drink 3 gallons of apple juice how many pints have I drank

2.1.8) If the fish I caught was 3 feet and 4 inches long and there are 2.53 centimeters in a inch how long is the fish in centimeters

2.1.9) How many fluid ounces are there in 4 liters if 1 ounce has 29.6 milliliters

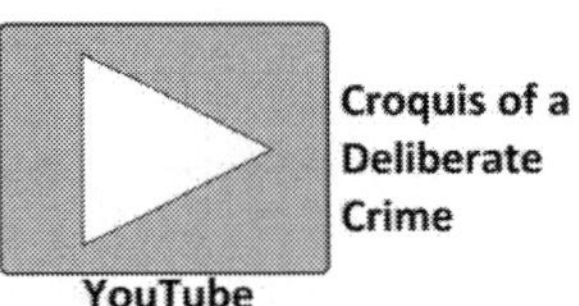

3 ARITHMETIC

3.1 Addition-Single Digits

3.1.1) 1+3=	3.1.2) 2+0=	3.1.3) 4+6=	3.1.4) 5+8=	3.1.5) 3+2=	3.1.6) 7+3=
3.1.7) 3+0=	3.1.8) 7+9=	3.1.9) 1+8=	3.1.10) 5+5=	3.1.11) 7+4=	3.1.12) 2+6=
3.1.13) 4+5=	3.1.14) 5+9=	3.1.15) 2+5=	3.1.16) 6+9=	3.1.17) 4+2=	3.1.18) 3+8=
3.1.19) 2+2=	3.1.20) 4+8=	3.1.21) 8+2=	3.1.22) 9+5=	3.1.23) 6+4=	3.1.24) 8+5=
3.1.25) 4+7=	3.1.26) 8+7=	3.1.27) 9+9=	3.1.28) 9+0=	3.1.29) 6+6=	3.1.30) 2+7=
3.1.31) 1+2=	3.1.32) 7+8=	3.1.33) 6+2=	3.1.34) 3+4=	3.1.35) 9+4=	3.1.36) 1+5=
3.1.37) 7+6=	3.1.38) 8+8=	3.1.39) 9+6=	3.1.40) 1+6=	3.1.41) 6+5=	3.1.42) 9+2=
3.1.43) 7 +3	3.1.44) 9 +4	3.1.45) 3 +6	3.1.46) 5 +9	3.1.47) 8 +5	3.1.48) 5 +7
3.1.49) 8 +8	3.1.50) 7 +2	3.1.51) 6 +4	3.1.52) 7 +7	3.1.53) 3 +2	3.1.54) 2 +9

3.2 Addition-Two Digits

3.2.1)11+23=	3.2.2)22+20=	3.2.3)34+16=	3.2.4)65+68=	3.2.5)83+22=	3.2.6)33+60=
3.2.7)17+39=	3.2.8)81+48=	3.2.9)65+05=	3.2.10)37+74=	3.2.11)34+25=	3.2.12)85+39=
3.2.13)72+35=	3.2.14)16+49=	3.2.15)44+92=	3.2.16)92+12=	3.2.17)44+28=	3.2.18)28+32=
3.2.19)19+55=	3.2.20)36+54=	3.2.21)84+67=	3.2.22)98+27=	3.2.23)29+59=	3.2.24)19+40=
3.2.25)36+66=	3.2.26)11+62=	3.2.27)47+38=	3.2.28)76+12=	3.2.29)23+64=	3.2.30)79+54=
3.2.31)37+46=	3.2.32)18+88=	3.2.33)79+26=	3.2.34)31+56=	3.2.35)26+85=	3.2.36) 40+31=
3.2.37) 21 +34	3.2.38) 57 +56	3.2.39) 89 +32	3.2.40) 65 +67	3.2.41) 81 +83	3.2.42) 51 +17
3.2.43) 75 +46	3.2.44) 67 +76	3.2.45) 32 +88	3.2.46) 99 +37	3.2.47) 27 +28	3.2.48) 31 +98

3.3 Multiple Digit Addition

3.3.1)111+2365=	3.3.2)2227+201=	3.3.3)343+160	3.3.4)165+6825=
3.3.5)8301+22=	3.3.6)331+602=	3.3.7)1775+39=	3.3.8)811+483=
3.3.9)6523+105=	3.3.10)376+742=	3.3.11)345+255=	3.3.12)854+399=
3.3.13)726+355=	3.3.14)116+949=	3.3.15)44+192=	3.3.16)920+128=
3.3.17)445+287=	3.3.18)284+132=	3.3.19)119+855=	3.3.20)336+254=
3.3.21)284+367=	3.3.22)298+727=	3.3.23)29+2259=	3.3.24)119+409=
3.3.25)365+166=	3.3.26)110+627=	3.3.27)475+386=	3.3.28)768+129=
3.3.29)236+642=	3.3.30)790+543=	3.3.31)375+461=	3.3.32)182+888=
3.3.33)793+265=	3.3.34)314+5611=	3.3.35)2664+8551=	3.3.36)21+568=

3.3.37) 571 +343	3.3.38) 2889 +566	3.3.39) 1653 +327	3.3.40) 781 +679	3.3.41) 3256 +124
3.3.42) 245 +31	3.3.43) 175 +46	3.3.44) 267 +376	3.3.45) 132 +988	3.3.46) 199 +337

Decimal addition

3.12.1)11+2.3=
3.12.2).22+2.0=
3.12.3)3.4+16=
3.12.4)6.5+6.8=
3.12.5).83+2.2=
3.12.6)3.3+60=
3.12.7)1.7+3.9=
3.12.8)8.1+.48=
3.12.9).65+0.5=
3.12.10)3.7+74=
3.12.11)3.4+2.5=
3.12.12).85+39=
3.12.13).72+35=
3.12.14)1.6+4.9=
3.12.15).44+9.2=
3.12.16)9.2+12=
3.12.17)4.4+.28=
3.12.18)2.8+3.2=
3.12.19)11.1+2.365=
3.12.20)2.227+2.01=
3.12.21)34.3+16.0
3.12.22)16.5+68.25=
3.12.23)83.01+2.2=
3.12.24)3.31+60.2=
3.12.25)1.775+3.9=
3.12.26)81.1+4.83=
3.12.27)65.23+10.5=
3.12.28)37.6+.742=
3.12.29)34.5+25.5=
3.12.30).854+.399=

The table below shows the number of dogs with each color in a small town.

Color of dogs	Number of dogs
Black	215
white	167
yellow	132
brown	367
spotted	197

3.3.w1) How many dogs live in this small town?
3.3.w2) What is the total number of black, white and brown dogs living in this small town?
3.3.w3) How many spotted dogs live in this small town?
3.3.w4) What is the total number of brown and yellow dogs living in this small town?

The following table lists the number of lakes in each state

State	Number of Lakes
Illinois	23
Washington	71
California	82
Arizona	17
Kentucky	45
New York	67

3.3.w5) How many lakes are there in California?
3.3.w6) How many lakes are there in Arizona?
3.3.w7) What is the total number of lakes in Arizona Kentucky and New York?
3.3.w8) What is the total number of lakes listed in this table?

The following lists the number of vegetables Mary grew in her garden this year

onions 346
#carrots 157
#tomatoes 281

3.3.w9) How many carrots did Mary grow?
3.3.w10) What is the total number of vegetables Mary grew?
3.3.w11)What is the total number of onions and tomatoes that Mary grew?

The following is a series of numbers

6, 10, 14, 18

3.3.w12) What would be the next two numbers in this series

3.3.w13) What number would not be in this series?

a) 30, b) 38, c) 44, d) 50

3.3.w14) Which number represents the number 674

a) 200+400+65+9
b) 60+7+4
c) 342+472
d) 60+70+40

3.3.w15) You open a bank account with $127. The next week you deposit $312, followed by another $251 the next week. What is the amount in your bank account?

3.3.w16) I bought 1 cake for $12.83 and two pies for $15.61 each. What was the total cost of this purchase?

3.3.w17) The following table details the number of apples the school sold last week. What is the best estimate of the total number of apples sold last week?

DAY	NUMBER
Monday	132
Tuesday	247
Wednesday	331
Thursday	287
Friday	198

3.3.w18) The clock below shows the time I started to study.

If I study for 1 hour and 20 minutes which of the following digital clocks below shows the time of day I finished.

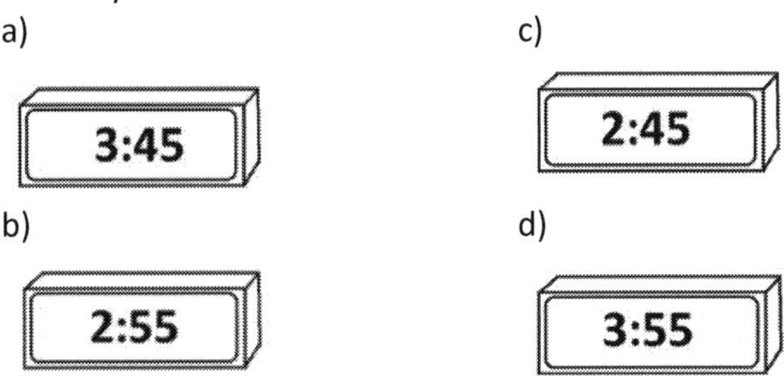

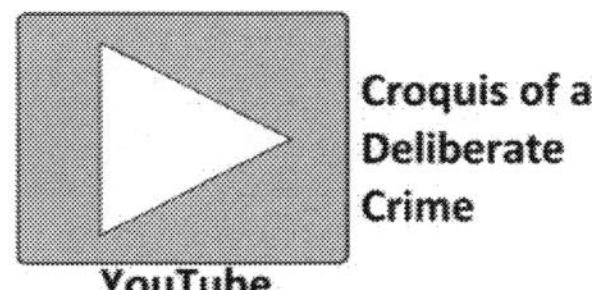

If you don't get the correct answer, and want an explanation on how to work the problem, go to YouTube and type in "MMT" then the problem number. An example would be, MMT 3.9.w12,. The video will show you how to work problem 3.9.w12.

For one on one tutoring via skype at $35.00/Hr.; contact me at marksmathtutoring@yahoo.com

3.3.w19) The clock below shown the time I started playing fetch with my dog.

If I played for 30 minutes which digital clock below shows the time I was finished?

a)

c) 

b)

d) 

3.3.w20) The following clock shows what time I started eating

If it takes me 45 minutes to eat which clock below shows the time I am finished

a)

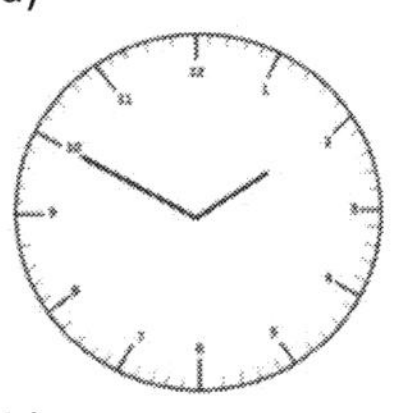

d)

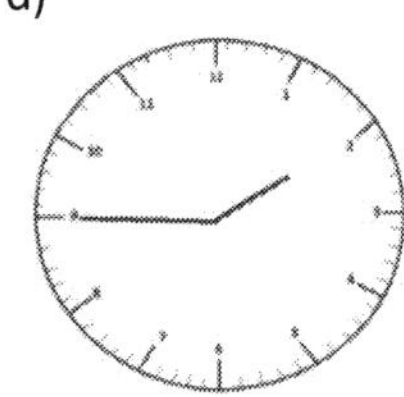

b)

c)

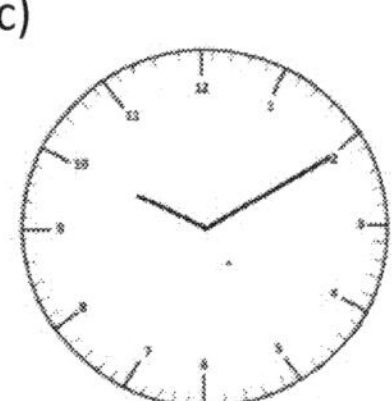

Croquis of a Deliberate Crime

3.3.w21) The clock below shows the time I started watching my favorite tv show.

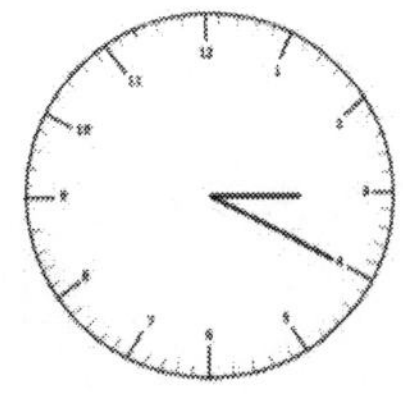

If I watch for 25 minutes, which clock below shows the time I am finished.

a)

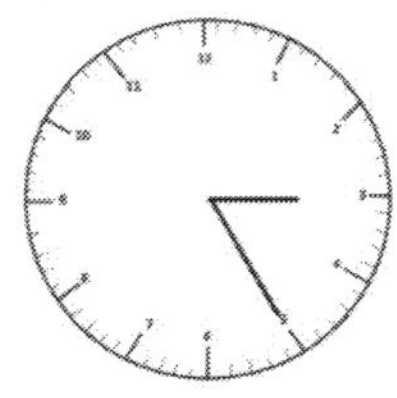

c)

b)

d)

3.3.w22) If the rule is add 48 to a number to get the answer which table below shows this relationship?

A)

NUMBER	EXPRESSION	ANSWER
48	48+1	49
48	48+2	50
48	48+3	51
48	48-4	52

B)

NUMBER	EXPRESSION	ANSWER
48	48x1	48
48	48-1	48
48	48+0	48
48	48-0	48

C)

NUMBER	EXPRESSION	ANSWER
1	1+48	49
2	2+48	50
3	3+48	51
4	4+48	52

d)

NUMBER	EXPRESSION	ANSWER
1	35+1	36
2	36+2	38
3	37+3	40
4	38+4	42

3.3.w23) A bakery makes 500 chocolate cupcakes per day . They make 135 more vanilla cupcakes per day than chocolate. Which equation below could be used to find X the total number of vanilla cupcakes per day.

a) x=500-135

b)x= 500+500+135

c) x= 500X135

d) x=500÷135

Croquis of a Deliberate Crime

3.3.w24) The table below shows the number of apples compared with the number of oranges

APPLES	ORANGES
82	114
95	127
64	96
47	79
78	110

Which statement below describes the relationship in the table
a) The number of apples + 32 = number of oranges
b) The number of apples - 32 = number of oranges
c) The number of apples + 23 = number of oranges
a) The number of apples - 23 = number of oranges

3.3.w25)You can earn an extra points on a test if you do a special project. Which table below best represents your final score for the relationship Y = 35 + X

A)

INITAIL TEST SCORE	FINAL TEST SCORE
35	70
45	75
55	90
63	100

B)

INITAIL TEST SCORE	FINAL TEST SCORE
35	70
45	80
55	90
63	100

C)

INITAIL TEST SCORE	FINAL TEST SCORE
35	70
45	80
55	95
63	100

D)

INITIAL TEST SCORE	FINAL TEST SCORE
35	70
45	80
55	90
63	98

3.3.W26) The table below shows the number of fish I caught on vacation. If the total number is 127 which equation below would be the best way to determine the number I caught on the 4th day.

INITAIL TEST SCORE	FINAL TEST SCORE
1	32
2	17
3	42
4	n

A) 127= (32+17+42)-N
B) 127=(32+17+42)+N
C) 127=(32+17+42)xN
D) 127=(32+17+42)÷N

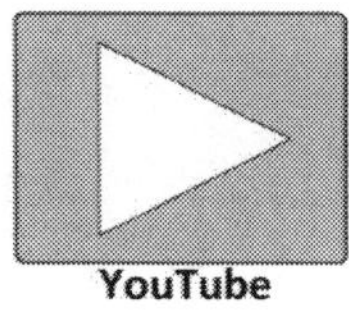

Croquis of a Deliberate Crime

3.3.w27) The relationship between y and x is defined by Y = 2.05 + X. Which table below best represents this relationship.

A)

X	Y
17.3	19.35
18.5	20.55
25.1	27.25
31.8	33.85

B)

X	Y
17.3	19.35
18.5	20.75
25.1	27.15
31.8	33.85

C)

X	Y
17.3	19.15
18.5	20.55
25.1	27.15
31.8	33.85

D)

X	Y
17.3	19.35
18.5	20.55
25.1	27.15
31.8	33.85

3.3.W28) Two sequences of number are listed in the table below.

Sequence A	7.8	12.3	14.7	16.4
Sequence B	13.1	17.6	20.0	21.7

Which statement below best represents this relationship

A) Sequence A is 5.3 less than Sequence B

B) Sequence B is 4.5 less than Sequence A

C) Sequence A is 5.3 more than Sequence B

D) Sequence B is 5.3 less than Sequence A

3.3.w29) If I start my homework at 2:45 and work for 1 hour and 45 minutes what time do I finish

3.3.w30) If I start to read at 5:20 and do it for 2 hours and 50 minutes what time do I finish

3.3.w31) If I start to do something at 1:30 and continue for 2hours and 30 minutes what time do I finish

3.3.w32) If I start to play with my dog at 3:15 and do so for 2 hours and 15 minutes what time do I finish

3.3.w33) The value of t can be determined by the equation t = x + 12.05. Which table below shows this relationship

A)

X	1	3	4	6
t	13.05	14.05	16.05	18.05

B)

X	1	3	4	6
t	13.05	15.05	17.05	18.05

C)

X	1	3	4	6
t	12.05	15.05	16.05	18.05

D)

X	1	3	4	6
t	13.05	15.05	16.05	18.05

3.3.W34) Given the information in the table below

X	0	1	2	3
y	7	8	9	10

Which statement below best describes this relationship
A) Y equals X +7
B) X equals Y + 7
C) X equals Y ÷ 7
D) Y equal X-7

3.3.w35) During a card game one team scored the following points

PLAYER	SCORE
Mike	-3
Susan	+2
Brad	-1
Karen	+4

Given this information what was the combined score of this team

3.3.w36) Given the data in the table below

D	6.3	7.8	9.1	10.4
U	7.5	9.0	10.3	11.6

Which of the following equations below best describes this relationship between D and U
A) D + U = 1.2
B) D – U = 1.2
C) D + 1.2 = U
D) U + 1.2 = D

3.4 Subtraction-Single Digits

3.4.1) 5-3=	3.4.2) 2-0=	3.4.3) 8-6=	3.4.4) 9-8=	3.4.5) 3-2=	3.4.6) 7-3=
3.4.7) 3-0=	3.4.8) 7-4=	3.4.9) 1-1=	3.4.10) 5-4=	3.4.11) 7-4=	3.4.12) 2-1=

3.4.55) 1-3=	3.4.56) 2-10=	3.4.57) 4-6=	3.4.58) 9-8=	3.4.59) 13-2=	3.4.60) 7-6=
3.4.61) 3-0=	3.4.62) 7-9=	3.4.63) 1-8=	3.4.64) 5-5=	3.4.65) 7-4=	3.4.66) 2-6=
3.4.67) 4-5=	3.4.68) 5-9=	3.4.69) 2-5=	3.4.70) 6-9=	3.4.71) 4-2=	3.4.72) 3-8=
3.4.73) 2-2=	3.4.74) 4-8=	3.4.75) 8-2=	3.4.76) 9-5=	3.4.77) 6-4=	3.4.78) 8-5=
3.4.79) 4-7=	3.4.80) 8-7=	3.4.81) 9-9=	3.4.82) 9-0=	3.4.83) 6-6=	3.4.84) 2-7=
3.4.85) 1-2=	3.4.86) 7-8=	3.4.87) 6-2=	3.4.88) 3-4=	3.4.89) 9-4=	3.4.90) 1-5=
3.4.91) 7-6=	3.4.92) 8-8=	3.4.93) 9-6=	3.4.94) 1-6=	3.4.95) 6-5=	3.4.96) 9-2=
3.4.97) 7 -9	3.4.98) 9 -4	3.4.99) 3 -6	3.4.100) 5 -9	3.4.101) 8 -5	3.4.102) 5 -7
3.4.103) 8 -8	3.4.104) 7 -2	3.4.105) 6 -4	3.4.106) 7 -7	3.4.107) 3 -2	3.4.108) 2 -9

Croquis of a Deliberate Crime

3.5 Subtraction-Two Digits

3.5.1)81-23=	3.5.2)22-20=	3.5.3)34-16=	3.5.4)65-28=	3.5.5)83-22=	3.5.6)33-20=
3.5.7)97-39=	3.5.8)81-48=	3.5.9)65-05=	3.5.10)87-74=	3.5.11)34-25=	3.5.12)85-39=
3.5.13)72-5=	3.5.14)56-49=	3.5.15)44-12=	3.5.16)92-2=	3.5.17)44-28=	3.5.18)88-32=
3.5.19)19-15=	3.5.20)86-54=	3.5.21)84-67=	3.5.22)98-27=	3.5.23)59-29=	3.5.24)79-40=
3.5.25)36-6=	3.5.26)61-10=	3.5.27)47-38=	3.5.28)76-2=	3.5.29)23-4=	3.5.30)79-54=
3.5.31)37-16=	3.5.32)18-9=	3.5.33)79-26=	3.5.34)31-6=	3.5.35)86-85=	3.5.36) 17-8

3.5.37) 81	3.5.38) 57	3.5.39) 89	3.5.40) 65	3.5.41) 81	3.5.42) 45
-34	- 6	-32	-47	-73	-1
3.5.43) 75	3.5.44) 67	3.5.45) 32	3.5.46) 99	3.5.47) 27	3.5.48) 67
-46	- 6	-18	-37	-18	-38

3.5.49)11-23=	3.5.50)22-30=	3.5.51)34-16=	3.5.52)65-48=	3.5.53)13-22=	3.5.54)33-60=
3.5.55)17-39=	3.5.56)81-48=	3.5.57)65-95=	3.5.58)37-74=	3.5.59)34-85=	3.5.60)85-39=
3.5.61)72-35=	3.5.62)16-49=	3.5.63)44-92=	3.5.64)92-12=	3.5.65)44-28=	3.5.66)28-32=
3.5.67)19-55=	3.5.68)36-54=	3.5.69)84-67=	3.5.70)98-27=	3.5.71)29-59=	3.5.72)19-40=
3.5.73)36-66=	3.5.74)11-62=	3.5.75)47-38=	3.5.76)76-12=	3.5.77)23-64=	3.5.78)79-54=
3.5.79)37-46=	3.5.80)18-88=	3.5.81)79-26=	3.5.82)31-56=	3.5.83)26-85=	3.5.84) 40-31=

3.5.85) 21	3.5.86) 57	3.5.87) 89	3.5.88) 65	3.5.89) 81	3.5.90) 51
-34	-56	-32	-67	-83	-17
3.5.91) 75	3.5.92) 67	3.5.93) 32	3.5.94) 99	3.5.95) 27	3.5.96) 31
-46	-76	-88	-37	-28	-98

3.6 Subtraction-Multiple digit

3.6.1)1111-365=	3.6.2)2227-201=	3.6.3)343-160	3.6.4)165-25=	3.6.5)8301-22=
3.6.6)1331-302=	3.6.7)1775-39=	3.6.8)811-483=	3.6.9)6523-105=	3.6.10)976-742=
3.6.11)345-255=	3.6.12)854-99=	3.6.13)726-355=	3.6.14)116-49=	3.6.15)244-192=
3.6.16)920-128=	3.6.17)445-287=	3.6.18)284-12=	3.6.19)1119-855=	3.6.20)336-254=
3.6.21)284-167=	3.6.22)798-727=	3.6.23)1129-159=	3.6.24)119-9=	3.6.25)365-166=
3.6.26)1110-627=	3.6.27)475-386=	3.6.28)768-129=	3.6.29)236-42=	3.6.30)790-543=
3.6.31)875-461=	3.6.32)882-288=	3.6.33)793-265=	3.6.34)5314-611=	3.6.35)9664-8551=
3.6.36)621-568=	3.6.37)1127-89=	3.6.38)187-129=	3.6.39)327-189=	3.6.40)1321-287=

3.6.41) 571	3.6.42) 2889	3.6.43) 1653	3.6.44) 781	3.6.45) 3256	3.6.46) 321
-343	- 66	-327	-679	-124	-264
3.6.47) 245	3.6.48) 175	3.6.49) 267	3.6.50) 1132	3.6.51) 3199	3.6.52) 127
- 31	-46	- 76	-988	-337	-89

3.6.53)111-2365=	3.6.54)2227-7201=	3.6.55)343-860	3.6.56)165-6825=
3.6.57)8301-9722=	3.6.58)331-602=	3.6.59)1775-1939=	3.6.60)811-483=
3.6.61)6523-105=	3.6.62)376-742=	3.6.63)345-1255=	3.6.64)854-999=
3.6.65)726-855=	3.6.66)116-949=	3.6.67)44-192=	3.6.68)920-1128=
3.6.69)445-3287=	3.6.70)284-8132=	3.6.71)119-855=	3.6.72)336-654=
3.6.73)284-367=	3.6.74)298-727=	3.6.75)29-2259=	3.6.76)119-409=
3.6.77)365-166=	3.6.78)110-627=	3.6.79)475-386=	3.6.80)768-129=

Subtraction Decimals

3.13.1)11-2.3=
3.13.2).22-2.0=
3.13.3)3.4-16=
3.13.4)6.5-6.8=
3.13.5).83-2.2=
3.13.6)3.3-60=
3.13.7)1.7-3.9=
3.13.8)8.1-.48=
3.13.9).65-0.5=
3.13.10)3.7-74=
3.13.11)3.4-2.5=
3.13.12).85-39=
3.13.13).72-35=
3.13.14)1.6-4.9=
3.13.15).44-9.2=
3.13.16)9.2-12=
3.13.17)4.4-.28=
3.13.18)2.8-3.2=
3.13.19)11.1-2.365=
3.13.20)2.227-2.01=
3.13.21)34.3-16.0
3.13.22)16.5-68.25=
3.13.23)83.01-2.2=
3.13.24)3.31-60.2=
3.13.25)1.775-3.9=
3.13.26)81.1-4.83=
3.13.27)65.23-10.5=
3.13.28)37.6-.742=
3.13.29)34.5-25.5=
3.13.30).854-.399=

Add/Subtraction Complex Signs

3.16.1)-1+2=
3.16.2)-2-2=
3.16.3)-3+1=
3.16.4)6-(-6)=
3.16.5)-8+2=
3.16.6)-3-6=
3.16.7)-1-(-3)=
3.16.8)-8+4=
3.16.9)-6-5=
3.16.10)-3-(-7)=
3.16.11)3-(-2)=
3.16.12)-8+3=
3.16.13)-7-3=
3.16.14)-1-4=
3.16.15)-4-(-9)=
3.16.16)-9+12=
3.16.17)-4-(-2)=
3.16.18) 2-(-3)=
3.16.19)-1-(-2)=
3.16.20)-2-2=
3.16.21)-3+16
3.16.22)-1-(-6)=
3.16.23)-8-2=
3.16.24)-3+6=
3.16.25)-1-3=
3.16.26)-8-(-4)=
3.16.27)-6-1=
3.16.28)-3-7=
3.16.29)-3+2=
3.16.30)-8-(-3)=

3.6.w1) Sue back 827 cookies

#She sold 127 of the cookies

#Her brother Mike sold 81 of the cookies

What is the best way to figure out how many cookies she has left over

a) 827-127-81=, b) 127-827-81=, c) 827+127+81=, d) 127+81-827=
b) How many cookies are left over

3.6.w2) Mark picked 427 apples on Monday, the 328 pears on Tues. What is the difference between the number of apples and pears he picked?

3.6.w3)Mike goal is to mow 125 lawns this summer

In June he mows 35

In July he mows 61

How many lawns must he mow in August to make his goal?

3.6.w38) The table below shows the number of cats and dogs for three different public school

School	Cats	dogs
Harrison	126	217
Casis	118	187
Baker	153	254

What is the total difference between the number of cats and dogs?

3.6.w4)Gilbert bought 87 flowers for his moms garden. He put 31 in the front yard and 27 in the back. How many flowers did he have left?

3.6.w5)Wanda saved the following amount of money in three months

#March she saved $827

#April she saved $294

May she saved $447

How much more money did she save in March than April and May combined?

3.6.w6)Rita had two boxes of cupcakes

#She made 85 chocolate

#She made 76 vanilla

#Her brother ate 28 of them

Which equation would be useful in finding the number of cupcakes she had left after her brother ate them.

a) 85+76-28=

b) 85+76+28=

c) 85-76+28=

d) 85-76-28=

How many cup cakes did she have left after her brother ate some?

3.6.w7) Sarah grew three vegetables in her garden last year. The list below shows the number of each she grew.

127 tomatoes

312 cucumbers

187 carrots

Which expression below is the best way to determine the difference between the number of carrots and tomatoes she grew?

a) 127-187, b) 187-127, c) 187+127, d) 127+187

3.6.w8) Mike rode his bike 431 miles in June and 277 mile in July. What is the difference in miles between these two months?

3.6.w9)Larimer save $841 in April, he spent $128 in May then saved another $56 in June. Which expression is best for determining the amount of money he has saved?

a)841-128+56=

b) 841-128-56=

c)841+128+56=

d)841+56-128=

3.6.w10) Brad has 841 apples in two boxes. He has 367 in one box. How many apples are in the other box?

3.6.w11) I ate 7 more oranges than apples. Which tables below shows this relationship.

A)

APPLES	ORANGES
4	11
6	13
8	15
10	17
15	24

C)

APPLES	ORANGES
4	11
6	13
8	15
10	17
15	22

B)

APPLES	ORANGES
4	11
6	12
8	15
10	17
15	22

D)

APPLES	ORANGES
4	12
6	14
8	16
10	17
15	22

3.6.w12) If you bake 4 cupcakes on Mon 6 on Tuesday, then 5 on Wednesday, how many cupcakes would you have?

3.6.w13) It took me three years to save $25,357. If the first year I saved $8,113, and $7,891, how much did I save in the third year?

3.6.w14) The table below shows the relationship between the miles I hiking and biking.

MONTH	BIKING	HIKING
June	28	15
July	32	19
August	35	22
September	41	28

Which equation below shows this relationship?
a) Miles biked – 13 = miles hiked
b) Miles biked - 11 = miles hiked
c) Miles biked - 12 = miles hiked
d) Miles biked - 15 = miles hiked

3.6.w15) I have two jars with penny's
Jar A has 27,315 pennies
Jar B has 8,465 pennies
What is the best estimate for the difference in the number of pennies in these two jars?

3.6.w16) I bought a bike to repair then sale. The following is the amount I spent and sold it for
Bought bike for $12.00
Repaired bike for $8.00
#Painted bike for $5.50
#sold bike for $30.00
What is the best estimate for the amount of profit I made?

3.6.w17) You sold pizza at a bake sale. The cost of making all the pizza was $10.35. They sold for a total of $21.11. What was your profit?

3.6.w18) My dog has $14.00 to spend on treats and toys. He buys on ball for $2.85, two cookies for $.65 each, and a chew toy for $1.97. What is the amount of money he has left over?

3.6.w19) The following is a list of the number of miles I walk each month.
#June 327
#July 451
#Aug 634
If my goal was 1500, how many more do I need to walk?

3.6.w20) If the clock below shows the time I stopped watching TV

If I started at 9:15 how long did I watch TV

3.6.w21) If the clock below shows the time I stopped walking

If I started at 11:10 how long did I walk

3.6.w22) The clock below shows the time I stopped playing football.

If I started at 8:10 how many hours and minutes did I play

3.6.w23) The clock below shows the time I stopped playing video games

If I started at 1:15 how long did I play?

3.6.W24) The table below shows the length and weight of the fish I caught on vacation.

	WEIGHT	LENGTH
BASS	6.8 lbs	13.4 in
TROUT	23.15 lbs	26.78 in

Based on this information which of the following statements is true
A) The combined weights is 29.75 lbs
B) the combined lengths of the fish is 40.18 in
C) The difference in the lengths of the bass and the trout is 16.38 in.
D) The Bass weighed 13.28 pounds less than the trout

3.6.w25) My cow weights 125.6 lbs and my sisters cow weights 78.13 lbs. What is the difference in their weights.

3.6.w26) I earned $21.35 for babysitting. I then earned an extra $12.30 for cleaning a house. If I then spent $18.93, what is the total amount I have left over?

3.6.w27) If I buy a hamburger for $8.37 and a coke for $1.87, and I pay with a $20.00 bill what is the change I have left over?

3.6.w28) The table below shows the population in three four different towns.

TOWN	POPULATION
Mercer	11,215
Bellevue	21,561
Tacoma	13,335
Everett	

If the population of Everett is 7,327 less than Bellevue what is the total population of all four towns.

3.6.w29) If I biked 12,348 miles last year and have put a total of 25,668 miles on the bike since buying it last year. How many miles did I bike this year.

3.6.w30) The length of two different biking distances are given below.

Monday 2.3 Kilometers

Tuesday 1250 meters

What is the differences in these distances

a) 1247.7 meters
b) 1252.3 meters
c) 1050 meters
d) 1020 meters

3.6.w31) I need to balance my budget to see how much extra money I have this month. The tables below show my expenses and income

Expenses		Income	
Food	$251.00	Mowing lawns	$342.00
Rent	$450.00	Baby Sitting	$235.00
Utilities	$50.00	House cleaning	$ 578.00

Based on this information how much money do I have left over after expenses?

3.6.w32) If I have a fish 4 meters long and cut it into three pieces. The first is 1.35 meters long, the second is 0.7 meters long, how long is the third piece?

3.6.w33) If I need to be at work at 7.15 a.m. and the drive is 1hour and 30 m minutes long what time should I leave the house?

3.6.w34) If I want to finish doing something at 3:30 and it will take me 2 hours and 45 minutes what time should I start

3.6.w35) If I want to finish walking at 2:15 and it will take me 1 hours and 35 minutes what time should I start

3.6.w36) If I want to finish reading something at 1:30 and it will take me 3 hours and 25 minutes what time should I start

3.6.w37) If I want to finish doing something at 3:30 and it will take me 2 hours and 45 minutes what time should I start

3.6.w38) If I eat 56 cookies in one day, 28 of which were in the morning. Which of the following equation below will help me figure out how many I ate, C, in the rest of the day.

A) 56 + 28 = C
B) 56 – 28 = C
C) 56 X 28 = C
D) 56 ÷ 28 = C

3.6.w39) I bought a cat and a dog.
I paid 128.31 for the dog
I paid a total of 131.27 for both pets
Given this information how much did I pay for the cat.

3.6.W40) The two tables below show my assets and liabilities(expenses)

ASSETS

ASSETS	VALUE
CASH	$105.41
SAVINGS	$23.16
STOCKS	$436.22
BONDS	$112.71

LIABILTY

LIABILITY	VALUE
RENT	$231.07
CAR	$56.89
FOOD	$45.67

What is the difference or my net worth

3.7 Multiplication-Single Digits

3.7.1) 1x3=	3.7.2) 2x0=	3.7.3) 4x6=	3.7.4) 5x8=	3.7.5) 3x2=	3.7.6) 7x3=
3.7.7) 3x0=	3.7.8) 7x9=	3.7.9) 1x8=	3.7.10) 5x5=	3.7.11) 7x4=	3.7.12) 2x6=
3.7.13) 4x5=	3.7.14) 5x9=	3.7.15) 2x5=	3.7.16) 6x9=	3.7.17) 4x2=	3.7.18) 3x8=
3.7.19) 2x2=	3.7.20) 4x8=	3.7.21) 8x2=	3.7.22) 9x5=	3.7.23) 6x4=	3.7.24) 8x5=
3.7.25) 4x7=	3.7.26) 8x7=	3.7.27) 9x9=	3.7.28) 9x0=	3.7.29) 6x6=	3.7.30) 2x7=
3.7.31) 1x2=	3.7.32) 7x8=	3.7.33) 6x2=	3.7.34) 3x4=	3.7.35) 9x4=	3.7.36) 1x5=
3.7.37) 7x6=	3.7.38) 8x8=	3.7.39) 9x6=	3.7.40) 1x6=	3.7.41) 6x5=	3.7.42) 9x2=

3.7.43) 7 x3	3.7.44) 9 x4	3.7.45) 3 x6	3.7.46) 5 x9	3.7.47) 8 x5	3.7.48) 5 x7
3.7.49) 8 x8	3.7.50) 7 x2	3.7.51) 6 x4	3.7.52) 7 x7	3.7.53) 3 x2	3.7.54) 2 x9

3.8 Multiplication-Two Digits

3.8.1)11x23=	3.8.2)22x20=	3.8.3)34x16=	3.8.4)65x68=	3.8.5)83x22=	3.8.6)33x60=
3.8.7)17x39=	3.8.8)81x48=	3.8.9)65x05=	3.8.10)37x74=	3.8.11)34x25=	3.8.12)85x39=
3.8.13)72x35=	3.8.14)16x49=	3.8.15)44x92=	3.8.16)92x12=	3.8.17)44x28=	3.8.18)28x32=
3.8.19)19x55=	3.8.20)36x54=	3.8.21)84x67=	3.8.22)98x27=	3.8.23)29x59=	3.8.24)19x40=
3.8.25)36x66=	3.8.26)11x62=	3.8.27)47x38=	3.8.28)76x12=	3.8.29)23x64=	3.8.30)79x54=
3.8.31)37x46=	3.8.32)18x88=	3.8.33)79x26=	3.8.34)31x56=	3.8.35)26x85=	3.8.36)84x16=

3.8.37) 21 x34	3.8.38) 57 x56	3.8.39) 89 x32	3.8.40) 65 x67	3.8.41) 81 x83	3.8.42) 27 x53
3.8.43) 45 x31	3.8.44) 75 x46	3.8.45) 67 x76	3.8.46) 32 x88	3.8.47) 99 x37	3.8.48) 56 x78

3.9 Multiple digit Multiplication

3.9.1)111x2365= 3.9.2)2227x201= 3.9.3)343x160 3.9.4)165x6825=
3.9.5)8301x22= 3.9.6)331x602= 3.9.7)1775x39= 3.9.8)811x483=
3.9.9)6523x105= 3.9.10)376x742= 3.9.11)345x255= 3.9.12)854x399=
3.9.13)726x355= 3.9.14)116x949= 3.9.15)44x192= 3.9.16)920x128=
3.9.17)445x287= 3.9.18)284x132= 3.9.19)119x855= 3.9.20)336x254=
3.9.21)284x367= 3.9.22)298x727= 3.9.23)29x2259= 3.9.24)119x409=
3.9.25)365x166= 3.9.26)110x627= 3.9.27)475x386= 3.9.28)768x129=
3.9.29)236x642= 3.9.30)790x543= 3.9.31)375x461= 3.9.32)182x888=
3.9.34)793x265= 3.9.35)314x5611= 3.9.36)2664x8551= 3.9.37)21x568=

3.9.38) 571 x343 3.9.39) 2889 x566 3.90.40)1653 x327 3.9.41) 781 x679 3.9.42) 3256 x124

3.9.43) 245 x31 3.9.44) 175 x46 3.9.45) 267 x376 3.9.46) 132 x988 3.9.47) 199 x337

Multiplication Decimals

3.14.1)11X2.3= 3.14.2).22X2.0= 3.14.3)3.4X16=
3.14.4)6.5X6.8= 3.14.5).83X2.2= 3.14.6)3.3X60=
3.14.7)1.7X3.9= 3.14.8)8.1X.48= 3.14.9).65X0.5=
3.14.10)3.7X74= 3.14.11)3.4X2.5= 3.14.12).85X39=
3.14.13).72X35= 3.14.14)1.6X4.9= 3.14.15).44X9.2=
3.14.16)9.2X12= 3.14.17)4.4X.28= 3.14.18)2.8X3.2=
3.14.19)11.1X2.365= 3.14.20)2.227X2.01= 3.14.21)34.3X16.0
3.14.22)16.5X68.25= 3.14.23)83.01X2.2= 3.14.24)3.31X60.2=
3.14.25)1.775X3.9= 3.14.26)81.1X4.83= 3.14.27)65.23X10.5=
3.14.28)37.6X .742= 3.14.29)34.5X25.5= 3.14.30).854X.399=

The following table details the number of cookies baked on each pan.

Number of cookie pans	Number of cookies
2	12
3	18
4	
6	36
8	48

3.9.w1) How many cookies where baked on 4 pans?
3.9.w2) How many cookies on 7 pans?
3.9.w3) How many cookies on each pan?

3.9.w4) Brad put four turtles in each pond. He has 6 ponds. How many turtle does he have?
3.9.w5) Elizabeth gave 6 rhinos 7 carrots each, how many carrots did she give the rhinos?

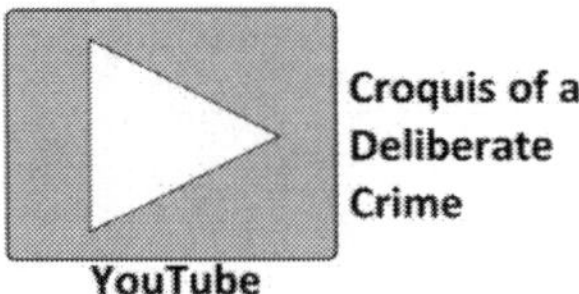

3.9.w6) There are four pairs of socks in each package. Which table below shows the relationship between the number of socks and the number of packages.

a)

Number of Packages	4	5	6	8
Number of Socks	12	15	18	21

b)

Number of Packages	4	5	6	8
Number of Socks	16	18	20	22

c)

Number of Packages	4	5	6	8
Number of Socks	16	20	24	32

d)

Number of Packages	4	5	6	8
Number of Socks	1	13	24	35

3.9.w7) There are two different types of cupcakes for sale

5 boxes with 6 chocolate cupcakes in each

there are 42 vanilla cup cakes on the table

What is the total number of cupcakes on sale?

3.9.w8) What number goes in the box to make the mathematical statement true ◯X6=42

3.9.w9) The baseball team bought 7 boxes of candy bars to sell. Each box has 9 candy bars in them. How many bars do they have to sell?

3.9.w10) In the equations below, the Δ always represents the same number.

⌂ + Δ = 8

Δ X Δ = 4

What is the value of ⌂?

3.9.w11) The following table describes the number of potatoes in a bag.

Number of bags	1	4	6	7
Number of Potatoes	15	60		105

Each bag has the same number of potatoes in it. How many potatoes are in 6 bags?

a) 45, because 105-60=45
b) 90, because 6X15=90
c) 45, because 60-15=45
d) 75, because 15+60=75

3.9.w12) At the bakery the cupcakes are in boxes with 12 cupcakes each. If you count in groups of 12 which numbers will you use?

a) 12, 24, 38, 42
b) 10, 20, 30, 40
c) 12, 24, 36, 48
d) 36, 48, 59, 61

3.9.W13) The table below show the total number of horses for different number of stalls

Number of stalls	1	3	5	7
Number of Horses	5	15		35

There is a equal number of horses in each stall. Which equation is the best way to determine the number if horses in 5 stalls?

a) 3+15=, b) 5X15=, c) 5+15=, d) 5X5=

3.9.w14) You made cupcakes for your school and put them in 8 boxes. There are 73 cupcakes in each box. How many cupcakes did you make.

3.9.w15) The table below show the total number of apples in different number of bags

Number of bags	1	2	3	5
Number of apples	12	24		60

There is a equal number of apples in each bag. How many apples are in 3 bags?

3.9.w16) The school sells 96 cookies every day. How many cookies will they sell in 8 days?

3.9.w17) There are 28 apple pies, and 17 peach pies. Each is for sale for $7.00. How much money will it take to buy all of the pies?

3.9.w18) The table below lists the number of rabbits in different number of cages.

Number of cages	Number of rabbits
3	12
5	20
7	28
8	
10	40

Each cage contains the same number of rabbits. What is one way to determine the number of rabbits in 8 cages

a) find the difference between 40 and 28
b) find the product of 8X4
c) find the sum of 40 and 28
d)find the difference between 40 and 10.

3.9.w19) The table below shows the number of people that enter a public bus each hour.

Number of hours	**Number of people**
1	16
2	32
4	
5	80
8	128

Each hour the same number of people enter the bus. How many people entered the bus in 5 hours?

a) 48, because 128-80=48
b) 64, because 4X16=64
c) 48, because 32+16=48
d) 16, because 32÷16=2

3.9.w20) While on a field trip to the ocean, 5 kids collect 15 shells each, which expression can be used to determine the total number of shells collected?

a) 15÷5=
b) 15X5=
c) 15+5=
d) 15-5=

How many shells in total where collected?

3.9.w21) The table below shows the total number of kids in different number of buses.

Number of buses	Number of Kids
2	24
5	60
6	
7	84
9	108

Each bus has the same number of kids in it. How many kids total will be in 6 buses?

3.9.w22) Andy practices math 2 hours a day. How many hours will he practice in 9 days?

3.9.w23) Michelle practices math 3 hours a day, and history 2 hours a day. What is the total number of hours in 7 days she practices?

3.9.w24) Emery drew 6 rows of dogs. Each row has 8 dogs in it. How many dogs did she draw?

3.9.w25) The table below shows the number of dogs of different colors.

Color of Dog	Number of Dogs
Black	48
Yellow	32
Brown	24
Spotted	56

The picture graph below represents the same information

Color of Dogs	Number of Dogs
Black	X X X X X X
Yellow	X X X X
Brown	X X X
Spotted	X X X X X X X

Which Key completes the picture graph?
a) Each X means 6 dogs
b) Each X means 8 dogs
c) Each X means 4 dogs
d) Each X means 2 dogs.

3.9.w26) John has 16 packages a baseball cards. Each pack has 6 cards in it. He gives 12 to a friend. Which mathematical stamen below will help determine the amount of cards he has left?
a) 16x12-6=186
b) 16x6-12=84
c) 12+6+16=34
d) 12X6-16=56

Croquis of a Deliberate Crime

For one on one tutoring via skype at $35.00/Hr.; contact me at marksmathtutoring@yahoo.com

3.9.w27) I eat 4 apple a day. Which table below describes the number of apples total I have eaten in 4, 6, 7 days

A)

NUMBER OF DAYS	TOTAL NUMBER OF APPLES
4	16
6	24
7	28

C)

NUMBER OF DAYS	TOTAL NUMBER OF APPLES
4	16
6	22
7	28

B)

NUMBER OF DAYS	TOTAL NUMBER OF APPLES
4	16
6	24
7	26

D)

NUMBER OF DAYS	TOTAL NUMBER OF APPLES
4	18
6	24
7	28

3.9.w28) If a restaurant charges $6.00 per meal which table below describes the cost for a specific number of meals

A)

Number of Meals	4	5	7	9
Total Cost of Meals	$24	$30	$44	$54

C)

Number of Meals	4	5	7	9
Total Cost of Meals	$24	$30	$42	$54

B)

Number of Meals	4	5	7	9
Total Cost of Meals	$24	$28	$42	$48

D)

Number of Meals	4	5	7	9
Total Cost of Meals	$26	$28	$42	$52

3.9.w29) I sold pies at a rate of $7.00 per pie. Which tables below show this relationship?

A)

NUMBER OF PIES	TOTAL COST
2	$14
4	$26
6	$42
7	$49
8	$56

C)

NUMBER OF PIES	TOTAL COST
2	$14
4	$28
6	$42
7	$49
8	$56

B)

NUMBER OF PIES	TOTAL COST
2	$14
4	$28
6	$42
7	$48
8	$56

D)

NUMBER OF PIES	TOTAL COST
2	$14
4	$32
6	$42
7	$48
8	$56

3.9.w30) My sister put 3 apples and 4 oranges in each lunch bag. There are 8 lunch bags. What is the total number of pieces of fruit.

Croquis of a Deliberate Crime

If you don't get the correct answer, and want an explanation on how to work the problem, go to YouTube and type in "MMT" then the problem number. An example would be, MMT 3.9.w12,. The video will show you how to work problem 3.9.w12.

For one on one tutoring via skype at $35.00/Hr.; contact me at marksmathtutoring@yahoo.com

3.9.w31) Given the mathematical statement below.

◇ X 10 = ○

Which table below represents this relationship

a)

◇	○
26	36
34	44
57	67
69	79

c)

◇	○
26	260
34	340
57	570
69	690

b)

◇	○
26	27
34	35
57	58
69	70

d)

◇	○
26	2.6
34	3.4
57	5.7
69	6.9

3.9.w32) Your soccer tem plays 16 games a year. How many games will they play in 24 years?

3.9.w33) Each box has 16 rocks in it. If there are 37 boxes how many rocks total are there?

3.9.w34) If you sell boxes of cookies. The table below shows the number of cookies in each box.

BOXES	27	35	69	121
COOKIES	2,700	3,500		12,100

How many cookies will be in 69 boxes?

3.9.w35) If you mow 6 lawns a day, 7 days a week for 8 weeks and earn $12.00 per lawn how much money have you earned?

3.9.w36) Given the numerical sequence shown below

18, 21, 24, 27

Which of the tables below shows this relationship

a)

NUMBER	RELATIONSHIP	ANSWER
17	17+1	18
20	20+1	21
23	23+1	24
26	26+1	27

c)

NUMBER	RELATIONSHIP	ANSWER
18	18+0	18
21	21+0	21
24	24+0	24
27	27+0	27

b)

NUMBER	RELATIONSHIP	ANSWER
6	6X3=	18
7	7X3=	21
8	8X3=	24
9	9X3=	27

d)

NUMBER	RELATIONSHIP	ANSWER
18	18X1=	18
21	21X1=	21
24	24X1=	24
27	27X1=	27

3.9.w37) There are 36 kids in a class rooom. There are 25 class rooms. How many kids in this school?

3.9.w38) If I put 100 cupcakes in each box and there are 48 boxes, how many cupcakes do I have?

3.9.w39) Given the numerical relationship shown below

◇ X 15 = ○

Which table below best describes this relationship.

a)

◇	2	4	6	8
○	17	19	21	23

c)

◇	2	4	6	8
○	13	11	9	7

b)

◇	2	4	6	8
○	15	30	45	60

d)

◇	2	4	6	8
○	30	60	90	120

3.9.w40) It cost $14.00 to paint a bike. The following list details how many bikes I painted
Thursday I painted 337 bikes
Friday I painted 181 bikes
Saturday I painted 257 bikes
What is the total cost of painting these bikes?

3.9.w41) The following table shows the number of apples in each pie.

NUMBER OF PIES	NUMBER OF APPLES
1	32
2	64
3	96
4	128

Which of the following equations best described this relationship
a) total number of pies + 31 = total number of apples
b) total number of pies X 32 = total number of apples
c) total number of pies ÷ 31 = total number of apples
d) total number of pies - 31 = total number of apples

3.9.w42) If I throw the ball for my dog 34 times a day for 56 days. How many times have I thrown the ball for him?

3.9.w43) A season pass for the movie theater cost $100. If 125 people buy one how much money did the theater make?

3.9.w44) There are 49 boxes of light bulbs. Each box has 24 bulbs in it. What is the total number of light bulbs?

3.9.w45) If I buy 6 boxes of cookies and each has 8 cookies in it. What is the total number of cookies I have bought?

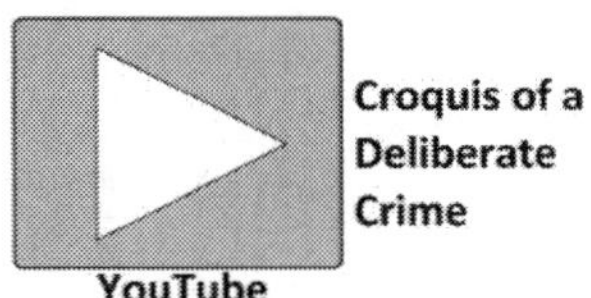

For one on one tutoring via skype at $35.00/Hr.; contact me at marksmathtutoring@yahoo.com

3.9.w46) I put the same number of chocolate chips in each cookie, and the relationship[describing how many each cookie gets is described in the table below.

NUMBER OF COOKIES	20	25	30	35
NUMBER OF CHIPS	300	375	450	525

Which of the following equations below describes this relationship?
a) Number of Cookies + 250 = Number of Chips
b) Number of Cookies - 250 = Number of Chips
c) Number of Cookies X 15 = Number of Chips
d) Number of Cookies ÷ 15 = Number of Chips

3.9.w47) Given the drawing below

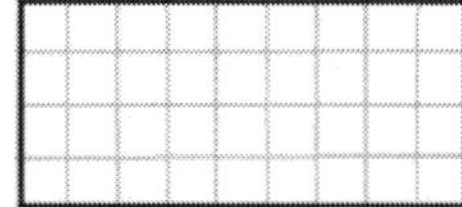

Which of the following boxes would have the same number of squares in it?

a)

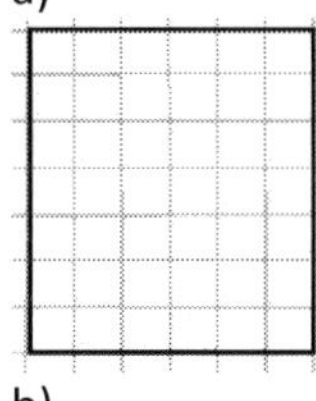

c)

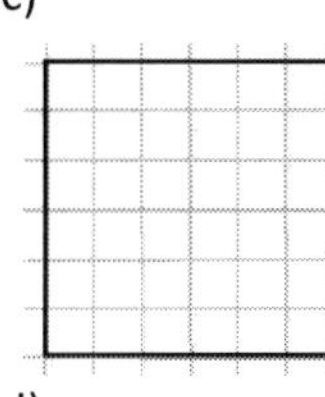

b) d)

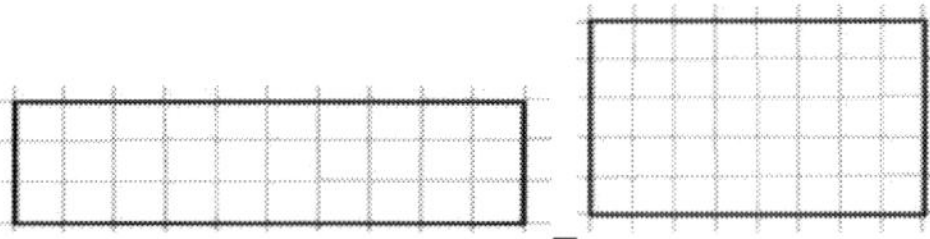

3.9.w48) There are 420 tress in a orchards. Which of the following equations can describe the shape of the orchard?
a) 7 rows of 70 tress = 420
b) 6 rows of 70 tress = 420
c) 8 rows of 54 tress = 420
d) 9 rows of 50 trees = 420

3.9.w49) Which table below best describes the relationship Y = 4 X

A)

X	Y
3	9
5	20
6	24
8	32

B)

X	Y
3	12
5	15
6	24
8	32

C)

X	Y
3	12
5	20
6	24
8	28

D)

X	Y
3	12
5	20
6	24
8	32

3.9.W50) What is the total if I subtract 27 from the product of 23 and 17

3.9.W51) On Monday I caught 31 fish, and on Tues I caught 127 fish. If each fish weighs 8 pounds how much in pounds did I catch between the two days.

3.9.W52) If I bike 25 miles a week for 5 weeks what is the total distance?

3.9.w53) I measured the weights all the dogs in my neighborhood. 27 weighted 18 pounds and 13 weighted 27 pounds. What is the total weight of these dogs?

3.9.W54) The table below shows the process of admittance to a theme park

TYPE OF ADMISSION	ADULT	CHILD
GENERAL ADMISSION	$12.00	$10.00
SPECIAL	$10.00	$8.00
OFF SEASSON	$7.00	$5.00
LATE NIGHT	$9.00	$7.00

Based on this information if I bought 2 adult tickets and three child tickets and payed a total of $29.00, what kind of tickets did I buy?

3.9.w55) If I play video games at the arcade for $1.25 per hour, for 3 hours a day and for 5 days how much money did I spend?

3.9.w56) I pet 321 dogs a year, for 32 years. What is the total amount of dogs I pet?

3.9.w57) If I eat 3.7 pounds of fish a month for 1.3 months how many pounds of fish have I eaten.

3.9.w58) Which of the following table best described the relationship y = 0.15 X

A)

X	Y
5	50
10	100
15	150
20	200
25	250

B)

X	Y
5	75
10	150
15	175
20	300
25	325

C)

X	Y
5	.75
10	1.50
15	1.75
20	3.00
25	3.25

D)

X	Y
5	.075
10	.150
15	.175
20	.300
25	.325

3.9.W59) I have 139 cookies in the kitchen then add 28 more boxes. Each box has 24 cookies in it. What is the total number of cookies in the kitchen?

3.9.w60) If it take me 1:45 to mow a single lawn and I have 3 to do, how much time will it take.

3.9.w61) If it take 45 minutes to bake a sheet of cookies and I have 5 sheets, how much time will it take

3.9.w62) If I it take 35 minutes to wash a car and I have 6 to do, and I start at 2:15 what time will I be done

3.9.w63) To walk a dog takes 1hour and 45 minutes. If I have 5 dogs to walk how much time will it take.

3.9.w64) If your math test has 50 questions and each one is worth 2 points, which equation best determine the final score, P, with # number questions correct.
A) 50 ÷ # = P
B) # X 2 = P
C) P X 2 = #
D) 2 ÷ P = #

3.9.w65) A hamburger joint uses N pounds of meat for M number of hamburgers as shown in the table below

Number of Hamburgers	20	40	50	80
Pounds of Meat	30	60	75	120

Which of the following statements is true
A) M + 10 = N
B) M X 10 = N
C) M ÷ N = 10
D) M X 1.5 = N

3.9.w66) The list below describes the number of cookies a student eats for three different activates.
Studying math 6 cookies per minute
watching tv 4 cookies per minute
playing with the dog 20 cookies per hour
Which of the following equation could calculate the total number of cookies eaten in 2 hours
A) (6X120)+(4X120)+2X20=total
B) (6X2)+(4X2)+20=total
C) (6X2)+(4X2)+(20X2)=total
D) (6X120)+(4X60)X20=total

3.9.w67) The following table shows the amount of money a person earns for a given job

JOB	AVERAGE ANNUAL SALARY
COOK	$18,326
MUSCIAN	$26,533
REALATOR	$21,458
TEACHER	$32,766

With this information how much more money will a teacher earn than a cook in 12 years

3.9.w68) it cost $1.29 to buy one cookie. Which equation below can be used to find the total cost, P, for buying T number of cookies
A) 1.29 X T = P
B) 1.29 + P = T
C) 1.29 X P = T
D) T X P = 1.29

3.9.w69) If my dog eats one pound of food less then 3 times what I eat, I. Which equation below could be used to determine the amount my dog eats, E.
A) E=3I+1
B) E=3I-1
C) I=3E-3
D) I=3E+3

3.9.W70) If I have a sequence defined by the equation Y=4X+4. Which of the following numbers could be the dependent variable if the independent variable are { 1, 3, 5, 7, 9}
A) {8,12,22,32,40}
B) {8, 16, 24, 32, 40}
C) {8, 16, 24, 34, 40}
D) {8, 14, 22, 34, 42}

3.9.W71) If I need 35 pounds flour and it is sold in 5 pounds bags. I have collected 3 pounds so far. Which of the following equations could help me determine how many pounds of flour, Y, I still need to buy
A) 35= 5X+3
B) 35=5X+15
C) 35= 3X+5
D) 35=3X+15

3.9.W72) If I am buying 4.5 pounds of sugar at $1.2/pound how much change will I get from a $20 bill

3.9.W73) I took a taxi. He charged me a $7.00 pick up fee and $0.02 for each mile. Which of the following expression could be used to find the total amount, $, of the fare for a trip of 40 miles
A) $= 7+(40)(0.02)
B) $ = (7)(0.02) +40
C) $= 7-(40)(0.02)
D) $ = (7)(0.02) -40

3.9.W74) If a cow eats 35 pounds of oats a day. Who much will 4 cows eat in 3 days.

3.9.w75) Which of the following statements best fits the following expression 4X=600
A) There are 2400 items total
B) There are 596 items total
C) There are 604 items total
D) 600 items were divided into 4 even stacks

3.9.w76) If I spend $32 on cakes and pies. They cost the following

PASTRY	COST
Cake	$7.00
Pie	$6.00

If I bought 2 cakes how many pies did I buy

3.9.w77) If a goat eats and apple a day and a horse eats 3 apples a day, and I have 20 goats and 3 horses how many apples a day do I need.

3.9.w78) Which table below best represents the equation Y=4X+6

A)

X	2	4	6	9
Y	12	22	30	42

B)

X	2	4	6	9
Y	14	22	32	42

C)

X	2	4	6	9
Y	14	22	30	44

D)

X	2	4	6	9
Y	14	22	30	42

3.9.w79) I sell 128 cakes and 132 pies per day. If I sell at this rate for 4 days how many more pies will I sell than cakes.

3.9.w80) If I catch 8 fish by 6:00 a.m. and then catch 4 fish per hour until 12:00 noon. Which equation below will tell me how many fish , F, I have caught in total

A) F = 8 + 4(12-6)

B) F= 8 – 4(12-6)

C) F = 8 X 4(12-6)

D) F= 8 ÷ 4(12-6)

3.9.w81) If I have $50.00 to buy treats. I buy 12 cookies at $0.35 each and 7 cupcakes at $1.25 each How much change do I have left over.

3.9.w82) If I have two fish to start with and then catch 5 fish per hour which one of the answers below shows this relationship for different number of hours of fishing, H, and the number of fish I have, F.

A)

HOURS	FISH
2	10
4	20
5	25
6	30

B)

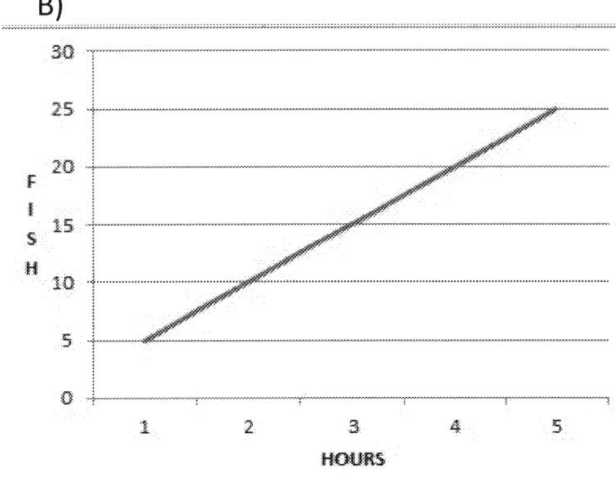

C)
F = 5H+2

D)
I catch 30 fish

3.9.w83) If 20 people owe me $12.50 each and 8 pay me, how much money is still due to me.

3.10 Division-no remainders

3.10.1) 2÷1= 3.10.2) 2÷2= 3.10.3) 3÷1= 3.10.4) 3÷3= 3.10.5) 4÷1= 3.10.6) 4÷2=
3.10.7) 4÷4= 3.10.8) 5÷1= 3.10.9) 5÷5= 3.10.10) 6÷1= 3.10.11) 6÷2= 3.10.12) 6÷3=
3.10.13) 6÷6= 3.10.14) 7÷1= 3.10.15) 7÷7= 3.10.16) 8÷1= 3.10.17) 8÷2= 3.10.18) 8÷4=
3.10.19) 8÷8= 3.10.20) 9÷1= 3.10.21) 9÷3= 3.10.22) 9÷9= 3.10.23) 10÷1= 3.10.24) 10÷2=
3.10.25) 10/5= 3.10.26) 10/10= 3.10.27) 12/1= 3.10.28) 12/2= 3.10.29) 12/3= 3.10.30) 12/4=
3.10.31) 12/6= 3.10.32) 12/12= 3.10.33) 14/1= 3.10.34) 14/2= 3.10.35) 14/7= 3.10.36) 14/14=
3.10.37) 15/1= 3.10.38) 15/3= 3.10.39) 15/5= 3.10.40) 15/15= 3.10.41) 18/3= 3.10.42) 18/6=

3.10.43) 20 ÷2 3.10.44) 9 ÷3 3.10.45) 6 ÷2 3.10.46) 15 ÷5 3.10.47) 8 ÷4 3.10.48) 10 ÷2

3.10.49) 8 ÷8 3.10.50) 8 ÷2 3.10.51) 6 ÷3 3.10.52) 7 ÷7 3.10.53) 8 ÷2 3.10.54) 2 ÷2

3.10.55) 136÷4= 3.10.56) 180÷5= 3.10.57) 64÷2= 3.10.58)112÷4=
3.10.59)280÷5= 3.10.60) 364÷7= 3.10.61) 488÷8= 3.10.62) 141÷3=
3.10.63)477÷9= 3.10.64) 232÷4= 3.10.65) 208÷8= 3.10.66) 267÷3=
3.10.67)581÷7= 3.10.68)455÷5= 3.10.69)86÷2= 3.10.70)312÷6=
3.10.71) 162÷2= 3.10.72) 192÷3= 3.10.73) 576÷9= 3.10.74) 536÷8=
3.10.75) 476÷7= 3.10.76)1840÷5= 3.10.77)1944÷9= 3.10.78) 72÷3=

3.10.79) 56/2= 3.10.80) 76/4= 3.10.81) 156/6= 3.10.82) 360/8=
3.10.83) 405/9= 3.10.84) 399/7= 3.10.85) 184/4= 3.10.86) 1296/6=
3.10.87) 128/8= 3.10.88) 651/7= 3.10.89) 370/5= 3.10.90) 156/3=
3.10.91) 894/6= 3.10.92) 130/5= 3.10.93) 112/2= 3.10.94)105/3=
3.10.95) 846/9= 3.10.96) 672/8= 3.10.97) 7784/7= 3.10.98) 4452/4=
3.10.99) 186/2= 3.10.100) 210/6= 3.10.101) 54/3= 3.10.102) 272/8=
3.10.103) 160/5= 3.10.104) 147/7= 3.10.105) 752/8= 3.10.106) 684/9=
3.10.108) 252/7= 3.10.109) 1435/5= 3.10.110) 140/4= 3.10.111) 134/2=

3.10.113) 4|544 3.10.114) 5|320 3.10.115) 7|2002 3.10.116) 9|1143
3.10.117) 8|1896 3.10.118) 3|51 3.10.119) 9|522 3.10.120) 6|1164
3.10.121) 7|546 3.10.122) 5|305 3.10.123) 3|186 3.10.124) 4|188
3.10.125) 8|768 3.10.126) 4|1132 3.10.127) 6|282 3.10.128) 7|252
3.10.129) 7|364 3.10.130) 6|510 3.10.131) 4|1132 3.10.132) 9|423
3.10.133) 3|81 3.10.134) 7|693 3.10.135) 3|123 3.10.136) 8|1184
3.10.137) 4|196 3.10.138) 9|288 3.10.139) 5|2430 3.10.140) 6|1164
3.10.141) 4|52 3.10.142) 9|756 3.10.143) 8|96 3.10.144) 5|185

Decimals

Round to the nearest tenths place

3.15.1)11÷2.3= 3.15.2).22÷2.0= 3.15.3)3.4÷16=
3.15.4)6.5÷6.8= 3.15.5).83÷2.2= 3.15.6)3.3÷60=
3.15.7)1.7÷3.9= 3.15.8)8.1÷.48= 3.15.9).65÷0.5=

Round to the nearest hundredths place

3.15.10)3.7÷74= 3.15.11)3.4÷2.5= 3.15.12).85÷39=
3.15.13).72÷35= 3.15.14)1.6÷4.9= 3.15.15).44÷9.2=
3.15.16)9.2÷12= 3.15.17)4.4÷.28= 3.15.18)2.8÷3.2=

Multiplication/Division Complex

3.17.1)(21)X(-3)= 3.17.2)(-9)X(-3)= 3.17.3)(26)X(-1)=
3.17.4)(-6)X(-6)= 3.17.5)(-83)X(2)= 3.17.6)(-3)X(-60)=
3.17.7)(-1)X(-3.9)= 3.17.8) (8)X(-4)= 3.17.9)(-6)X(5)=
3.17.10)(-3)X(-7)= 3.17.11)(-3)X(2)= 3.17.12)(85)X(-3)=
3.17.13)(72)X(-3)= 3.17.14)(-1)X(-4)= 3.17.15)(4)X(-9)=
3.17.16)(9)÷(-1)= 3.17.17)(-4)÷(-2)= 3.17.18)(2)÷(-1)=
3.17.19)(-1)÷(1)= 3.17.20)(-6)÷(-2)= 3.17.21)(3)÷(-3)
3.17.22)(-8)÷(-4)= 3.17.23)(2)÷(-2)= 3.17.24)(-9)÷(-3)=
3.17.25)(-16)÷(8)= 3.17.26)(-81)÷(-9)= 3.17.27)(65)÷(-5)=

3.10.w1) thru 3.10.w3) The picture blow shows how many flowers Sarah bought to put in her garden.

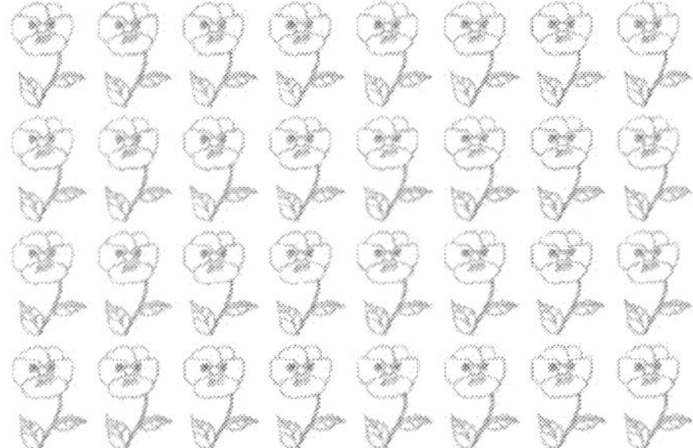

She will plant them in rows of 8 flowers.
3.10.w1) How many rows will she have once completed?
3.10.w2) How many rows will have 4 flowers?
3.10.w3) How many flowers are not in a row of 4 flowers?

3.10.w4) Mike has 15 tomatoes to but on 5 hamburgers. He wants to deposit the same amount of tomatoes on each burger. How many does each hamburger get?

3.10.w5) Mrs. Garcia has 42 cups. She wants to put them in 6 boxes each with the same amount of cups. How many cups does each box have?

3.10.w6) Aaron will place 45 rocks from his collection on a self. Each shelf will have 9 rocks. How many selves does he need?

3.10.w7) 6 students from your school go to the zoo with 11 carrots each. They want to feed 3 animals with equal number of carrots. Which equation is the best way to figure out how many carrots each animal will get.
a) 6X11÷3= b) 6X2÷11=, c) 2X11÷6=, d) 2X11X6=

3.10.w8) The bicycle shop has 42 bike for sale. They are arranged into 6 rows with an even number of bikes in each row. How many bikes are there in each row?

3.10.w9) The picture bellows shows the number of bike at a store.

The bike will be arranged in three rows with the same number in each. Which expression below will determine the number of bikes in each row.

a) 6, because 18÷3=6, b) 8, because 15÷3+3=8, c) 5, because 15÷3=5, d) 3, because 15÷5=3

3.10.w10) The band director has 28 trumpets

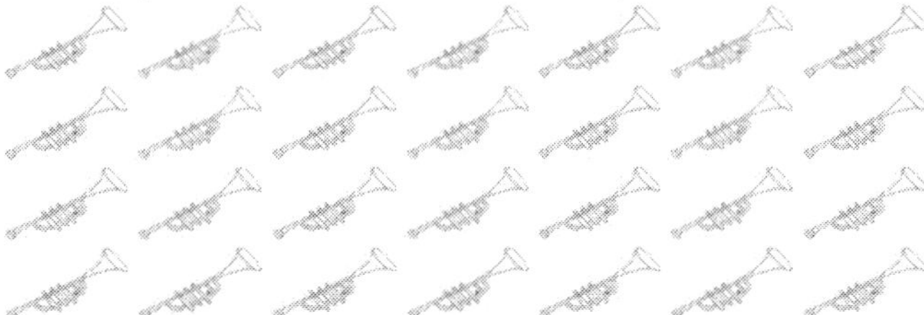

He will put a same number of trumpets on 7 selves. How many trumpets will be on each self?

a) 8, because 28÷7=8
b) 4, because 28÷7=4
c) 7, because 28÷4=7
d) 4, because 28÷7=7

3.10.w11) The candle shown below will be arranged in 4 rows.

Each row will have the same number of candles. Which mathematical express is best for determining the number of candles in each row?

a) 20÷4=5
b) 10÷5=2
c) 20÷5=4
d) 10÷2=5

3.10.W12) Nellie is putting on a dog show in her neighborhood. There are 16 dogs entered as shown below.

If she puts the dogs into 4 rows, Each row has the same number of dogs. How many dogs will be in each row?

a) 12, 16÷4=12
b) 4, 16÷4=4
c) 3, 6÷3=2
d) 8, 16÷2=8

3.10.w13) Verna bought 20 trees for his farm, as shown below.

He wants to plant them in 5 rows. Each row will have the same number of trees in it. Which mathematical expression will help in determining the number of trees in each row?
a) 20X4=100
b) 4X6=24
c) 20÷5=4
d) 20÷2=10

3.10.w14) Danielle sorted 40 greeting cards into 5 equally sized groups. Which statement below is **NOT** in the same fact family as 40÷5=8
a) 8X5=40
b) 5X4=8
c) 40÷8=5
d) 5X8=40

3.10.w15) John has 14 model boat to play with, as shown below.

While playing with them in the bath, he arranges them in 2 rows with equal number in each. Which statement below will help determine the number of boats in each row?
a) 14÷2=7
b) 2X14=28
c) 14-2=10
d) 14÷7=2

3.10.w16) I put 36 dozen cookies into 4 boxes. If each box has an even number of cookies how many cookies does each box have?

3.10.w17) I have 138 trees places in 6 rows. Each row has the same number of trees. How many trees are in each row?

3.10.w18) If I have 128 cupcakes to put into boxes. Each box can hold 8 cupcakes. How many boxes do I need.
a) 15, b) 16, c) 17, d) 8

3.10.w19) If I have 24 horses and put 6 hoarse in each field. How many field will I need?
a) 3, b) 4, c) 6, d) 23

3.10.w20) I have 146 pennies. I will stack them in groups of 8. How many stacks will I have?
a) 17, b)18, c)19, d)20

3.10.w21) If I have 35 dollars to but hamburgers. Each burger is 6 dollars. How many burgers can I buy?
a) 4, b) 5, c) 6, d) 7

3.10.w22) The table below show the number of feet in a given number of yards

NUMBER OF YARDS	NUMBER OF FEET
33	11
12	4
42	14
81	27

Which of the following equations best represents this relationship
a)Number of Yards – 21 = Number of feet
b)Number of Yards X 2 = Number of feet
c)Number of Yards – 8 = Number of feet
d)Number of Yards ÷ 3= Number of feet

3.10.w23) The table below show the number of fluid ounces in a given number of teaspoons

NUMBER OF TEASPOONS	NUMBER OF FLUID OUNCES
34	17
12	6
42	21
82	42

Which of the following equations best represents this relationship
a)Number of Teaspoons – 17 = Number of Fluid Ounces
b) Number of Teaspoons – 6 = Number of Fluid Ounces
c) Number of Teaspoons ÷ 6 = Number of Fluid Ounces
d) Number of Teaspoons ÷ 2 = Number of Fluid Ounces

3.10.w24) If I jog 108 minutes over 4 days. The same amount of time each day. How many minutes did I jog each day.

3.10.w25 There are 216 students in a school. They are divided evenly between 9 class. How many are in each class?

3.10.w26) You teacher orders apples to make pies. Each pie gets the same number of apples
There are 32 pies.
each pie gets 45 apples
#The apples are divided evenly between 8 boxes
How many apples are in each box?

3.10.w27) If the 6 elephants at the zoo eat a total 204 bananas, and each one ate the same amount, how many bananas did each elephant get to eat?

3.10.w28) You bought 34 cases of carrots for a trip to the zoo. Each case had 25 carrots each. If five rhino divided the carrots evenly how many did each one get?

3.10.w29) If I have 128 cookies to divide into piles of three cookies each. How many piles do I have?

3.10.w30) I have a bunch of toys. I divided them into 2 equal groups. Which equation can **NOT** be used to find the number of toys in each group.

a) ◯÷2=5
b) 2+5=◯
c) 2X5=◯
d) 5x2=◯

3.10.w31) I buy a computer and 3 video games for $560. If I spent $389 for the computer and the same amount for each video game, how much did each game cost?

3.10.w32) The following table shows how many pennies were in five different boxes

BOX	NUMBER OF PENNIES
A	87
B	24
C	56
D	76
E	17

If I divide the pennies into 4 equal piles, how many pennies will be in each group?

3.10.w33) I had 147 strawberries. If I divide them into 7 equal piles, how many are in each?

3.10.w34) Which diagram below represents the equation 27÷3?

a)

XXXX
XXXX
XXXX
XXXX
XXXX
XXXX

c)

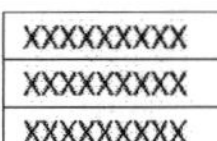

XXXXXXXXX
XXXXXXXXX
XXXXXXXXX

b)

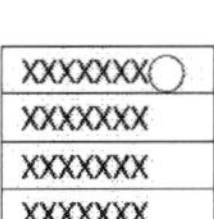

XXXXXXX◯
XXXXXXX
XXXXXXX
XXXXXXX

d)

XXXXXX◯
XXXXXX◯
XXXXXX◯
XXXXXX
XXXXXX

3.10.w35) The table below show a mathematical relationship

◯	Δ
25	5
15	3
40	8
10	2

Which of the following below best represents this relationship?

a) Δ - 20 = ◯
b) Δ ÷ 4 = ◯
c) Δ + 20 = ◯
d) Δ X 5 = ◯

3.10.w36) In the equation below the ◯ and the ⌂ represent different numbers

◯ X ⌂ = 42

Which of the following is in the same fact family

a) 42 X ◯ = ⌂
b) ⌂ X 42 = ◯
c) 42 ÷ ◯ = ⌂
d) ◯ ÷ ⌂ = 42

3.10.w37) I have 725 cookies. I separate them into 5 groups of equal amounts. How many cookies will be in two of the groups.

a) 145
b) 290
c) 730
d) 435

3.10.w38) I paid $76.20 for a magazine subscription that last 12 months. What is the cost of each issue?

3.10.w39) If I saved $187.50 over 5 weeks. If I saved the same amount each week how much did I save each week

3.10.w40) If I have 49 cupcakes that weight 2352 grams. How much does each cupcake weight if each has the same weight.

3.10.w41) The following number all have something in common. { 12, 126, 411, 873}

A) They are divisible by 4
B) They are divisible by 6
C) They are divisible by 3
D) They are divisible by 2

3.10.W42) The following table describes how many cupcakes I have vs the number of boxes.

CUPCAKES	BOXES
51	3
85	5
119	7
136	8

Which statement below is true about the relationship shown above

A) The number of boxes plus 28 equals the number of cupcakes
B) The number of cupcakes minus 28 equals the number of boxes
C) The number of cupcakes times 17 equals the number of boxes
D) The number of cupcakes divided by 17 equals the number of boxes

3.10.w43) If I have 864 pennies I want to put into 36 rows each with the same number of pennies. How many rows will I have.

3.10.w44) While going fishing I had 204 worms. I used 36 of them then divided the remaining evenly between 4 friends. Which equation below would be best to determine how many worms each friend received.

A) (204-36)x4=N
B) (204-36)-4=N
C) (204-36)÷4=N
D) (204-36) + 4=N

3.10.w45) What is the quotient when 0.93 is divided by 3

3.10.w46) I have 1995 fish to divide evenly between 15 tanks. How many fish will be in each tank.

3.10.w47) I have a rope 4.27 feet long. I cut it into 7 equal parts. How long is each in inches

3.10.w48) If I have 429 cupcakes and want to put 13 in a box. How many boxes will I need.

3.10.w49) If I buy a car for $1100.08 and makes 8 equal sized payments, what is the amount of each payment.

3.10.w50) If I have 508 can of soda and want to put them on four shelves in equal amounts. How many cans will be on each shelve.

3.10.w51) If I mowed 5 lawns in 4 hours and 35 minutes, how long did each lawn take

3.10.w52) If it took me 3 hours and 30 minutes to bake 6 sheet of cookies how long did it tale to bake each sheet

3.10.w53) If it take me 7 hours to do 4 jobs how long was each job

3.10.w54) If I walk 5 miles in 5 hours and 25 minutes than how long did each mile take
3.10.w55) If I have 45 pennies and I place them in stacks of 7, how many stacks of 7 do I have
3.10.w56) If I have 36 pennies and I place them in stacks of 7, how many stacks total do I have
3.10.w57) If I have 37 pennies and I place them in stacks of 5, how many stacks of 5 do I have
3.10.w58) If I have 61 pennies and I place them in stacks of 9, how many stacks total do I have
3.10.w59) If I have 24 pennies and I place them in stacks of 9, how many stacks of 9 do I have
3.10.w60) If I have 27 pennies and I place them in stacks of 4, how many stacks of 4 do I have
3.10.w61) If I have 12 pennies and I place them in stacks of 5, how many stacks of 5 do I have
3.10.w62) If I have 83 pennies and I place them in stacks of 5, how many stacks of 5 do I have

3.10.w63) If I have 120 cookies I want to share evenly between my friends. Which table below shows the relationship between the number of friends, F, and the number of cookies each will get, N.

A)

NUMBER OF FRIENDS	NUMBER OF COOKIES
2	60
3	40
4	30
6	10

B)

NUMBER OF FRIENDS	NUMBER OF COOKIES
2	60
3	40
4	35
6	20

C)

NUMBER OF FRIENDS	NUMBER OF COOKIES
2	60
3	50
4	30
6	20

D)

NUMBER OF FRIENDS	NUMBER OF COOKIES
2	60
3	40
4	30
6	20

3.10.w64) If I make 100 cookies, and used 25 eggs how many cookies did I make per egg.
A) 10
B) 4
C)20
D)50

3.10.w65) If I pay $150.12 for a gym yearly membership, what is the monthly cost?

3.10.w66) If my aquarium has 465 gallons and 25 fish how many gallons does each fish get
A) 20.6 fish per gallon
B) 18.6 fish per gallon
C) 13.7fish per gallon
D) 21.4 fish per gallon

3.10.w67) If I divide the number 7 by 5, which equation below could **NOT** be used to find the result.
A) 7÷5=
B) 7/5=
C) 5÷7=
D) $5\overline{)7}$

3.10.w68) At a party I will give each adult 2 cupcakes and each child 1 cupcake. If there are 25 adults and 40 children and 15 cupcakes per box how many boxes do I need.

3.10.w69) If 14 cupcakes cost $10.92 what is the cost of one cupcake

3.11 Inequalities

State if these are true or false

3.11.1) 3<1	3.11.2) 5>5	3.11.3) 7≤7	3.11.4) 14<7	3.11.5) 56<81	3.11.6) 4>8
3.11.7) 81<45	3.11.8) 85≥51	3.11.9) 3<9	3.11.10) 43>67	3.11.11) 2<8	3.11.12) 41<41
3.11.13) 76≤76	3.11.14) 78<98	3.11.15) 8<4	3.11.16) 9≤12	3.11.17) 76≤67	3.11.18) 543>73
3.11.19) 0<1	3.11.20) 13<7	3.11.21) 67>43	3.11.22) 13≥31	3.11.23)45<45	3.11.24) 123>237

3.11.25) 3.01<-3.10	3.11.26) 5.0>-5.00	3.11.27) 7.11≤-71.1	3.11.28) -14.30<7.30

3.11.29) 4.15>4.25	3.11.30) 5.167<5.168	3.11.31) 7.2456>7.3345	3.11.32) 2.34<2.24
3.11.33) 5.551<5.450	3.11.34) 6.28>6.38	3.11.35) 1.25>1.26	3.11.36) 4.445>4.545
3.11.37) 6.01>6.010	3.11.38) 8.291<8.190	3.11.39) 3.24>3.25	3.11.40) 6.01≥6.010
3.11.41) 4.556>4.555	3.11.42) 3.6>2.65	3.11.43) 6.779<6.778	3.11.44)7.3>8.2
3.11.45) 8.667<8.668	3.11.46) 7.89<7.88	3.11.47) 2.356>2.365	3.11.48) 3.225>3.252

3.11.49)-6.45<-5.45	3.11.50) -3.56<-3.66	3.11.51)-1.235<-1.236	3.11.52) -7.68<-7.58
3.11.53) -9.551<-9.550	3.11.54) -5.67<-5.68	3.11.55) -5.336>-5.363	3.11.56)-6.344>-6.343
3.11.57) -3.778>-3.768	3.11.58)6.00≤6.0	3.11.59) –4.25<-4.26	3.11.60) -9.446>-9.436
3.11.61) -6.67<-6.87	3.11.62) -7.667>-7.578	3.11.63)-5.01>-5.10	3.11.64) -4.326<-4.437
3.11.65)-3.11>-31.1	3.11.66) -4.01<-4.10	3.11.67) -7.89>-7.81	3.11.68) -5.6>-4.7
3.11.69) -66.8>-69.4	3.11.70) -3.45<-3.450	3.11.71)-2.34>-2.36	3.11.72) -89.90<-89.901

3.11.w1) A group of number is shown below

2467	2586	2775	2911

Which statement below is true:
a) 2586 >2476 because the 5>4.
b) 2467>2911 because 67>11
c) 2775>2467 because 75 is greater than 67
d) 2467<2586 because 67<86

3.11.w2) A groups of number is shown below

137	366	415	110

Which statement below is true
a) 415<366 because 66<15
b) 137>415 because 37 is greater than 15
c) 366>415 because 6>5
d) 110<366 because 1<3

3.11.w3) A group of numbers is shown below

4	8	9	5

Which statement below is **NOT** true
a) 4<8
b)9>4
c) 9>8
d)4>9

3.11.w4) A group of numbers is shown below

827	199	1127	531

Which statement below is true
a) 827>1127 because the 8 > 11
b) 199>531 because 1>5
c) 531>1127 because 53>11
d) 1127>827 because 1>0

3.11.w5) The following list shows three clues about a number I am thinking about.
the number is greater than 3578
the number is less than 5587
There is a 6 in the hundreds place
Which of the following could be this number
a) 6156
b) 4729
c) 4699
d)2687

3.11.w6) The following list shows three clues about a number I am thinking about.
the number is greater than 379
the number is less than 421
There is a 8 in the tens place
Which of the following could be this number
a) 581
b) 381
c) 289
d)417

3.11.w7) The following list shows three clues about a number I am thinking about.
the number is greater than 28
the number is less than 54
There is a 7 in the ones place
Which of the following could be this number
a) 42
b) 73
c) 47
d)31

3.11.w8) The sum of 6 thousands 4 hundreds 5 tens and 2 ones is which of the following
a) 6542
b) 2546
c)6452
d) 17

3.11.w9) The sum of 8 thousands 3 hundreds 0 tens and 1 ones is which of the following
a) 8031
b) 1038
c) 8301
d) 12

3.11.w10) I have 12.25 pounds of potatoes and my friend has 15.7 pounds. Which number below is between these two numbers.
A) 11.37, B) 16.80, C) 12.37, D) 3.45

3.11.w11) If I go to the mall with \$45, and spend \$10 on a burger. Which of the following equations can be used to find the amount of money, \$, I have left to spend
A) 10 + \$ < 45
B) 45-\$>10
C) 10+\$ ≤ 45
D) 10-45>10

3.11.W12) I need \$15 for a trip this weekend. I have already saved \$8. The following equation will help me determine the amount,\$, I need to save

8+\$≥15

Which of the following equation is the same
A) \$≥23
B) \$<23
C) \$≥7
D) \$<7

3.11.W13) Which list below shows the weights of dogs from highest to lowest
A) -4, 0, -12, -123
B) 0, -4, -12, -123
C) -123, -12, -4, 0
D) -12, -4, 0, -123

Croquis of a Deliberate Crime

YouTube

3.11.w14) If I earn \$8.00 per hour and want to save \$48.00. Which one of the following equation below can help me determine the amount of hours, N, I need to work

A) $8xN \geq 48$

B) $8xN < 48$

C) $48-8 \geq N$

D) $8 \div N > 48$

3.11.w15) If I buy a bottle of milk for \$3.50 and cookies at \$0.45 each which expression below helps me determine how many cookies, x, I can buy with \$7.50

A) $7.5 < 3.5+0.45X$

B) $7.5 \leq 3.5+0.45X$

C) $7.5 > 3.5+0.45X$

D) $7.5 \geq 3.5+0.45X$

3.11.w16) If I am saving \$20.00/week and I started with \$180.00 which equation below helps me determine how much money, \$, I will have in, W, weeks

A) \$= 180+20W

B) \$= 180-20W

C) \$= 20+180W

D) \$= 20+-180W

Prime factors/GCT/LCF

What are the prime factors of the following numbers

3.18.1) 28	3.18.2) 135	3.18.3) 50	3.18.4) 98	3.18.5) 48	3.18.6) 96
3.18.7) 125	3.18.8) 27	3.18.9) 162	3.18.10) 375	3.18.11) 160	3.18.12) 405
3.18.13) 192	3.18.14) 54	3.18.15)375	3.18.16) 75	3.18.17) 44	3.18.18)9

What are the Least common factors (LCF) of the following

3.18.19) 28,192	3.18.20) 135, 375	3.18.21) 162, 160	3.18.22) 375, 192
3.18.23) 48, 54	3.18.24) 96, 162	3.18.25) 125, 27	3.18.26) 27, 192
3.18.27) 162, 28	3.18.28) 375, 162	3.18.29) 160, 44	3.18.30) 405, 192

What are the Greatest common factors (GCF) of the following

3.18.37) 28, 50	3.18.38) 125, 375	3.18.39) 375, 160	3.18.40) 44, 192
3.18.41) 162, 375	3.18.42) 160, 75	3.18.43) 192, 375	3.18.44) 28, 44
3.18.45) 192, 162	3.18.46) 125, 160	3.18.47) 405, 375	3.18.48) 75, 375

3.18.w1) What is the missing part of the prime factor of 180

2^2x3^2x _.

Exponents

3.19.1) $(2X10^{12})X(3X10^4)$	3.19.2) $(3.5X10^2)X(2X10^7)$	3.19.3) $(1.5X10^8)X(5X10^6)$
3.19.4) $(8X10^4)X(2X10^6)$	3.19.5) $(3.5X10^2)X(2X10^9)$	3.19.6) $(1.5X10^8)X(5X10^9)$
3.19.7) $(3X10^2)X(5X10^4)$	3.19.8) $(4.5X10^3)X(2X10^7)$	3.19.9) $(1X10^4)X(6X10^9)$
3.19.10) $(5X10^8)X(9X10^4)$	3.19.12) $(3X10^2)X(7X10^3)$	3.19.13) $(2X10^8)X(6.5X10^8)$
3.19.14) $(3.5X10^3)X(8X10^6)$	3.19.15) $(2X10^5)X(9X10^7)$	3.19.16) $(6X10^7)X(8X10^6)$

3.19.17) $(5X10^3)X(6X10^{-4})$	3.19.18) $(8X10^{-2})X(8X10^{-8})$	3.19.19) $(6X10^9)X(9X10^{-4})$
3.19.20) $(2X10^{-7})X(5X10^4)$	3.19.21) $(6X10^{-3})X(6X10^{-9})$	3.19.22) $(7X10^{-1})X(8X10^{-4})$
3.19.23) $(1X10^{-8})X(9X10^3)$	3.19.24) $(2X10^{-2})X(7X10^{-5})$	3.19.25) $(4X10^{-3})X(6X10^{-2})$
3.19.26) $(5X10^{-4})X(8X10^6)$	3.19.27) $(6X10^2)X(7X10^{-9})$	3.19.28) $(7X10^{-8})X(7X10^6)$

3.19.29) $(7X10^{6})\div(9X10^{4})$
3.19.30) $(4X10^{-2})\div(5X10^{8})$
3.19.31) $(3X10^{-8})\div(9X10^{-7})$
3.19.32) $(5X10^{-3})\div(5X10^{4})$
3.19.33) $(4X10^{-5})\div(8X10^{-8})$
3.19.34) $(5X10^{8})\div(7X10^{-2})$
3.19.35) $(3X10^{9})\div(6X10^{-3})$
3.19.36) $(3X10^{-3})\div(4X10^{-4})$
3.19.37) $(9X10^{-8})\div(4X10^{-9})$
3.19.38) $(1X10^{5})\div(7X10^{-7})$
3.19.39) $(8X10^{-1})\div(9X10^{7})$
3.19.40) $(2X10^{8})\div(2X10^{6})$

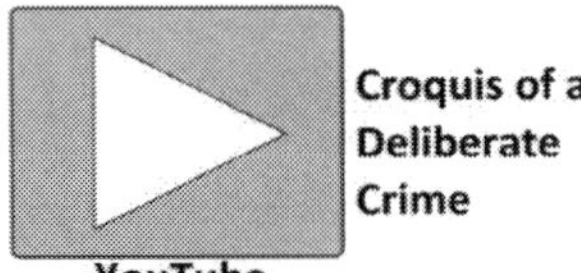

If you don't get the correct answer, and want an explanation on how to work the problem, go to YouTube and type in "MMT" then the problem number. An example would be, MMT 3.9.w12,. The video will show you how to work problem 3.9.w12.

For one on one tutoring via skype at $35.00/Hr.; contact me at marksmathtutoring@yahoo.com

4 GEOMETRY

4.1) Which of the following is not a Rhombus, trapezoid, rectangle or square?

A) B) C) D)

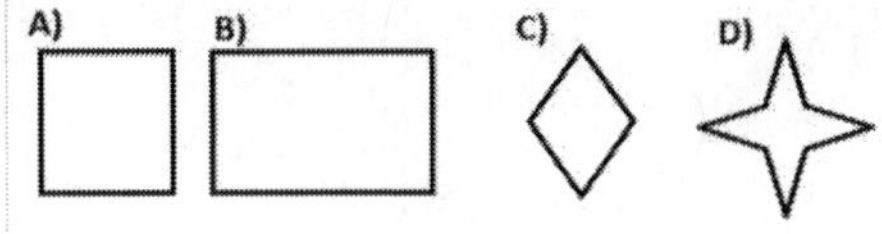

4.2) Which of the following is not a polygon?

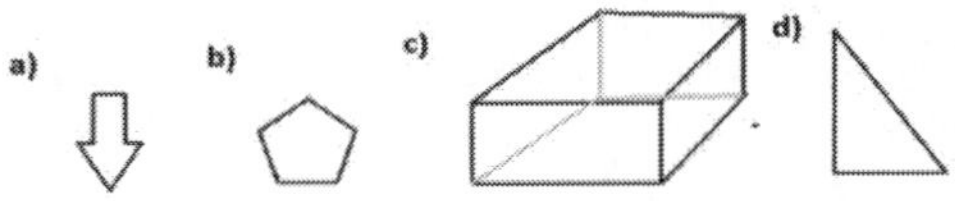

a) b) c) d)

4.3) Which of the following figures is not a quadrilateral?

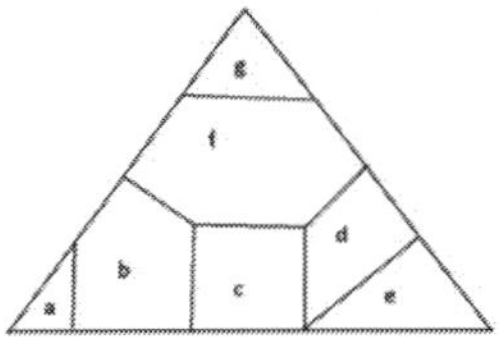

4.4) Which of the following is not a Rhombus, trapezoid, rectangle or square?

a)
b)
c)
d)

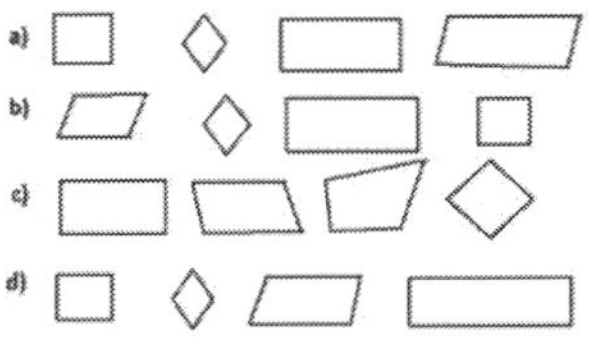

4.5) Which statement is true about the following figures?

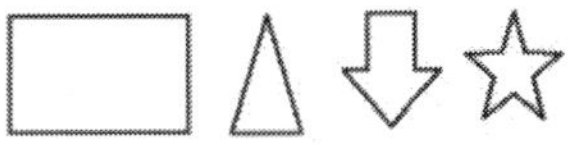

a) All the figures are Rhombuses
b) All the figures are polygons
c) All the figures are parallelograms
d) All figures are Quadrilaterals

4.61) Which of the following is required for a pentagon?
a) right angles
b) parallel lines
c) 4 vertices
d) five sides

4.62) The following figures share a common characteristic.

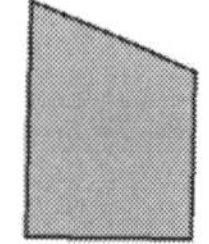

a) all are trapezoids
b) all are squares
c) all are triangles
d) all are quadrilaterals

4.39) Which of the following figure is not a pentagon

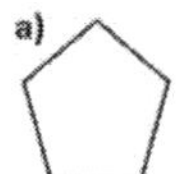

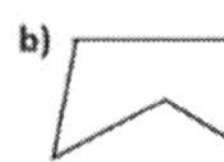

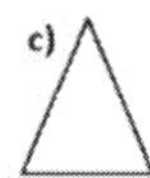

4.40) Which of the following figure is not a hexagon

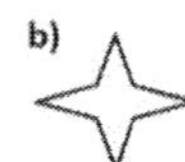

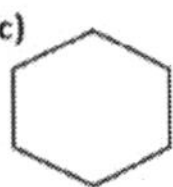

4.81) Which of the following is a rectangle?

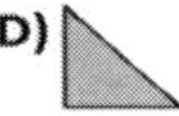

4.6) Which figure has symmetry

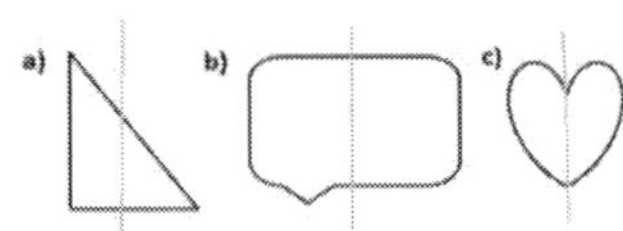

4.7) Which figure does not have symmetry

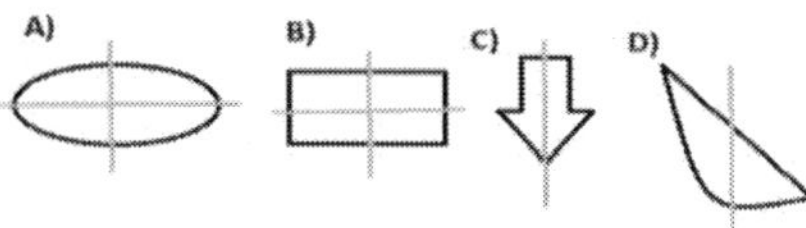

If you don't get the correct answer, and want an explanation on how to work the problem, go to YouTube and type in "MMT" then the problem number. An example would be, MMT 3.9.w12,. The video will show you how to work problem 3.9.w12.

For one on one tutoring via skype at $35.00/Hr.; contact me at marksmathtutoring@yahoo.com

4.65) The drawing below is only half of the figure. The rest of it is a symmetry about the line AB

Which one of the following could complete this figure

a)

b)

c)

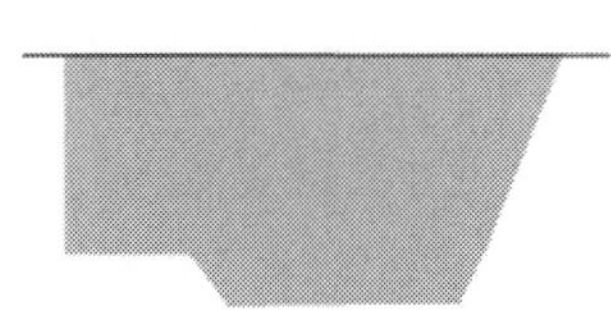

d)

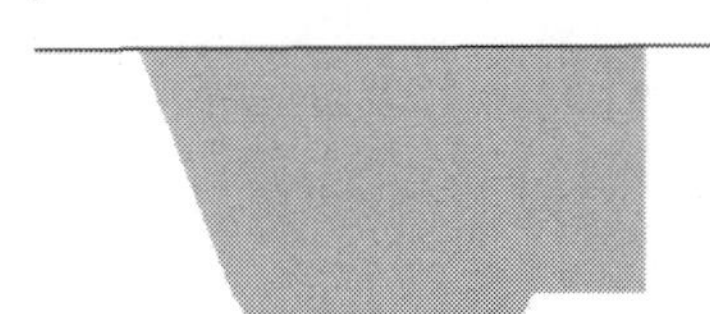

4.66) Which drawing below has two lines of symmetry?

A) 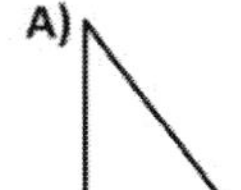
B) 
C) 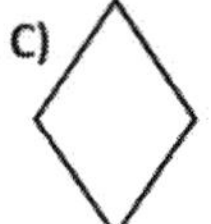
D) 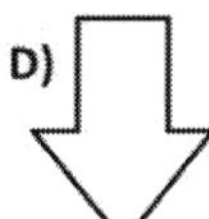

4.67) Which of the drawings below has only one line of symmetry?

A) 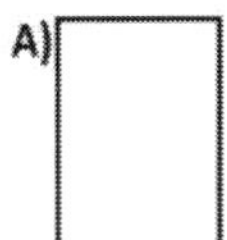
B) 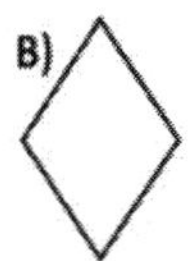
C) 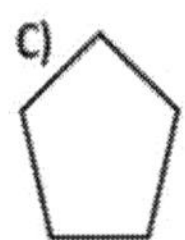
D) 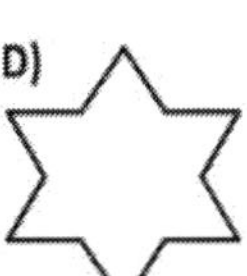

4.68) Which of the following figures has both a horizontal and a vertical line of symmetry?

A) 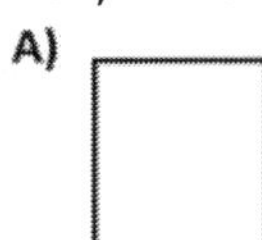
B) 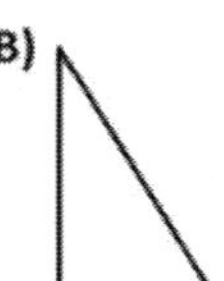
C) 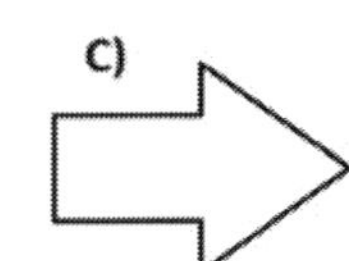
D) 

4.69) Which figure below has only a horizontal line of symmetry, no vertical?

A) 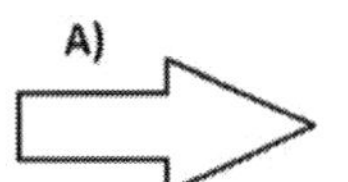
B) 
C) 
D) 

If you don't get the correct answer, and want an explanation on how to work the problem, go to YouTube and type in "MMT" then the problem number. An example would be, MMT 3.9.w12,. The video will show you how to work problem 3.9.w12.

4.70) Which figure below does not have a vertical line of symmetry, no horizontal?

A)  B) 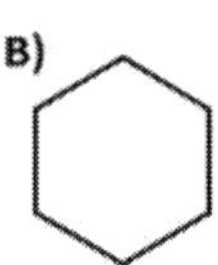 C)  D) 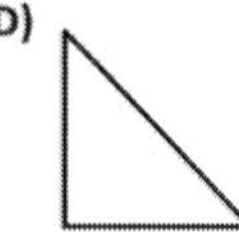

4.8) How many edges does the figure have?

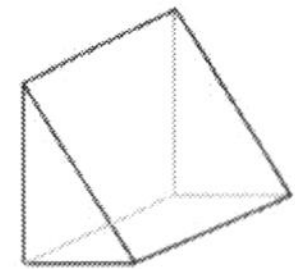

4.9) How many edges does the figure have?

4.10) How many edges does the figure have?

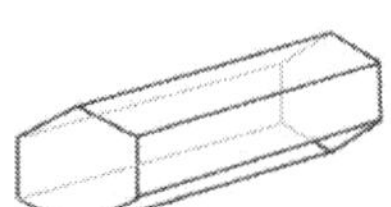

4.11) How many edges does the figure have?

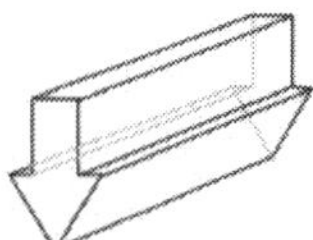

4.41) How many edges does the figure have?

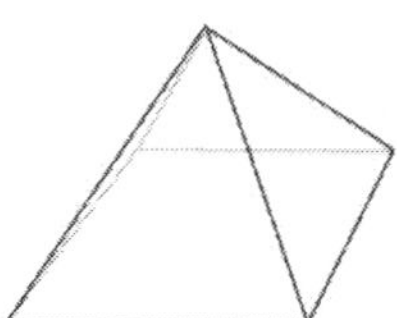

4.42) How many edges does the figure have?

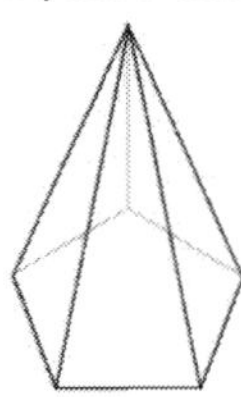

4.12) Which of the following figures is made of four congruent shapes

a) b) 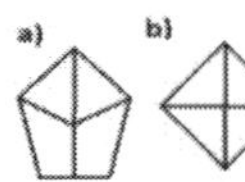 c)  d) 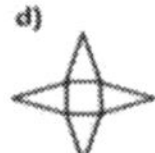

4.13) Given the figure below:

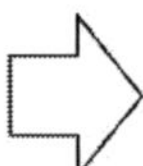

Which figure below appears to be congruent?

a) b) 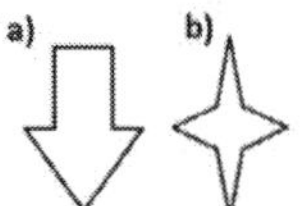 c)  d) 

4.14) A triangle has three equal sides. If the perimeter is 18 cm how long is each side?

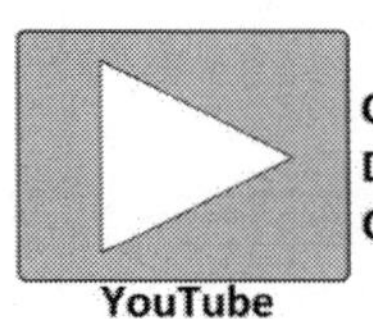

Croquis of a Deliberate Crime

4.15) The following figure was created with two congruent triangle on each end of a rectangle. What is the perimeter of this shape?

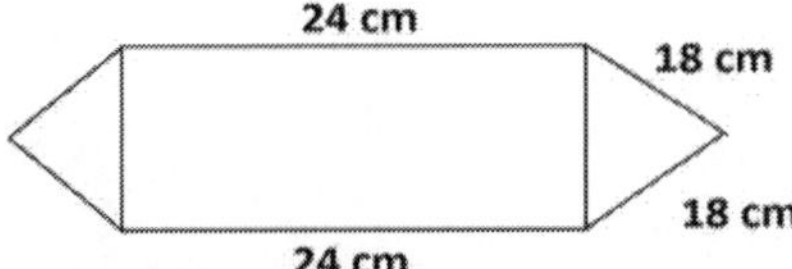

4.16) The following figure has a line of symmetry as shown. What is the perimeter of this figure?

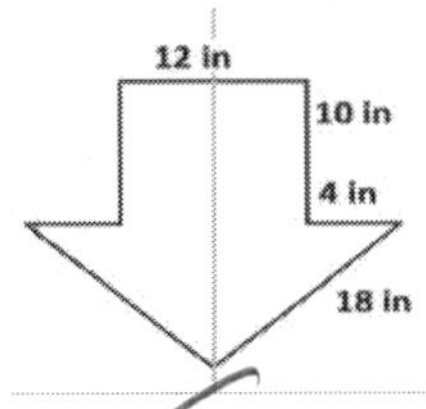

4.17) Ed needs to fence his back yard in. The dimensions of the yard are shown below

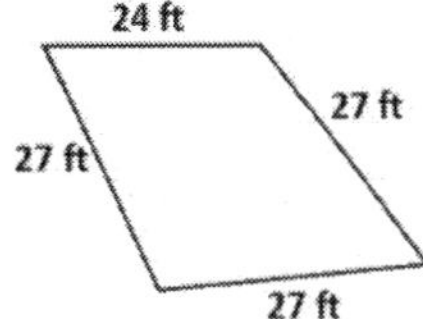

If he has 103 feet of fence does he have enough to do the job?

4.18) Given the drawings of two rectangles below

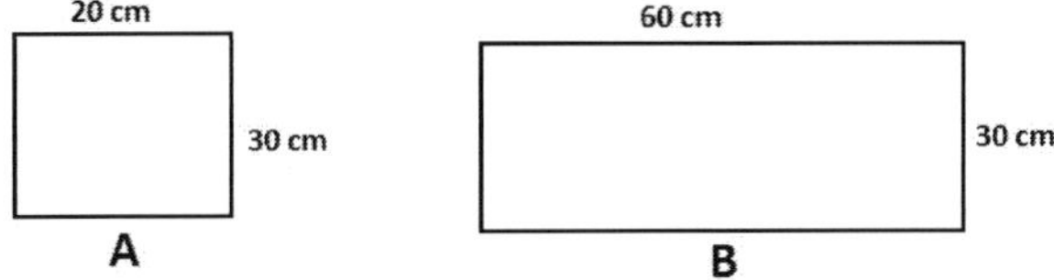

What statement below is true
a) The perimeter of A is 40 cm less than the perimeter of B
b) The perimeter of B is 40 cm less than the perimeter of A
c) The perimeter of A is 80 cm less than the perimeter of B
d) The perimeter of B is 80 cm less than the perimeter of A

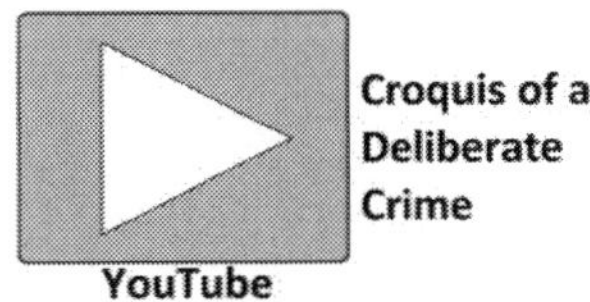

If you don't get the correct answer, and want an explanation on how to work the problem, go to YouTube and type in "MMT" then the problem number. An example would be, MMT 3.9.w12,. The video will show you how to work problem 3.9.w12.

For one on one tutoring via skype at $35.00/Hr.; contact me at marksmathtutoring@yahoo.com

4.19) The two figures below are drawn with congruent sides.

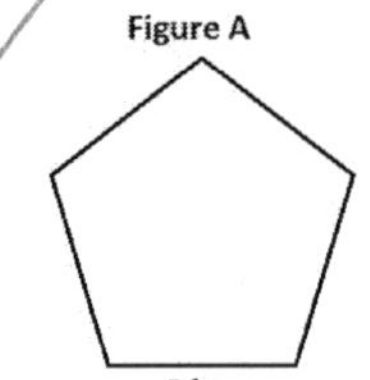

Which statement below is true
a)The perimeter of Figure A is 16 inches larger the Figure B
b)The perimeter of Figure B is 16 inches larger the Figure A
c)The perimeter of Figure A is 24 inches larger the Figure B
d)The perimeter of Figure B and A are the same

4.20) Sarah needs to fence in her garden to keep animals out. The garden has the dimensions shown below

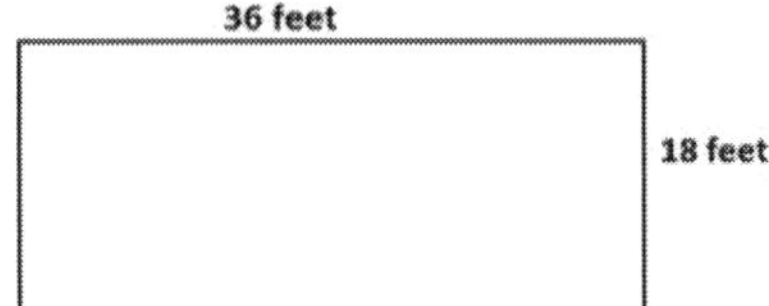

If she has 110 feet of fence, does she have enough?

4.21) Steve has a garden he needs to fence in. He has 64 feet of fence. Which in of the following figure could not be the dimensions of his garden?

a)

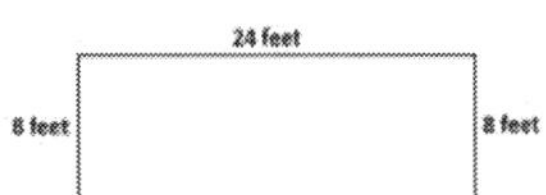

c)

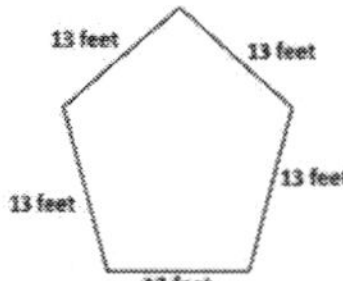

b)

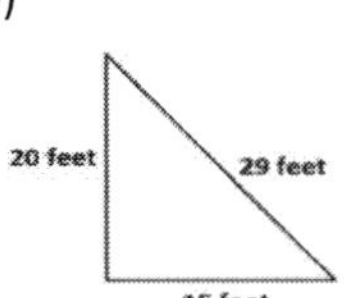

d)

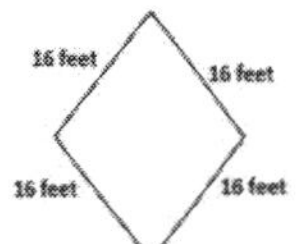

4.22) Which of the following figures does not have a perimeter of 120 cm?

a)

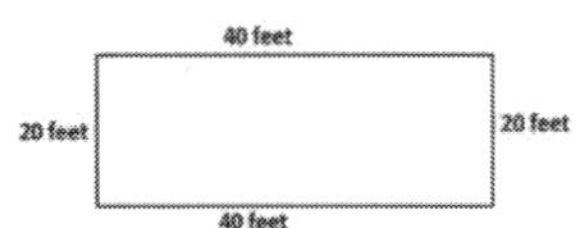

c)

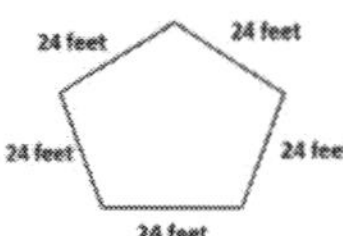

b)

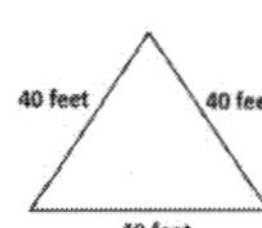

d)

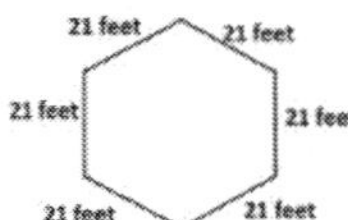

4.23) If a triangle has a perimeter of 26 inches, and two sides are 11 inches each. What is the length of the third side?

4.24) What is the area of the letter H below if each square is 1 foot square

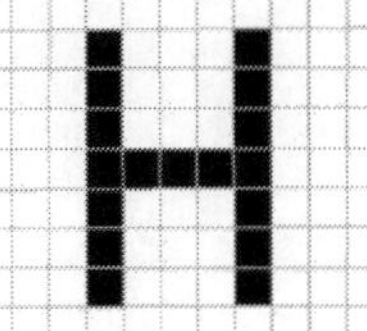

4.25) What is the area of the letter L below if each square is 1 foot square

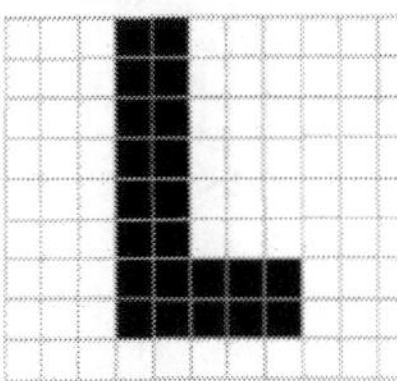

4.26) What is the difference between the area of the letter O and the letter T shown below if each square is I Meter squared

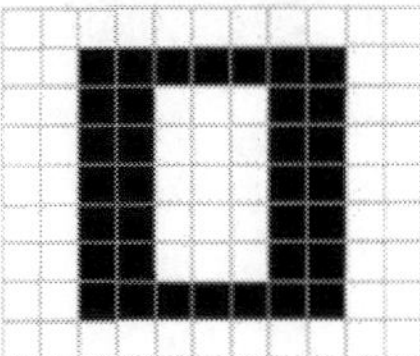

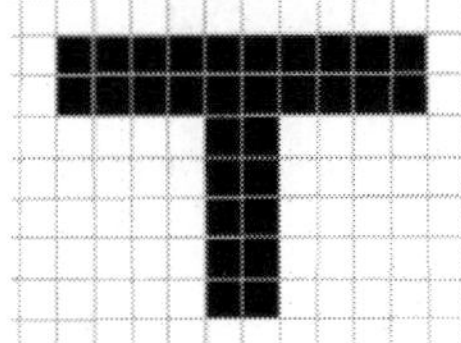

4.27) Which equation below best describes the mathematical equation to determine the area of the shaded box below?

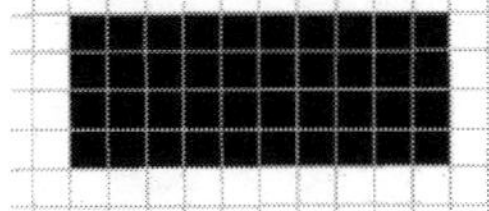

a) 6-4=2
b) 10X4=40
c) 24÷4=6
d) 6+4=10

4.28) I started to tie my kitchen floor as shown in the diagram below. Each small square is 1 foot square.

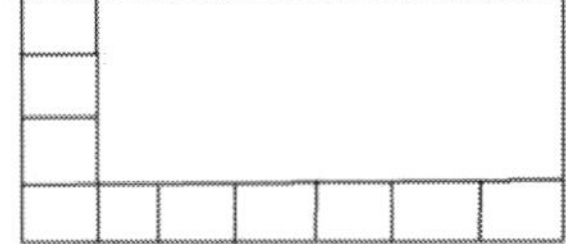

Once finished tiling the floor how many ties will be used?

4.29) Given the diagram below what is the area of the rectangle?

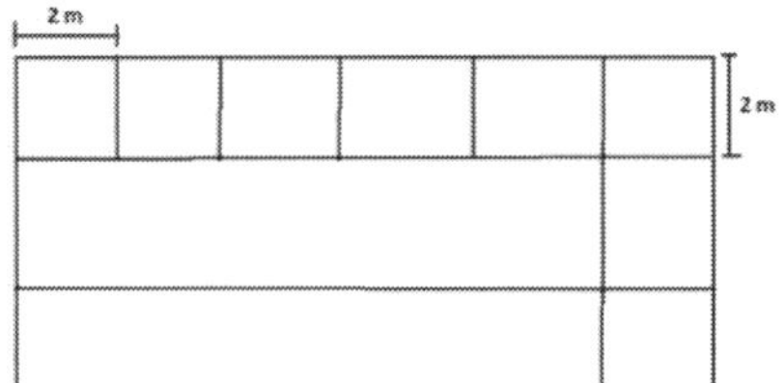

4.30) Which of the following rectangles has an area of 42?

a)

c)

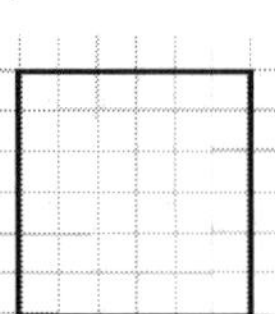

b)

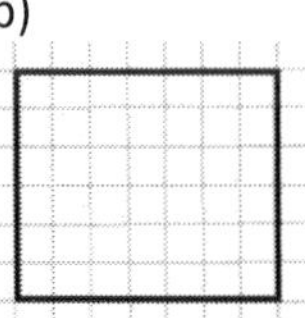

d)

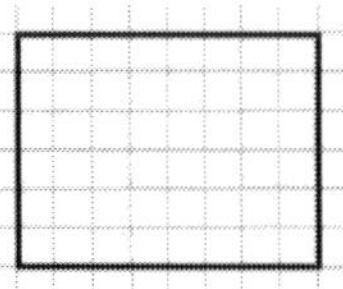

4.31) If your floor measures 9 feet by 17 feet, what is the area of this floor in feet square?

4.32) If a garden has the shape of the drawing below and each square is 1 meter square, what is the area of the garden?

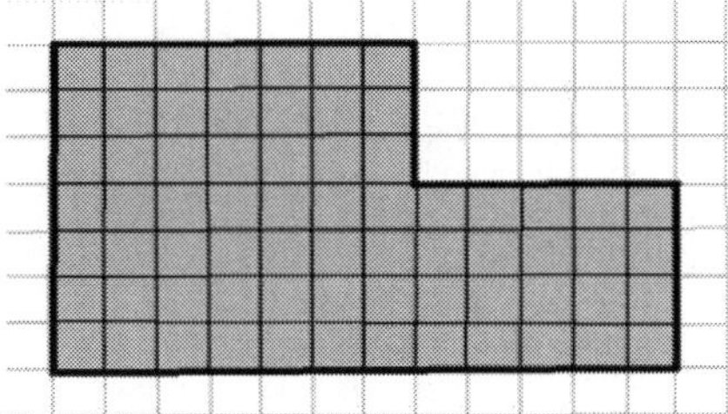

4.33) Which statement below is true about the two figures below

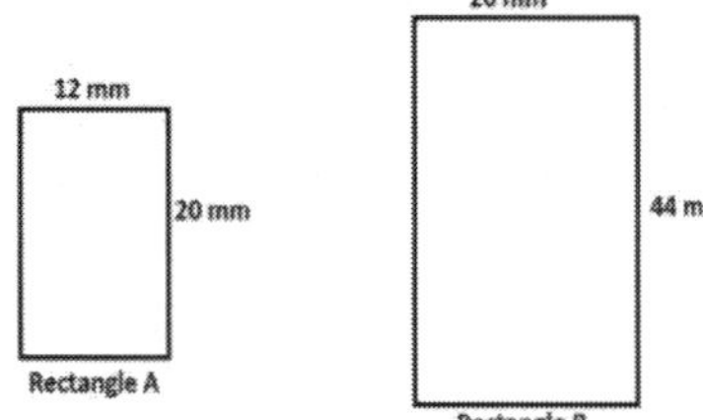

a) The perimeter rectangle A is 56 mm small than rectangle B
b) The perimeter rectangle A is 64 mm small than rectangle B
c) The perimeter rectangle A is 32 mm small than rectangle B

4.53) I a rectangle has sides 45 mm and 20 mm and the smaller side is cut in half, what is its new area?

4.54) If a square has sides 45 inches and is cut to 1/3 what is its new area?

4.55) What is the perimeter of a rectangular poster with one side 18 inches and the other 8 inches.

4.56) If your garden is square with sides 39 feet, what is the perimeter?

4.43) How many smaller blocks are in this cub?

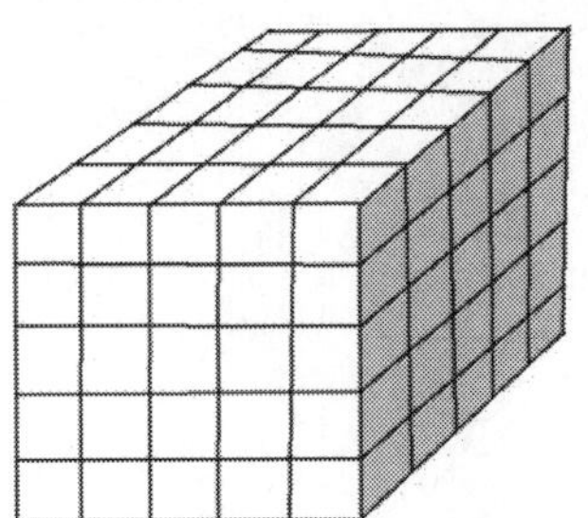

4.44) How many smaller blocks are in this cub?

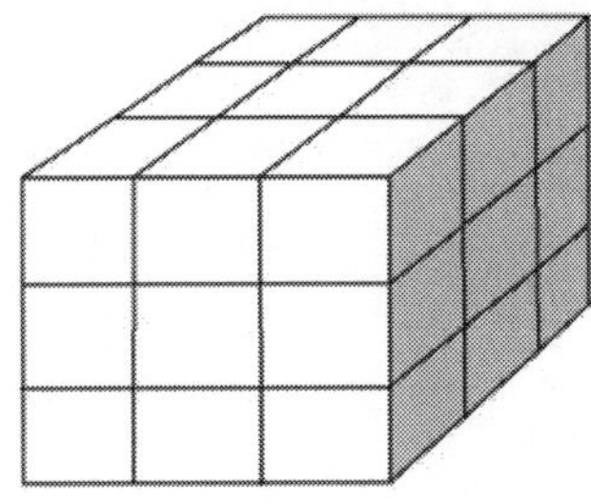

4.45) How many smaller blocks are in this cub?

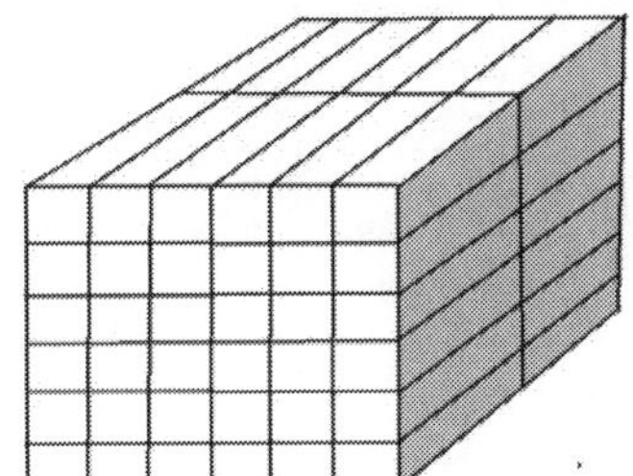

4.46) How many smaller blocks are in this cub?

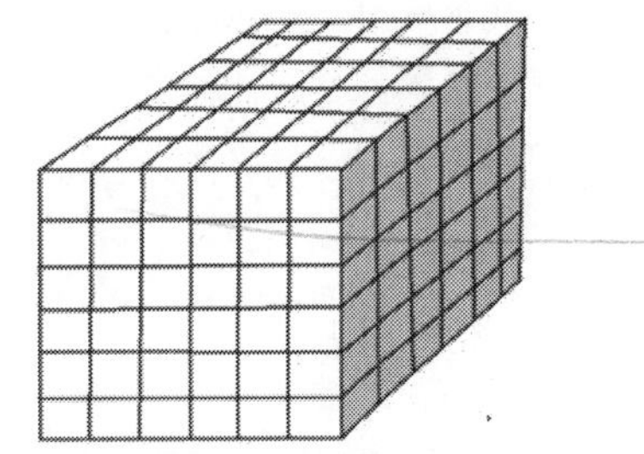

4.47) How many smaller blocks are in this cub?

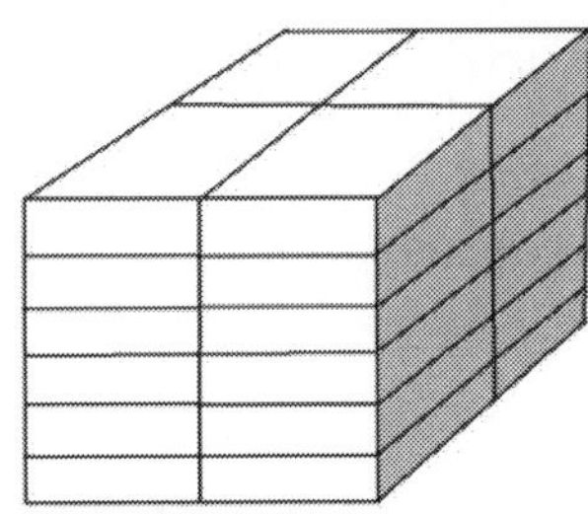

4.48) How many smaller blocks are in this cub?

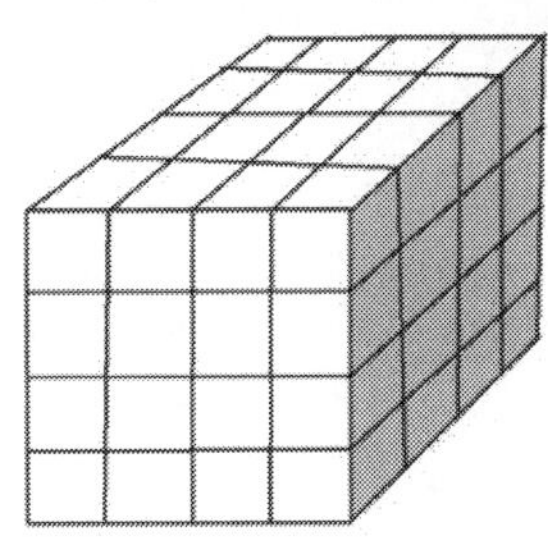

4.49) What is the volume of this cube?

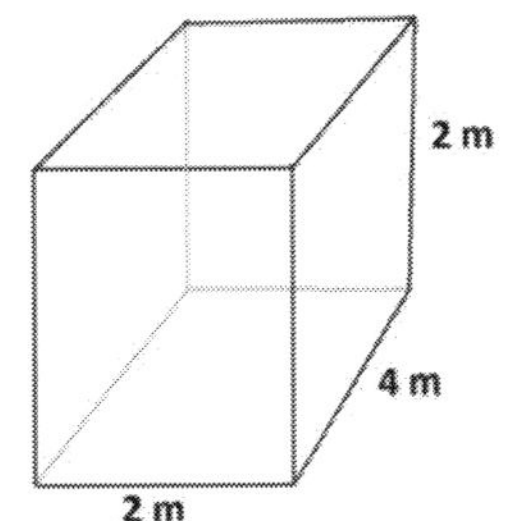

4.50) What is the volume of this cube?

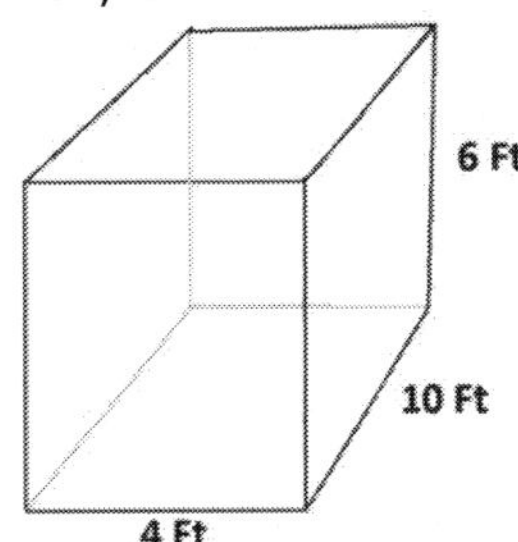

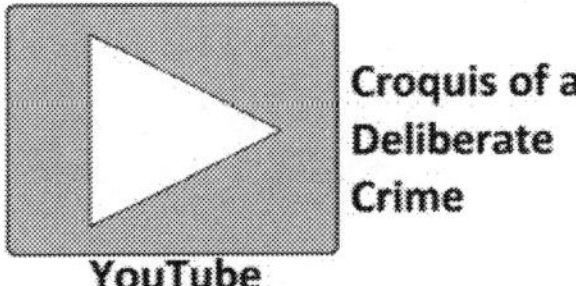

4.51) What is the volume of this cube?

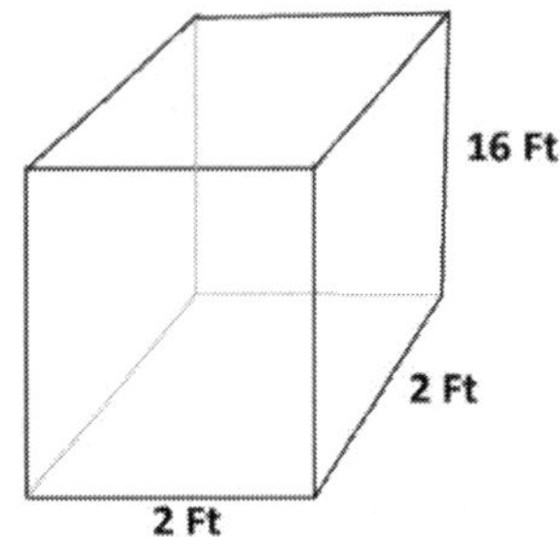

4.52) What is the volume of this cube?

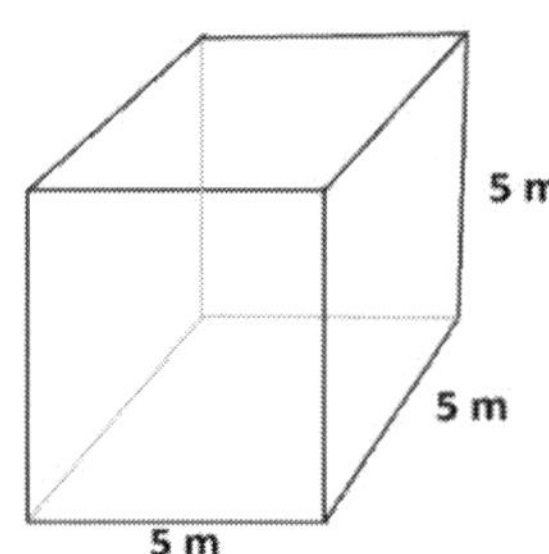

Units

4.34) What would be the best unit of measurement for the size of your dog?
a) Gallons, b) pounds, c) pints, d) Quart

4.35) What would be the best unit of measurement for the distance between you and your school?
a) Gallons, b) miles, c) pints, d) feet

For one on one tutoring via skype at $35.00/Hr.; contact me at marksmathtutoring@yahoo.com

4.36) What would be the best unit of measurement for the amount of milk in your refrigerator?
a) Gallons, b) pounds, c) miles, d) feet

4.37) What would be the best unit of measurement for the distance between you and your TV?
a) Gallons, b) pounds, c) pints, d) feet

Interest

4.38) You parents borrowed $5,000.00 from the bank to buy a car. They repaid $6,500.00. Which statement best explains why they paid the extra $1,500.00
a) They wanted to donate $1,500.00 to the bank to be nice
b) They repaid the loan on a week day and the bank charges money for these days
c) They had extra money and nothing to do with it.
d) The bank charged $1,500.00 in interest for a $6,000.00 loan

If you don't get the correct answer, and want an explanation on how to work the problem, go to YouTube and type in "MMT" then the problem number. An example would be, MMT 3.9.w12,. The video will show you how to work problem 3.9.w12.

For one on one tutoring via skype at $35.00/Hr.; contact me at marksmathtutoring@yahoo.com

4.57) Which of the following is a rotational transformation

a)

b)

c)

d)

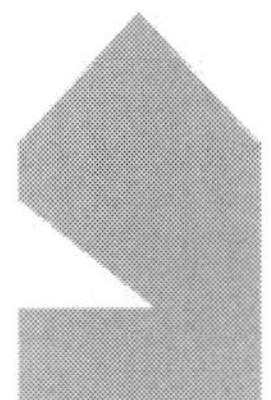 

4.58) In the drawing below which angle are right angles?

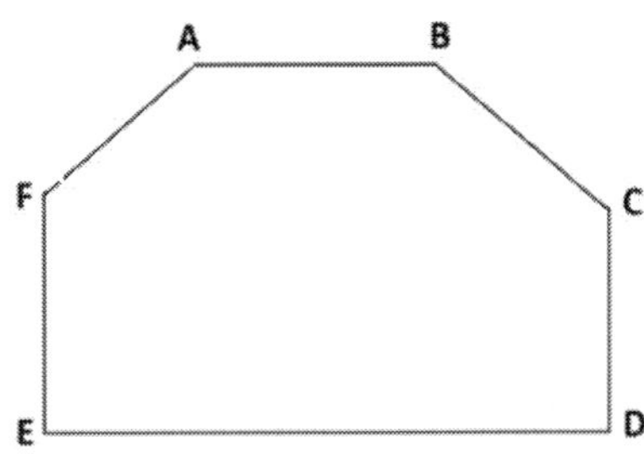

a) <FED, and <EDC
b) <EFA and <FED
c) < CDE and <DCB
d) <FAB and <BCD

4.70) Which two lines in the drawing below appear to be parallel?

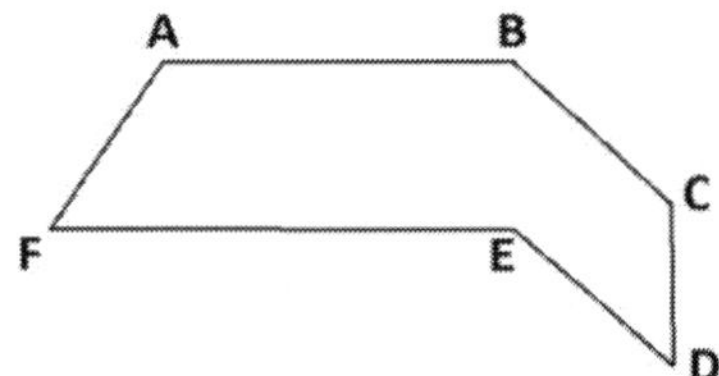

a) AB and BC
b) FE and BC
c) BC and ED
d) CD and AB

4.64) Given the drawing below which two lines appear to be parallel

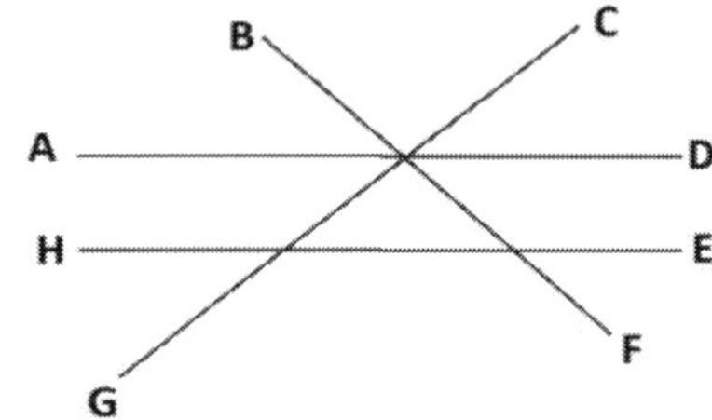

a) Lines BF and CG
b) Lines AD and HE
c) Lines BF and HE
d) Lines AD and BF

4.71) In the figure below which of the following statements is true about the labeled angles

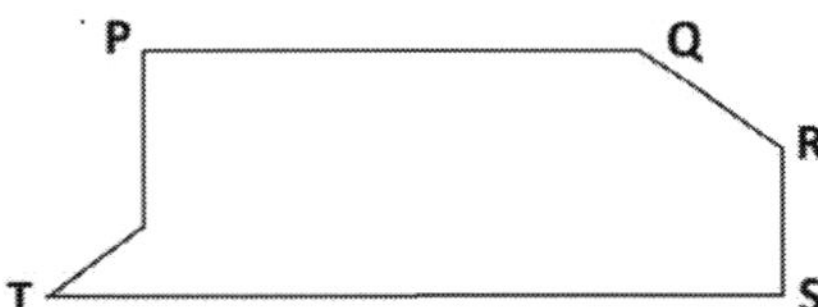

a) 1 right angle, 2 obtuse angles, 2 acute angles
b) 2 right angle, 1 obtuse angles, 2 acute angle
c) 2 right angle, 2 obtuse angles, 1 acute angles
d) 1 right angle, 1 obtuse angles, 3 acute angles

4.72) Which of the following triangle appears to be acute?

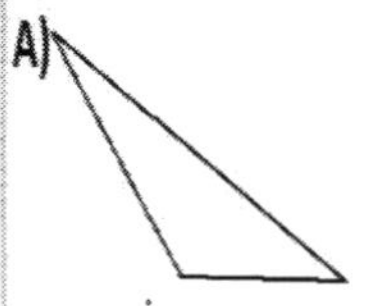

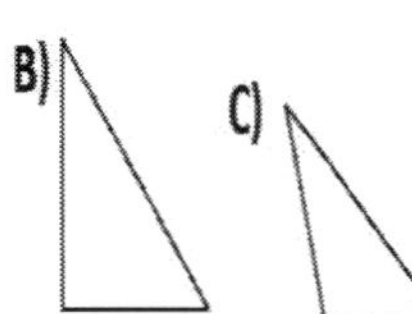

4.73) Which of the following triangle appears to be a right angle?

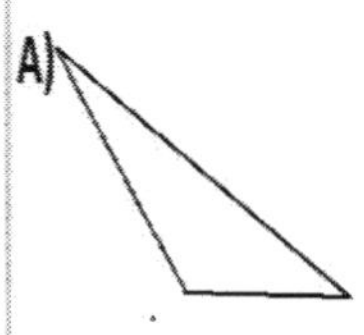

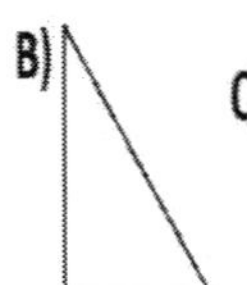

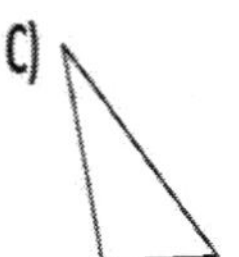

4.74) Which of the following angles appears to be perpendicular?

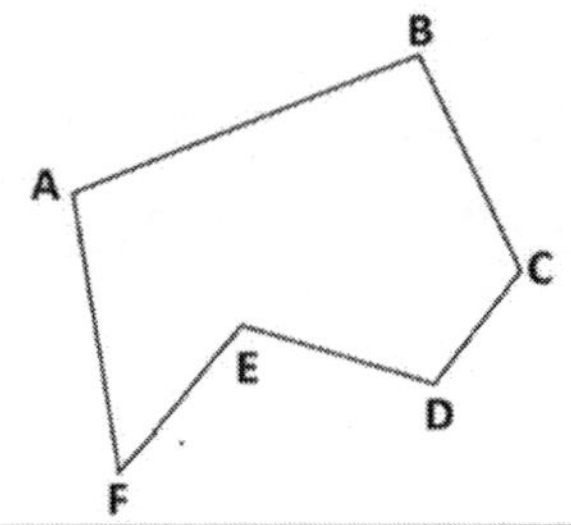

4.75) If I make a triangle with one 90 degrees angle and two acute angles, which statement below describes the figure?

a) Acute triangle
b) Obtuse triangle
c) Right triangle
d) Figure is not a triangle

4.76) If angle <ABC is 41 degrees and angle <CBD is a right angle what is the angle of <ABD

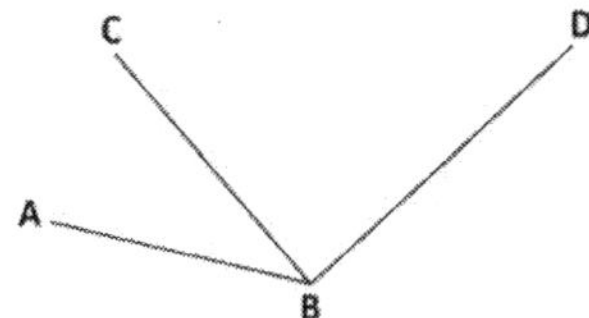

4.77) What is the translation shown in the drawing below?

a) Rotation
b) Translation
c) Reflection
d) none of the above

Croquis of a Deliberate Crime

For one on one tutoring via skype at $35.00/Hr.; contact me at marksmathtutoring@yahoo.com

4.78) Which of the following is not a translation of the following diagram?

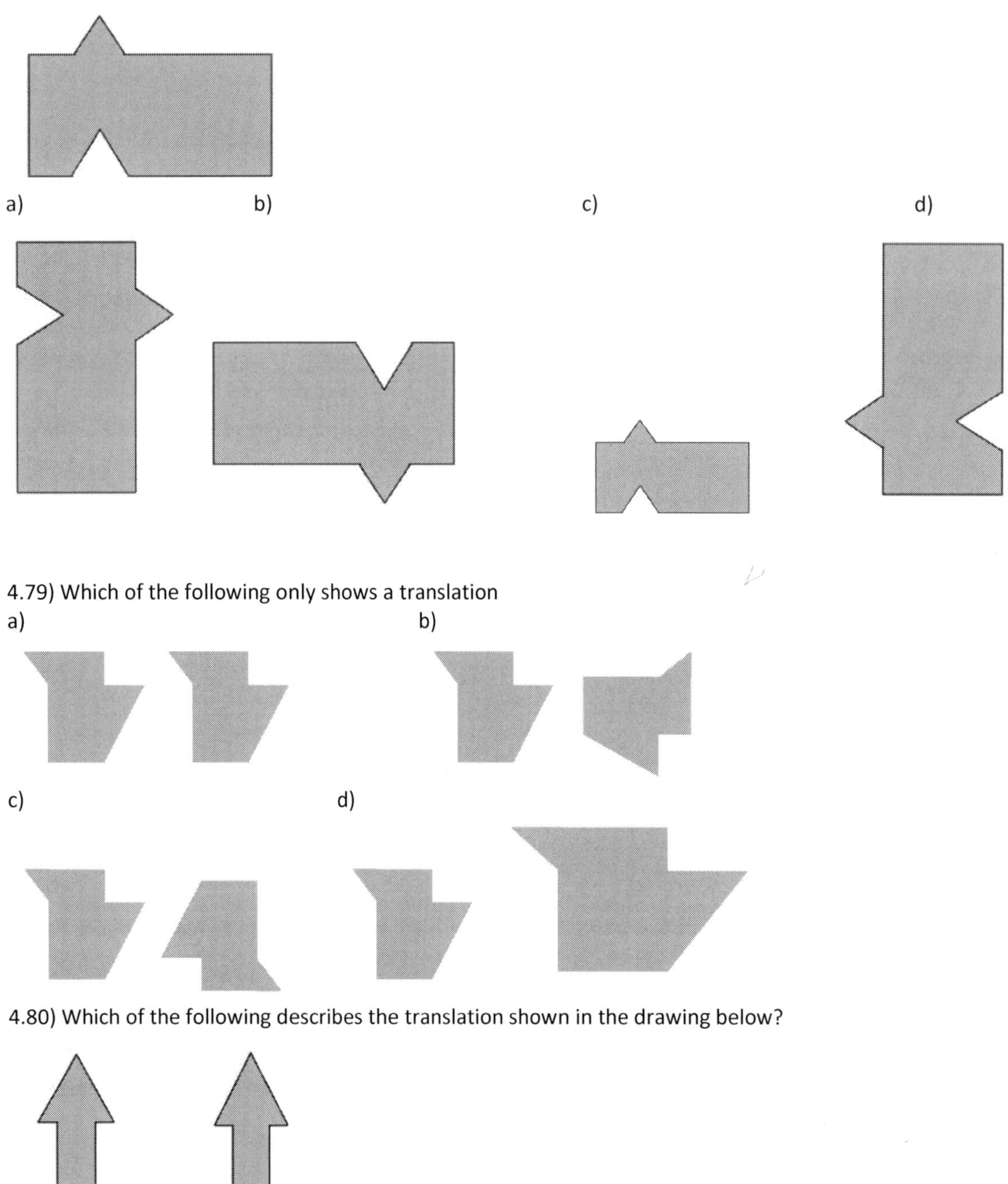

4.79) Which of the following only shows a translation

4.80) Which of the following describes the translation shown in the drawing below?

A) Translation
B) Reflection
c) Rotation
d) no translation

4.81) Which of the following describes the translation shown in the drawing below?

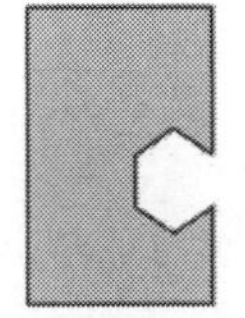
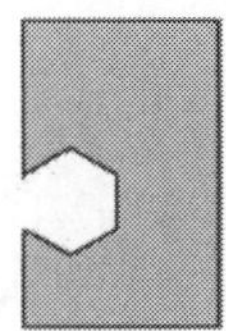

A) Translation
B) Reflection
c) Rotation
d) no translation

4.82) Which of the following describes the translation shown in the drawing below?

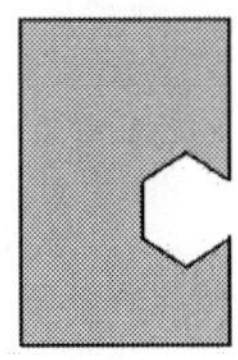
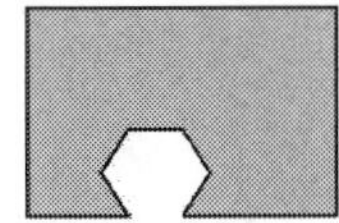

A) Translation
B) Reflection
c) Rotation
d) no translation

4.83) Which statement below best describes the three polygons drawn here?

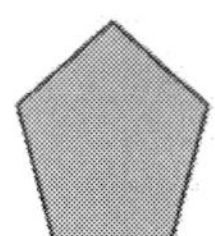
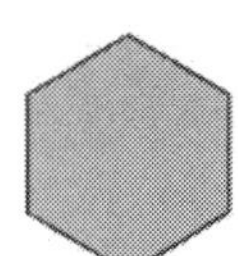

a) All have right angles only
b) All have obtuse only
c) All have acute angles only
d) all of them have parallel lines

4.84) I am going to tile my floor. Part of it is already done and is shaded grey in the diagram below.

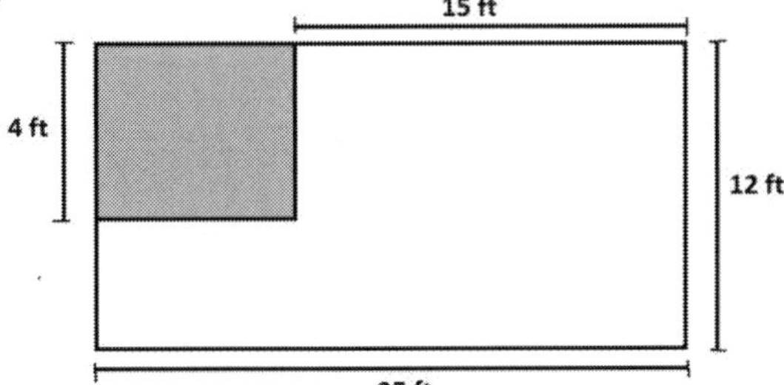

What is the area in square feet to be tiled?

For one on one tutoring via skype at $35.00/Hr.; contact me at marksmathtutoring@yahoo.com

4.85) I made a dog kennel. I divided it into three parts as shown in the diagram.

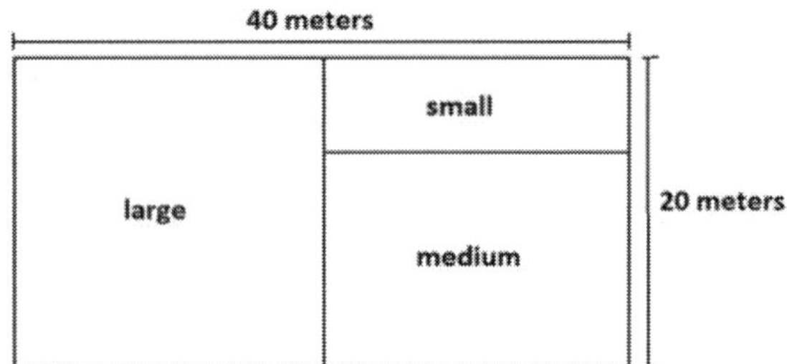

If the area of the small dogs cage is 100 meters square, and the area of the medium dog cage is 250 meters square what is the area of the large dog cage?

4.86) If a square has a side of 15 inches which of the following statements is not true
A) The perimeter is 60 inches
B) The length of the other sides are 15 inches
C) The area of the square is 225 inches square
D) We don't know the length of the other sides

4.87) If my garden has an area of 72 feet square and one side is 9 feet, what is the length of the other side

4.88) The radius if a circle is 20, which equation below could be used to find the circumference.
A) $\Pi X20^2 =$
B) $2X\Pi X20=$
C) $\Pi X4=$
D) $2X\Pi X20^2=$

4.89) A bunch of rectangular prisms have a length of 6 cm and a width of 4 cm. The table below shows the relationship between the height, h, and the volume, v

Height h	Volume, v
2	48
4	96
5	120
7	168

Which equation below can be used to find v for a given value of h
A) h=24v
B) 24h = v
C) 6h=v
D) 4v=h

4.87) The circle drawn below has a diameter of 16 inches and segments AB and DE are 3 inches. What is the length of the radius. The point C is in the center of both circles.

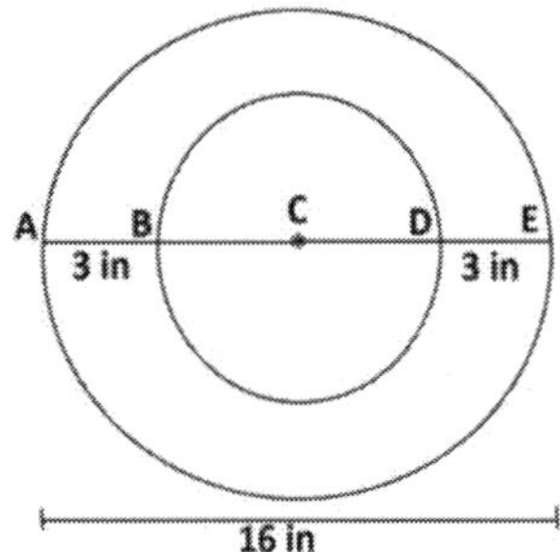

4.88) Three circle are described below

circle A has a radius of 16 cm
circle B has a radius of 32 cm
circle C has a diameter of 32 cm

Which statement below is true

A) Radius of B is the same as radius of C
B) The diameter of A is the same as diameter of B
C) The diameter of A is the same as the diameter of C
D) Diameter of A and B are the same

4.89) If the perimeter of a circle is 48 in; which of the following could be the radius of the circle

A) 6.4 in
B) 8.3 in
C) 7.6 in
D) 12.5 in

4.90) If a circle has a circumference of 64 feet which equation below could be used to determine the radius.

A) ΠXR=64
B) 32 x Π = R
C) 32/Π=R
D) 64/Π=R

4.91) What is the measure of the angle, V

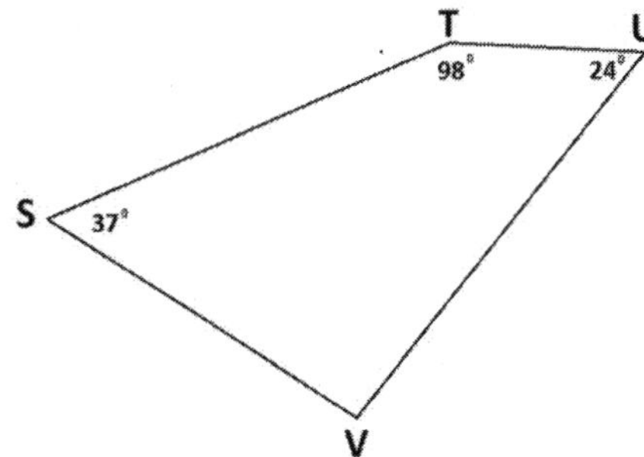

4.92) A pipe has a diameter of 28.9 inches. Which of the following is the best estimate of the circumference

A)91
B)78
C)34
D)1124

4.93) What is the circumference of the circle drawn below

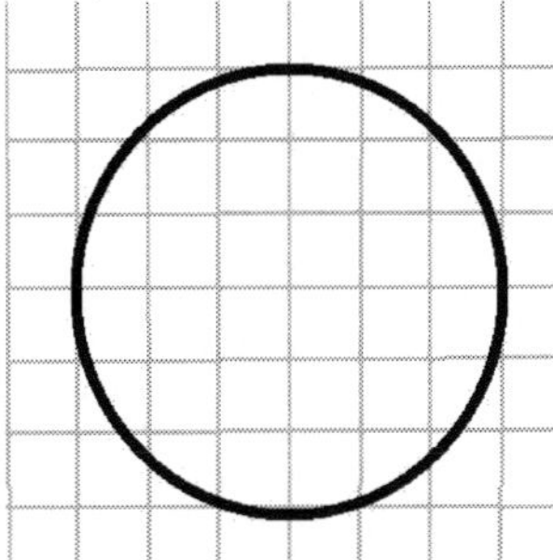

4.94) If gear A does 125 revolutions how many does gear C do

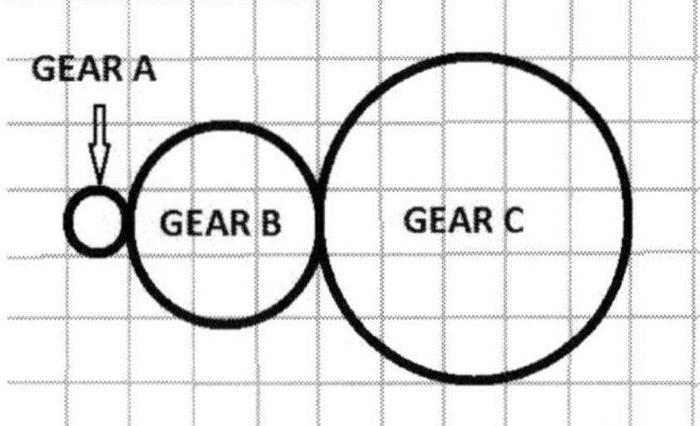

4.95) What is the diameter of the circle drawn below

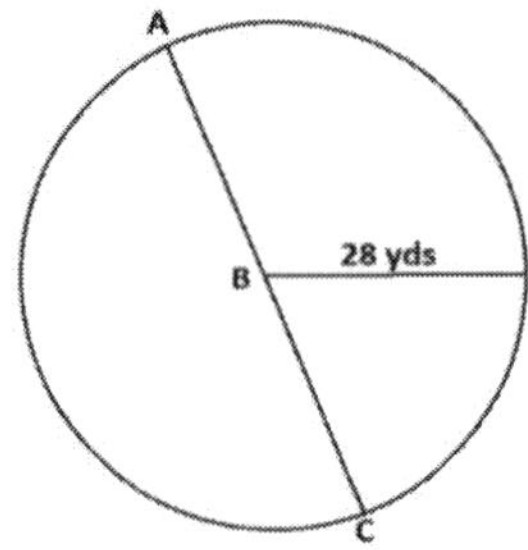

4.96) If I use the equation 18 x Π to find the circumference what would be the radius of the circle.

4.97) Given the drawing below of a triangle what is the value of the angle market Θ

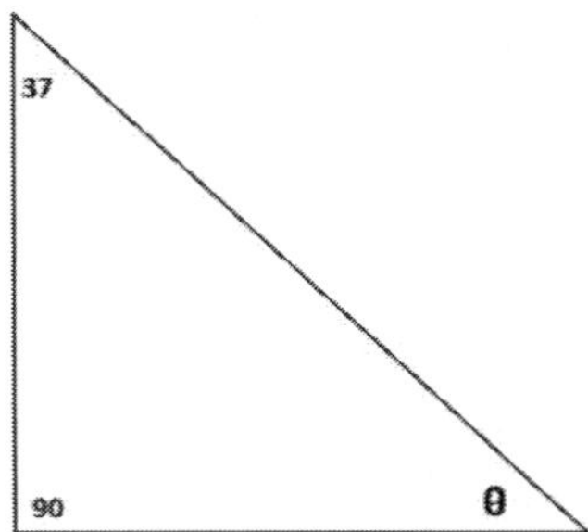

4.98) The table below shows the relationship between perimeter,. P, and area, A, of a square

Perimeter P	Area A
12	9
16	16
20	25
24	36

Which equation below could be used to show this relationship

A) $(A)^{1/2}$=4P

B) Px4 = A

C) $(A \div 4)^2$= P

D) A÷ P= 4

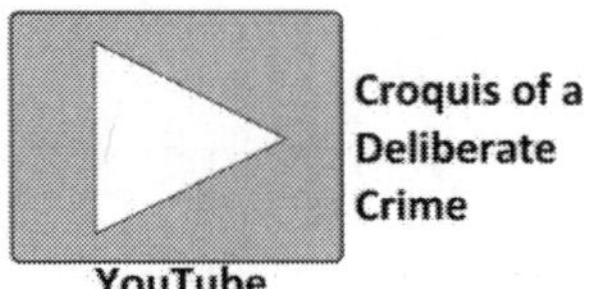

4.99) What is the area of the triangle drawn below

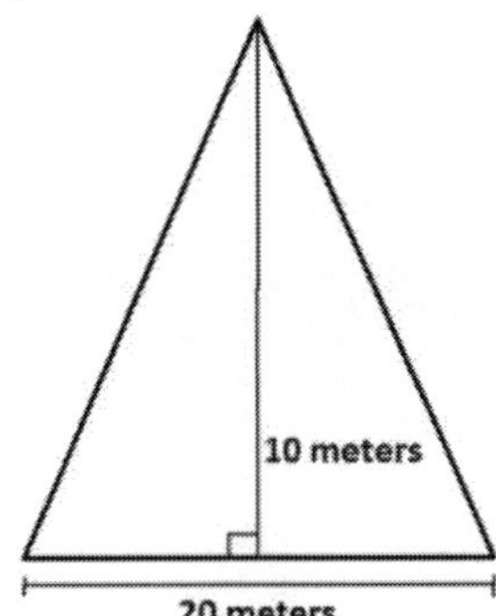

4.100) Given the drawing of a triangle below what is the value of the missing angle

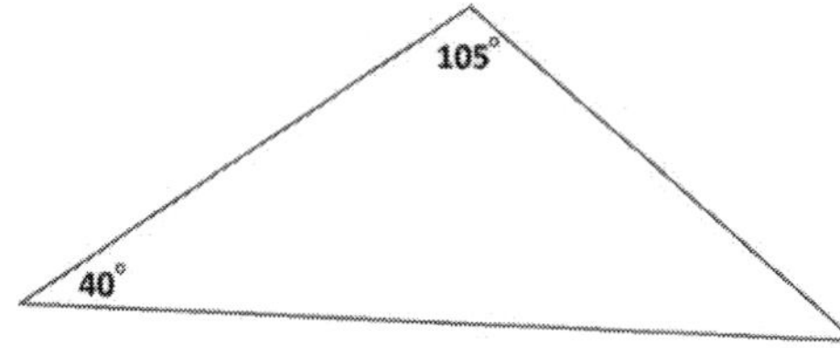

4.101) What is the area of the trapezoid drawn below

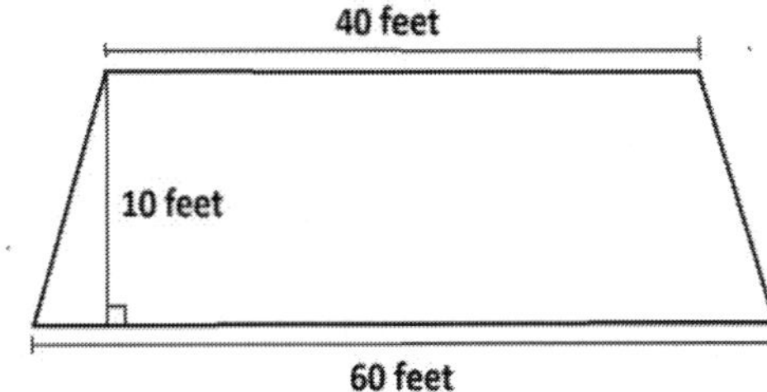

4.102) In a triangle the measure of angle XYZ is 92 degrees, and YZX is 37 degrees, what is the measure of angle ZXY

4.103) Given the drawing below what is the difference between angle D and angle B

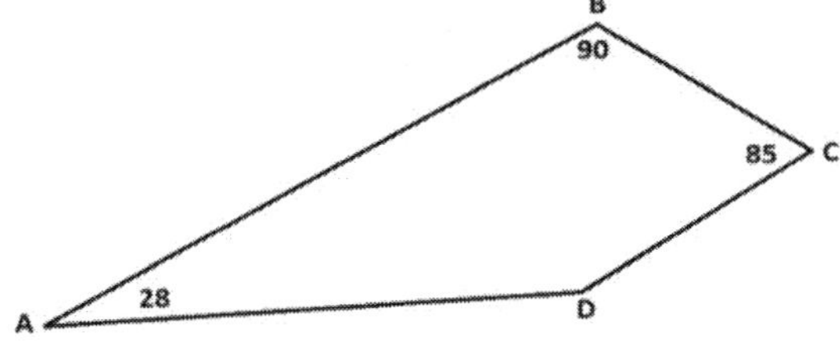

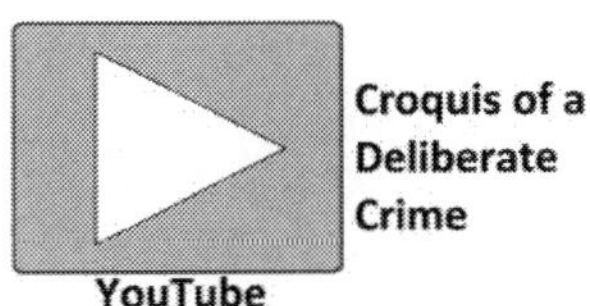

4.104) Given the diagram below

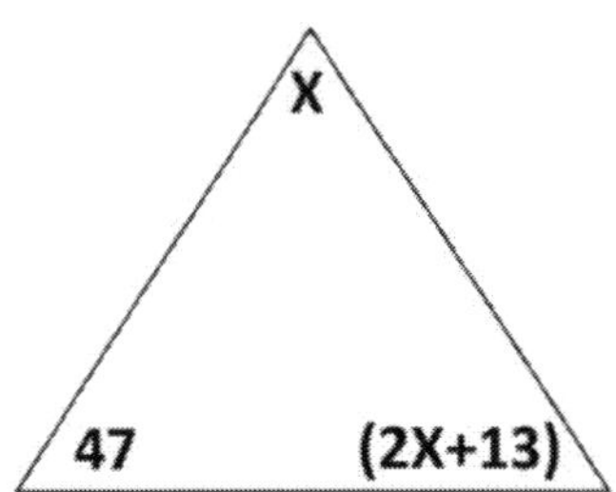

What is the value of X

4.105) Given the diagram below

3X

what is the value of X

4.106) Given the diagram below

2X

35

2X-15

what is the value of X

4.107) Given the diagram below

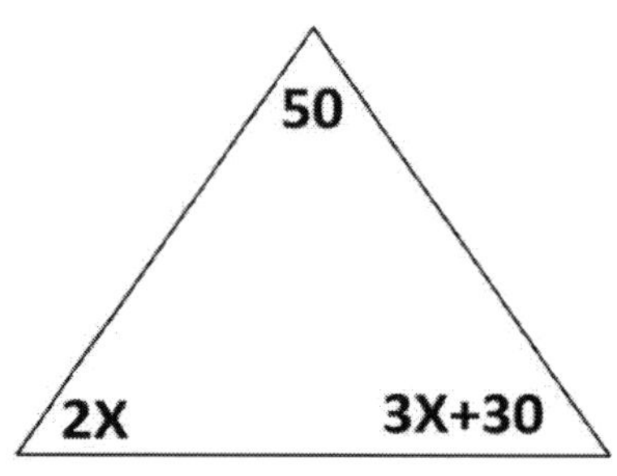

what is the value of X

4.108) Given the diagram below

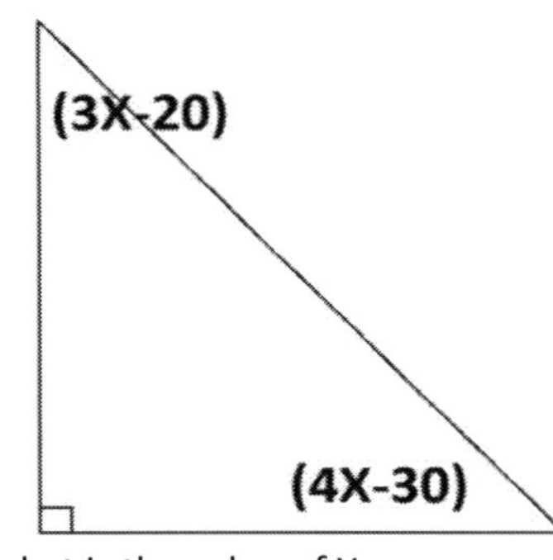

what is the value of X

4.109) Given the diagram below

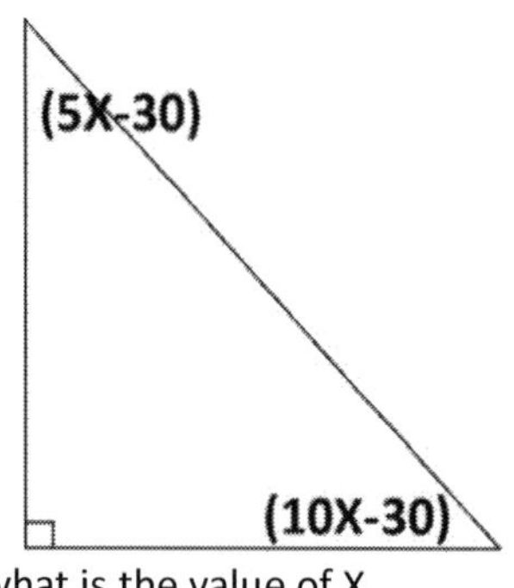

what is the value of X

YouTube

Croquis of a Deliberate Crime

4.110) Given the graph below

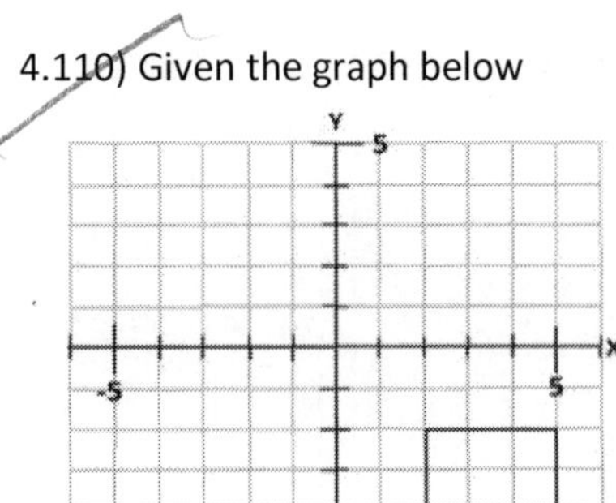

Which of the following shows a translation of six left four up

A)

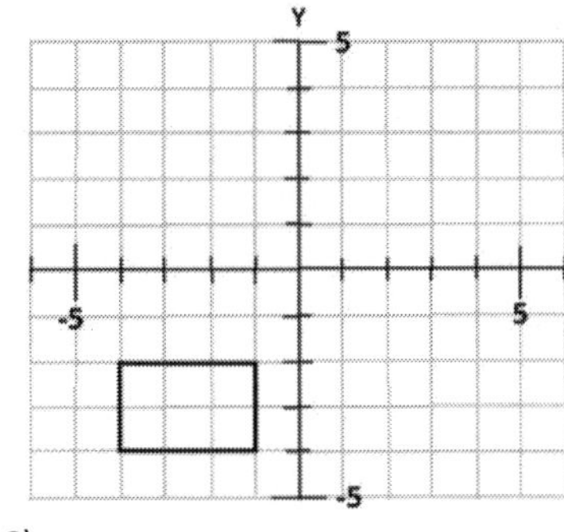

B)

C)

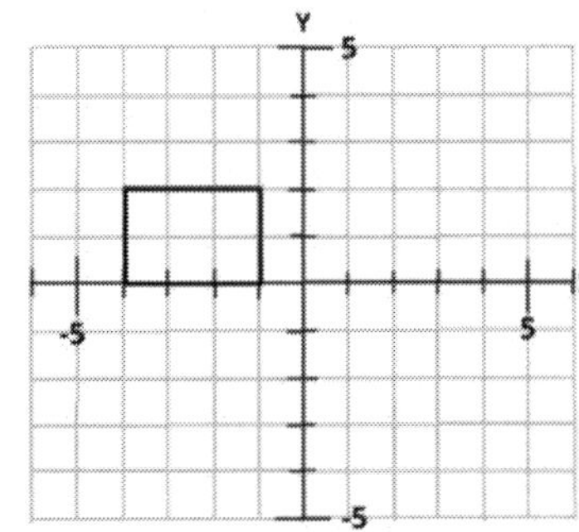

D)

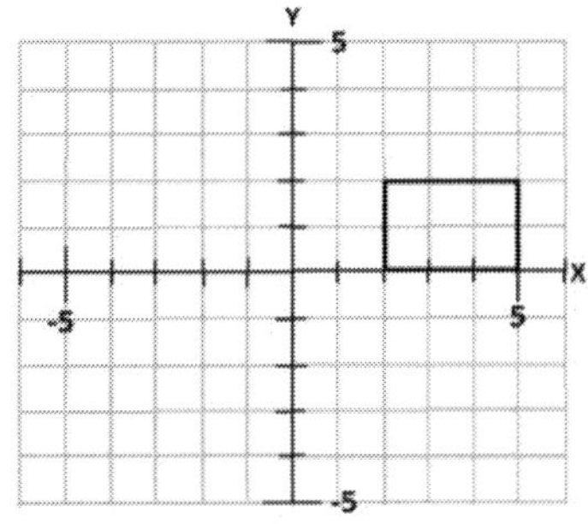

Croquis of a Deliberate Crime

If you don't get the correct answer, and want an explanation on how to work the problem, go to YouTube and type in "MMT" then the problem number. An example would be, MMT 3.9.w12,. The video will show you how to work problem 3.9.w12.

For one on one tutoring via skype at $35.00/Hr.; contact me at marksmathtutoring@yahoo.com

4.111) I make a scale model of a town where one inch eqauls 1.25 miles. Which of the graphs below show this relationship

A)

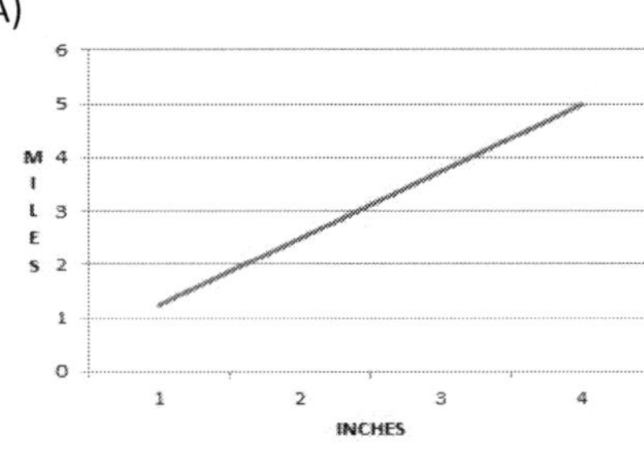

B)

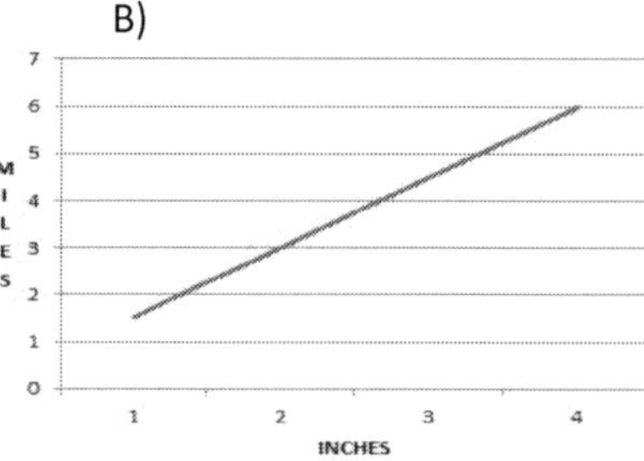

C)

D)

4.112) Given the drawing below

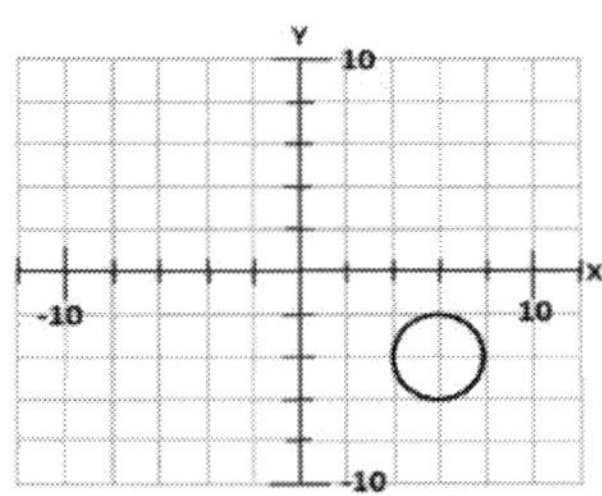

Which of the following is a translation six left seven up

A)

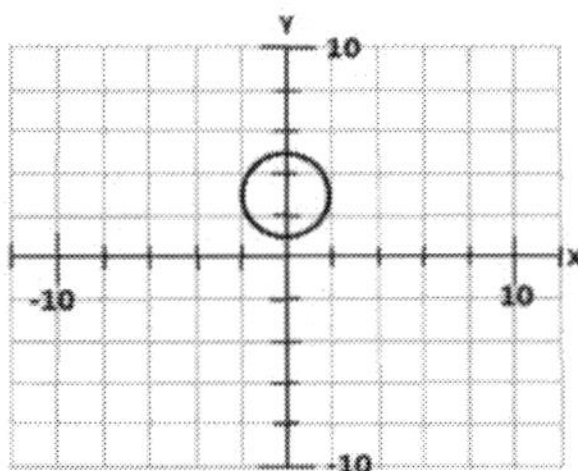

B)

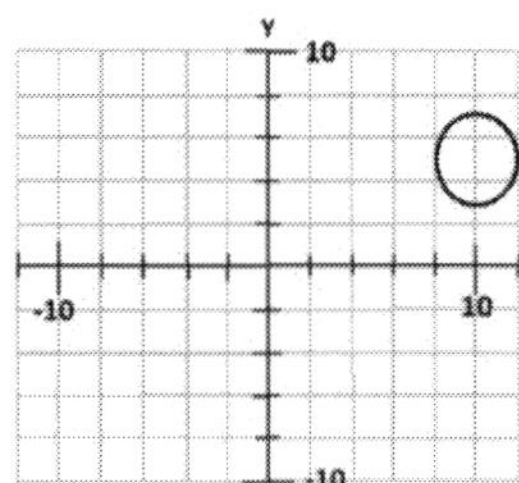

C)

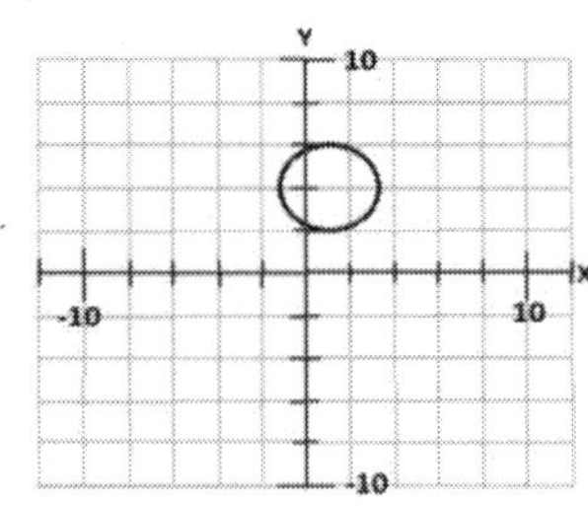

D)

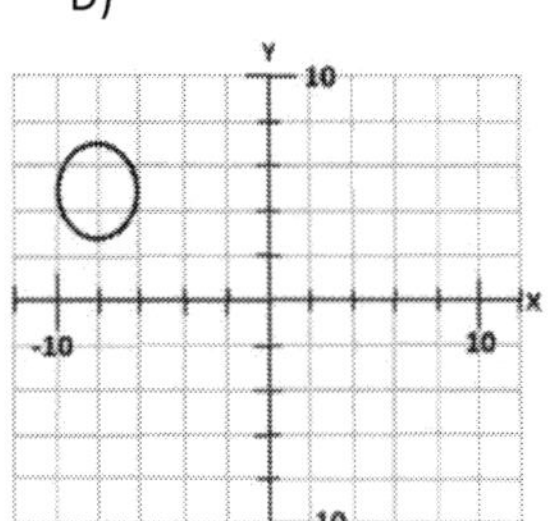

4.113) Given the graph below

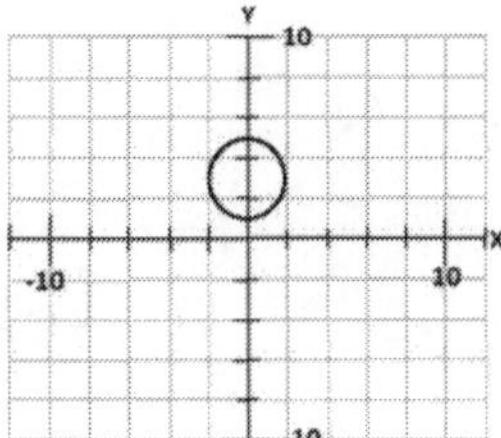

If the circle is translated right 4 and down 6 which of the following coordinates would be on the circles perimeter

A) (11,4)
B) (5,0)
C) (4,11)
D) (4, -5)

4.114) The two triangle drawn below are similar

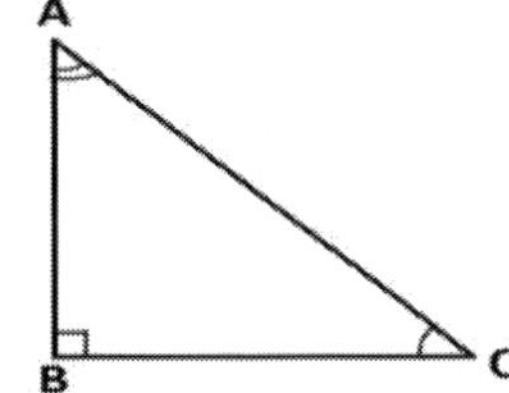

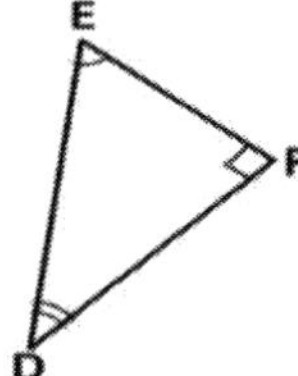

Which line segment corresponds to line AB
A) BC
B)DE
C)EF
D)FD

4.115) Which of the following graphs would represent a mirror reflection about the X axis of figure with coordinates (3,1), (2,2), (4,2), (3,3)

A)

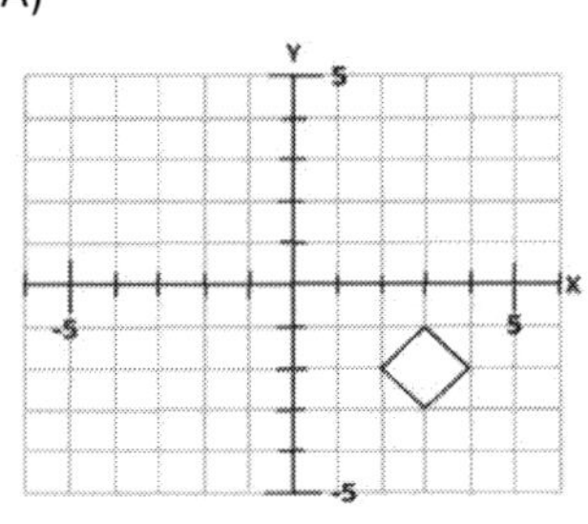

B)

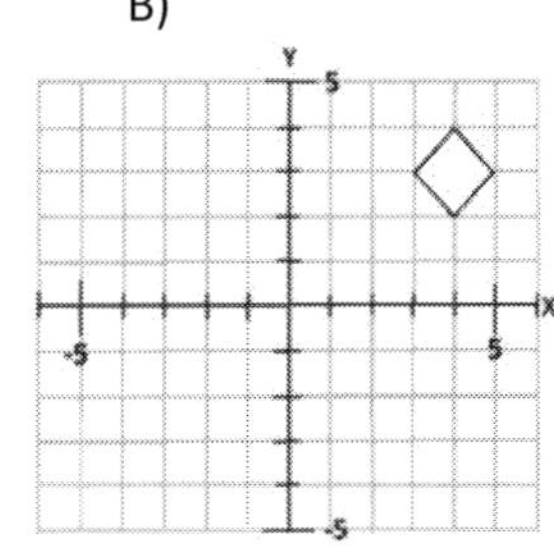

C)

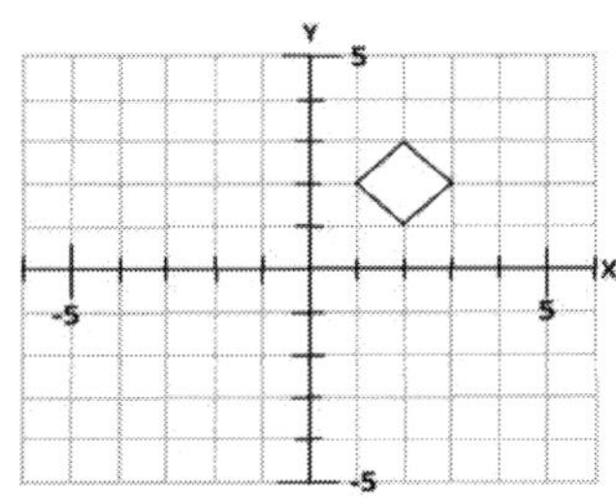

D)

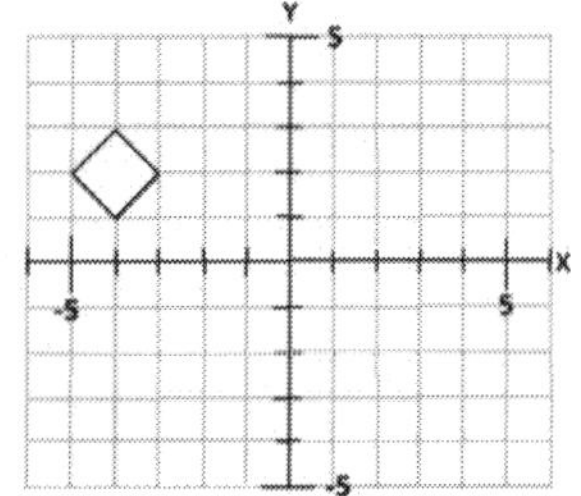

4.116) If angel <A id 42° what would an angel that is complementary to <A

4.117) If an angel <B is 87°, what would be an angel That is supplementary to <B

4.118) Which translation describes the relationship graphed below

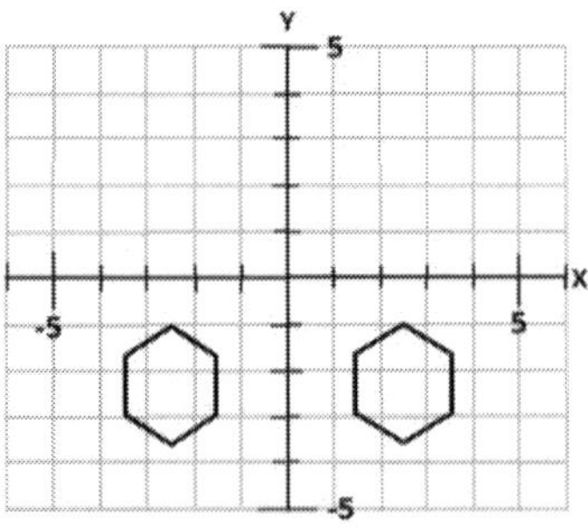

A) Reflection about the X axis
B) Reflection about the Y axis
C) Translation across X axis
D) Translation about Y axis

4.119) If two angles of a isosceles triangle is 54° which of the following equations could be used to find the value of the third angel, A
A) A= 180-2(54)
B) A= 180+2(54)
C) A=180+54
D) A=180-54

4.120) If I draw two triangle with similar angles which of the following statements must be true.
A) The triangle are the same size and shape
B) They have corresponding angle that are congruent
C) They are same size but different shape
D) They have corresponding side that are congruent

4.121) If the two triangle shown below are similar

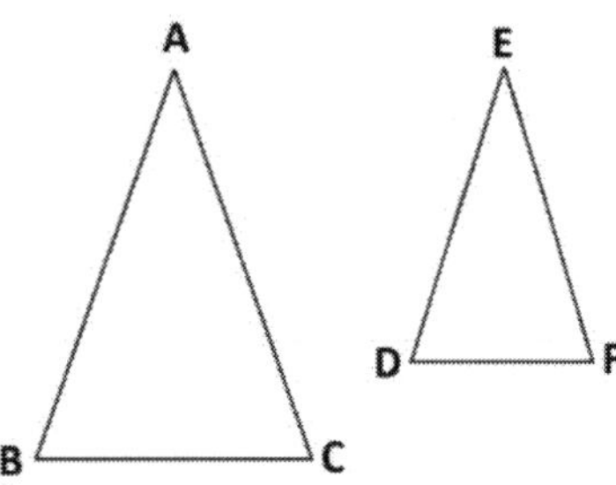

Which of the following relationships must be true
A) ${}^{BD}/_{CF}={}^{BE}/_{FA}$
B) ${}^{BD}/_{BA}={}^{FA}/_{FE}$
C) ${}^{BC}/_{BA}={}^{DF}/_{DE}$
D) ${}^{BE}/_{CD}={}^{BA}/_{DE}$

4.122) If a circle has a radius of 6 inches what is the area of the circle

4.123) If two rectangles are similar and one has sides 4 inches and 7 inches. Which of the following could be the dimensions of the second rectangle
A) 5 by 8
B) 6 by 10
C) 8 by 14
D) 12 by 20

4.124) What is the height of a rectangle prism with a volume of 24 feet cubed and a length of 2 feet and a width of 3 feet.

4.125) What is the area of a circle with a radius of 25 feet.

4.126) What is the volume of a triangular prism with height of 10 inches a base of 20 inches and a width of 3 inches as drawn below

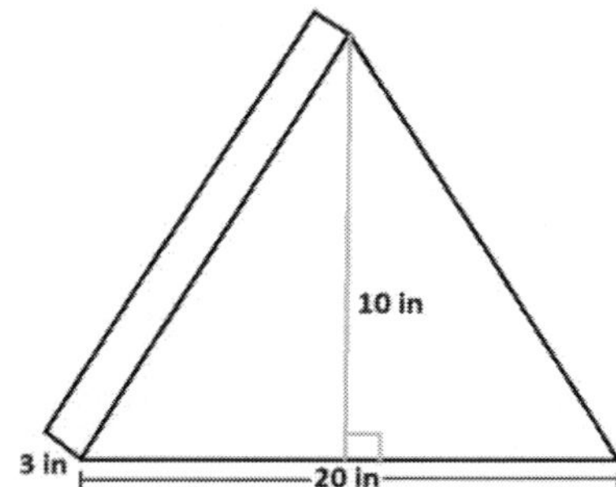

4.127) What is the base of the triangular prism shown below if the height is 5 meters, and the volume is 200 m^2. Remember V = BH

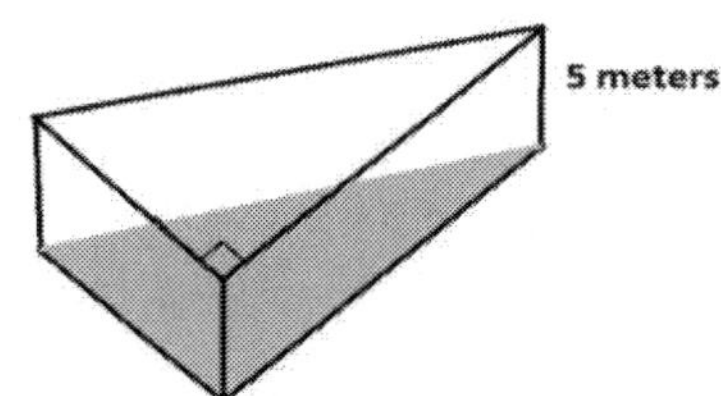

4.128) Given the drawing below

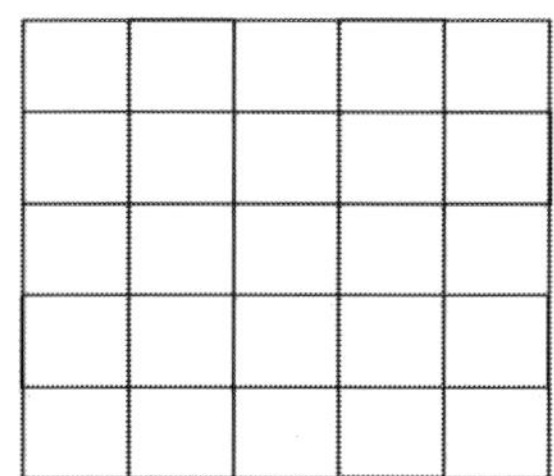

What is the best description of the side of this square
A) $\sqrt{20}$ B) $\sqrt{10}$ C) $\sqrt{25}$ D) $\sqrt{5}$

4.129) What is the volume of a cylinder with a height of 15 feet and a radius of 7 feet

For one on one tutoring via skype at $35.00/Hr.; contact me at marksmathtutoring@yahoo.com

4.130) Given the drawing of two similar triangles below

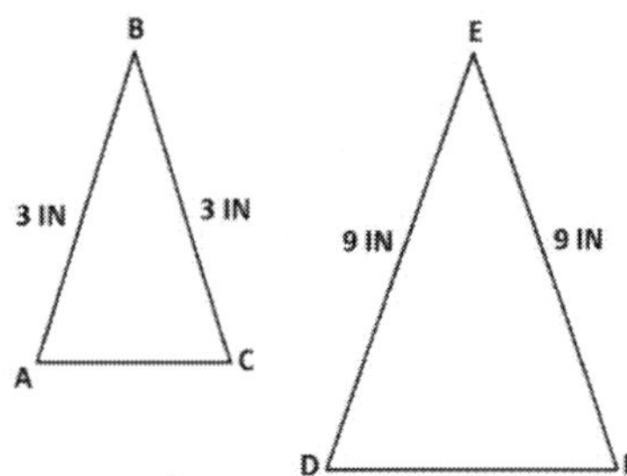

Which statement below must be true

A) Line DF must be 9 inches

B) Line AC must be 3 inches

C) <A+<C+<E must be 180 degrees

D) Line AC must be twice as long as line DF

4.131) Given the drawing below

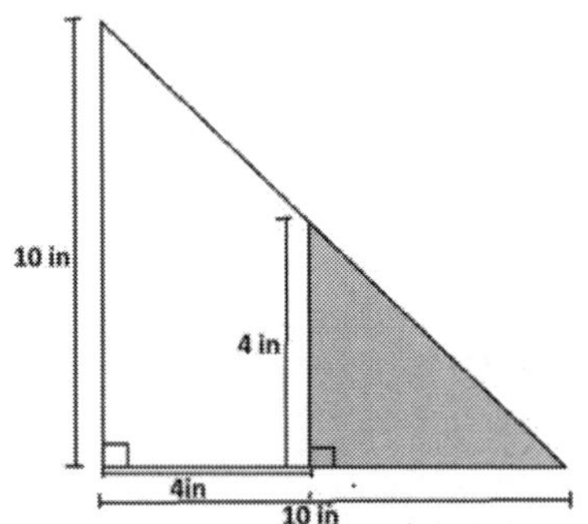

What is the area of the unshaded part of the triangle.

4.132) Given the drawing below

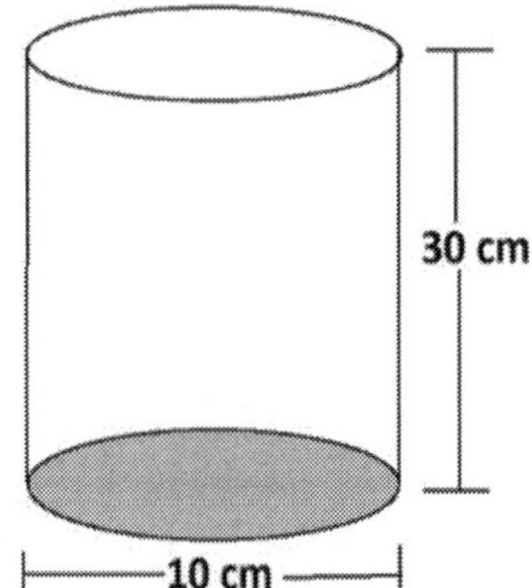

What is the volume of this cylinder

4.133) Given the drawing below

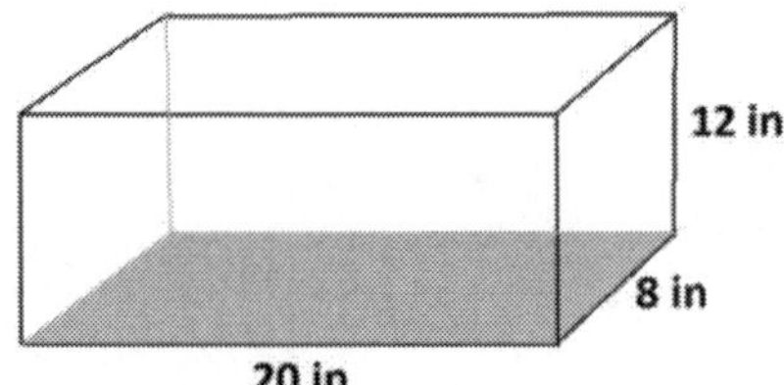

What is the volume of this figure

4.134) Given the figure below

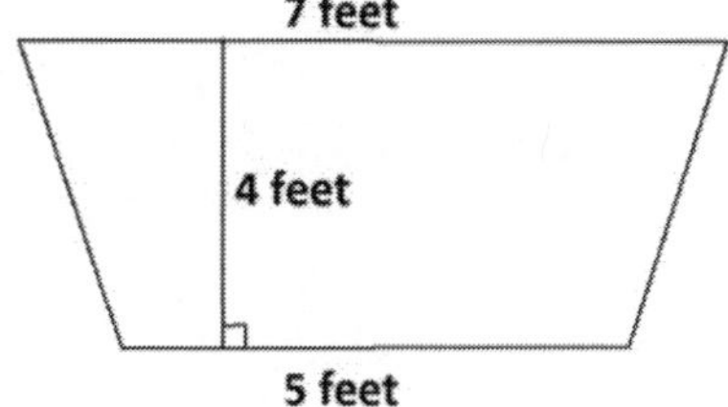

What is the area of this figure

4.135) Given the figure below

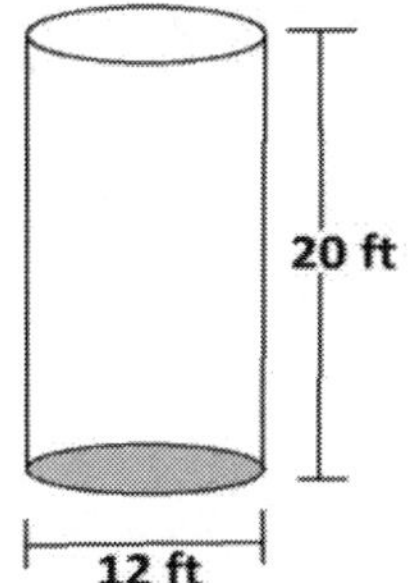

What is the volume of is figure

4.136) Given the two similar triangle drawn below

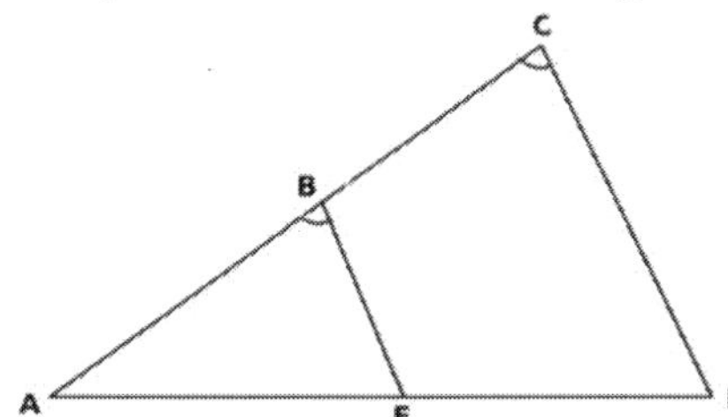

Which of the following statements must be true

A) BE/BC=AE/DE

B) AE/AB=BC/BE

C) DC/DE= BA/AE

D) CD/BE=DA/EA

4.137) Given the drawing below

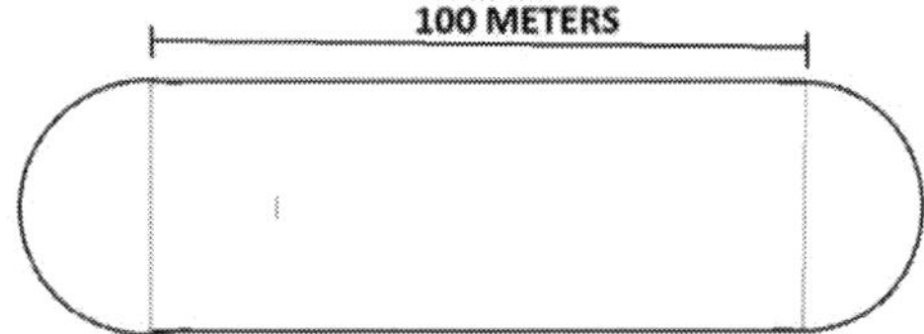

If the area of the rectangle is 1000 meters square What is the area of the complete figure

For one on one tutoring via skype at $35.00/Hr.; contact me at marksmathtutoring@yahoo.com

4.138) Given the drawing below

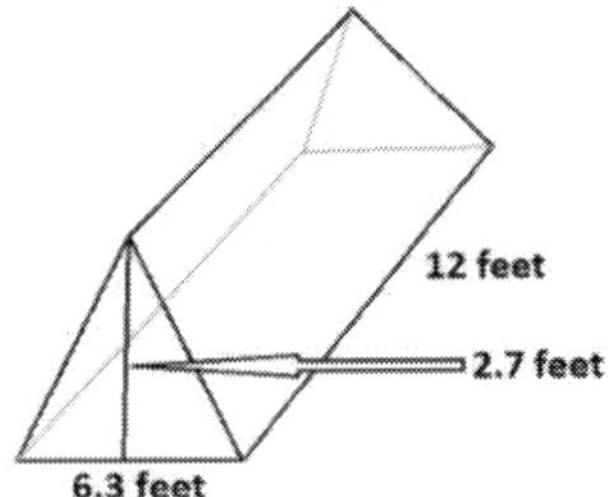

What is the volume of this figure

4.139) If a rectangle prism has a width of 3.5 inches and a height of 2.4 inches and a length of 4 inches what is the volume

4.140) what is the measure of an angle that is supplementary to 48.6 degrees

4.141) In the following diagram the circle has a radius of 10 cm and all three triangles are congruent

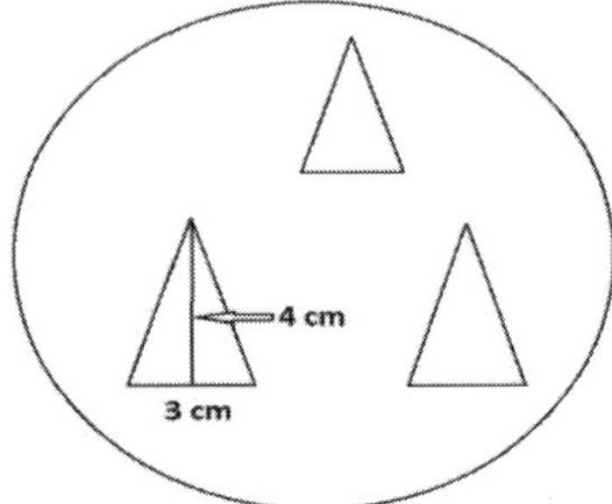

What is the area of the circle that is not covered by a triangle

4.142) Given the drawing below, the cylinder has a diameter of 10 feet and a height of 4 feet

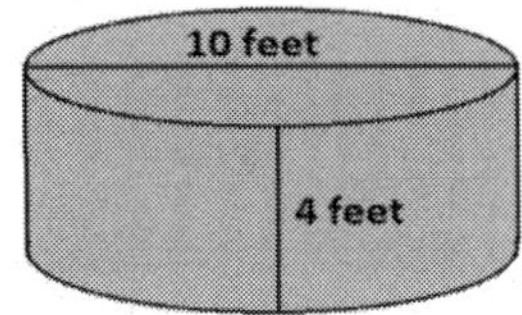

What is the volume of this cylinder

4.143) Given the drawing below of a piece of a paper to be folded into rectangle prism. What is the area of paper

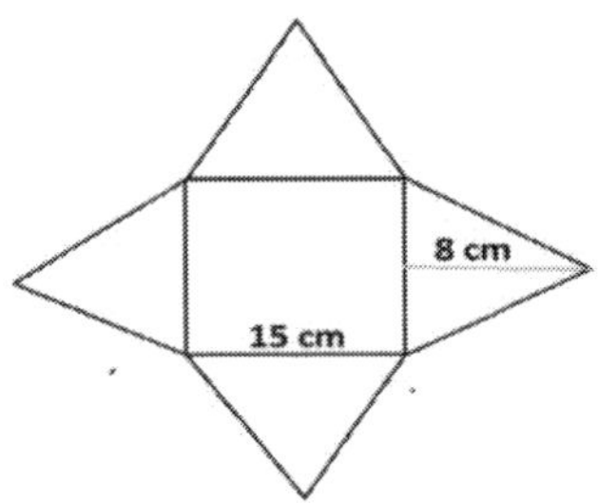

4.144) What is the circumference of a circle with a diameter of 15 meters

For one on one tutoring via skype at $35.00/Hr.; contact me at marksmathtutoring@yahoo.com

4.145) Given the drawing below

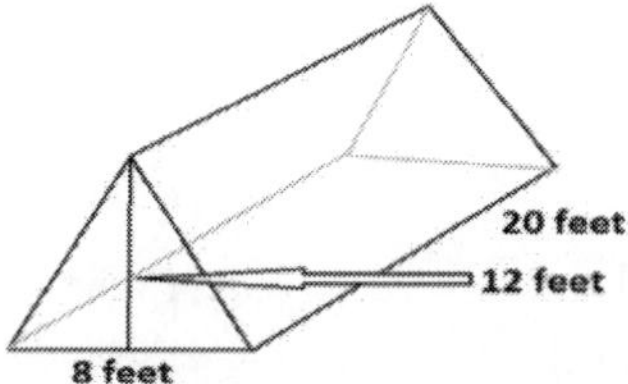

What is the volume of this figure

4.146) Given the drawing below with a base 12 feet by 12 feet and a heights of 20 feet

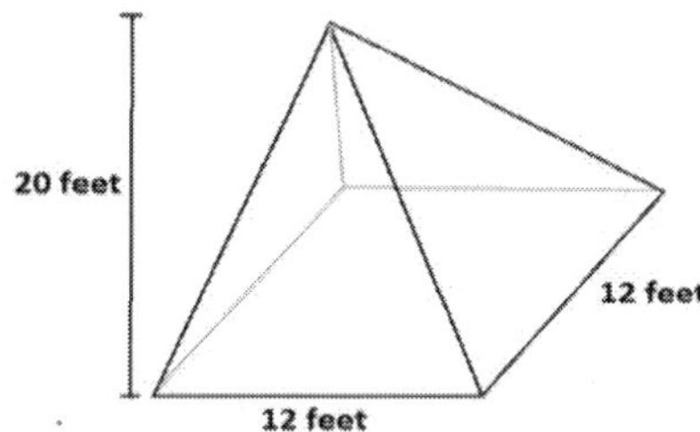

What is the volume of this figure

4.147) What is the area of the figure below

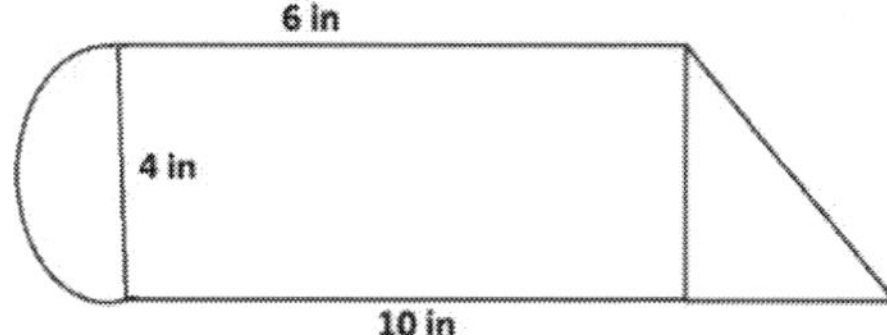

4.148) If a box has a volume of 200 feet cubed and a base of 20 feet square what is the height of the box

4.149) What is the measure of the third angle of a isolates triangle if two of the angle are 48 degrees

4.150) Given the drawing of two similar triangles below

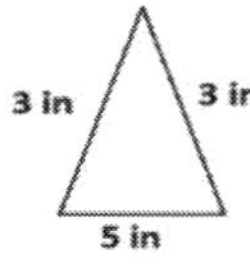

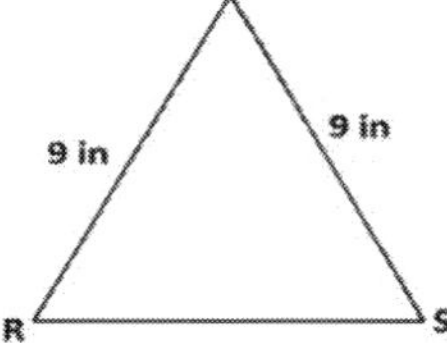

What is the value of line RS

4.151) What is the circumference of a circle with a radius of 3.5 inches.

4.152) Given two cubes each with sides of 6 inches. What is the total volume of both cubes combined

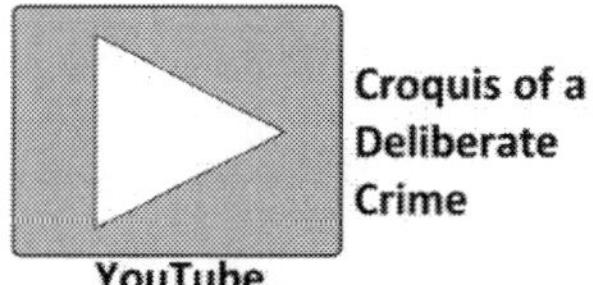

4.153) If the area of the shaded area in the drawing below is 56 inches square and the volume is 1400 inches cubed what is the height.

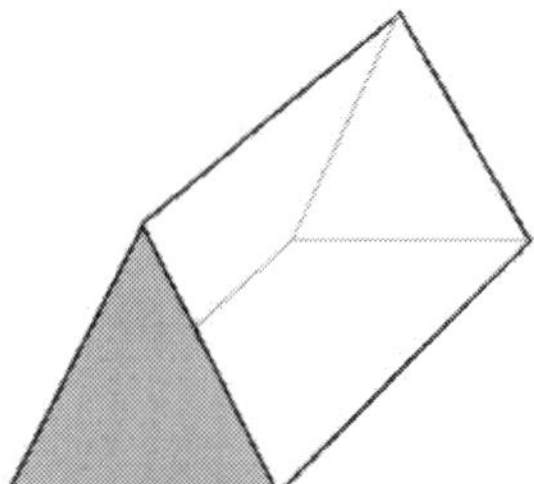

4.154) The fallowing drawing is of a piece of paper to be folded into a rectangle prism. What is the area of this piece of paper

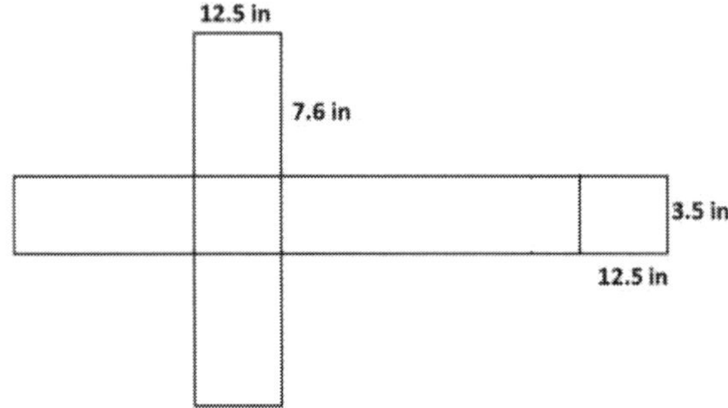

4.155) What is the area of a circle with a diameter of 10 feet.

4.156) If a rectangle drawn below

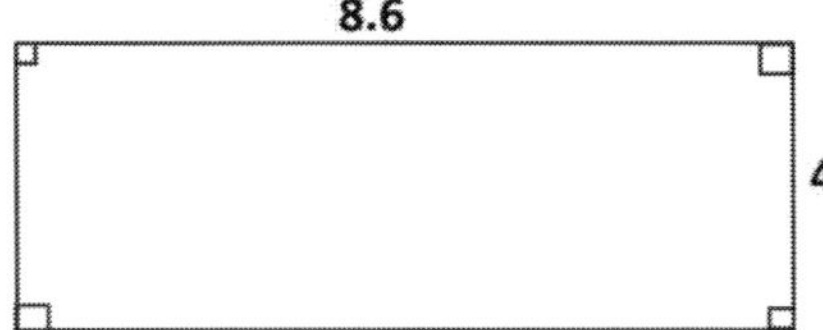

What would be the dimension is it is dilated by 2.5

4.157) If a rectangle drawn below

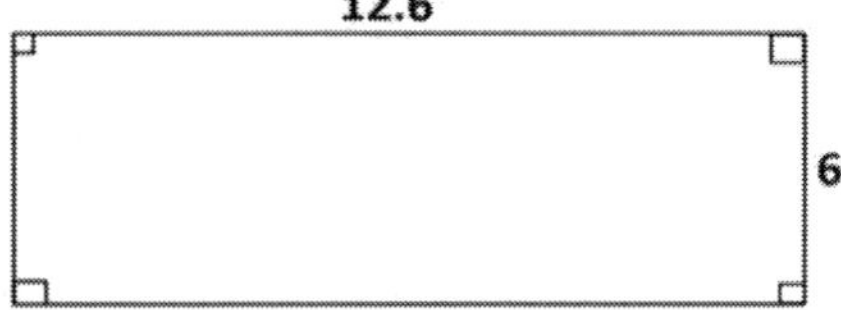

If the rectangle is dilated by 1/3 what are the new dimensions

4.158) If a circle with a radius of 6 is dilated by ½ what is the new radius

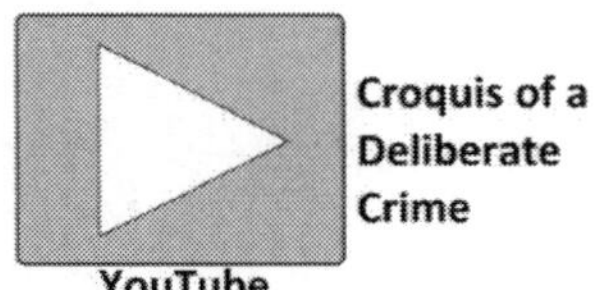

4.159) What was the dilation of a rectangle that started with dimension of 14.6 by 4.8 if its final dimension were as below

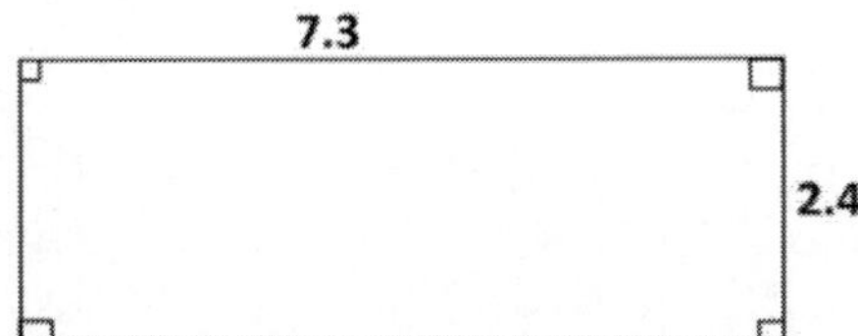

4.160) If a rectangle is dilated by 3 what is the increase in the area of this rectangle
4.161) If a circle is dilated by 2 what is the increase in the area of this circle
4.162) If a rectangle is dilated by 1/2 what is the increase in the area of this rectangle
4.163) If a circle is dilated by 1/3 what is the increase in the area of this circle

4.164) If a rectangle is dilated by 3 what is the increase in the perimeter of this rectangle
4.165) If a circle is dilated by 2 what is the increase in the perimeter of this circle
4.166) If a rectangle is dilated by 1/2 what is the increase in the perimeter of this rectangle
4.167) If a circle is dilated by 1/3 what is the increase in the perimeter of this circle

4.168) What is the dilation of the triangles below

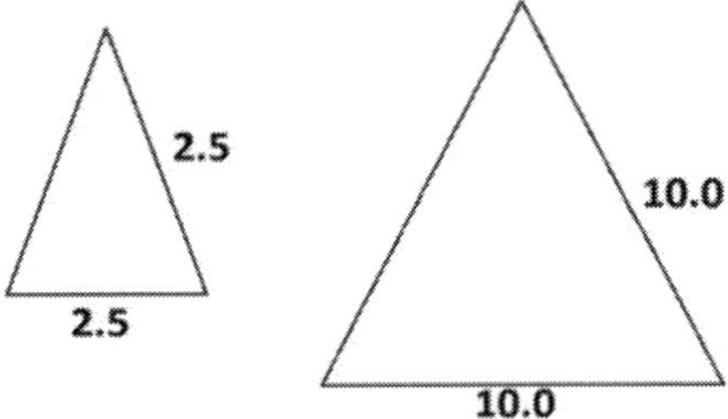

4.169) What is the dilation of the circles drawn below

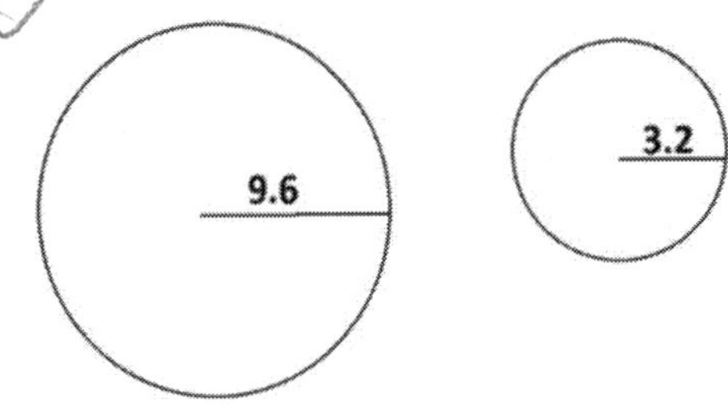

4.170) What is the length of a side of a square if the area is 64 feet square

4.171. What is the value of X in the diagram below

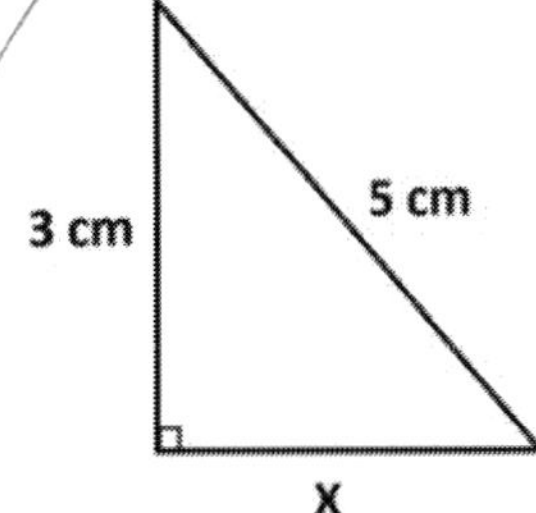

4.172) What is the surface area of the figure drawn below

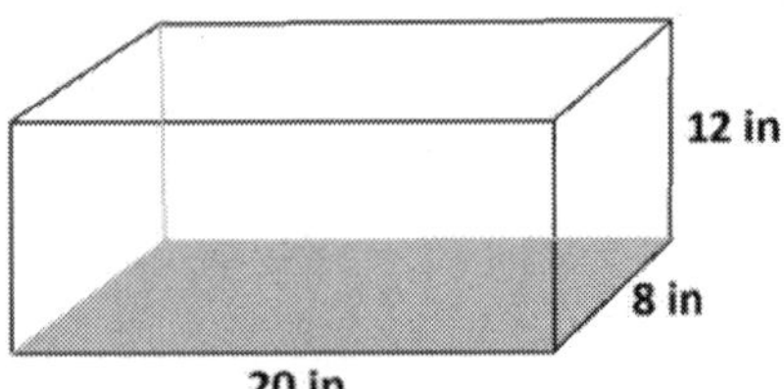

4.173) What is the volume of a cylinder with a radius of 6 and a height of 10.

4.174) What is the surface area of a box 3ft by 6 ft by 4 ft in dimensions.

4.175) If a sphere is dilated by 2.83, how much does the volume increase
A) The volume increases by 2.83
B) The volume increases by $(2.83)^2$
C) The volume increases by $(2.83)^3$
D) There is no increase in the volume

4.176) What is the volume of a doughnut of height 3 cm outside radius of 12 cm and the hole with a radius of 6 cm

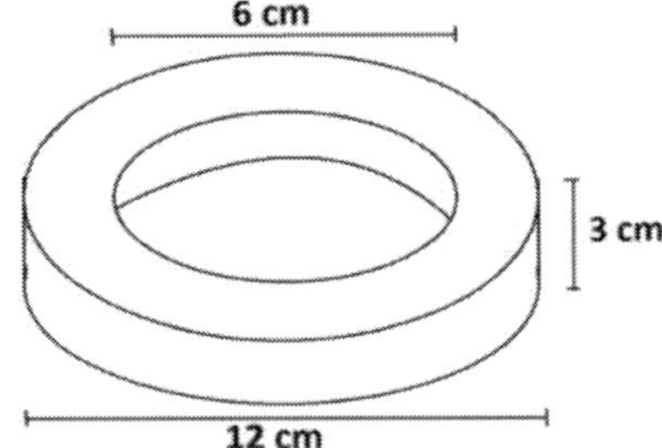

4.177) What is the volume of a cone with a radius at the bottom of 6 inches and a height of 12 inches.

4.178) If the cylinder drawn below is dilated by 2.5 what are the new dimensions

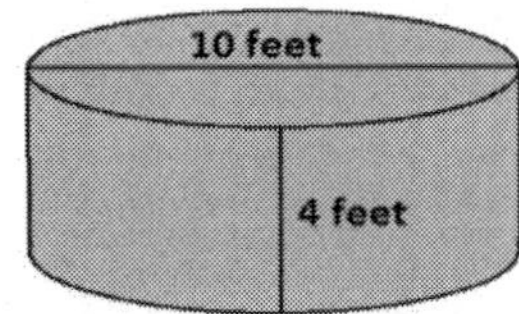

4.179) What is the volume of a cone with a diameter of 10 inches and a height of 20 inches.

4.180) What is the lateral surface area of the following drawing (calculator is allowed on this problem)

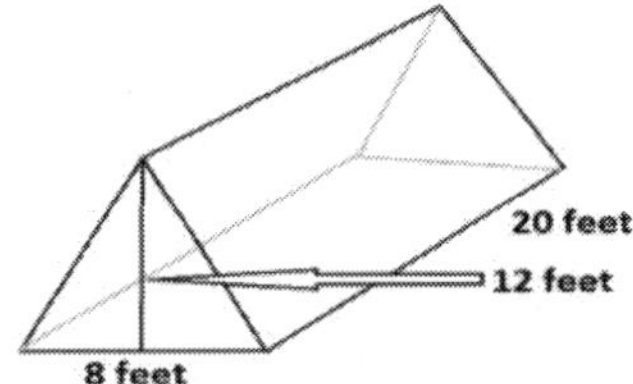

4.181) What is the length of a side of a square with an area of 81 feet square

4.182) A cube of sides 4 inches and a hole in each side with a radius of 2 inches has what surface area. Calculator is allowed for this problem

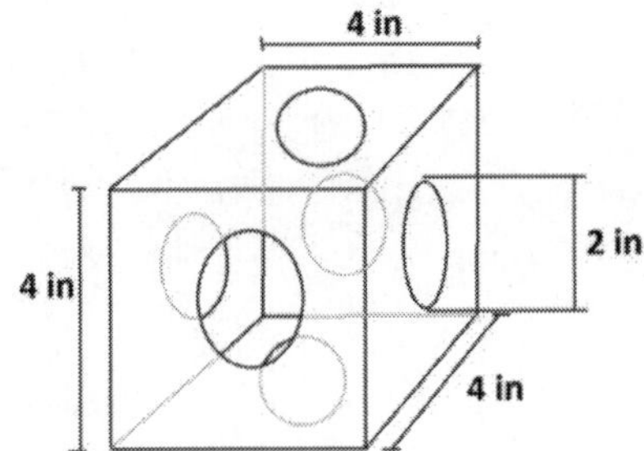

4.183) If a sphere has a radius of $3\ ^1/_3$ feet, what is its volume (calculator allowed)

4.184) Given the dilation shown below, what is the value of X (calculator allowed)

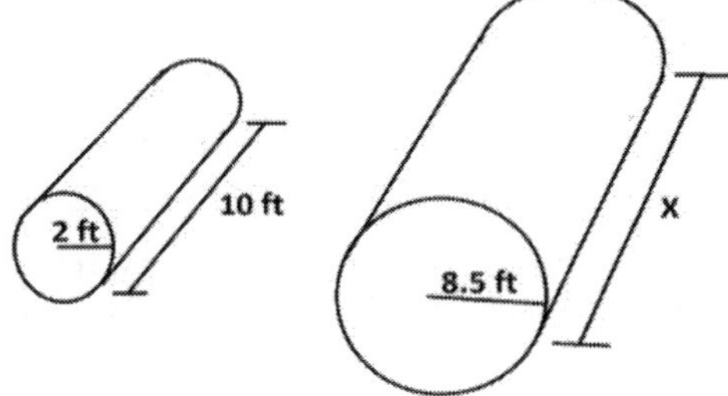

4.185) If a sphere is dilated by ¾ what is the change in the surface area
A) 3/4
B) 6/8
C) 9/16
D) 4/3

4.186) If a sphere is dilated by ¾ what is the change in the volume
A) 3/4
B) 9/12
C) 27/64
D) 4/3

4.187) If a cube is dilated by $1\ ^1/_2$ what is the change in the surface area
A) 3/2
B) 6/4
C) 9/4
D) 3/2

4.188) If a cube is dilated by $1\ ^1/_2$ what is the change in the volume
A) 3/2
B) 6/8
C) 12/16
D) 27/8

4.189) Given the figures below which has a volume shown in this equation: V= $(1/3)(10)^2(20)$

A)

20 cm

10 cm

C)

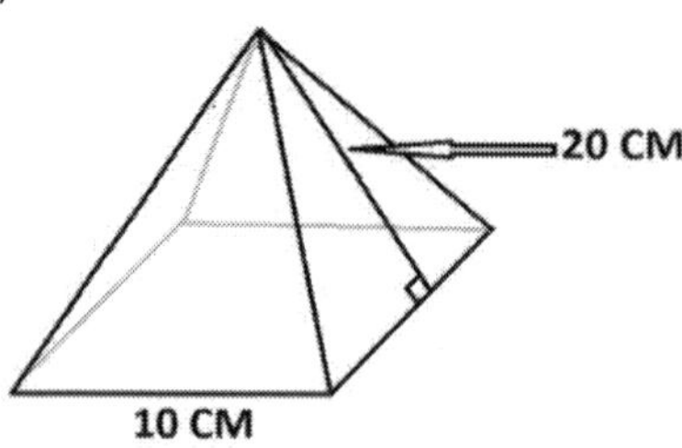

B)

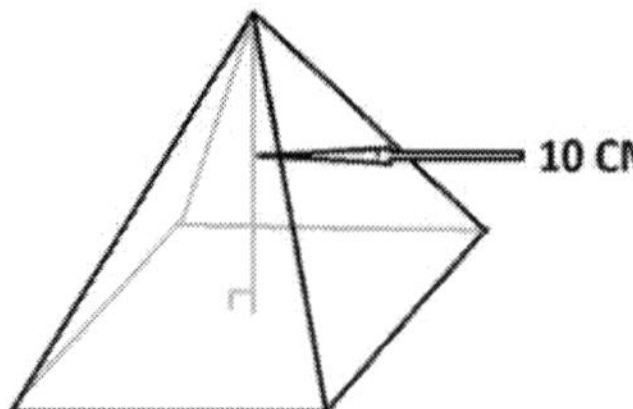

D)

10 CM

20 CM

4.190) What would be the lateral surface area of the following diagram

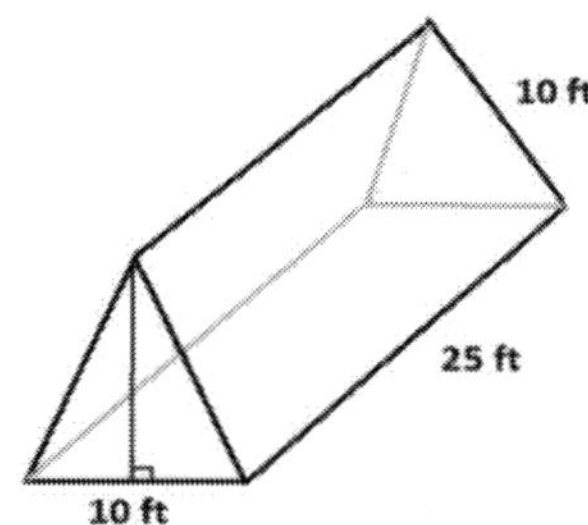

4.191) Two squares with a ratio in dimensions of 1:5. Which of the following statements is true

A) The perimeter of one is 2 times greater than the other

B) The area of one is 25 greater than the other

C) The area of one is 5/3 greater than the other

D) The perimeter of one is 3/5 greater than the other

4.192) A ball has a radius of 4.5 feet, what is its volume (calculator is allowed)

4.193) Given the diagram below what is the value of W

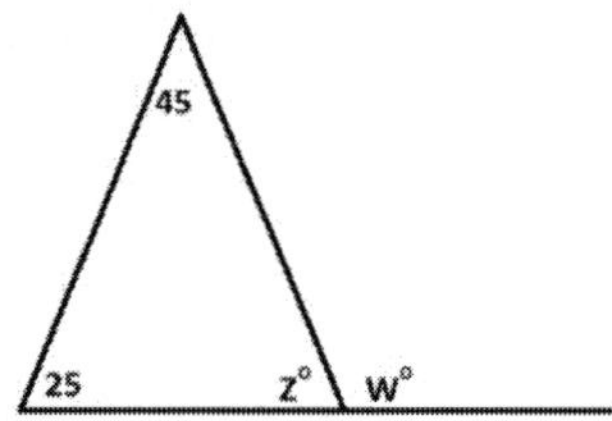

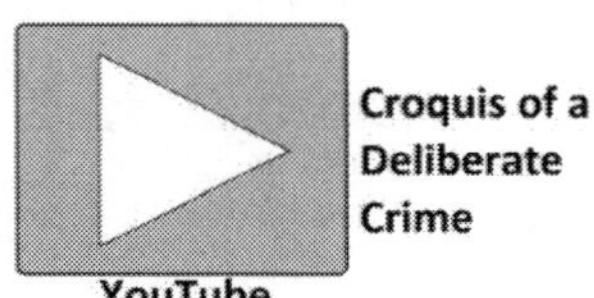

4.194) What is the surface area of this figure

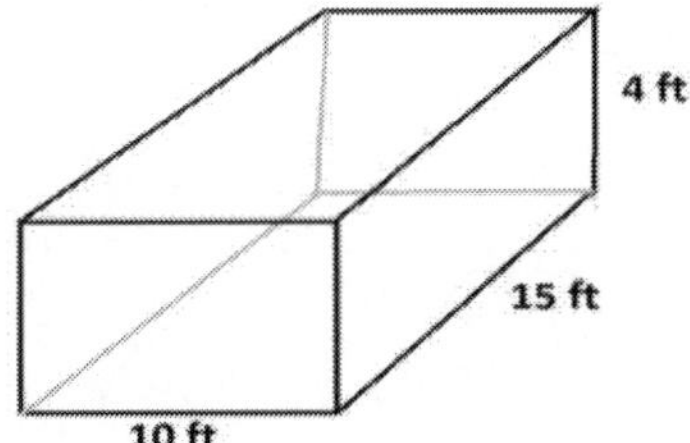

4.195) What is the volume of the figure drawn below (calculators allowed)

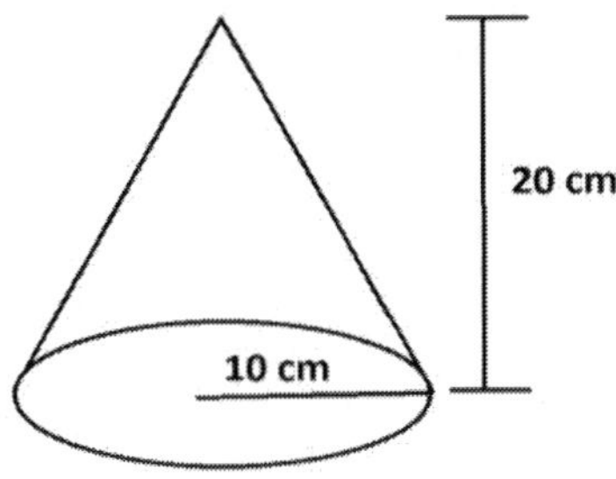

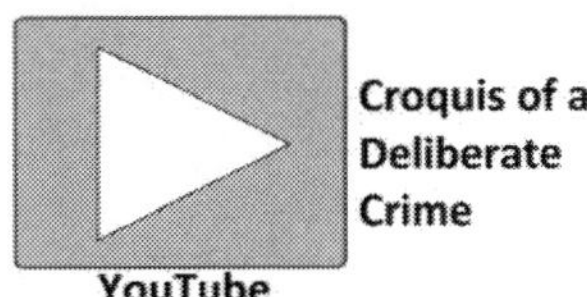

If you don't get the correct answer, and want an explanation on how to work the problem, go to YouTube and type in "MMT" then the problem number. An example would be, MMT 3.9.w12,. The video will show you how to work problem 3.9.w12.

For one on one tutoring via skype at $35.00/Hr.; contact me at marksmathtutoring@yahoo.com

5.0 FRACTIONS

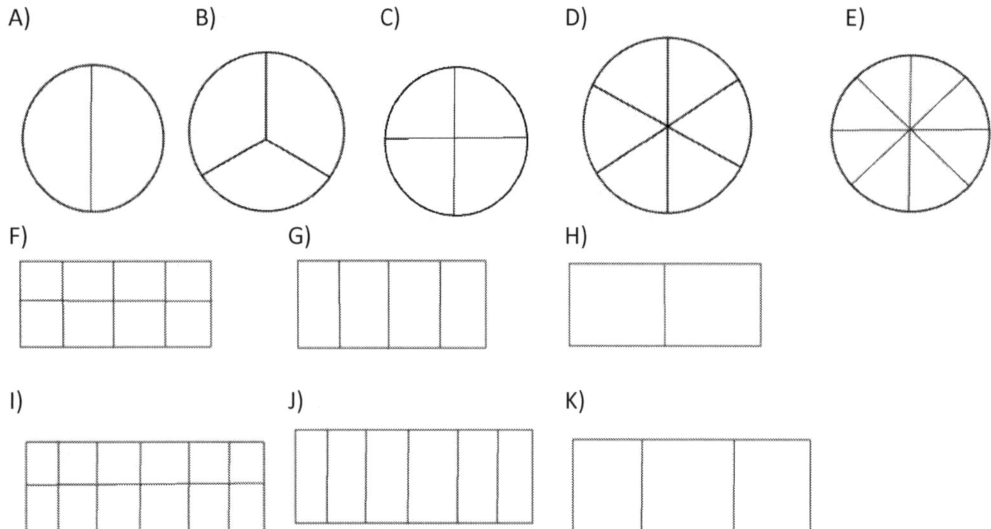

For the following problems redraw each figure before shading in the parts. This way you can reuse them.
5.1) for figure A) color ½ of the circle
5.2) for figure B) color 2/3 of the circle
5.3) for figure I) color 7/12 of the square
5.4) for figure J) color 5/6 of the square
5.5) for figure F) color 5/8 of the square
5.6) for figure E) color 5/8 of the circle

5.7) color 2/4 of figure C) and 1/2 of Figure A) Are they the same?
5.8) color 3/4 of figure C) and 6/8 of Figure E) Are they the same?
5.9) color 2/3 of figure B) and 3/6 of Figure D) Are they the same?
5.10) color 2/8 of figure E) and 1/4 of Figure C) Are they the same?
5.11) color 2/4 of figure G) and 2/8 of Figure F) Are they the same?
5.12) color 6/12 of figure I) and 3/4 of Figure G) Are they the same?
5.13) color 2/3 of figure K) and 4/6 of Figure J) Are they the same?

5.14) color 2/4 of figure C) and 3/8 of Figure E) Are they the same? If not which one is greater?
5.15) color 2/3 of figure B) and 3/6 of Figure D) Are they the same? If not which one is less?
5.16) color 3/8 of figure E) and 3/4 of Figure C) Are they the same? If not which one is less?
5.17) color 1/3 of figure B) and 3/8 of Figure E) Are they the same? If not which one is greater?
5.18) color 3/4 of figure G) and 1/2 of Figure H) Are they the same? If not which one is greater?
5.19) color 1/3 of figure K) and 1/3 of Figure J) Are they the same? If not which one is less?
5.20) color 4/12 of figure I) and 1/3 of Figure K) Are they the same? If not which one is greater?
5.21) color 2/12 of figure I) and 2/6 of Figure J) Are they the same? If not which one is greater?
5.22) color 2/6 of figure J) and 2/3 of Figure K) Are they the same? If not which one is greater?
5.23) color 2/4 of figure G) and 4/8 of Figure F) Are they the same? If not which one is greater?
5.24) color 4/6 of figure J) and 1/2 of Figure H) Are they the same? If not which one is less?
5.25) color 6/12 of figure I) and 3/6 of Figure J) Are they the same? If not which one is less?
5.27) color 2/12 of figure I) and 2/6 of Figure J) Are they the same? If not which one is greater?
5.28) color 1/3 of figure K) and 2/6 of Figure J) Are they the same? If not which one is less?
5.29) color 1/8 of figure F) and 1/4 of Figure G) Are they the same? If not which one is greater?

5.30) Sarah shaded the following figure

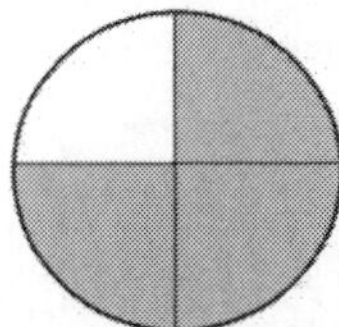

Which fraction best representents the shaded area
a) 2/3, b) 3/4, c) 1/2, d) 4/4

5.31) Edward shaded the following figure

Which fraction best represents the shaded area
a) 1/4, b) 3/2, c) 2/3, d) 1/3

5.32) Mike saded th following figure

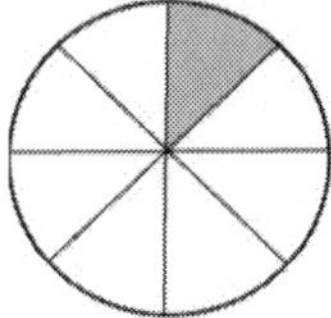

Which fraction best represents the saded area
a) 1/8, b) 1/4, c) 1/2, d) 7/8

5.33) Jonny shaded the following figure

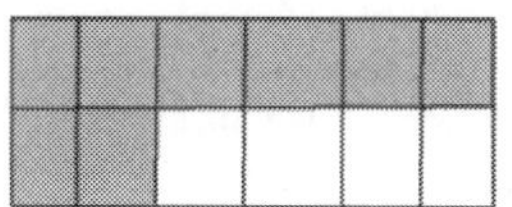

Which fraction best represents the saded area
a) 5/8, b) 8/12, c) 2/3, d) 3/4

5.34) Lynne saded the following figure

Which fraction best represents the shaded area
a) 4/6, b) 3/4, c) 2/3, d) 3/5

5.35) Lynne saded the following figure

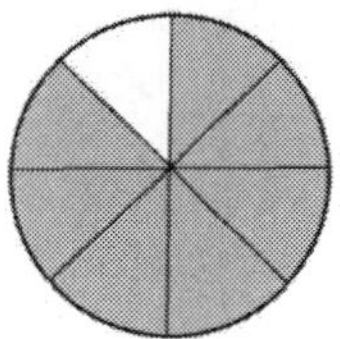

Which fraction best represents the shaded area
a) 7/8, b) 1/8, c) 3/4, d) 5/8

5.36) Sarah ate 1/3 of a cake and her brother ate 1/4 of a pie. Which one ate the most cake?
5.37) If one apple is 3/4 of a pound and the other is 3/5 of a pound. Which apple is bigger?
5.38) If I buy 2/5 of a pound of sugar and you buy 2/3 of a pound of sugar, who bought the most?
5.39) If Al pays 3/4 of a dollar and Sue pays 3/5 of a dollar who pays the most?
5.40) Which number is smaller 1/2 or 1/3?
5.41) Which number is larger 2/3 or 2/5?
5.42) which number is larger 3/5 or 3/8?
5.43) Which number is smaller 5/8 or 5/9

5.44) Which fraction is larger 2/5 or 3/5?
5.45) which fraction is larger 1/3 or 2/3?
5.46) Which fraction is smaller 3/8 or 6/8?
5.47) which fraction is smaller 5/6 or 3/6?

Croquis of a Deliberate Crime

5.48) Verna shaded the following two figures

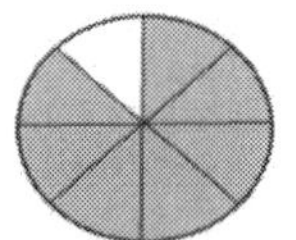 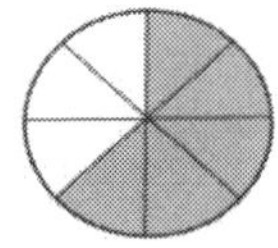

Which statements best describes the shaded areas
a) 7/8<5/8
b) 3/4>5/8
c)3/4>7/8
d) 7/8>5/8

5.49) Verna shaded the following two figures

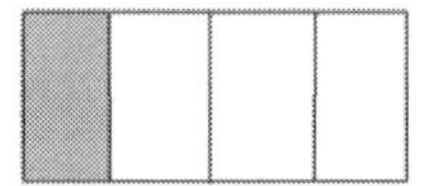 

Which statements best describes the shaded areas
a) 3/4>1/4
b) 1/4>3/4
c) 1/2<1/4
d) 1/4<3/4

5.50) the following shapes are shaded as shown.

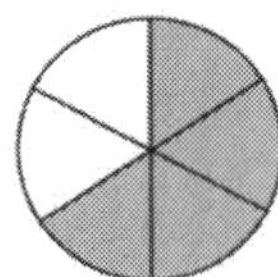 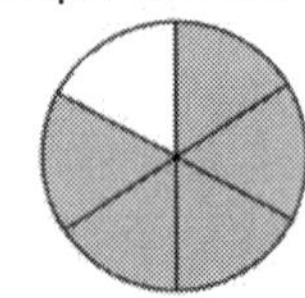

Which stament below best describes this shading
a)5/6>4/6, b) 2/6>3/6, c) 3/4< 2/3, d) 5/6=4/6

5.51) the following shapes are shaded as shown.

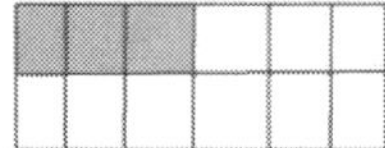 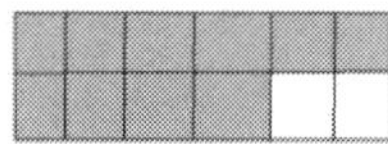

Which stament below best describes this shading
a)5/6>4/6, b) 3/8>3/6, c) 10/12< 3/12, d)10/12>3/12

5.52) the following shapes are shaded as shown.

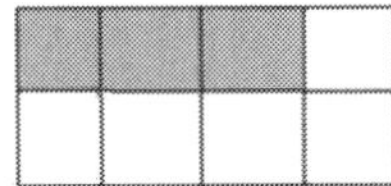 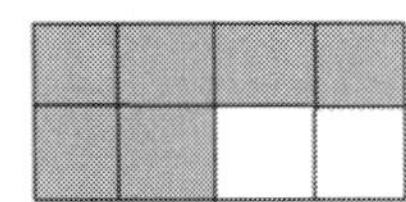

Which stament below best describes this shading
a)3/8>6/8, b) 3/8<6/8, c) 2/4< 2/8, d) 5/6<4/6

5.53) the following shapes are shaded as shown.

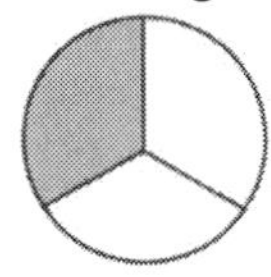 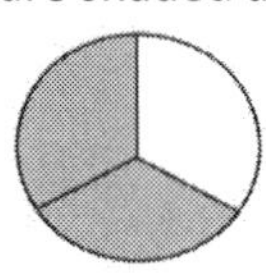

Which stament below best describes this shading
a)2/3>1/3, b) 2/3<1/3, c) 1/4>2/6, d) 4/6<2/6

5.54) Which statement is true
a) 1/8<1/5<1/4<1/3, b) 1/3<1/4<1/6<1/9, c) 2/5<2/4<2/6<2/8, d) 3/5>3/7>3/8>3/2

5.55) Which statement is true
a) 3/5<3/4<3/2<3/7, b) 3/4>3/5>3/7>3/8, c) 4/5<4/6<4/7<4/9, d) 4/5>4/6>4/3>4/8

5.56) Which statement is true
a) 5/7>5/8>5/4>5/6, b) 4/5>4/6>4/7>4/9, c) 3/5<3/4<3/7<3/9 d) 6/7<6/4<6/5<6/9

5.57) Which statement is true
a) 2/3<3/3<4/3<5/3, b) 3/9>5/9>6/9<1/9, c) 6/7>5/7>7/7>3/7, d) 5/6>5/4>5/3>5/2

5.58) Which statement is true
a) 5/8<7<8<3/8<6/8, b) 3/7<9/7<6/7<8/7, c) 7/8>6/8>5/8>3/8, d) 12/4<3/4<6/4<3/4

5.59) The diagram below show the amount of money I found in the street today.

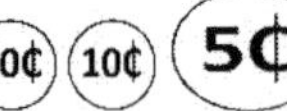

How much money is this
a) $\$1^{\underline{51}}$
b) $\$1^{\underline{96}}$
c) $\$1^{\underline{47}}$
d) $\$1^{\underline{37}}$

5.60) I want to buy a candy bar. It cost $\$1^{\underline{86}}$. If the diagram below shows how much money I have in my pocket do I have enough money?

$1 25¢ 10¢ 10¢ 10¢ 5¢ 5¢ 1¢ 1¢

5.61) Is the amount of money shown below more than $\$0^{\underline{87}}$?

25¢ 25¢ 10¢ 10¢ 5¢ 5¢ 5¢ 1¢ 1¢

5.62) The drawing below shows four different amounts of money. Which one has a 7 in the tenths place?

a)

$5 25¢ 25¢

$1 25¢ 10¢ 5¢ 1¢

b)

$1 25¢

$1 10¢ 10¢ 5¢ 5¢ 1¢ 1¢ 1¢

c)

$5 25¢ 10¢ 10¢ 5¢ 5¢ 5¢ 1¢

d)

$1 25¢ 25¢ 10¢ 5¢ 5¢ 1¢ 1¢ 1¢

5.63) The drawing below represents which relationship?

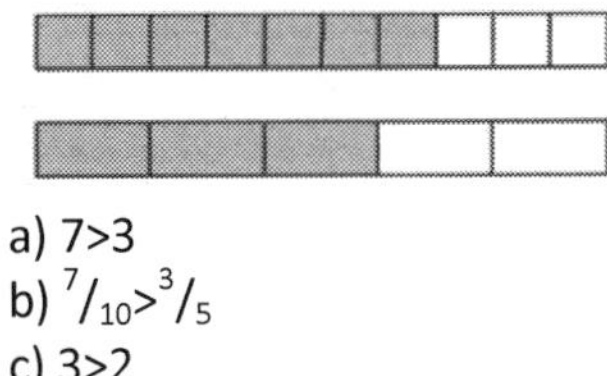

a) 7>3
b) $^7/_{10} > ^3/_5$
c) 3>2
d) $^3/_{10} > ^2/_5$

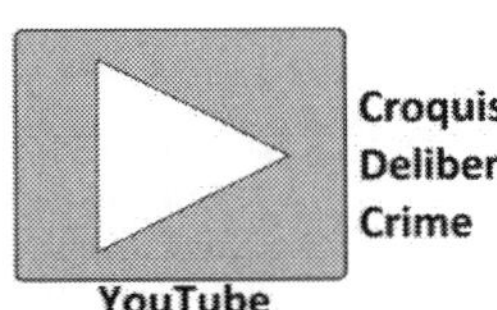

Croquis of a Deliberate Crime

5.64) Given the diagram below

1					
1/2			1/2		
1/3		1/3		1/3	
1/4	1/4		1/4	1/4	
1/5	1/5	1/5	1/5	1/5	
1/6	1/6	1/6	1/6	1/6	1/6

Which of the following statements is true
a) 1/6>1/5>1/4>1/3
b) 2/6< 2/5< 1/4< 2/3
c) 4/6>3/5>2/4<1/3
d) 1/2>2/3>3/4>4/5

5.65) Given the following statements which one is greater than $0.93.

A)

25¢ 25¢ 25¢ 10¢ 5¢ 1¢

B)

25¢ 25¢ 25¢ 10¢ 5¢ 1¢ 1¢

C)

25¢ 25¢ 10¢ 10¢ 10¢ 5¢ 5¢ 5¢ 5¢ 1¢

D)

25¢ 10¢ 10¢ 10¢ 10¢ 5¢ 5¢ 1¢ 1¢

Fraction Addition

5.2.1) 1/2+1/2 5.2.2) 2/3+3/3 5.2.3) 5/6+1/6 5.2.4) 3/4+2/4
5.2.5) 5/8+2/8 5.2.6) 6/9+4/9 5.2.7) 1/5+3/5 5.2.8) 2/6+4/6
5.2.9) 3/9+ 2/9 5.2.10) 4/7+2/7 5.2.11) 1/3+1/3 5.2.12) 4/6+1/6
5.2.13) 3/8+2/8 5.2.14) 4/7+1/7 5.2.15) 2/11+6/11 5.2.16) 5/16+4/16
5.2.17) 2/8+4/8 5.2.18) 3/7+2/7 5.2.19) 6/12+5/12 5.2.20) 5/13+7/13
5.2.21) 4/12+6/12 5.2.22) 4/15+8/15 5.2.23) 6/11+3/11 5.2.24) 7/10+4/10

5.2.25)3/4+1/3 5.2.26)2/3+1/6 5.2.27)3/4+4/5 5.2.28)2/7+1/2
5.2.29)5/7+2/3 5.2.30)2/3+2/7 5.2.31)3/7+5/6 5.2.32)3/5+1/2
5.2.33)2/5+1/4 5.2.34)3/7+7/8 5.2.35)3/7+3/5 5.2.36)2/7+1/4
5.2.37)5/7+1/5 5.2.38)1/8+1/3 5.2.39)2/7+1/3 5.2.40)1/6+3/8
5.2.41)3/7+1/3 5.2.42)3/7+2/3 5.2.43)6/7+5/8 5.2.44)6/7+3/4
5.2.45)1/3+5/6 5.2.46)1/3+1/2 5.2.47)2/5+1/6 5.2.48)3/4+5/6
5.2.49)1/6+1/3 5.2.50)1/4+1/6 5.2.51)2/5+5/6 5.2.52)3/7+4/5
5.2.53)2/3+1/5 5.2.54)3/4+2/3 5.2.55)1/3+5/7 5.2.56)5/8+5/6

5.2.57)$1\,^{2}/_{3}+2\,^{1}/_{4}$ 5.2.58)$2\,^{1}/_{6}+2\,^{3}/_{4}$ 5.2.59)$3\,^{1}/_{5}+1\,^{1}/_{4}$ 5.2.60)$2\,^{1}/_{8}+1\,^{1}/_{7}$
5.2.61)$2\,^{5}/_{8}+1\,^{1}/_{3}$ 5.2.62)$1\,^{5}/_{7}+3\,^{5}/_{6}$ 5.2.63)$2\,^{2}/_{7}+3\,^{1}/_{2}$
5.2.64)$1\,^{3}/_{5}+2\,^{3}/_{8}$ 5.2.65)$1\,^{3}/_{5}+2\,^{6}/_{7}$ 5.2.66)$1\,^{1}/_{4}+1\,^{1}/_{3}$ 5.2.67)$1\,^{1}/_{3}+3\,^{1}/_{5}$
5.2.68)$1\,^{2}/_{7}+4\,^{1}/_{5}$ 5.2.69)$1\,^{4}/_{7}+3\,^{2}/_{3}$ 5.2.70)$1\,^{5}/_{8}+2\,^{4}/_{7}$ 5.2.71)$2\,^{1}/_{4}+2\,^{5}/_{6}$
5.2.72)$2\,^{1}/_{2}+3\,^{5}/_{7}$ 5.2.73)$3\,^{1}/_{7}+2\,^{1}/_{6}$ 5.2.74)$1\,^{3}/_{8}+4\,^{2}/_{3}$ 5.2.75)$1\,^{1}/_{6}+2\,^{1}/_{5}$

5.2.76) $2\,{}^{4}/_{7}+2\,{}^{2}/_{5}$
5.2.77) $1\,{}^{2}/_{5}+1\,{}^{1}/_{6}$
5.2.78) $2\,{}^{7}/_{8}+2\,{}^{1}/_{6}$
5.2.79) $1\,{}^{2}/_{5}+3\,{}^{7}/_{8}$
5.2.80) $1\,{}^{2}/_{7}+4\,{}^{1}/_{5}$
5.2.81) $1\,{}^{4}/_{7}+3\,{}^{2}/_{3}$
5.2.82) $1\,{}^{5}/_{8}+2\,{}^{4}/_{7}$
5.2.83) $2\,{}^{1}/_{4}+2\,{}^{5}/_{8}$
5.2.84) $2\,{}^{5}/_{8}+3\,{}^{4}/_{5}$
5.2.85) $2\,{}^{1}/_{4}+2\,{}^{4}/_{5}$
5.2.86) $1\,{}^{4}/_{5}+3\,{}^{6}/_{7}$
5.2.87) $1\,{}^{3}/_{8}+2\,{}^{3}/_{7}$

5.2.88) $3+2{}^{3}/_{7}$
5.2.89) $1+6{}^{5}/_{8}$
5.2.90) $5+8{}^{7}/_{8}$
5.2.91) $8+3{}^{1}/_{6}$
5.2.92) $9+2{}^{5}/_{8}$
5.2.93) $9{}^{8}/_{9}+4$
5.2.94) $3+1{}^{2}/_{9}$
5.2.95) $5{}^{3}/_{7}+4$
5.2.96) $4+2{}^{3}/_{5}$
5.2.97) $2{}^{4}/_{7}+6$
5.2.98) $1+8{}^{2}/_{9}$
5.2.99) $2{}^{4}/_{9}+7$

5.2.100) (2/3)+(-1/4)
5.2.101) (-2/5)+(-1/3)
5.2.102) (1/5)+(-1/4)
5.2.103) (-1/8)+(1/4)
5.2.104) (-5/6)+(1/3)
5.2.105) (-4/7)+(-2/3)
5.2.106) (2/5)+(-5/7)
5.2.107) (-1/2)+(-4/5)
5.2.108) (-3/4)+(2/3)
5.2.109) (6/8)+(-2/3)
5.2.110) (-3/5)+(-5/6)
5.2.111) (-1/2)+(2/6)

5.2.112) $(1{}^{2}/_{3})+(-1{}^{3}/_{4})$
5.2.113) $(-2\,{}^{4}/_{5})+(-1{}^{1}/_{3})$
5.2.114) $(-2\,{}^{1}/_{3})+({}^{5}/_{6})$
5.2.115) $(3\,{}^{1}/_{3})+(-1\,{}^{4}/_{5})$
5.2.116) $(-2\,{}^{1}/_{3})+(-2\,½)$
5.2.117) $(-3\,¼)+(-2/3)$
5.2.118) $(-1\,{}^{2}/_{3})+(-1\,{}^{3}/_{5})$
5.2.119) $(-1{}^{3}/_{4})+(2\,{}^{1}/_{3})$
5.2.120) $(-2\,¼)+(-2\,{}^{3}/_{5})$
5.2.121) $(-1\,{}^{6}/_{8})+(2\,½)$
5.2.122) $(-3\,{}^{2}/_{3})+(-1\,{}^{3}/_{5})$
5.2.123) $(2\,½)+(-3\,¼)$

5.2.124) $(2)+(-1{}^{3}/_{4})$
5.2.125) $(-3)+(-1{}^{1}/_{3})$
5.2.126) $(-1)+({}^{5}/_{6})$
5.2.127) $(2)+(-1\,{}^{4}/_{5})$
5.2.128) $(-2\,{}^{1}/_{3})+(-1)$
5.2.129) $(-3\,¼)+(-2)$
5.2.130) $(-1\,{}^{2}/_{3})+(-1)$
5.2.131) $(-1{}^{3}/_{4})+(2)$

5.2.w1) If I share a cake with a friend in the proportions shown below.
Me   my friend

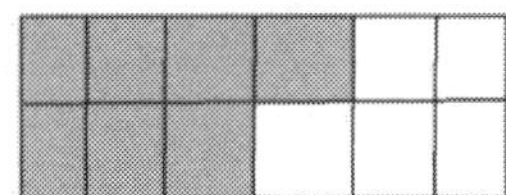

What fraction best describes the amount of cake eaten?
a) 11/12 b) 8/12 c) 2/3 d) ¾

5.2.w2) If I have 2/3 of a pound and you have 3/4 of a pond how much do we have combined

5.2.w3) If I walk 5/6 of a mile before lunch and 3/5 of a mile after lunch how far did I walk

5.2.w4) If my fish weights 4/5 of a pound and my friends weights 2/3 of a pound how much do they weight together

5.2.w5) If I have 5/6 a dollar and borrow another 2/5 of a dollar how much do I have

5.2.w6) If one piece of paper is 7/8 foot long and the other is 2/3 foot long how long are they combined

5.2.w7) My dog eat 5/6 pound of food and yours eats 2/3 pound how much did they eat combined

5.2.w8) If I have ¾ pound of grapes and you have $2\,{}^{2}/_{3}$ pound of grapes how much do we have combined

5.2.w9) If I have $4\,{}^{5}/_{6}$ dollar in my pocket and 2 ¾ in my piggy bank how much do I have total

5.2.w10) My fish weights $12\,{}^{4}/_{5}$ pound and another guys weights 5 ¾ how much do they weight combined

5.2.w11) I have 3 feet of rope and you have 1 ¾ foot piece how long are they combined

Fraction Subtraction

5.3.1) 1/2-1/2
5.3.2) 2/3-1/3
5.3.3) 5/6-1/6
5.3.4) 3/4-1/4
5.3.5) 5/8-3/8
5.3.6) 6/9-4/9
5.3.7) 4/5-3/5
5.3.8) 5/6-4/6
5.3.9) 3/9- 2/9
5.3.10) 4/7-2/7
5.3.11) 1/3-1/3
5.3.12) 4/6-1/6
5.3.13) 3/8-2/8
5.3.14) 4/7-1/7
5.3.15) 2/11-1/11
5.3.16) 5/16-4/16
5.3.17) 12/8-4/8
5.3.18) 3/7-2/7
5.3.19) 6/12-5/12
5.3.20) 5/13-2/13
5.3.21) 7/12-6/12
5.3.22) 8/15-5/15
5.3.23) 6/11-3/11
5.3.24) 7/10-4/10

5.3.25)3/4-1/3
5.3.26)2/3-1/6
5.3.27)3/4-4/5
5.3.28)2/7-1/2
5.3.29)5/7-2/3
5.3.30)2/3-2/7
5.3.31)3/7-5/6
5.3.32)3/5-1/2
5.3.33)2/5-1/4
5.3.34)3/7-7/8
5.3.35)3/7-3/5
5.3.36)2/7-1/4
5.3.37)5/7-1/5
5.3.38)1/8-1/3
5.3.39)1/8-1/9
5.3.40)1/6-3/8
5.3.41)3/7-1/3
5.3.42)3/7-2/3
5.3.43)6/7-5/8
5.3.44)6/7-3/4
5.3.45)1/3-5/6
5.3.46)1/3-1/2
5.3.47)2/5-1/6
5.3.48)3/4-5/6
5.3.49)1/6-1/3
5.3.50)1/4-1/6
5.3.51)2/5-5/6
5.3.52)3/7-4/5
5.3.53)2/3-1/5
5.3.54)3/4-2/3
5.3.55)1/3-5/7
5.3.56)5/8-5/6

5.3.57)$1\frac{2}{3}-2\frac{1}{4}$
5.3.58)$2\frac{1}{6}-2\frac{3}{4}$
5.3.59)$3\frac{1}{5}-1\frac{1}{4}$
5.3.60)$2\frac{1}{8}-1\frac{1}{7}$
5.3.60)$2\frac{5}{8}-3\frac{2}{5}$
5.3.61)$2\frac{5}{8}-1\frac{1}{3}$
5.3.62)$1\frac{5}{7}-3\frac{5}{6}$
5.3.63)$2\frac{2}{7}-3\frac{1}{2}$
5.3.64)$1\frac{3}{5}-2\frac{3}{8}$
5.3.65)$1\frac{3}{5}-2\frac{6}{7}$
5.3.66)$1\frac{1}{4}-1\frac{1}{3}$
5.3.67)$1\frac{1}{3}-3\frac{1}{5}$
5.3.68)$1\frac{2}{7}-4\frac{1}{5}$
5.3.69)$1\frac{4}{7}-3\frac{2}{3}$
5.3.70)$1\frac{5}{8}-2\frac{4}{7}$
5.3.71)$2\frac{1}{4}-2\frac{5}{6}$
5.3.72)$2\frac{1}{2}-3\frac{5}{7}$
5.3.73)$3\frac{1}{7}-2\frac{1}{6}$
5.3.74)$1\frac{3}{8}-4\frac{2}{3}$
5.3.75)$1\frac{1}{6}-2\frac{1}{5}$
5.3.76)$2\frac{4}{7}-2\frac{2}{5}$
5.3.77)$1\frac{2}{5}-1\frac{1}{6}$
5.3.78)$2\frac{7}{8}-2\frac{1}{6}$
5.3.79)$1\frac{2}{5}-3\frac{7}{8}$
5.3.80)$1\frac{2}{7}-4\frac{1}{5}$
5.3.81)$1\frac{4}{7}-3\frac{2}{3}$
5.3.82)$1\frac{5}{8}-2\frac{4}{7}$
5.3.83)$2\frac{1}{4}-2\frac{5}{8}$
5.3.84)$2\frac{5}{8}-3\frac{4}{5}$
5.3.85)$2\frac{1}{4}-2\frac{4}{5}$
5.3.86)$1\frac{4}{5}-3\frac{6}{7}$
5.3.87)$1\frac{3}{8}-2\frac{3}{7}$
5.3.88) $3-2\frac{3}{7}$
5.3.89) $1-6\frac{5}{8}$
5.3.90) $5-8\frac{7}{8}$
5.3.91) $8-3\frac{1}{6}$
5.3.92) $9-2\frac{5}{8}$
5.3.93) $9\frac{8}{9}-4$
5.3.94)$3-1\frac{2}{9}$
5.3.95)$5\frac{3}{7}-4$
5.3.96) $4-2\frac{3}{5}$
5.3.97) $2\frac{4}{7}-6$
5.3.98) $1-8\frac{2}{9}$
5.3.99)$2\frac{4}{9}-7$

5.3.100) 2/3-(-1/4)
5.3.101) (-2/5)-(-1/3)
5.3.102) (1/5)-(-1/4)
5.3.103) (-1/8)-(1/4)
5.3.104) (-5/6)-(1/3)
5.3.105) (-4/7)-(-2/3)
5.3.106) (2/5)-(-5/7)
5.3.107) (-1/2)-(-4/5)
5.3.108) (-3/4)-(2/3)
5.3.109) (6/8)-(-2/3)
5.3.110) (-3/5)-(-5/6)
5.3.111) (-1/2)-(2/6)

5.3.112) $(1\frac{2}{3})-(-1\frac{3}{4})$
5.3.113) $(-2\frac{4}{5})-(-1\frac{1}{3})$
5.3.114) $(-2\frac{1}{3})-(\frac{5}{6})$
5.3.115) $(3\frac{1}{3})-(-1\frac{4}{5})$
5.3.116) $(-2\frac{1}{3})-(-2\frac{1}{2})$
5.3.117) $(-3\frac{1}{4})-(-2/3)$
5.3.118) $(-1\frac{2}{3})-(-1\frac{3}{5})$
5.3.119) $(-1\frac{3}{4})-(2\frac{1}{3})$
5.3.120) $(-2\frac{1}{4})-(-2\frac{3}{5})$
5.3.121) $(-1\frac{6}{8})-(2\frac{1}{2})$
5.3.122) $(-3\frac{2}{3})-(-1\frac{3}{5})$
5.3.123) $(2\frac{1}{2})-(-3\frac{1}{4})$

5.3.124) $(2)-(-1\frac{3}{4})$
5.3.125) $(-3)-(-1\frac{1}{3})$
5.3.126) $(-1)-(\frac{5}{6})$
5.3.127) $(2)-(-1\frac{4}{5})$
5.3.128) $(-2\frac{1}{3})-(-1)$
5.3.129) $(-3\frac{1}{4})-(-2)$
5.3.130) $(-1\frac{2}{3})-(-1)$
5.3.131) $(-1\frac{3}{4})-(2)$

5.3.w1) If I cut pieces of paper into two shapes shown below
○○⌂○○
⌂⌂○○⌂
What is the best way to determine the fractional differences between these two shapes?
a)10/10-6/10=
b)10/10-4/10=
c)6/10-4/10=
d)6/10+4/10=

5.3.w2) I am 6 ½ away from a fountain. My dog is 4 1/3 feet away from the fountain. What is the distance between me and my dog.

For one on one tutoring via skype at $35.00/Hr.; contact me at marksmathtutoring@yahoo.com

5.3.w4) given the diagram below

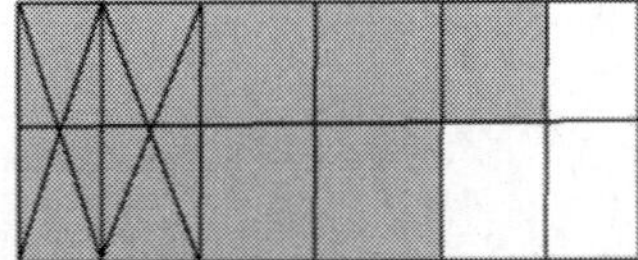

Which statement below best represents the difference shown?
a) 9/12-4/12
b)12/12-9/12
c) 12/12-4/12
d) 9/12+4/12

5.3.w5) If I have ${}^{4}/_{5}$ dollar and buy a burger for ¾ dollar how much do I have left over

5.3.w6) If I my mom sends me to the store for 3/5 pound of grapes but they only have 1/2 pound how much more do I need

5.3.w7) If I am making cookies and they require ¾ pound of butter and I have 7/9 pound how much will I have left over

5.3.w8) If I have a rope that is 8/9 foot long and I cut ½ foot out of it how long in her piece left over

5.3.w9) If I need 3/5 of a dollar to buy a candy bar and have 8/9 of a dollar how much change will I have left over

5.3.w10) What is the difference between the weight of my fish and my friends if mine weights $3\,{}^{6}/_{7}$ and his weights $2\,{}^{4}/_{5}$

5.3.w11) If I have $4\,{}^{4}/_{5}$ dollar and buy a burger for 2 ¾ dollar how much do I have left over

5.3.w12) If I have a rope 5 3/5 foot long and cut a piece 2 4/5 out of it how much rope do I have left

Fraction Multiplication

5.4.1) 1/2X1/2
5.4.2) 2/3X1/3
5.4.3) 5/6X1/6
5.4.4) 3/4X1/4
5.4.5) 5/8X3/8
5.4.6) 6/9X4/9
5.4.7) 4/5X3/5
5.4.8) 5/6X4/6

5.4.9)3/4X1/3
5.4.10)2/3X1/6
5.4.11)3/4X4/5
5.4.12)2/7X1/2
5.4.13)5/7X2/3
5.4.14)2/3X2/7
5.4.15)3/7X5/6
5.4.16)3/5X1/2
5.4.17)2/5X1/4
5.4.18)3/7X7/8
5.4.19)3/7X3/5
5.4.20)2/7X1/4
5.4.21)5/7X1/5
5.4.22)1/8X1/3
5.4.23)3/8X2/3
5.4.24)1/6X3/8
5.4.25)3/7X1/3
5.4.26)3/7X2/3
5.4.27)6/7X5/8
5.4.28)6/7X3/4
5.4.29)1/3X5/6
5.4.30)1/3X1/2
5.4.31)2/5X1/6
5.4.32)3/4X5/6
5.4.33)1/6X1/3
5.4.34)1/4X1/6
5.4.35)2/5X5/6
5.4.36)3/7X4/5
5.4.37)2/3X1/5
5.4.38)3/4X2/3
5.4.39)1/3X5/7
5.4.40)5/8X5/6

5.4.41)$1\,{}^{2}/_{3}$X$2\,{}^{1}/_{4}$
5.4.42)$2\,{}^{1}/_{6}$X$2\,{}^{3}/_{4}$
5.4.43)$3\,{}^{1}/_{5}$X$1\,{}^{1}/_{4}$
5.4.44)$2\,{}^{1}/_{8}$X$1\,{}^{1}/_{7}$
5.4.45)$2\,{}^{5}/_{8}$X$3\,{}^{2}/_{5}$
5.4.46)$2\,{}^{5}/_{8}$X$1\,{}^{1}/_{3}$
5.4.47)$1\,{}^{5}/_{7}$X$3\,{}^{5}/_{6}$
5.4.48)$2\,{}^{2}/_{7}$X$3\,{}^{1}/_{2}$
5.4.49)$1\,{}^{3}/_{5}$X$2\,{}^{3}/_{8}$
5.4.50) $1\,{}^{3}/_{5}$X$2\,{}^{6}/_{7}$
5.4.51) $1\,{}^{1}/_{4}$X$1\,{}^{1}/_{3}$
5.4.52)$1\,{}^{1}/_{3}$X$3\,{}^{1}/_{5}$
5.4.53)$1\,{}^{2}/_{7}$X$4\,{}^{1}/_{5}$
5.4.54) $1\,{}^{4}/_{7}$X$3\,{}^{2}/_{3}$
5.4.55) $1\,{}^{5}/_{8}$X$2\,{}^{4}/_{7}$
5.4.56)$2\,{}^{1}/_{4}$X$2\,{}^{5}/_{6}$
5.4.57)$2\,{}^{1}/_{2}$X$3\,{}^{5}/_{7}$
5.4.58) $3\,{}^{1}/_{7}$X$2\,{}^{1}/_{6}$
5.4.59) $1\,{}^{3}/_{8}$X$4\,{}^{2}/_{3}$
5.4.60)$1\,{}^{1}/_{6}$X$2\,{}^{1}/_{5}$
5.4.61)$2\,{}^{4}/_{7}$X$2\,{}^{2}/_{5}$
5.4.62)$1\,{}^{2}/_{5}$X$1\,{}^{1}/_{6}$
5.4.63)$2\,{}^{7}/_{8}$X$2\,{}^{1}/_{6}$
5.4.64)$1\,{}^{2}/_{5}$X$3\,{}^{7}/_{8}$
5.4.65)$1\,{}^{2}/_{7}$X$4\,{}^{1}/_{5}$
5.4.66)$1\,{}^{4}/_{7}$X$3\,{}^{2}/_{3}$
5.4.67)$1\,{}^{5}/_{8}$X$2\,{}^{4}/_{7}$
5.4.68)$2\,{}^{1}/_{4}$X$2\,{}^{5}/_{8}$
5.4.69)$2\,{}^{5}/_{8}$X$3\,{}^{4}/_{5}$
5.4.70)$2\,{}^{1}/_{4}$X$2\,{}^{4}/_{5}$
5.4.71)$1\,{}^{4}/_{5}$X$3\,{}^{6}/_{7}$
5.4.72)$1\,{}^{3}/_{8}$X$2\,{}^{3}/_{7}$

5.4.73) $3X2^{3}/_{7}$
5.4.74) $1X6^{5}/_{8}$
5.4.75) $5X8^{7}/_{8}$
5.4.76) $8X3^{1}/_{6}$
5.4.77) $9X2^{5}/_{8}$
5.4.78) $9^{8}/_{9}X4$
5.4.79) $3X1^{2}/_{9}$
5.4.80) $5^{3}/_{7}X4$
5.4.81) $4X2^{3}/_{5}$
5.4.82) $2^{4}/_{7}X6$
5.4.83) $1X8^{2}/_{9}$
5.4.84) $2^{4}/_{9}X7$

5.4.100) 2/3x(-1/4)
5.4.101) (-2/5)x(-1/3)
5.4.102) (1/5)x(-1/4)
5.4.103) (-1/8)x(1/4)
5.4.104) (-5/6)x(1/3)
5.4.105) (-4/7)x(-2/3)
5.4.106) (2/5)x(-5/7)
5.4.107) (-1/2)x(-4/5)
5.4.108) (-3/4)x(2/3)
5.4.109) (6/8)x(-2/3)
5.4.110) (-3/5)x(-5/6)
5.4.111) (-1/2)x(2/6)

5.4.112) $(1^{2}/_{3})x(-1^{3}/_{4})$
5.4.113) $(-2\ ^{4}/_{5})x(-1^{1}/_{3})$
5.4.114) $(-2\ ^{1}/_{3})x(^{5}/_{6})$
5.4.115) $(3\ ^{1}/_{3})x(-1\ ^{4}/_{5})$
5.4.116) $(-2\ ^{1}/_{3})$x(-2 ½)
5.4.117) (-3 ¼)x(-2/3)
5.4.118) $(-1\ ^{2}/_{3})x(-1\ ^{3}/_{5})$
5.4.119) $(-1^{3}/_{4})x(2\ ^{1}/_{3})$
5.4.120) (-2 ¼)x$(-2\ ^{3}/_{5})$
5.4.121) $(-1\ ^{6}/_{8})$x(2 ½)
5.4.122) $(-3\ ^{2}/_{3})x(-1\ ^{3}/_{5})$
5.4.123) (2 ½)x(-3 ¼)

5.4.124) $(2)x(-1^{3}/_{4})$
5.4.125) $(-3)x(-1^{1}/_{3})$
5.4.126) $(-1)x(^{5}/_{6})$
5.4.127) $(2)x(-1\ ^{4}/_{5})$
5.4.128) $(-2\ ^{1}/_{3})x(-1)$
5.4.129) (-3 ¼)x(-2)
5.4.130) $(-1\ ^{2}/_{3})x(-1)$
5.4.131) $(-1^{3}/_{4})x(2)$

Fraction Division

5.5.1) 1/2÷1/2
5.5.2) 2/3÷1/3
5.5.3) 5/6÷1/6
5.5.4) 3/4÷1/4
5.5.5) 5/8÷3/8
5.5.6) 6/9÷4/9
5.5.7) 4/5÷3/5
5.5.8) 5/6÷4/6

5.5.9)3/4÷1/3
5.5.10)2/3÷1/6
5.5.11)3/4÷4/5
5.5.12)2/7÷1/2
5.5.13)5/7÷2/3
5.5.14)2/3÷2/7
5.5.15)3/7÷5/6
5.5.16)3/5÷1/2
5.5.17)2/5÷1/4
5.5.18)3/7÷7/8
5.5.19)3/7÷3/5
5.5.20)2/7÷1/4
5.5.21)5/7÷1/5
5.5.22)1/8÷1/3
5.5.23)1/9÷1/2
5.5.24)1/6÷3/8
5.5.25)3/7÷1/3
5.5.26)3/7÷2/3
5.5.27)6/7÷5/8
5.5.28)6/7÷3/4
5.5.29)1/3÷5/6
5.5.30)1/3÷1/2
5.5.31)2/5÷1/6
5.5.32)3/4÷5/6
5.5.33)1/6÷1/3
5.5.34)1/4÷1/6
5.5.35)2/5÷5/6
5.5.36)3/7÷4/5
5.5.37)2/3÷1/5
5.5.38)3/4÷2/3
5.5.39)1/3÷5/7
5.5.40)5/8÷5/6

5.5.41) $1\ ^{2}/_{3}\div 2\ ^{1}/_{4}$
5.5.42) $2\ ^{1}/_{6}\div 2\ ^{3}/_{4}$
5.5.43) $3\ ^{1}/_{5}\div 1\ ^{1}/_{4}$
5.5.44) $2\ ^{1}/_{8}\div 1\ ^{1}/_{7}$
5.5.45) $2\ ^{5}/_{8}\div 3\ ^{2}/_{5}$
5.5.46) $2\ ^{5}/_{8}\div 1\ ^{1}/_{3}$
5.5.47) $1\ ^{5}/_{7}\div 3\ ^{5}/_{6}$
5.5.48) $2\ ^{2}/_{7}\div 3\ ^{1}/_{2}$
5.5.49) $1\ ^{3}/_{5}\div 2\ ^{3}/_{8}$
5.5.50) $1\ ^{3}/_{5}\div 2\ ^{6}/_{7}$
5.5.51) $1\ ^{1}/_{4}\div 1\ ^{1}/_{3}$
5.5.52) $1\ ^{1}/_{3}\div 3\ ^{1}/_{5}$
5.5.53) $1\ ^{2}/_{7}\div 4\ ^{1}/_{5}$
5.5.54) $1\ ^{4}/_{7}\div 3\ ^{2}/_{3}$
5.5.55) $1\ ^{5}/_{8}\div 2\ ^{4}/_{7}$
5.5.56) $2\ ^{1}/_{4}\div 2\ ^{5}/_{6}$
5.5.57) $2\ ^{1}/_{2}\div 3\ ^{5}/_{7}$
5.5.58) $3\ ^{1}/_{7}\div 2\ ^{1}/_{6}$
5.5.59) $1\ ^{3}/_{8}\div 4\ ^{2}/_{3}$
5.5.60) $1\ ^{1}/_{6}\div 2\ ^{1}/_{5}$
5.5.61) $2\ ^{4}/_{7}\div 2\ ^{2}/_{5}$
5.5.62) $1\ ^{2}/_{5}\div 1\ ^{1}/_{6}$
5.5.63) $2\ ^{7}/_{8}\div 2\ ^{1}/_{6}$
5.5.64) $1\ ^{2}/_{5}\div 3\ ^{7}/_{8}$
5.5.65) $1\ ^{2}/_{7}\div 4\ ^{1}/_{5}$
5.5.66) $1\ ^{4}/_{7}\div 3\ ^{2}/_{3}$
5.5.67) $1\ ^{5}/_{8}\div 2\ ^{4}/_{7}$
5.5.68) $2\ ^{1}/_{4}\div 2\ ^{5}/_{8}$
5.5.69) $2\ ^{5}/_{8}\div 3\ ^{4}/_{5}$
5.5.70) $2\ ^{1}/_{4}\div 2\ ^{4}/_{5}$
5.5.71) $1\ ^{4}/_{5}\div 3\ ^{6}/_{7}$
5.5.72) $1\ ^{3}/_{8}\div 2\ ^{3}/_{7}$

5.5.73) $3\div 2^{3}/_{7}$
5.5.74) $1\div 6^{5}/_{8}$
5.5.75) $5\div 8^{7}/_{8}$
5.5.76) $8\div 3^{1}/_{6}$
5.5.77) $9\div 2^{5}/_{8}$
5.5.78) $9^{8}/_{9}\div 4$
5.5.79) $3\div 1^{2}/_{9}$
5.5.80) $5^{3}/_{7}\div 4$
5.5.81) $4\div 2^{3}/_{5}$
5.5.82) $2^{4}/_{7}\div 6$
5.5.83) $1\div 8^{2}/_{9}$
5.5.84) $2^{4}/_{9}\div 7$

5.5.100) 2/3÷(-1/4)
5.5.101) (-2/5)÷(-1/3)
5.5.102) (1/5)÷(-1/4)
5.5.103) (-1/8)÷(1/4)
5.5.104) (-5/6)÷(1/3)
5.5.105) (-4/7)÷(-2/3)
5.5.106) (2/5)÷(-5/7)
5.5.107) (-1/2)÷(-4/5)
5.5.108) (-3/4)÷(2/3)
5.5.109) (6/8)÷(-2/3)
5.5.110) (-3/5)÷(-5/6)
5.5.111) (-1/2)÷(2/6)

5.5.112) $(1^{2}/_{3})\div(-1^{3}/_{4})$
5.5.113) $(-2\ ^{4}/_{5})\div(-1^{1}/_{3})$
5.5.114) $(-2\ ^{1}/_{3})\div(^{5}/_{6})$
5.5.115) $(3\ ^{1}/_{3})\div(-1\ ^{4}/_{5})$
5.5.116) $(-2\ ^{1}/_{3})\div$(-2 ½)
5.5.117) (-3 ¼)÷(-2/3)
5.5.118) $(-1\ ^{2}/_{3})\div(-1\ ^{3}/_{5})$
5.5.119) $(-1^{3}/_{4})\div(2\ ^{1}/_{3})$
5.5.120) (-2 ¼)÷$(-2\ ^{3}/_{5})$
5.5.121) $(-1\ ^{6}/_{8})\div$(2 ½)
5.5.122) $(-3\ ^{2}/_{3})\div(-1\ ^{3}/_{5})$
5.5.123) (2 ½)÷(-3 ¼)

5.5.124) $(2)\div(-1^{3}/_{4})$
5.5.125) $(-3)\div(-1^{1}/_{3})$
5.5.126) $(-1)\div(^{5}/_{6})$
5.5.127) $(2)\div(-1\ ^{4}/_{5})$
5.5.128) $(-2\ ^{1}/_{3})\div(-1)$
5.5.129) (-3 ¼)÷(-2)
5.5.130) $(-1\ ^{2}/_{3})\div(-1)$
5.5.131) $(-1^{3}/_{4})\div(2)$

5.5.w1) I have 1/3 of a pie and I divide it into 6 equal parts. How much of a pie does each piece have?

5.5.w2) If I have 1/6 pound of candy and want to divide it into 4 equal piles. How much does each pile have?

5.5.w3) If I cut a 34 foot rope into ¼ foot pieces. How many pieces will I have?

5.5.w4) When I practice math I do it for 4/5 hour each time. If last month I practiced for 12 hours how many hours did I practice?

5.5.w5) If I bought 225 cupcakes and ate 2/9 on the way home how many do I have left over.

5.5.w6) If I eat 1 ½ cupcakes in 3 hours how many did I eat in 2 hours

5.5.w7) If I have 6 $^2/_5$ pounds of sugar to be divided evenly between three bags how much goes into each bag.

5.5.w8) If in 3 test I answer 4/5 of the questions correct. If there were 55 questions on each test how many questions did I get correct

5.5.w9) If I drink ¾ gallon of water a day how many will I drink in 11 days

5.5.w10) The diameter of a quarter is 5/8 of an inch. What is the length of a row of 12 quarters

5.5.w11) There are 120 dogs in my neighborhood.

¼ are black
$^2/_3$ are yellow
The rest are brown

Based on this how many are brown.

5.5.w12) If 3 ¾ pound sugar makes 24 cupcakes how many pounds do I need for 48 cakes

Fraction Reduction

Convert each improper fraction to a mixed fraction

5.5.132) 11/2	5.5.133) 4/3	5.5.134) 9/4	5.5.135) 12/4	5.5.136) 15/3	5.5.137) 13/2
5.5.138) 45/3	5.5.139) 21/7	5.5.140) 31/7	5.5.141) 75/5	5.5.142) 14/2	5.5.143) 32/8
5.5.144) 21/3	5.5.145) 76/6	5.5.146) 41/4	5.5.147) 65/7	5.5.148) 56/5	5.5.149) 79/4
5.5.150) 98/8	5.5.151) 17/5	5.5.152) 65/3	5.5.153) 86/4	5.5.154) 127/3	5.5.155) 67/6
5.5.156) 78/5	5.5.157) 14/4	5.5.158) 99/9	5.5.159) 165/3	5.5.160) 81/3	5.5.161) 145/8

Reduce fractions to reduced forms

5.5.162) 10/2	5.5.163) 12/3	5.5.164) 20/4	5.5.165) 4/12	5.5.166) 3/15	5.5.167) 6/12
5.5.168) 3/45	5.5.169) 7/21	5.5.170) 7/35	5.5.171) 5/75	5.5.172) 2/14	5.5.173) 8/32
5.5.174) 3/21	5.5.175) 6/78	5.5.176) 4/44	5.5.177) 7/49	5.5.178) 125/5	5.5.179) 4/14
5.5.180) 12/8	5.5.181) 6/18	5.5.182) 66/33	5.5.183) 88/4	5.5.184) 3/126	5.5.185) 6/16
5.5.186) 80/15	5.5.187) 14/4	5.5.188) 99/9	5.5.189) 3/165	5.5.190) 3/81	5.5.191) 8/168

Convert the Decimal to Fractions and Percent

5.7.1)1.4	5.7.2)6.1	5.7.3)2.67	5.7.4)3.45	5.7.5)1.878	5.7.6)9.35
5.7.7) 142.36	5.7.8) 2.25	5.7.9) 4.325	5.7.10) 13.45	5.7.11) 0.71	5.7.12) 7.66
5.7.13) 3.578	5.7.14) 0.0055	5.7.15) 0.37	5.7.16) 12.35	5.7.17) 0.32	5.7.18) 0.016

5.7.19) 11.3 5.7.20) 10 5.7.21) 2.7676 5.7.22) 6.257 5.7.23) 17.35 5.7.24) 6.3
5.7.25) 9.1 5.7.26) 3.46 5.7.27) 3.990 5.7.28) 1.01 5.7.29) 3.41 5.7.30) 0.125

Convert the Fractions to Decimals and Percent

5.8.1) $^{4}/_{100}$ 5.8.2) $^{27}/_{100}$ 5.8.3) $^{13}/_{1000}$ 5.8.4) $^{3}/_{10}$ 5.8.5) $^{67}/_{100}$ 5.8.6) $^{12}/_{1000}$
5.8.7) 1 $^{27}/_{100}$ 5.8.8) $^{3}/_{100}$ 5.8.9) 2 $^{34}/_{1000}$ 5.8.10)1 $^{7}/_{10}$ 5.8.11) 3 $^{4}/_{100}$ 5.8.12) 1 $^{2}/_{1000}$
5.8.13) $^{6}/_{10}$ 5.8.14) 2 $^{3}/_{10}$ 5.8.15) 3 $^{5}/_{10}$ 5.8.16) $^{4}/_{100}$ 5.8.17) 4 $^{1}/_{100}$ 5.8.18) 2 $^{47}/_{1000}$
5.8.19)2 $^{137}/_{1000}$ 5.8.20) 3 $^{4}/_{10}$ 5.8.21) 16 $^{7}/_{10}$ 5.8.22) 3 $^{3}/_{1000}$ 5.8.23) $^{89}/_{100}$ 5.8.24) $^{127}/_{100}$
5.8.25) $^{14}/_{100}$ 5.8.26) $^{6}/_{1000}$ 5.8.27) $^{29}/_{100}$ 5.8.28) $^{9}/_{1000}$ 5.8.29) 16 $^{23}/_{100}$ 5.8.30)1 $^{45}/_{1000}$

Convert the Fractions to Decimals and Percent (round decimals to the tenths place)

5.8.31) 4/6 5.8.32) 6/9 5.8.33) 2/3 5.8.34) 1/2 5.8.35) 8/7 5.8.36) 7/3
5.8.37) 3/4 5.8.38) 1/5 5.8.39) 2/7 5.8.40)4/3 5.8.41) 1/6 5.8.42)4/5
5.8.43) 4/7 5.8.44) 2/6 5.8.45) 2/9 5.8.46)4/4 5.8.47) 8/6 5.8.48) 3/9
5.8.49) 7/5 5.8.50) 5/3 5.8.51) 3/6 5.8.52)2/5 5.8.53) 2/2 5.8.54) 5/2
5.8.55) 6/4 5.8.56) 3/2 5.8.57) 3/7 5.8.58)1/3 5.8.59)5/4 5.8.60)3/5

Convert the Percent to a Fraction and a decimal

5.8.61) 36% 5.8.62) 128% 5.8.63) 2% 5.8.64) 65% 5.8.65) 12% 5.8.66) 39%
5.8.67) 161% 5.8.68) 23% 5.8.69) 51% 5.8.70) 146% 5.8.71) 436% 5.8.72)225%
5.8.73) 87% 5.8.74) 177% 5.8.75) 218% 5.8.76) 4% 5.8.77) 169% 5.8.78) 47%
5.8.79) 301% 5.8.80) 259% 5.8.81) 326% 5.8.82) 269% 5.8.83) 251% 5.8.84) 78%

5.8.w1) If I buy a bag of cookies and 9/12 of them are chocolate. Which fraction below is equivalent to this fraction
a) 4/6 b) 3/3 c) 3/4 d) 5/8

5.8.w2) If I buy a car for $3321 what is 6% of this

5.8.w3) If I buy something for $15.50, how much change will I get from a $20.00 if the tax is 8%.

5.8.w4) If a bag of cookies has 220 in it and 25% are chocolate, how many are not chocolate

5.8.w5) 50 cars arrived for the pick nick. Each car had three people in it. If 30% of them had a fishing rod how many people brought a fishing rod.

5.8.w6) What is the percentage 17% written in a decimal form

5.8.w7) Which of the following is equivalent to 136%
A) 13 $^{6}/_{100}$
B) $^{136}/_{1}$
C) 1 $^{36}/_{10}$
D) 1 $^{36}/_{100}$

5.8.W8) If I score a 95% on a test and got 190 questions correct how many question were on this test.

5.8.w9) If I pay $2.35 for a gallon of gas and buy 4 gallons. I then use 70% of it. What was the value of the gas I used.

5.8.w10) If I have a $25,000 loan at 8% simple interest how much interest do I pay in 3 years.

5.8.w11) I want to buy something. I found it at three stores each having a sale as described below

store A is having 18% sale
store B is $6.00 off
store C is $^{1}/_{10}$ off

If the original price at all stores was $40.00 which store is cheaper after the sale.

5.8.w12) The following diagram details the how I spend my money based on percentages

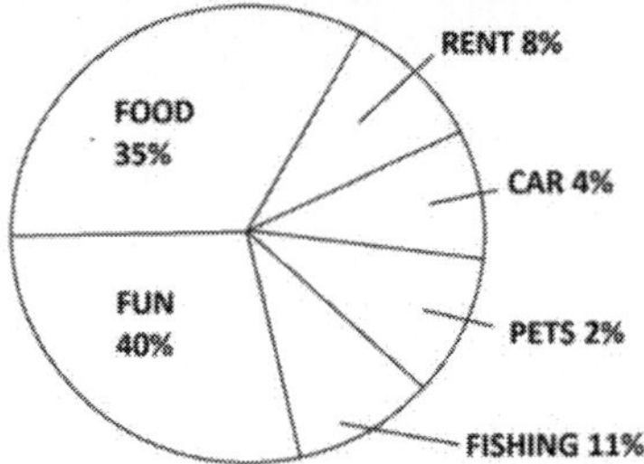

If I have $120 per month how much do I spend of fishing and pets combined.

5.8.w13) The following table shows how I spend my time per day

EVENT	HOURS
SLEEPING	8
EATING	5.5
STUDYING	6
PLAYING	2.5
TRAVELING	2

Based on this information which of the following statements is **NOT** true

A) 33 % spent sleeping
B) 23 % eating
C) 25 % studying
D) 14 % traveling

5.8.w14) A new computer was reduced in price from $450 to $400. What percentage was this discount

5.8.w15) A dinner was reduced from $45 to $35, What percentage was this discount

5.8.w16) The following table shows how I spend my money each month

ITEM	AMOUNT
RENT	$725
FUN	$125
SCHOOL	$400
FOOD	$345
CAR	$405

Which of the following is **NOT** true

A) 36.25% Rent
B) 20 % School
C) 19.25% Food
D) 6.25% Fun

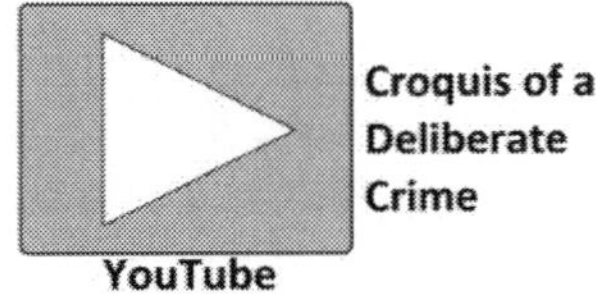

Croquis of a Deliberate Crime

Inequalities

State which symbol (<,>,≤,≥,=) best describes the relationship between the two fractions shown:

5.6.1) 1/2,2/2
5.6.2) 2/3,1/3
5.6.3) 5/6,7/6
5.6.4) 3/4,1/4
5.6.5) 5/8,7/8
5.6.6) 3/9,4/9
5.6.7) 4/5,3/5
5.6.8) 7/6,4/6
5.6.9) 3/9, 2/9
5.6.10) 4/7,6/7
5.6.11) 1/3,1/3
5.6.12) 4/6,4/6
5.6.13) 3/8,2/8
5.6.14) 2/7,1/7
5.6.15) 2/11,3/11
5.6.16) 8/16,4/16
5.6.17) 12/8,14/8
5.6.18) 3/7,5/7
5.6.19) 1/12,5/12
5.6.20) 5/13,7/13
5.6.21) 7/12,11/12
5.6.22) 8/15,5/15
5.6.23) 6/11,12/11
5.6.24) 7/10,4/10

5.6.25) 3/4,3/2
5.6.26) 2/3,2/5
5.6.27) 3/6,3/5
5.6.28) 3/4,3/8
5.6.29) 5/8,5/6
5.6.30) 6/9,6/10
5.6.31) 4/5,4/2
5.6.32) 5/6, 5/8
5.6.33) 3/9, 3/4
5.6.34) 4/7, 4/8
5.6.35) 1/3, 1/4
5.6.36) 4/6, 4/5
5.6.37) 3/8, 3/9
5.6.38) 4/7, 4/6
5.6.39) 2/11, 2/3
5.6.40) 5/16, 5/12
5.6.41) 12/8, 12/18
5.6.42) 3/7, 3/2
5.6.43) 6/12, 6/4
5.6.44) 5/13, 5/8
5.6.45) 7/12, 7/10
5.6.46) 8/15, 8/9
5.6.47) 6/11, 6/8
5.6.48) 7/10, 7/3

5.6.w9) If I sell 6 out of 8 cupcakes which fraction below best represents this fraction
a) 6/16
b) 12/16
c) 12/8
d) 1/2

Using <, >, ≤, ≥ to complete the following statements

5.6.66) 35, 51
5.6.67) 21, 68
5.6.68) 13, 54
5.6.69) 65, 89
5.6.70) 135, 21
5.6.71) 2134, 321
5.6.72) 12, 138
5.6.73) 789, 46
5.6.74) 533, 267
5.6.75) 887, 4567
5.6.76) 12, 476
5.6.77) 12.1, 33.7
5.6.78) 34, 34.2
5.6.79) 67.01, 67.1
5.6.80) 889.25, 889.2
5.6.81) 12.01, 13.01
5.6.82) 128.3, 128.03
5.6.83) 1.225, 1.252
5.6.84) 3.1, 4.5
5.6.85) 56.7, 65.7

State which symbol (<,>,≤,≥,=) best describes the relationship between the two fractions shown:

5.6.119)3/4,1/3
5.6.120)2/3,1/6
5.6.121)3/4,4/5
5.6.122)2/7,1/2
5.6.123)5/7,2/3
5.6.124)2/3,2/7
5.6.125)3/7,5/6
5.6.126)3/5,1/2
5.6.127)2/5,1/4
5.6.128)3/7,7/8
5.6.129)3/7,3/5
5.6.130)2/7,1/4
5.6.131)5/7,1/5
5.6.132)1/8,1/3
5.6.133)1/8,3/4
5.6.134)1/6,3/8
5.6.135)3/7,1/3
5.6.136)3/7,2/3
5.6.137)6/7,5/8
5.6.138)6/7,3/4
5.6.139)1/3,5/6
5.6.140)1/3,1/2
5.6.141)2/5,1/6
5.6.142)3/4,5/6
5.6.143)1/6,1/3
5.6.144)1/4,1/6
5.6.145)2/5,5/6
5.6.146)3/7,4/5
5.6.147)2/3,1/5
5.6.148)3/4,2/3
5.6.149)1/3,5/7
5.6.150)5/8,5/6

5.6.251) $1\frac{2}{3}, 2\frac{1}{4}$
5.6.252) $2\frac{1}{6}, 2\frac{3}{4}$
5.6.253) $3\frac{1}{5}, 1\frac{1}{4}$
5.6.254) $2\frac{1}{8}, 1\frac{1}{7}$
5.6.255) $2\frac{5}{8}, 3\frac{2}{5}$
5.6.256) $2\frac{5}{8}, 1\frac{1}{3}$
5.6.257) $1\frac{5}{7}, 3\frac{5}{6}$
5.6.258) $2\frac{2}{7}, 3\frac{1}{2}$
5.6.259) $1\frac{3}{5}, 2\frac{3}{8}$
5.6.260) $1\frac{3}{5}, 2\frac{6}{7}$
5.6.261) $1\frac{1}{4}, 1\frac{1}{3}$
5.6.262) $1\frac{1}{3}, 3\frac{1}{5}$
5.6.263) $1\frac{2}{7}, 4\frac{1}{5}$
5.6.264) $1\frac{4}{7}, 3\frac{2}{3}$
5.6.265) $1\frac{5}{8}, 2\frac{4}{7}$
5.6.266) $2\frac{1}{4}, 2\frac{5}{6}$
5.6.267) $2\frac{1}{2}, 3\frac{5}{7}$
5.6.268) $3\frac{1}{7}, 2\frac{1}{6}$
5.6.269) $1\frac{3}{8}, 4\frac{2}{3}$
5.6.270) $1\frac{1}{6}, 2\frac{1}{5}$
5.6.271) $2\frac{4}{7}, 2\frac{2}{5}$
5.6.272) $1\frac{2}{5}, 1\frac{1}{6}$
5.6.273) $2\frac{7}{8}, 2\frac{1}{6}$
5.6.274) $1\frac{2}{5}, 3\frac{7}{8}$
5.6.275) $1\frac{2}{7}, 4\frac{1}{5}$
5.6.276) $1\frac{4}{7}, 3\frac{2}{3}$
5.6.277) $1\frac{5}{8}, 2\frac{4}{7}$
5.6.278) $2\frac{1}{4}, 2\frac{5}{8}$
5.6.279) $2\frac{5}{8}, 3\frac{4}{5}$
5.6.280) $2\frac{1}{4}, 2\frac{4}{5}$
5.6.281) $1\frac{4}{5}, 3\frac{6}{7}$
5.6.282) $1\frac{3}{8}, 2\frac{3}{7}$

5.6.283) $3, 2\frac{3}{7}$
5.6.284) $1, 6\frac{5}{8}$
5.6.285) $5, 8\frac{7}{8}$
5.6.286) $8, 3\frac{1}{6}$
5.6.287) $9, 2\frac{5}{8}$
5.6.288) $9\frac{8}{9}, 4$
5.6.289) $3, 1\frac{2}{9}$
5.6.290) $5\frac{3}{7}, 4$
5.6.291) $4, 2\frac{3}{5}$
5.6.292) $2\frac{4}{7}, 6$
5.6.293) $1, 8\frac{2}{9}$
5.6.294) $2\frac{4}{9}, 7$

5.6.w1) If four friends bought a box of cookies each the table show how many were chocolate.

FRIEND	CHOCOLATE
Mike	2/5
Mary	3/10
Sue	5/20
David	11/40

Which person had the highest fraction of chocolate cookies?

5.6.w2) If the box of cookies had 6/10 chocolate which statement below is true
a) out of 100 cookies 6 were chocolate
b) out of 20 cookies 15 were chocolate
c) out of 15 cookies 9 were chocolate
d) out of 40 cookies 25 were chocolate

5.6.w3) I ate 38/54 cookies in one day. Which fraction below is the same fraction
a) 19/27 b) 6/9 c) 2/3 d) 12/15

5.6.w4) If I drink 3/5 of a bottle of water which fraction below is greater than 3/5
a) 5/10 b) 4/7 c) 9/14 d) 1/3

5.6.w5) I count the kinds of fish in a tank. The results are shown in the table below.

FISH TYPE	FRACTION
Guppy	2/5
Angle	3/10
Sword	1/10
Gold	1/5

Which fish has the largest population in the tank

5.6.w6) I finish 35 out of 60 math problems in my homework. Which fraction below is **NOT** the same fraction
a) 7/12 b) 70/120 c) 57/90 d) 105/180

5.6.w7) I read 4/6 of a book. What fraction below is equivalent to this fraction
a) 8/13 b) 11/18 c) 2/3 d) 13/24

5.6.w8) I spend 2/5 of an hour mowing the lawn. Which fraction below is less than this
a) 4/10 b) 5/15 c) 2/3 d) 8/20

5.6.w9) Which set of numbers are in the correct order from least to greatest.
A) 0, -4, $^{1}/_{3}$, 3 $^{16}/_{5}$, 4
B) -4, 0, $^{1}/_{3}$, 3, 4, $^{16}/_{5}$
C) -4, 0, $^{1}/_{3}$, $^{16}/_{5}$, 3, 4
D)-4, 0, $^{1}/_{3}$, 3, $^{16}/_{5}$, 4

Croquis of a Deliberate Crime

5.10.w1) The model below represents the number $1^{13}/_{100}$

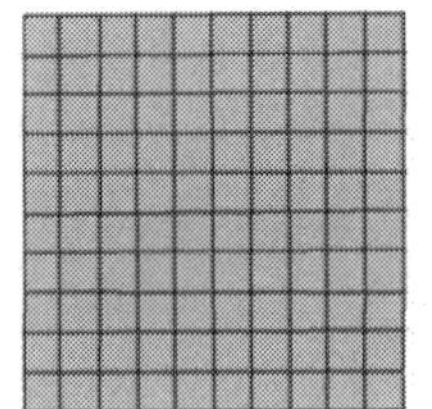 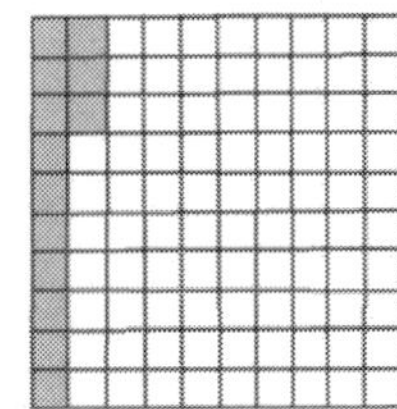

Which statement below represents the same value
a) 1.87
b) 1.13
c) 1.15
d) 1.31

5.10.w2) The model below $1\ ^{4}/_{100}$

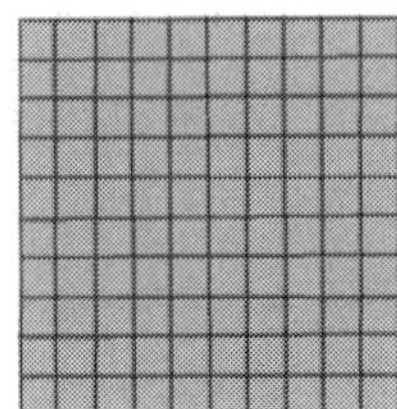 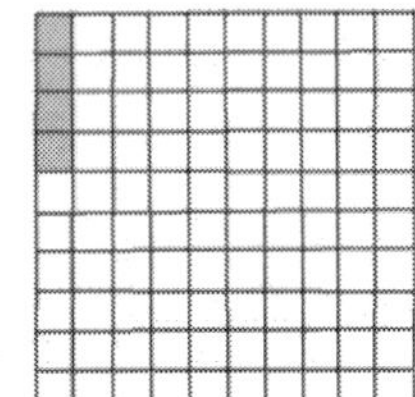

Which decimal represents the same value
a) 1.4
b) 1.04
c) 1.44
d) 4.01

5.10.w3) The drawing below is colored to show a fraction

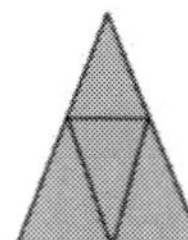 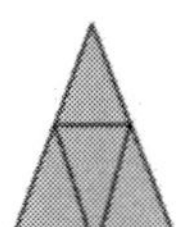 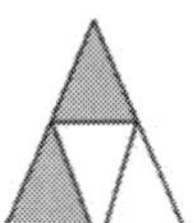

Which statement below explains this drawing
a) $^{2}/_{3}$
b) $2\ ^{2}/_{3}$
c) 2 ¾
d) $2\ ^{2}/_{4}$

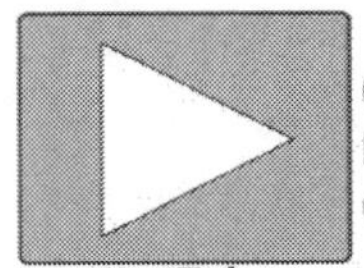

5.10.w4) The drawing below is colored to show a fraction

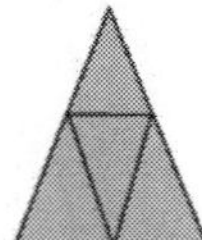 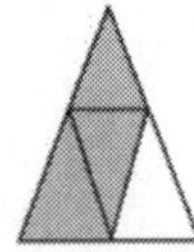

Which of the following best represents this fraction

a) $^{1}/_{8}$
b) ¾
c) 1 ¾
d) 1 $^{1}/_{8}$

5.10.w5) The drawing below has been colored to represent a number

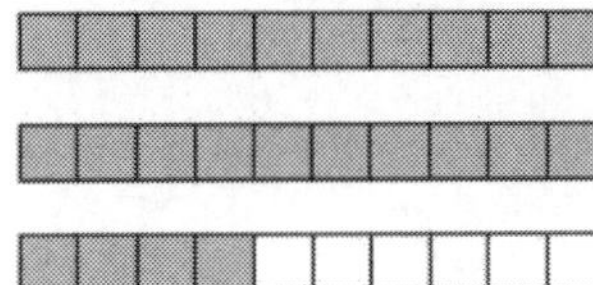

Which number below best represents this drawing?

a) $^{6}/_{10}$ or 0.6
b) 2 $^{6}/_{10}$ or 2.6
c) 2 $^{4}/_{10}$ or 2.4
d) 1 $^{4}/_{10}$ or 1.4

5.10.w6) The drawing below has been colored to show a number

Which of the numbers below best represents this number

a) $^{2}/_{10}$ or 0.2
b) 1 $^{2}/_{10}$ or 1.2
c) 1 $^{8}/_{10}$ or 1.8
d) $^{8}/_{10}$ or 0.8

5.10.w7) The drawing below has been colored to show a number

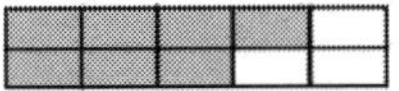

Which of the numbers below best represents this number

a) $^{7}/_{10}$ or 0.7
b) $^{5}/_{10}$ or 0.5
c) 1 $^{3}/_{5}$ or 1.6
d) $^{3}/_{5}$ or 0.3

5.10.w8) The drawing below has been colored to show a number

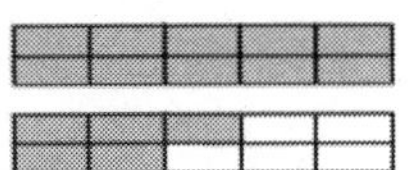

Which of the numbers below best represents this number

a) 1$^{5}/_{10}$ or 1.5
b) $^{5}/_{10}$ or 0.5
c) 1 $^{4}/_{5}$ or 1.8
d) $^{3}/_{5}$ or 0.6

5.10.w9) The drawing below is colored to represent a number

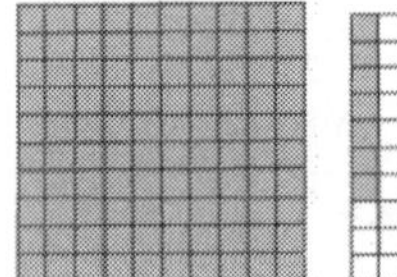 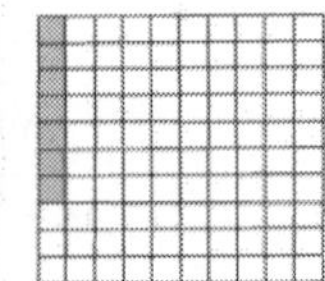

Which stamen below best describes this number in words
a) one and seven hundredths
b) six hundredths
c) ninety four hundredths
d) one and ninety four hundredths

5.10.w10)The drawing below is colored to represent a number

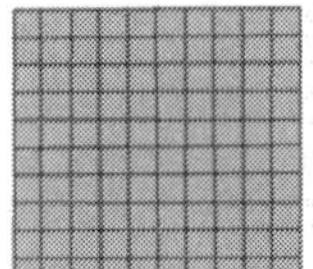 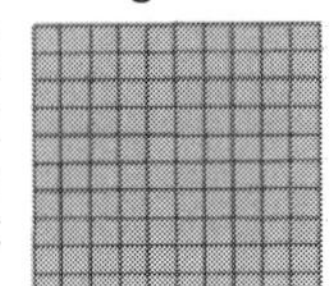 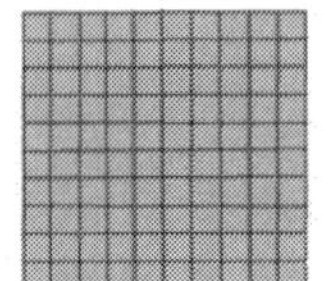 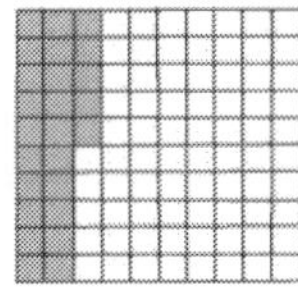

Which stamen below best describes this number in words
a) three and twenty five hundredths
b) fifteen hundredths
c) three hundreds and fifteen
d) eighty five hundredth

5.10.w11) The drawing below is colored to represent a number

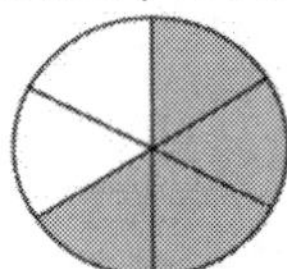

Which statement below best describes this number in words
a) three sixths
b) four sixth
c) two tenths
d) four tenths

5.10.w12) The drawing below is colored to represent a number

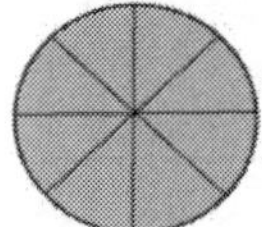 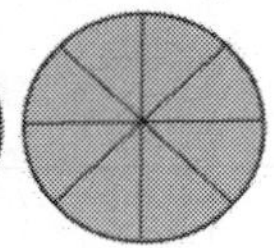 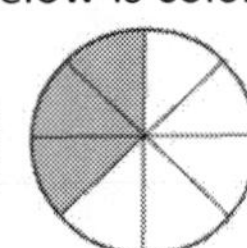

Which statement below best describes this number in words
a) five eights
b) three eights
c) two and three eights
d) two and three tenths

Croquis of a Deliberate Crime

5.10.w13) The drawing below is colored to represent a number

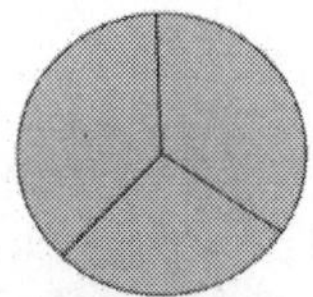 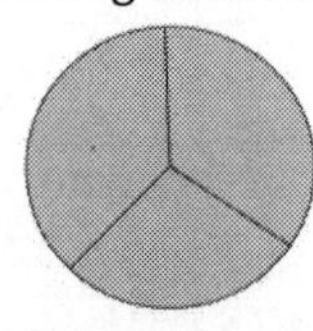 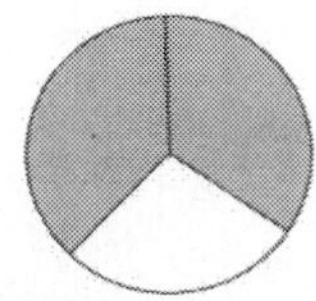

Which statement below best describes this number in words
a) one thirds
b) two and two thirds
c) two and one third
d) two thirds

5.10.w14) The drawing below is colored to represent a number

  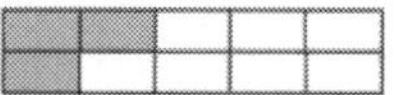

Which statement below best describes this number in words
a) seven tenths
b) two and seven tenths
c) two and seven hundredths
d) two and three tenths

5.10.w15) The drawing below is colored to represent a number

Which statement below best describes this number in words
a) three tenths
b) one and seven tenths
c) one and three tenths
d) two tenths

5.10.w16) The drawing below is shaded to represent a number

a) 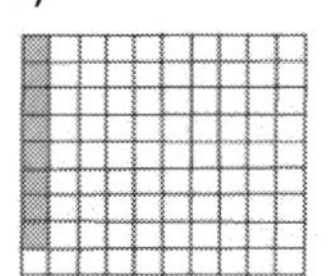
b) 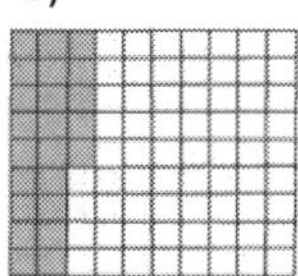
c) 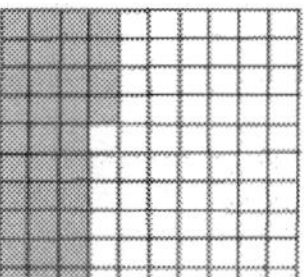
d) 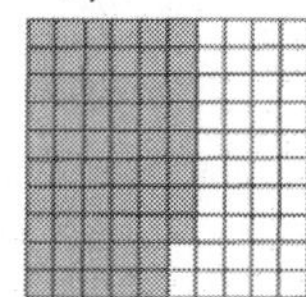

Which of the following represents these drawing in decimal form
a) 0.37, 0.45, 076, 0.89
b) 0.08, 0.25, 0.34, 0.58
c) 0.8, 0.25, 0.34, 0.58
d) 0.08, 0.05, 0.04, 0.08

Croquis of a Deliberate Crime

For one on one tutoring via skype at $35.00/Hr.; contact me at marksmathtutoring@yahoo.com

5.10.w17) The drawing below is shaded to represent a number

a) b) c) d)

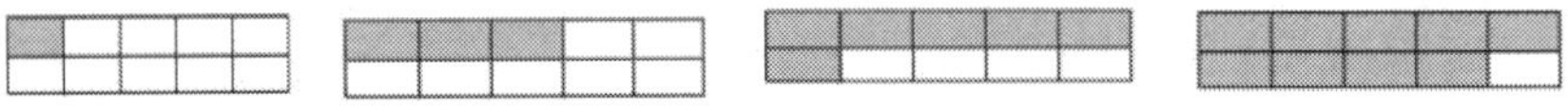

Which of the following represents these drawing in decimal form

a) 0.1, 0.3, 0.6, 0.9
b) 0.01, 0.03, 0. 06, 0.09
c) 1.1, 3.3, 6.6, 9.9
d) 1.9, 3.7, 6.4, 9.1

5.10.w18) Which diagram below represents the fraction 67/100

a) c)

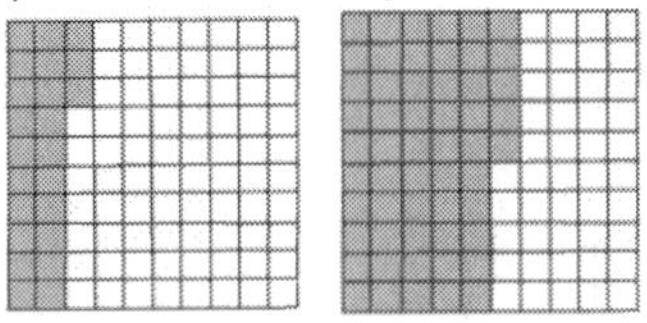

b) d)

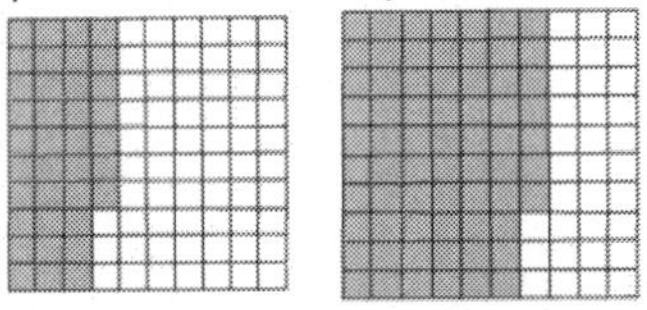

5.10.w19)The drawing below has been colored to represent the fraction 2 $^{6}/_{10}$

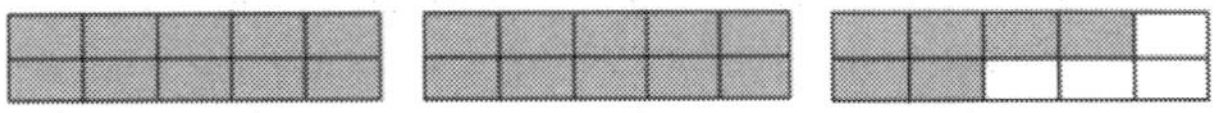

Which decimal best represents this number?

a) 1.4
b) 2.6
c) 0.6
d) 0.4

5.10.w20)Which of the following represents the same fraction

a) c)

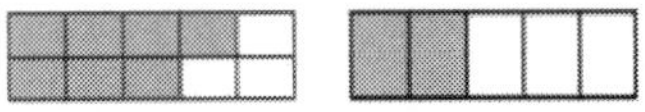

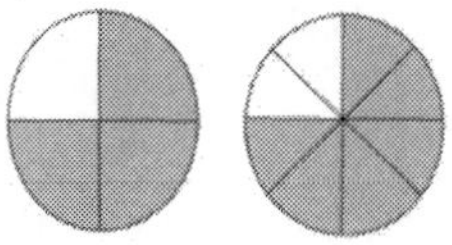

b) 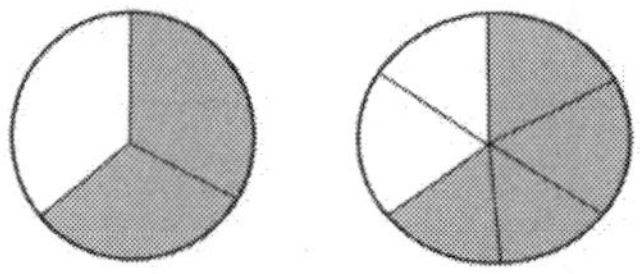 d)

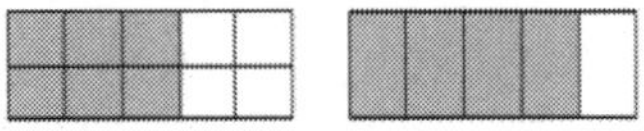

5.10.w21) Which of the following represents the fraction 6/10

a) 0.06
b) 0.6
c) 1.6
d) 1.06

5.10.w22) Which of the following represents the fraction 85/100
a) 1.85
b) 0.85
c) 85.0
d) 8.5

5.10.w23) If my dog weights 0.37 KG what is this in a fraction
a) $^{37}/_{10}$
b) $^{37}/_{100}$
c) $3\ ^{7}/_{100}$
d) $^{37}/_{1000}$

5.10.w24) Which of the following are equivalent?
a) 27/100=0.027
b) 1/10=0.01
c) 13/1000=0.013
d) 25/100=0.025

5.10.w25) Which of the following best represents them fraction $3\ ^{12}/_{100}$
a) 3.12
b) 312.100
c) 3.012
d)0.0312

5.10.W26) Given the two sets of numbers below

SET A

0.7	$\frac{70}{100}$
$\frac{7}{9}$	0.93

SET B

0.56	$\frac{56}{100}$
$\frac{6}{7}$	0.61

Which one of the following statments is true
A) All numbers in set A are less than 0.75
B) All number is set B are greater than 0.87
C) All numbers is set A are greater than 0.78
D) All number is set B are less than 0.86

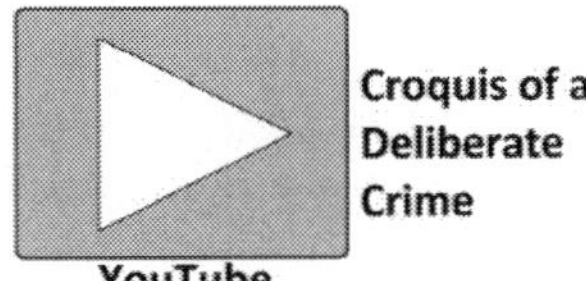

If you don't get the correct answer, and want an explanation on how to work the problem, go to YouTube and type in "MMT" then the problem number. An example would be, MMT 3.9.w12,. The video will show you how to work problem 3.9.w12.

For one on one tutoring via skype at $35.00/Hr.; contact me at marksmathtutoring@yahoo.com

5.10.w27) Which diagram below best represent the equation $^{2}/_{6}+^{5}/_{8}$

A)

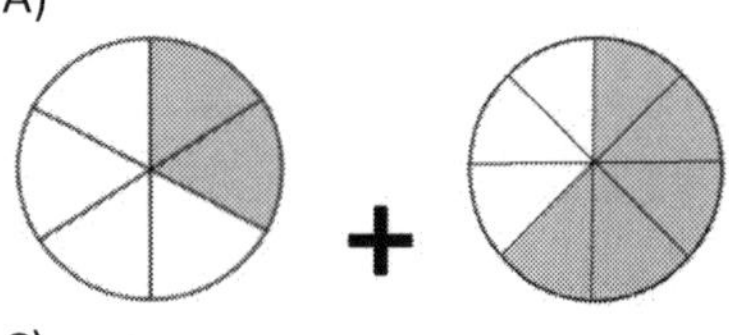

B)

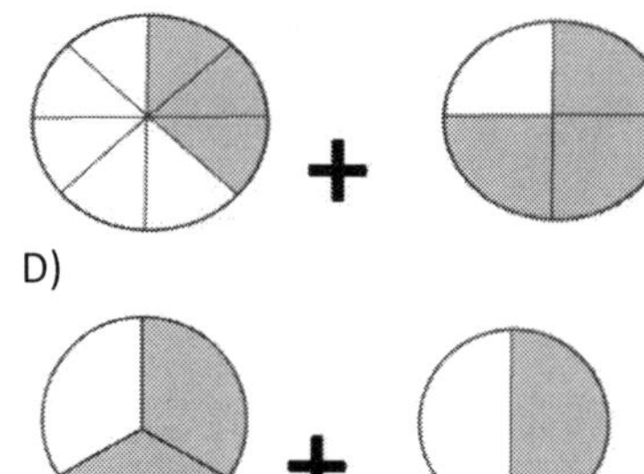

C)

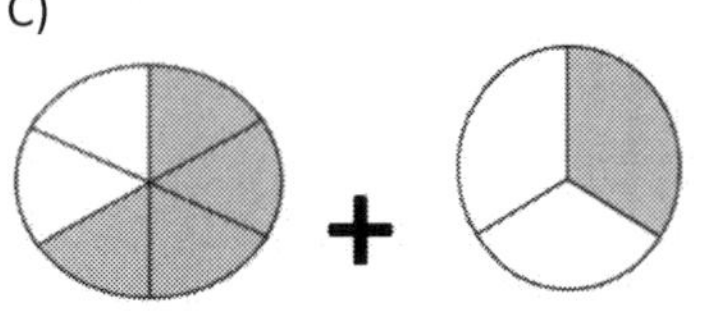

D)

5.10.w28) If I spend 85% of a dollar, what decimal equals this percentage

5.10.w29) Given the following equations

#1) $7\ ^{1}/_{3} = ^{22}/_{3}$

#2) $7.33 = ^{22}/_{3}$

#3) $6\ ^{1}/_{3} = ^{22}/_{3}$

A) Equation #1 only

B) Equation #2 only

C) Equation #1, and #2

D) Equation #2, and #3

Which of the following is true

5.10.w30) My dog weights 9 pounds. He than eats and gains 1 2/3 pounds. He then drinks water and gains another 1/2 pound. What is his final weight.

5.10.w31) I go to a party. There are 50 people there and I know 29 of them. If I start a converstion with one choosen at random what are the odds it will be someon I know.

5.10.w32) Which number below is equevalent to $^{16}/_{3}$

A) 5.1, because three goes into 16 five times with a remainder of 1

B) 5.3 because thre goes into 16 five times with a remainder of one times three

C) $5\ ^{1}/_{3}$, because three goes into 16 five times with a remainder of 1

D) 5.01, because three goes into 16 five times with a remainder of 1

5.10.w33) Given the table below

P	1/32	1/16	1/8	1/4
H	17/32	9/16	5/8	3/4

Given this inforation which of the following equation best describes the relationship between P and H

A) P + 1/4 = H

B)P + 1/2 = H

C) P + 1/8 = H

D) P + 1/16 = H

5.10.W34) Given the tabel bellow, what percentager of the fish are Trout

FISH TYPE	NUMBER
Bass	12
Trout	8
Salmon	16
Tuna	4

5.10.w35) I eat 1/3 of a pie after lunch and another 25% after dinner. What percent of the pie is left?

5.10.w36) Given the information in the drawing below

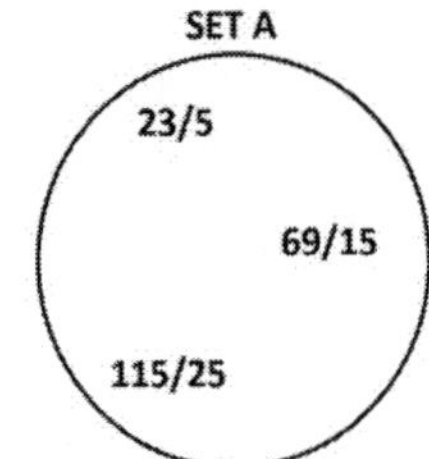

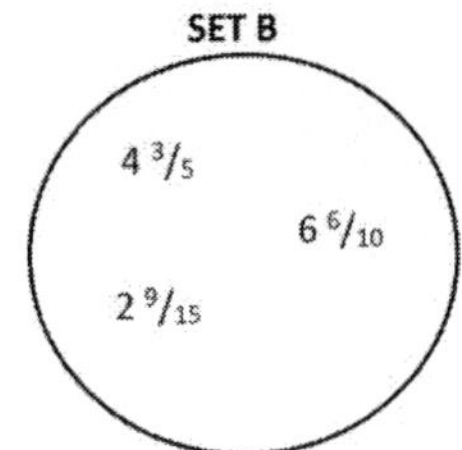

Which statement below is true
A) All numbers is both Set A and Set B are equal to 4.6
B) All numbers in Set A but not all number is Set B are equal to 4.6
C) Non of the number are equal to 4.6
D) All numbers in Set A and Set B are equal to 46%

5.10.w37) In my neigborhood 7% of the pets are fish. What decimal is equal to this percentage

5.10.w38) Which of the following equation is true
A) $^{8}/_{100}$=0.8
B) 1 $^{8}/_{10}$ = 1.08
C) 2 ¾ = 2.75
D) 3 $^{1}/_{100}$= 3.1

5.10.W39) If I caught 3.75 pounds of fish but my friend caught 3 times more how much did he catch.

5.10.w40) Which of the following is equarvalnat to $^{3}/_{4}\div{}^{5}/_{8}$
A) $^{3}/_{4}\text{x}{}^{5}/_{8}$
B) $^{4}/_{3}\div{}^{5}/_{8}$
C) $^{3}/_{4}\text{x}{}^{8}/_{5}$
D) $^{4}/_{3}\text{x}{}^{8}/_{5}$

5.10.W41) I received 5/8 of a pound of candy. What percentage of a pound is this

5.10.w42) Place the following mixed fractions in order from least to greatest

$2\,^{1}/_{4}$, $2\,^{3}/_{8}$, $2\,^{5}/_{6}$, $2\,^{2}/_{3}$

5.10.w43) Which shaed drawing represents 25%

A)

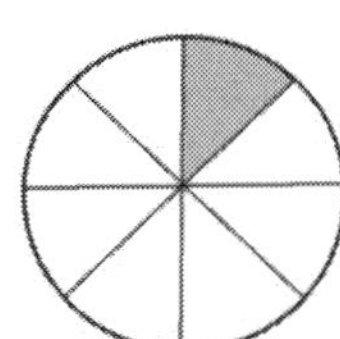

B)

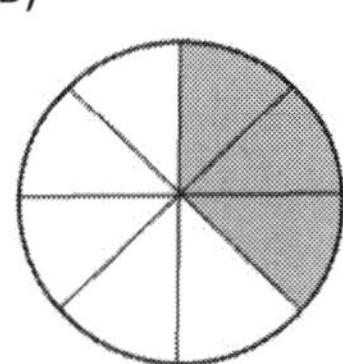

C)

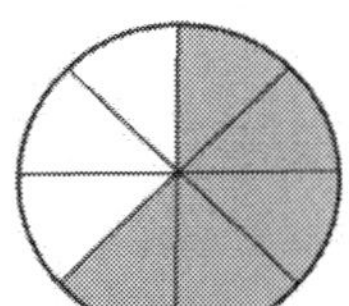

D)

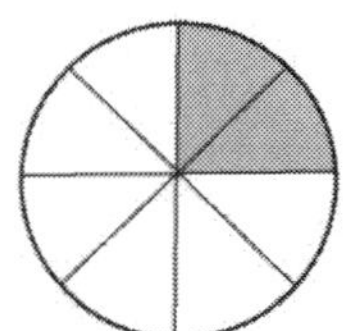

5.10.W44) If I received 0.95 of a dollar which fraction below is the same value
A) 95/10
B) 95/100
C) 95/1000
D) 95/1

5.10.w45) What percentage represents the shaded area of the drawing

5.10.w46) If I have 4/5 of a dollar and I want to spend 3/4 of it. What fraction of a dollar can I spend

5.10.w47) I put the following four numbers, {1.7. 2 ¼, 2.05, 2 $^{1}/_{10}$} on the number line below

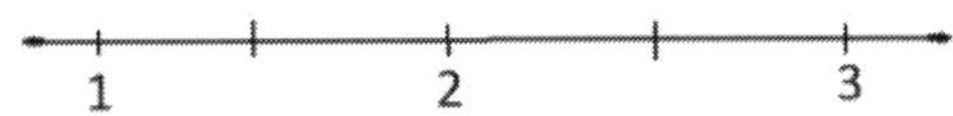

Which of the following numbers is closest to the number 2

5.10.w48) At my school 2 out of 9 eat lunch in the cafeteria. What percentage is this.

5.10.w49) If I interview the kids at your school and 75% said they prefer pizza over hamburger Which of the following is true
A) 75 out of those I interviewed prefer pizza
B) seven out of ten prefer pizza
C) three out of four prefer pizza
D) 100 people were interviewed

5.10.W50) Given these numbers {2 $^{7}/_{20}$, 2 $^{35}/_{100}$, 235%, $^{235}/_{100}$, 2.35}, Which of the following is the same value
A) 214%
B) 2 $^{14}/_{40}$
C) 27.20
D) 0.235

5.10.w51) If I get 24 out of 25 questions correct on a test what percentage did I receive.

5.10.w52) If I spend 24 minutes of two hours walking to my fishing spot, what percent of the time did I walk

5.10.w53) What value is equal to 244%
A) 24.4
B) 24 $^{4}/_{10}$
C) 2.44
D) 244/10

5.10.W54) If my weight is 250 pounds and loss 25 pounds. What percentage of my weight did I loss.

For one on one tutoring via skype at $35.00/Hr.; contact me at marksmathtutoring@yahoo.com

5.10.W55) Given The diagram below generated when I surveyed the dogs in my neighborhood

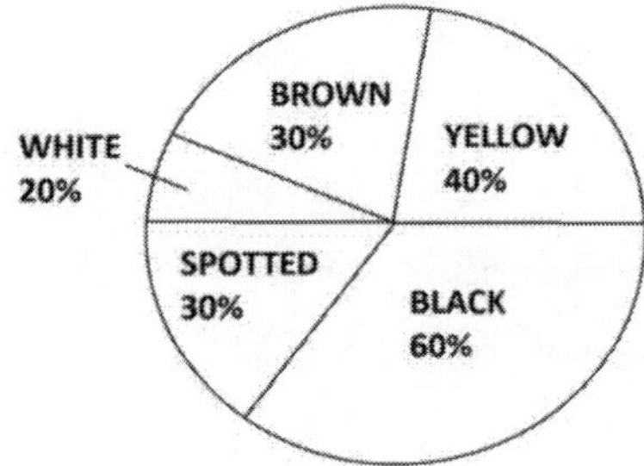

Given this data if I looked at 225 dogs how many were either brown or spotted

5.10.w56) Place the following numbers in order of least to greatest { $1\ ^{3}/_{5}$, 1.70, 156%}

5.10.w57) If I deposited $6,000 and in 4 years I have 7440, what was the simple interest rate.
A) 5%
B) 6%
C) 7%
D) 8%

5.10.W58) If a square with a side of $2\ ^{3}/_{8}$ is dilated by 3/5 what is the length of the new square

5.10.w59) I feed 25 monkeys at the zoo a banana. 20% are howler monkey. How many is this

5.10.w60) I have 64 coins in my pocket. 39% are pennies. How many pennies do I have.

5.10.w61) If I have $60.00, and I spend 1/3 of it. I then spend another 20% of what is left. I then get $5.00 from a friend. How much money do I have in my pocket.
5.10.w62) List the following is order of least to greatest { 1/9, 1/6, 12%, .013}

5.10.w63) Given the pie graph below detailing the types of pets people have

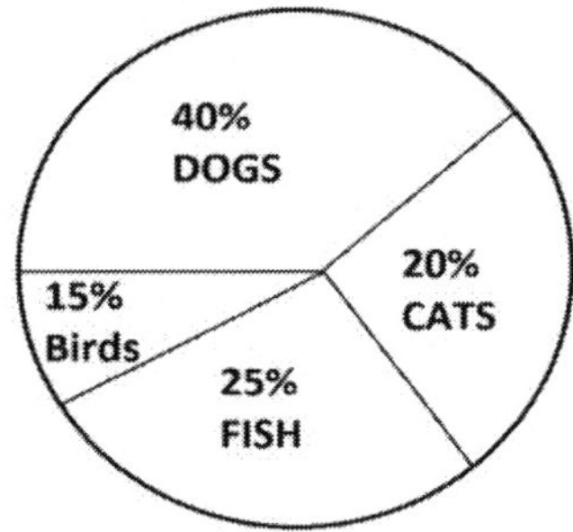

If 125 people where interviewed how many people picked Dogs.
5.10.w64) Place the following numbers in order from highest to lowest {0.23, -1.12, .36, -0.57,1.4}

5.10.w65) I start with $56.20 in my account. I spend $1.25 on bus fair and $4.35 on a burger. I then give half of the remainder to a friend, who much did I have left over.

5.10.w66) I interview the people in my neighborhood, asking them what was the color of their car. The results are as follows

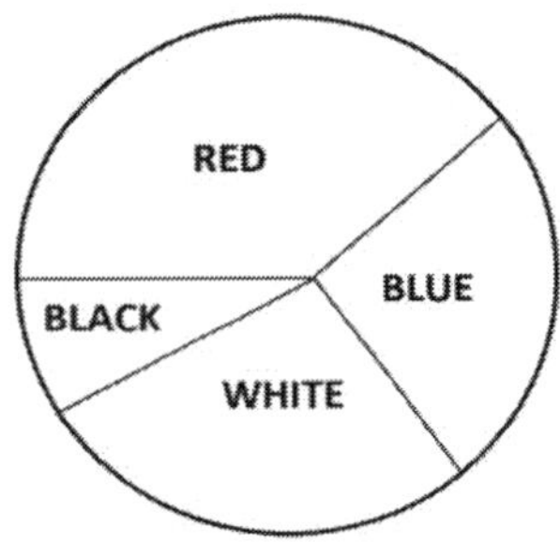

Which of the following is not true
A) Blue is 25%
B) White is 40%
C) Red is 50%
D) Black is less than 15%

5.10.w67) If a car mechanic charges $60.00 for the first hour and $45.00 for each additional hour and the final bill is $172.50, did the mechanic work for 3.5 hours?

5.10.w68) Place the following in order of least to greatest { 1/13, -0.086, 0.13, -52%)

5.10.W69) If the following figure is dilated by 9/6 what is the new measure of AB

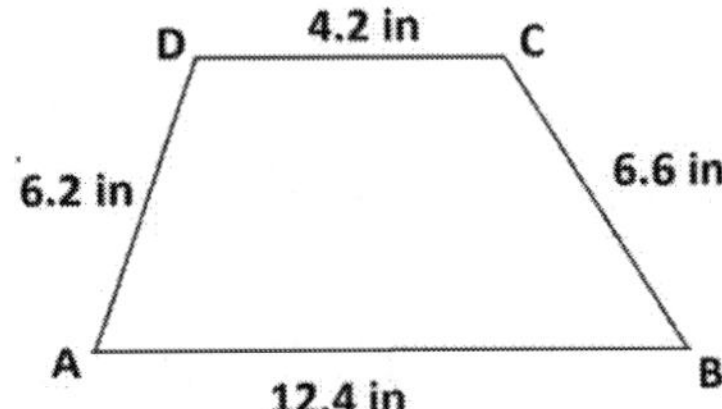

5.10.w70) If I am selling cookies for a school project. 30% of 140 people buy a package of cookies and there are 3 cookies in each package, how many cookies did I sell

5.10.w71) Given the table below showing types of fish I caught while on vacation

FISH TYPE	NUMBERS
BASS	10
TROUT	5
SALMON	15
HALIBUT	20

If I catch a total of 400 fish how many will be trout.

5.10.w72) Which of the following values is less than $1\ ^3/_5$
A)1.60
B) 8/5
C) 160%
D)16/11

5.10.W73) Place the following numbers in order from least to greatest { $3\ ^2/_3$, 350%, -4.5, $^{850}/_{200}$ }

5.10.w74) Place the following number is order from highest to least { 3/5, 4/9, .5, 55%}

5.10.W75) If I put $20,000 into a bank account earning 3.5% simple interest per year, how much will the account have in it after 4 years if no additional funds are deposited

5.10.w76) If college will cost $8,000 for the first year and you have a 85% scholarship, who much do you need to save each month for 2 years to save the remaining amount

5.10.w77) If I have $1000.00 to deposit into two different bank accounts. I put $500 into account 1 which pays 3.5% simple interest and $500 into account 2 that pays 3% interest compounded annually. Who much do I have total after 3 years. (calculators allowed)

5.10.w78) If I have $5000 in a account that pays 4% interest compounded annually how much will I have in the account after 5 years.

If you don't get the correct answer, and want an explanation on how to work the problem, go to YouTube and type in "MMT" then the problem number. An example would be, MMT 3.9.w12,. The video will show you how to work problem 3.9.w12.

For one on one tutoring via skype at $35.00/Hr.; contact me at marksmathtutoring@yahoo.com

6.0 GRAPHING

6.1)The graph below shows the number of cookies your brother ate.

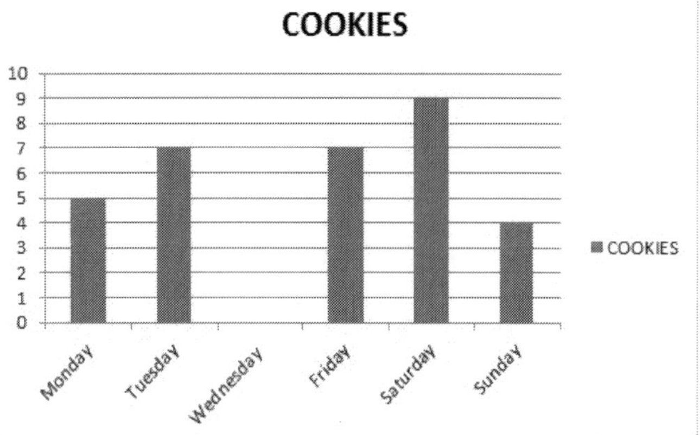

If the total of cookies eaten was 36, how many cookies were eaten on Wednesday?

6.2) What is the total weight of all the dogs shown in the graph below?

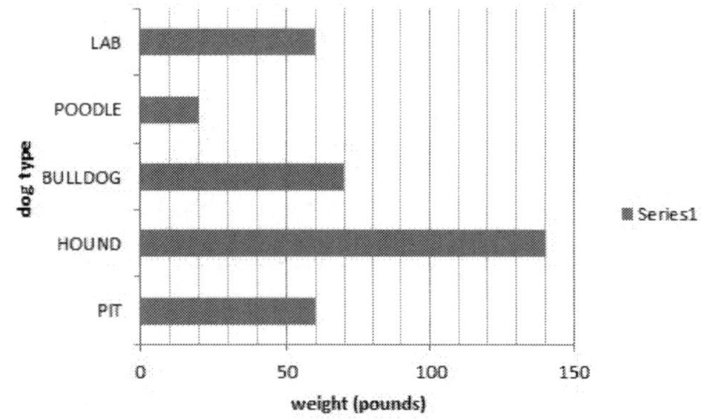

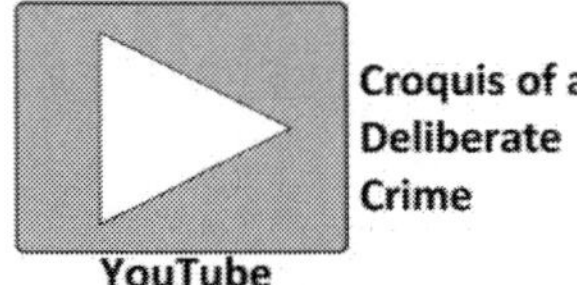

If you don't get the correct answer, and want an explanation on how to work the problem, go to YouTube and type in "MMT" then the problem number. An example would be, MMT 3.9.w12,. The video will show you how to work problem 3.9.w12.

For one on one tutoring via skype at $35.00/Hr.; contact me at marksmathtutoring@yahoo.com

6.3) Given the graph below

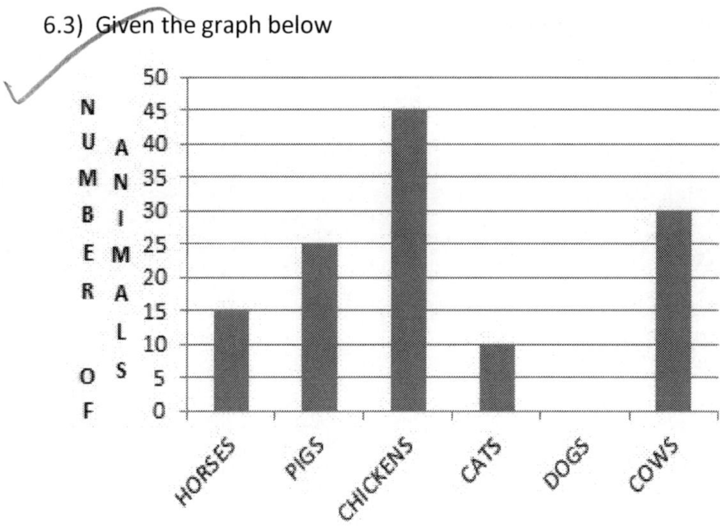

If there are 140 animals total on this farm which graph below indicated the number of cats

a) b) c) d)

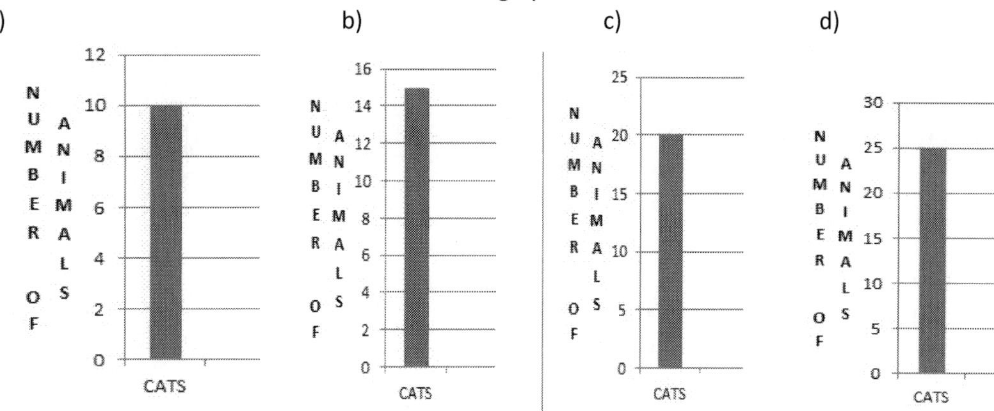

6.4) The following table describes the number of fruit trees on a farm

Type of fruit tree	Number of trees
Apple	11,256
Pear	8,765
Plum	12,367
Cherry	10,018
Peach	9,672

Which stamen is not true based on the data in the above table

a)Apples>Pear, b) Plums>Cherry, c) Peach<Cherry, d) Plum<Apple

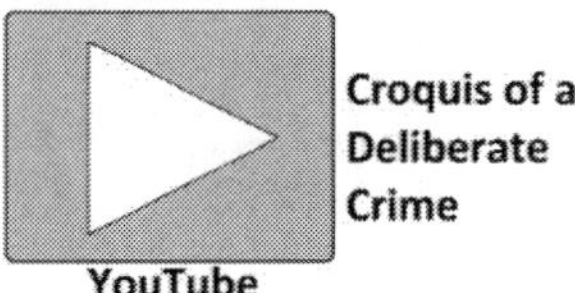

For one on one tutoring via skype at $35.00/Hr.; contact me at marksmathtutoring@yahoo.com

6.5) The graph below indicates the number of cars of each type for sale at a lot.

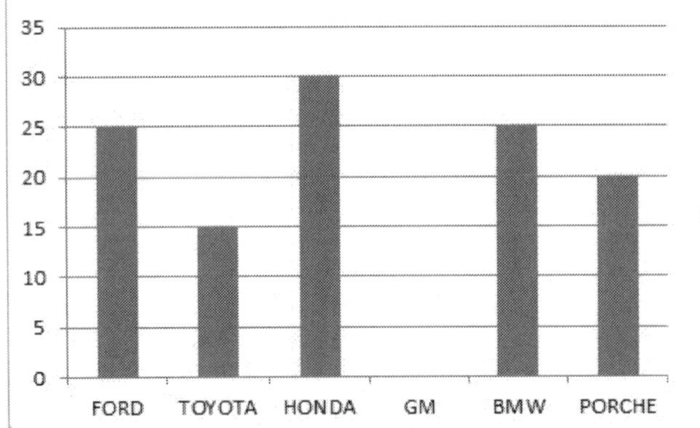

If there are 135 cars total on the lot for sale which graph below shows the number of GMs

a)  b)  c)  d) 

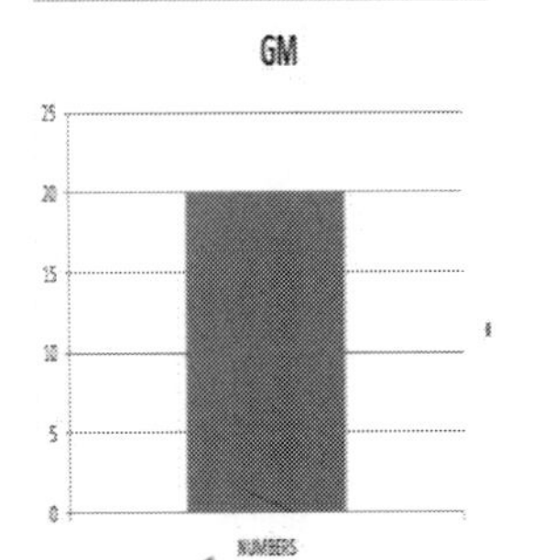

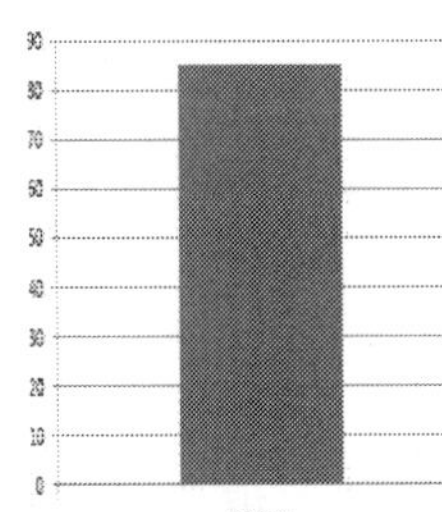

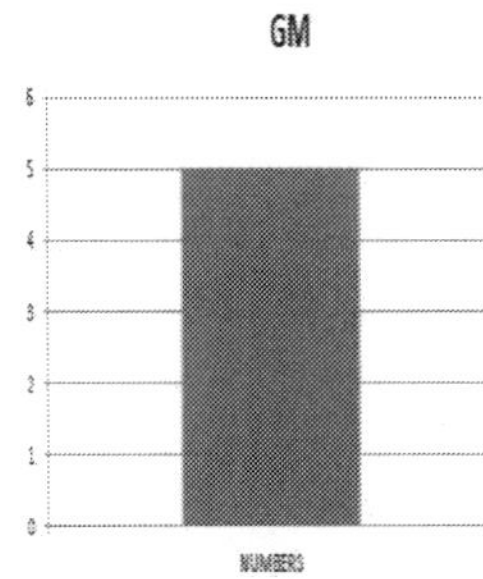

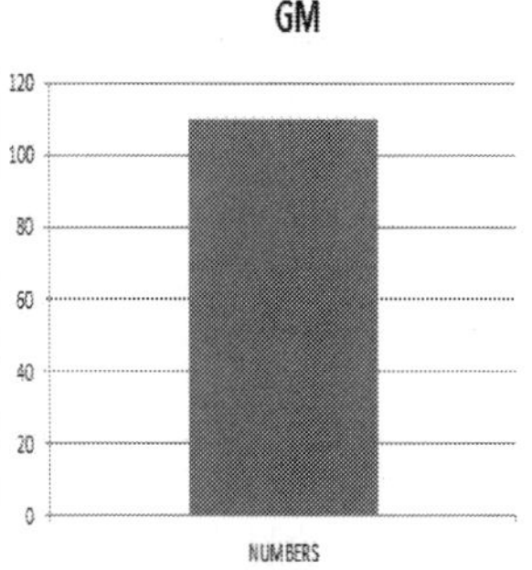

6.6) The graph below shows the number of tons of garbage collected by the city per month

	X			
	X		X	
X	X		X	X
X	X	X	X	X
X	X	X	X	X
May	June	July	Aug	May

Each **X** represented 500 pounds

Based on the graph above how many more pounds of garbage did the city collect in August than May?

6.7) The table below details the number of games for each sport

SPORT	NUMBER
SOCCER	35
FOOTBALL	17
BASEBALL	176
BASKETBALL	125

Based on the information in the table organize the sports from high to low

a) baseball, soccer, basketball, football
b) baseball, basketball, soccer, football
c) football, soccer, basketball, baseball
d) basketball, baseball, football, soccer

6.8) The following table details the number of minutes Mike did choirs.

		X	
X		X	
X		X	
X	X	X	X
X	X	X	X

Mon. Tues. Wed. Thur.

Each X represents 10 minutes of work

How many more minutes of work did Mike do on Mon compared to Thur.?

6.9) The following table describes the number of different types of fish 4 kids have in their aquariums.

AQUARIUM	GUPPIES	ANGLES
Mary	12	4
Steve	15	5
Susan	21	7
Mark	9	3

Which statement below is correct based on the information in the tables

a) There are three time the number of guppies as angles

b) There are eight more guppies than angle

c) There are three time the number of angles as guppies

d) There is no relationship in the number of guppies and angles.

6.10) The following graph describes the number of kids in each grade who bring a sandwich to school for lunch.

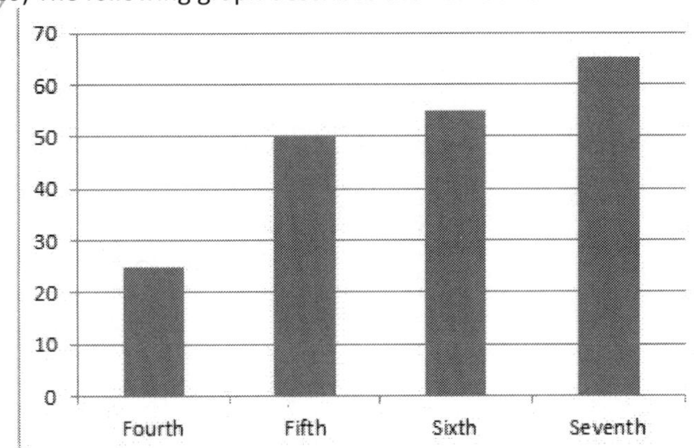

Based on the table above which statement is true

a) A total of 65 kids from the fourth and fifth grades had sandwiches

b) No grade brought 55 sandwiches

c) A total of 195 kids brought sandwiches

d) The difference between the seventh and fifth grades who brought sandwiches is 15

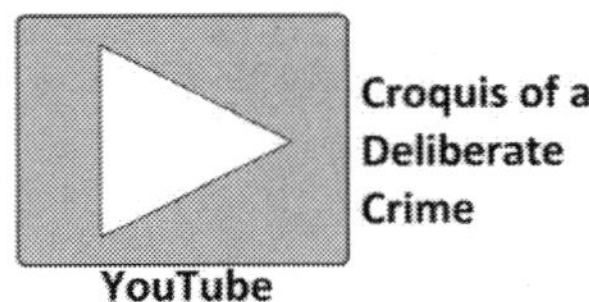

For one on one tutoring via skype at $35.00/Hr.; contact me at marksmathtutoring@yahoo.com

6.11) The following table details the amount of a discount a store is giving based on the amount you buy.

AMOUNT OF PURCHASE	AMOUNT AFTER DISCOUNT
$23.00	$18.00
$28.00	$23.00
$33.00	$28.00
$38.00	$33.00
$43.00	$38.00

Based on the information given in the table which statement is true
a) The amount after discount minus $5.00 equals the amount of purchase
b) There is no relationship between the two values
c) The amount after discount minus $5.00 equals the amount of purchase
d) The amount after discount is always $5.00 less than the amount of purchase

6.12)The following table describes the number of kids with each name in a school

NAMES	NUMBERS
Mike	35
James	25
John	15
Elmer	40

Which table below describes this data best

A)

NAMES	NUMBERS
Mike	XXXXXXX
James	XXXXX
John	XXXX
Elmer	XXXXXXXX

Each X is equal to 5 students

C)

NAMES	NUMBERS
Mike	XXXXXX
James	XXXXX
John	XXXXX
Elmer	XXXXXXXX

Each X is equal to 5 students

B)

NAMES	NUMBERS
Mike	XXXXXXX
James	XXXXX
John	XXX
Elmer	XXXXXXXX

Each X is equal to 5 students

D)

NAMES	NUMBERS
Mike	XXXXXXXX
James	XXXXX
John	XXX
Elmer	XXXXXXX

Each X is equal to 5 students

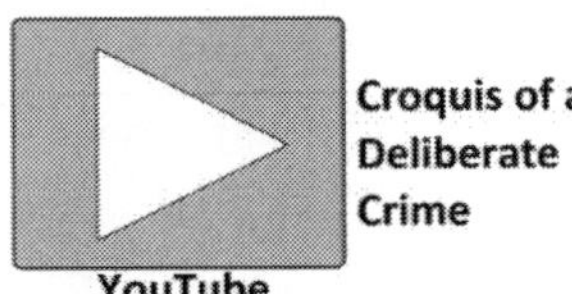

If you don't get the correct answer, and want an explanation on how to work the problem, go to YouTube and type in "MMT" then the problem number. An example would be, MMT 3.9.w12,. The video will show you how to work problem 3.9.w12.

For one on one tutoring via skype at $35.00/Hr.; contact me at marksmathtutoring@yahoo.com

6.13) The following graph describes the number of hamburger I ate each weekday.

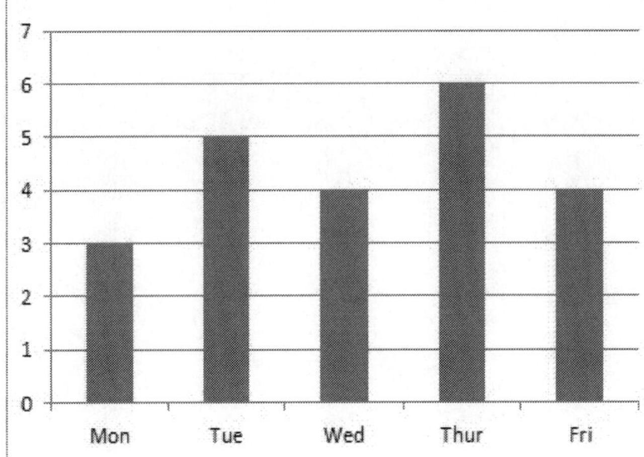

Which of the following tables best represents this data

a)

DAY	Mon	Tue	Wed	Thur	Fri
NUMBER	3	5	6	4	6

b)

DAY	Mon	Tue	Wed	Thur	Fri
NUMBER	3	6	5	7	5

c)

DAY	Mon	Tue	Wed	Thur	Fri
NUMBER	3	5	4	6	4

d)

DAY	Mon	Tue	Wed	Thur	Fri
NUMBER	3	7	4	7	5

6.14) The following table details the number of fish dinner a resturant sales

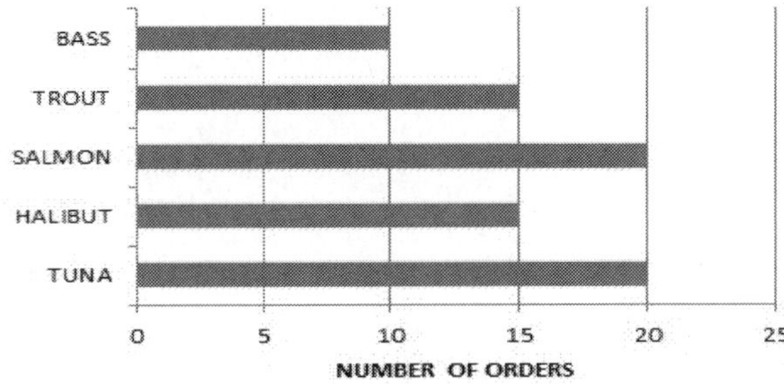

Which of the following tables best describes the data in the graph above

A)

FISH DINNER	NUMBER
BASS	10
TROUT	20
SLAMON	15
HALIBUT	15
TUNA	20

B)

FISH DINNER	NUMBER
BASS	10
TROUT	15
SLAMON	20
HALIBUT	25
TUNA	20

C)

FISH DINNER	NUMBER
BASS	10
TROUT	15
SLAMON	20
HALIBUT	15
TUNA	20

D)

FISH DINNER	NUMBER
BASS	10
TROUT	15
SLAMON	20
HALIBUT	15
TUNA	10

6.15) The following graph details the number of books I read per year I read

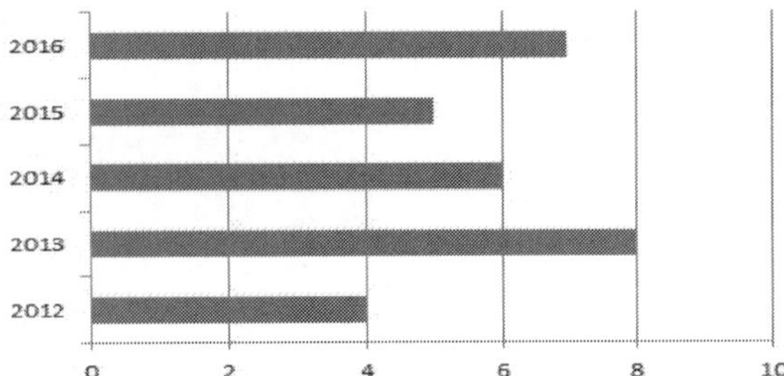

Which of the following tables best represents this data

A)

YEAR	NUMBER
2016	7
2015	5
2014	6
2013	8
2012	4

C)

YEAR	NUMBER
2016	7
2015	5
2014	8
2013	6
2012	4

B)

YEAR	NUMBER
2016	7
2015	5
2014	8
2013	8
2012	4

D)

YEAR	NUMBER
2016	7
2015	5
2014	6
2013	8
2012	6

6.16) The following tables describes the number of times a number was picked at randon from the deck of cards

DAY OF THE WEEK	NUMBER OF TIMES
One	4
Two	6
Three	5
Four	4
Five	3
Six	2

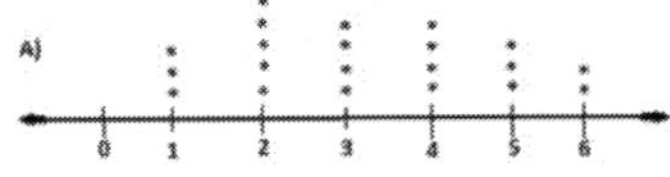

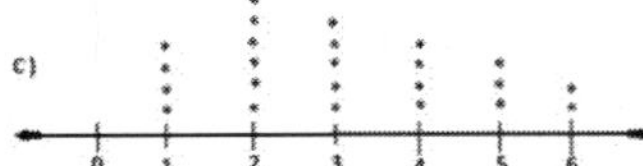

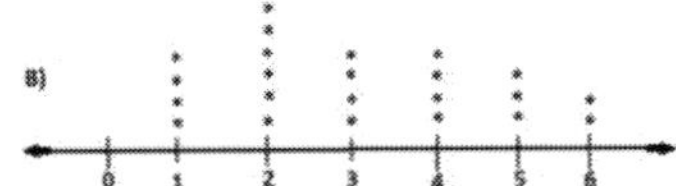

Croquis of a Deliberate Crime

6.17) The following table details the number of miles I ran in one day

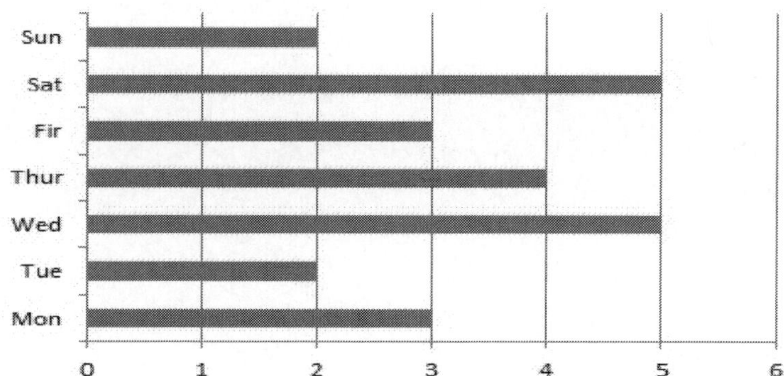

Which table below best describes this data?

A)

DAY	MILES
MON	3
TUE	2
WED	4
THUR	5
FRI	3
SAT	5
SUN	2

C)

DAY	MILES
MON	2
TUE	5
WED	3
THUR	4
FRI	5
SAT	2
SUN	3

B)

DAY	MILES
MON	3
TUE	2
WED	5
THUR	4
FRI	3
SAT	5
SUN	3

D)

DAY	MILES
MON	3
TUE	2
WED	5
THUR	4
FRI	3
SAT	5
SUN	2

6.18) The following list of numbers represents the card that was pulled from a deck.

3,2,7,6,6,7,5,10,2,3,7,3,7,1,3,

Which dot diagram below best represents this data

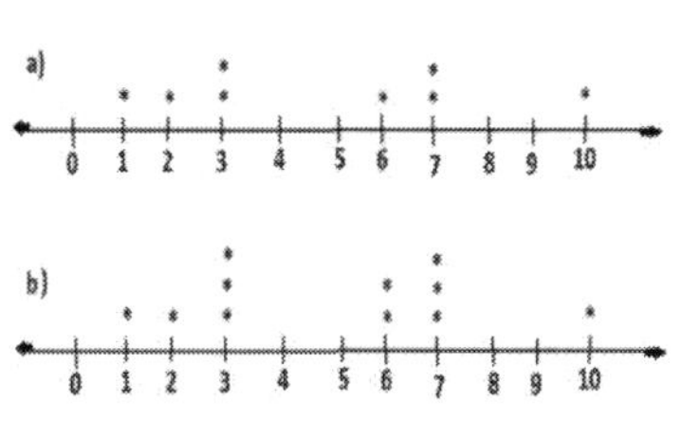

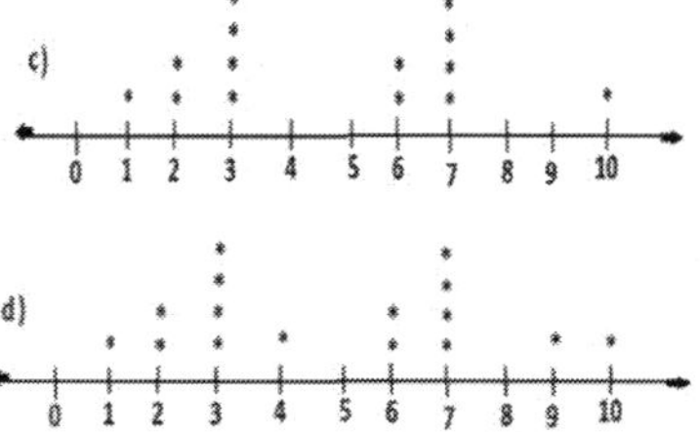

b)

0 1 2 3 4 5 6 7 8 9 10

d)

0 1 2 3 4 5 6 7 8 9 10

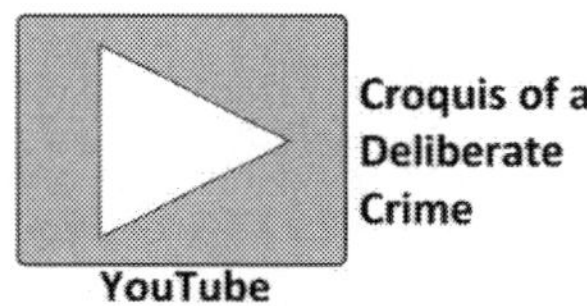

Croquis of a Deliberate Crime

6.19) Based on the graph below, how many more chocolate cupcakes were sold than vanilla

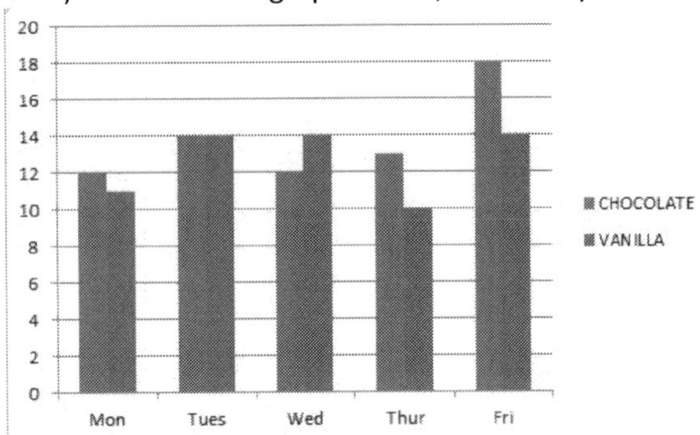

a) 5
b) 4
c) 6
d) 8

6.20) The graph below shows the number of fruits a grocery has on the shelf. Based on the this information how many more oranges than pears does the grocery have

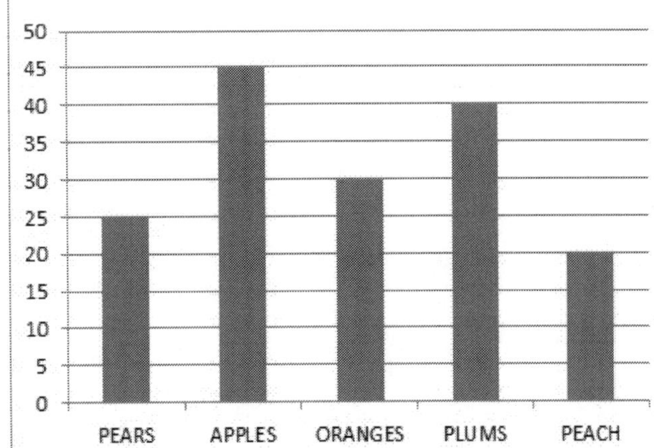

6.21) The graph below shows the number of hours I spent playing with my dog and cat.

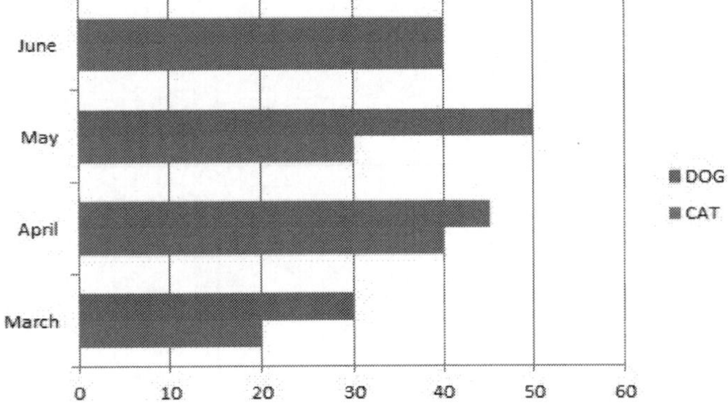

Based on this graph how many more hours in April did I play with my dog vs my cat?

For one on one tutoring via skype at $35.00/Hr.; contact me at marksmathtutoring@yahoo.com

6.22) The graph below show the number of cookies I are in each weekday.

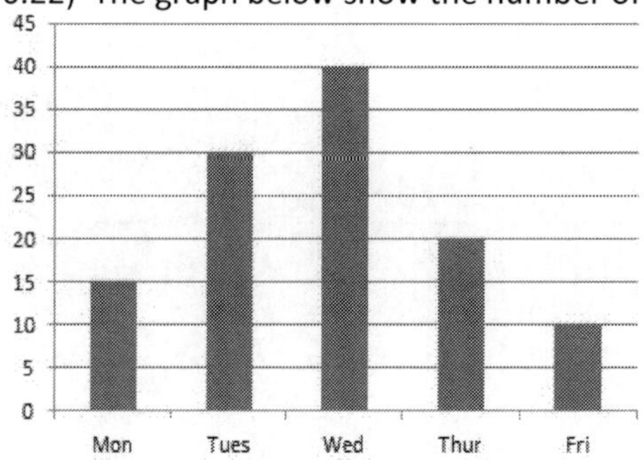

If I want to eat the same number of cookies each day how many more should I eat on Tues to equal the number I arte oh Wed?

6.23) The graph below shows the amount of money I earned mowing lawns and washing cars for four months.

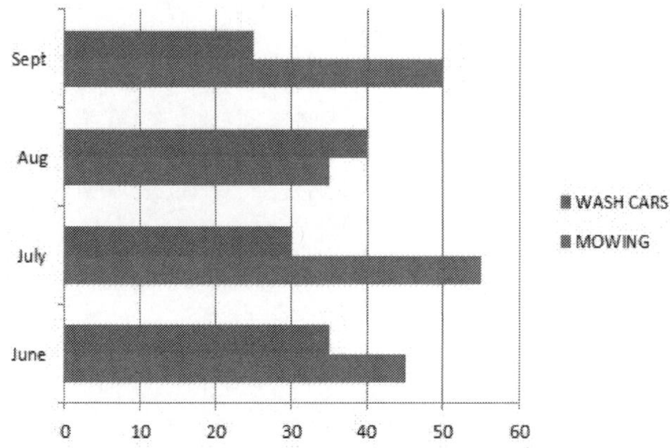

What is the difference in the amount of money I earned mowing lawns than washing cars?

6.24) The following graph shows the number of fish I caught each day during the summer.

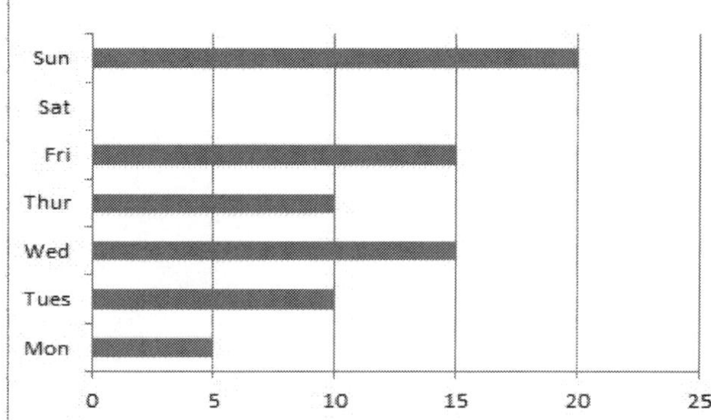

If I caught a total of 85 fish, how many must I have caught on Sat?

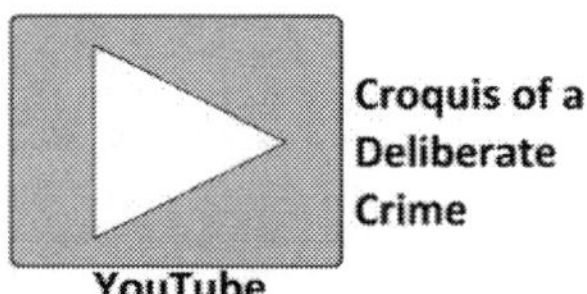

6.25) The following is a list of the length in inches of the fish I caught this summer.
12,14,16,12,18,22,16,24,16,18,13,23
Which of the table below best represents this data

a)

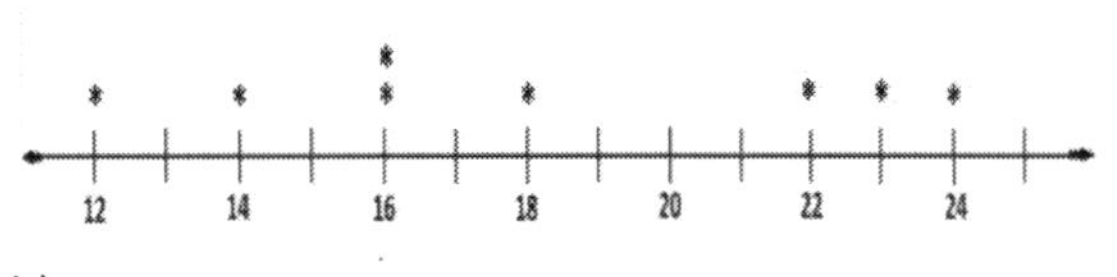

c) 

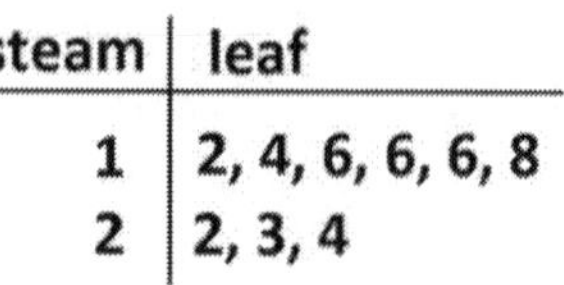

steam	leaf
1	2, 4, 6, 6, 6, 8
2	2, 3, 4

b)

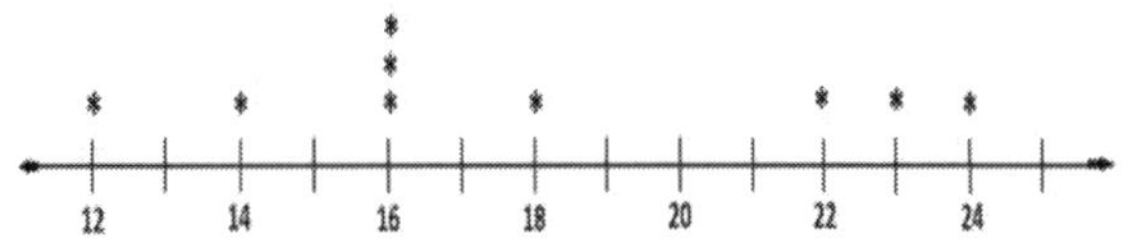

d)

steam	leaf
1	2, 4, 6, 8
2	2, 3, 4
3	0

6.26) The following table list the amount of fruit a farmer produced last year

FRUIT TYPE	NUMBER
Apples	125,835,266
Pears	217,346,893
Oranges	187,663,524
Peaches	237,894,332
Plums	109,475,872

Based on the information in this table which list below organizes this data from lowest to highest.
a) Plums, Oranges, Apples, Pears, Peaches
b) Plums, Apples, Oranges, Pears, Peaches
c) Peaches, Pears, Oranges, Apples, Plums
d) Plums, Apples, Oranges, Peaches, Pears

6.27) The following table list the number of fish I caught this summer based on their type.

FISH TYPE	NUMBER
Bass	45
Trout	
Salmon	17

If I caught a total of 63 fish how many Trout must I have caught?

Croquis of a Deliberate Crime

If you don't get the correct answer, and want an explanation on how to work the problem, go to YouTube and type in "MMT" then the problem number. An example would be, MMT 3.9.w12,. The video will show you how to work problem 3.9.w12.

6.28)The steam and leaf plot shown below show the weights of dogs in my neighborhood.

steam	leaf
1	3, 6, 8, 8
2	2, 6
3	5,5,8
4	1,5
5	0, 6, 7

Based on the information in this table what is the difference between the lightest and the heaviest dog?

6.29) The following two pictures detail the size of my friends back yards

Mary

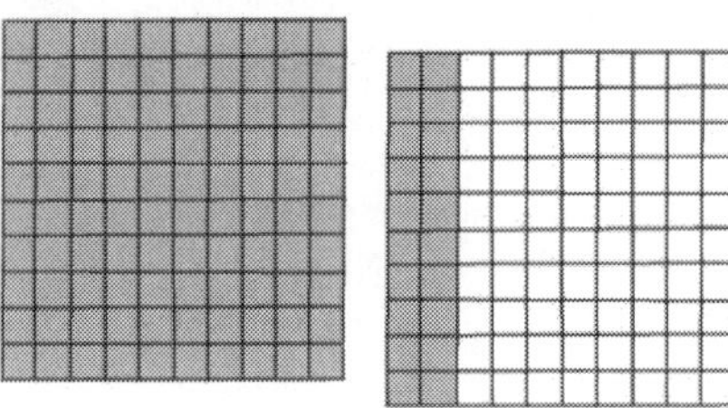

Sam

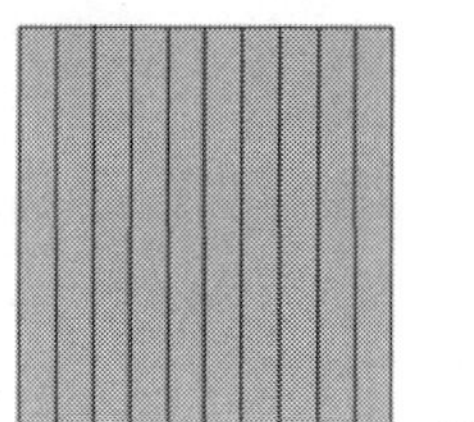

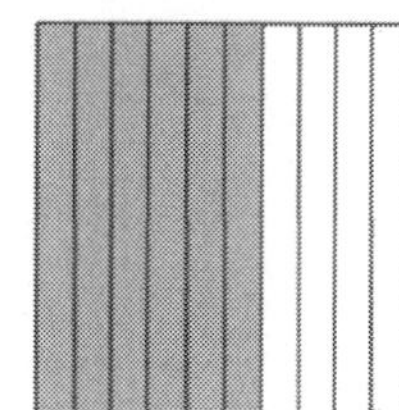

Susan

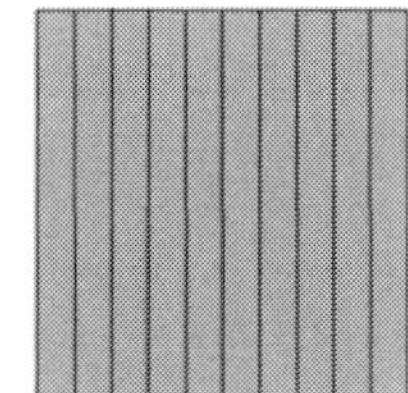

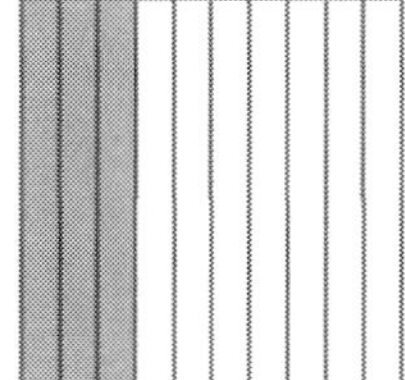

Mike

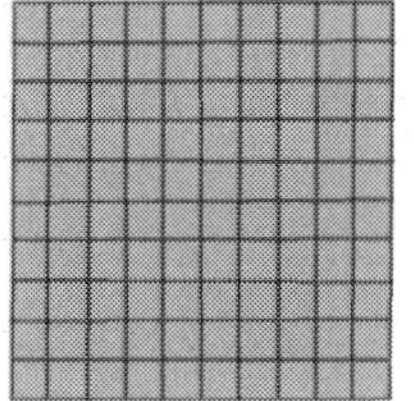

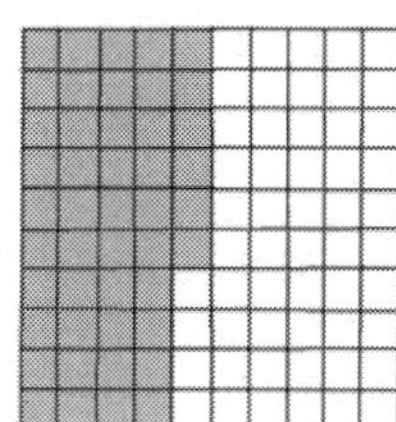

List these numbers in order of highest to lowest

a)1.6, 1.46, 1.3, 1.2

b) 1.2, 1.3, 1.46, 1.6

c) 1.46, 1.6, 1.3, 1.2

d) 1.2, 1.3, 1.6, 1.46

Croquis of a Deliberate Crime

If you don't get the correct answer, and want an explanation on how to work the problem, go to YouTube and type in "MMT" then the problem number. An example would be, MMT 3.9.w12,. The video will show you how to work problem 3.9.w12.

For one on one tutoring via skype at $35.00/Hr.; contact me at marksmathtutoring@yahoo.com

6.30) Given the information in the table below

WEIGHT	½	1	1 ½	2	2 ½	3	3 ½	4
NUMBER	2	4	0	3	6	2	1	4

a)

b)

c)

d)

6.31)The following table illustrates the number of biscuits my dog can eat for a specific number of hours

NUMBER OF HOURS	NUMBER OF BUSCUITS
1	15
2	30
3	45

A) B)

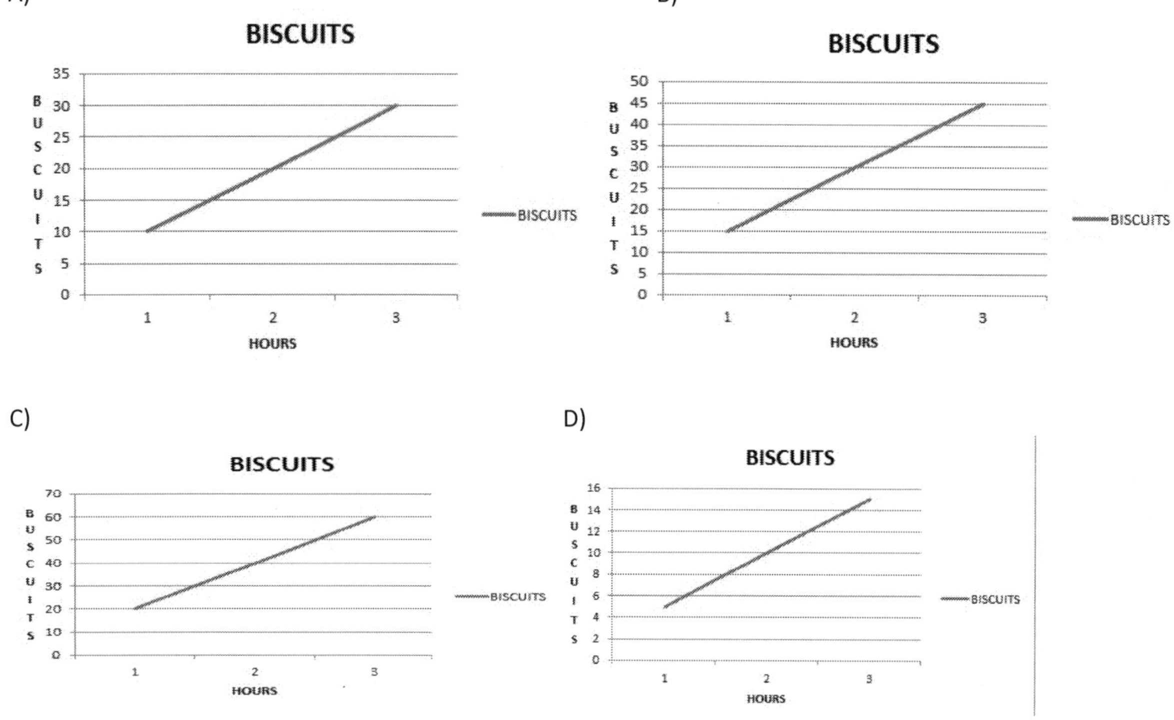

For one on one tutoring via skype at $35.00/Hr.; contact me at marksmathtutoring@yahoo.com

6.32) Given the graph below which table best represents this data.

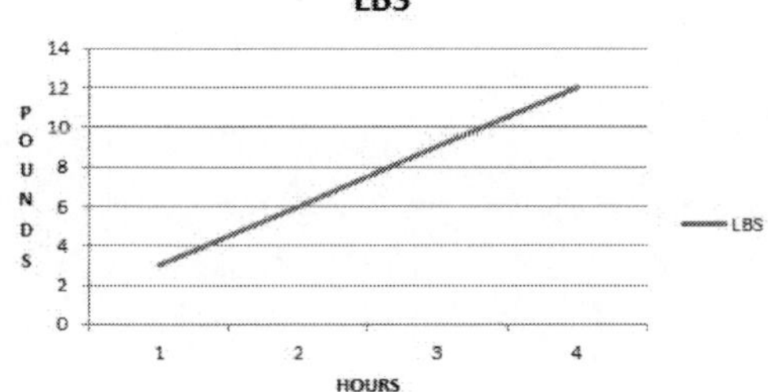

A)

HOURS	POUNDS
1	2
2	4
3	6
4	8

B)

HOURS	POUNDS
1	2
3	4
5	6
6	8

C)

HOURS	POUNDS
1	3
2	6
3	9
4	12

D)

HOURS	POUNDS
1	4
2	8
3	12
4	16

6.33) Which of the following points has the coordinates of (7,3)

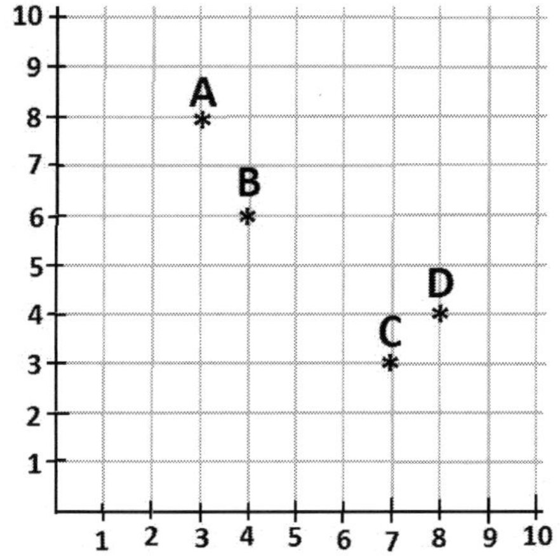

Croquis of a Deliberate Crime

6.34) What is the coordinates of the point in the graph below

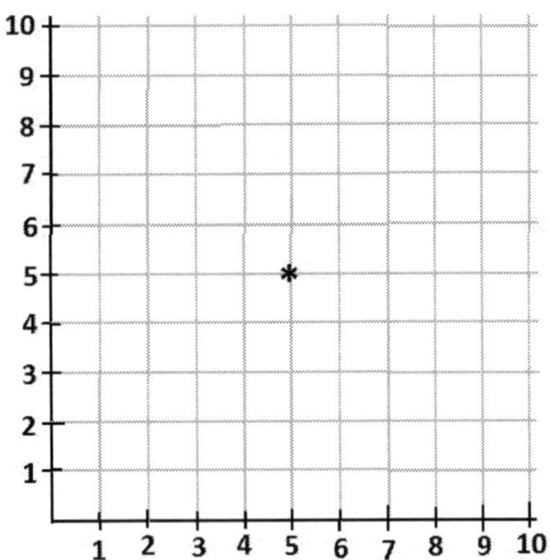

6.35) which point has the coordinates of (2,7)

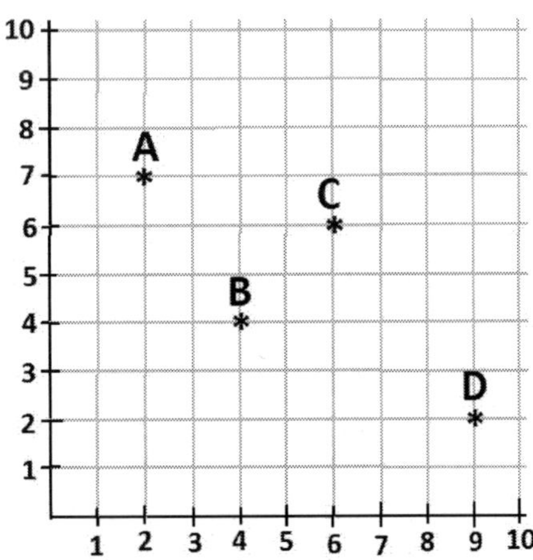

6.36) Which coordinate is **NOT** on the line of the graph below

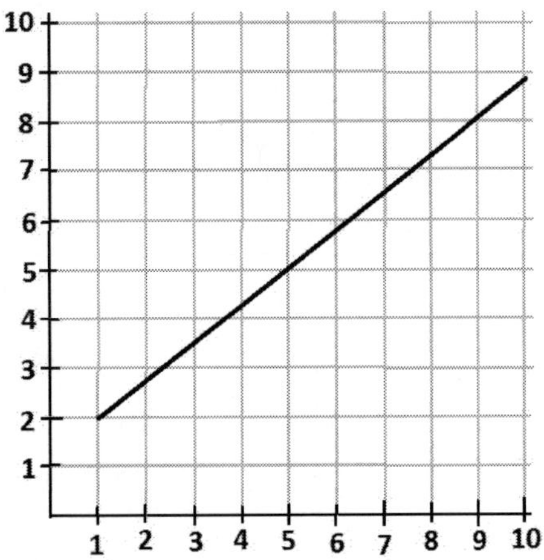

A) (5,5)
B)(9,8)
C) (2,2)
D) (3,4)

6.37) Which of the graphs below best represent the data presented in the following table

X	Y
2	5
8	6
9	8
10	10

A)

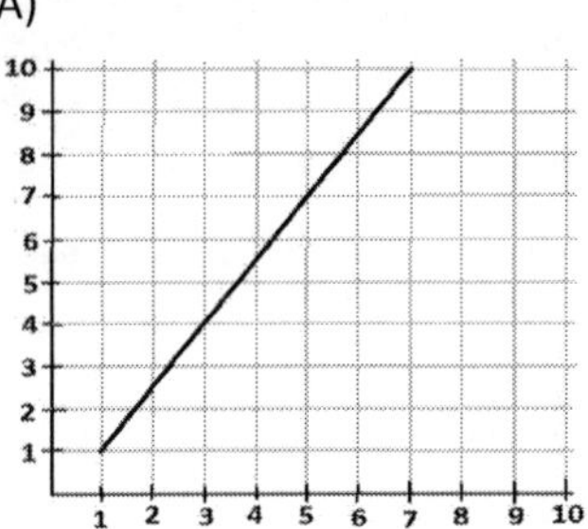

B)

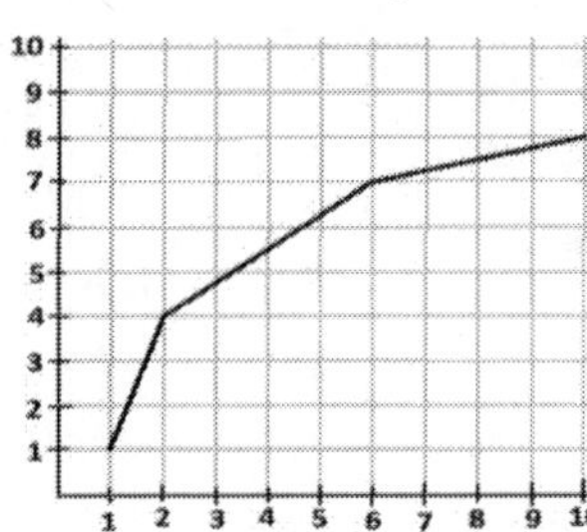

C)

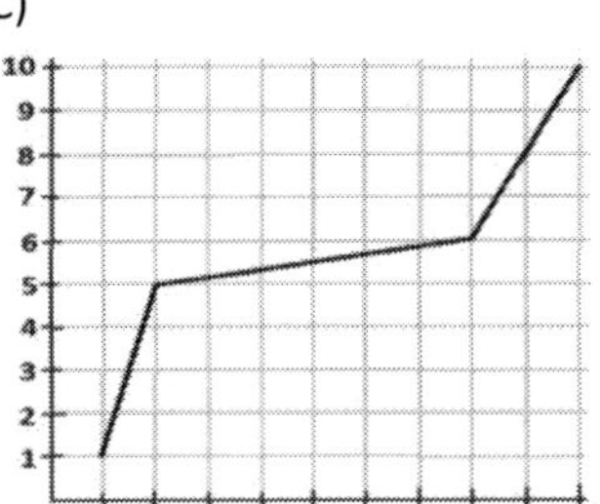

D)

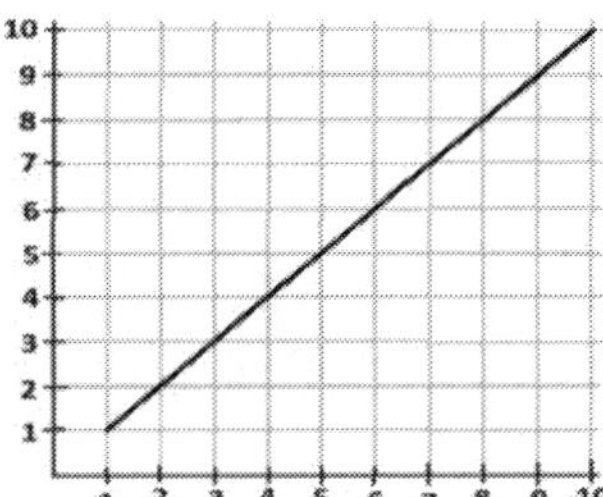

6.38) I measured the weight of my new puppy and recorded the results in the table below

#First week she gained 2 pound

each week after that she gained 3 pounds

Which graph below shows this data

A)

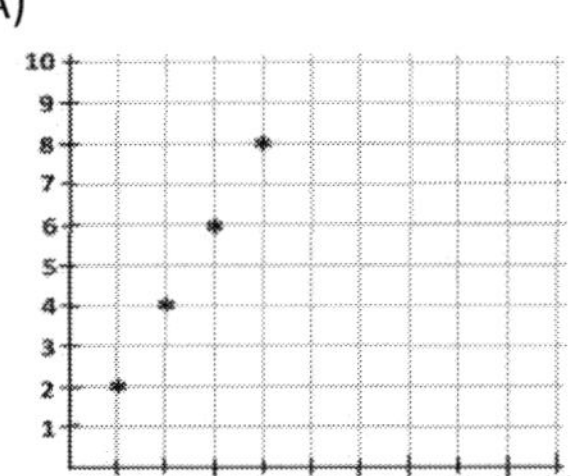

B)

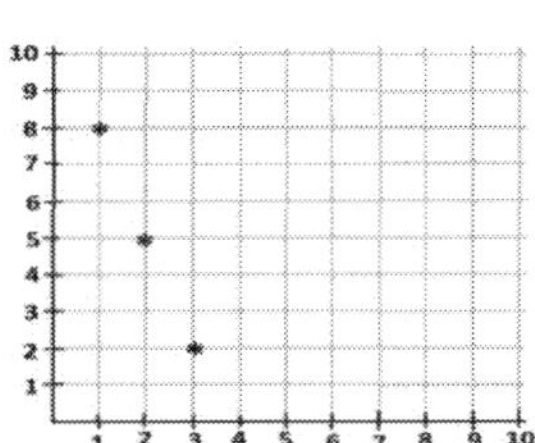

C)

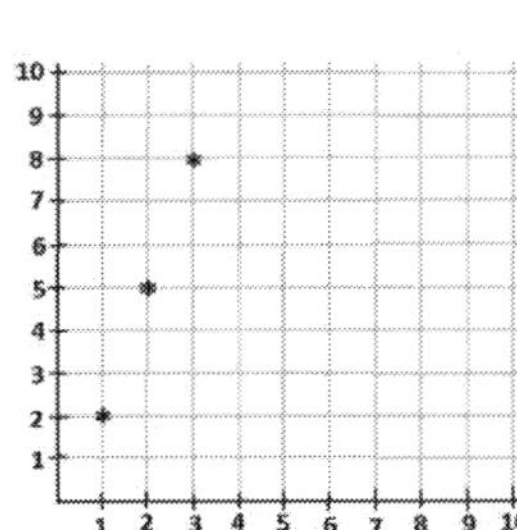

D)

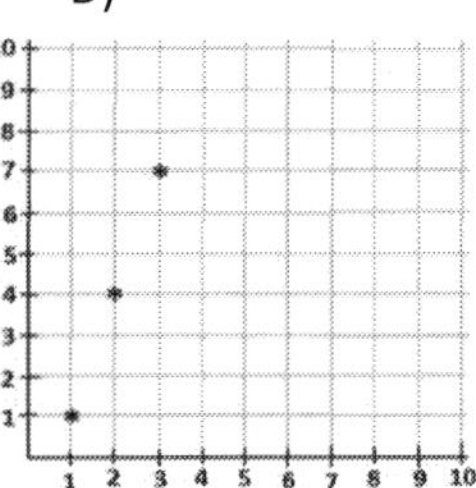

6.39) Given the information in the graph below

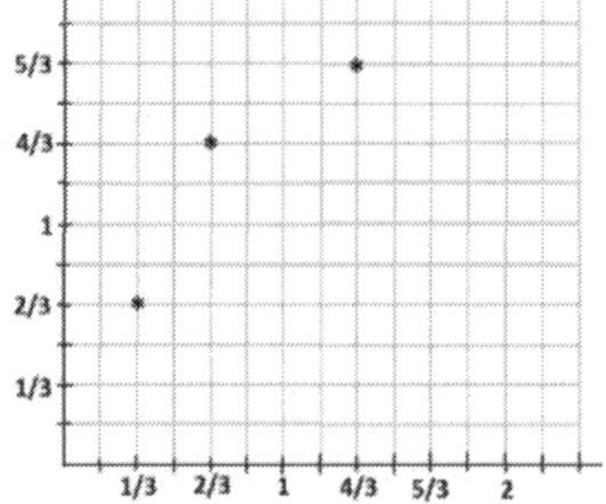

Which table below best describes this information

A)

X	1/3	2/3	5/3
Y	2/3	4/3	5/3

B)

X	1/3	2/3	5/3
Y	2/3	5/3	4/3

C)

X	1/3	2/3	4/3
Y	2/3	2/3	5/3

D)

X	1/3	2/3	4/3
Y	2/3	4/3	5/3

6.40) The following table show the number of soda pops sold vs atterndence at the theam park

TEMPERATURE	SODAS SOLD
75	20
80	40
85	30
90	70
95	50
100	80

A)

B)

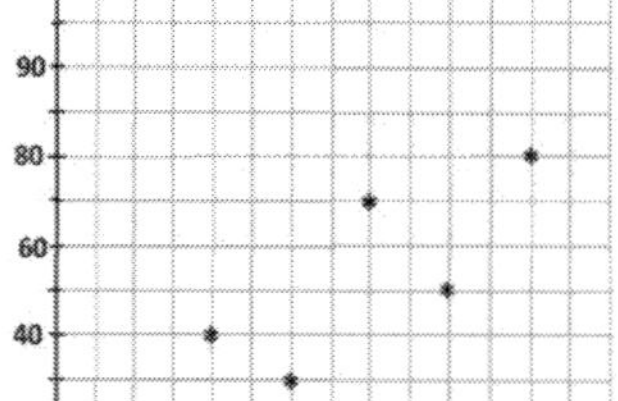

C)

D)

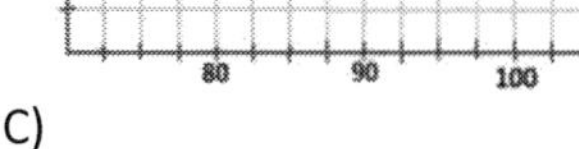

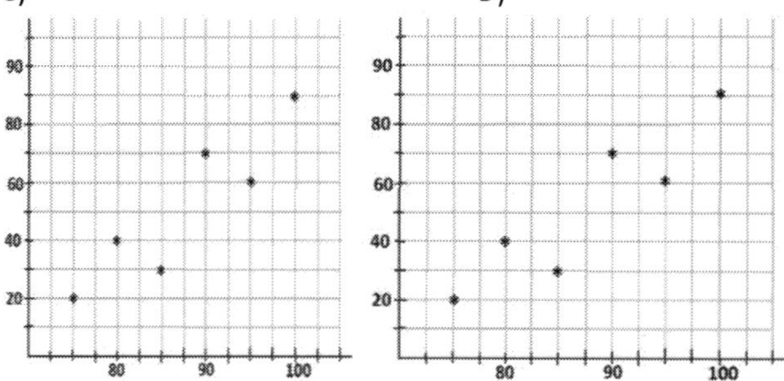

For one on one tutoring via skype at $35.00/Hr.; contact me at marksmathtutoring@yahoo.com

6.41) Given The graph below

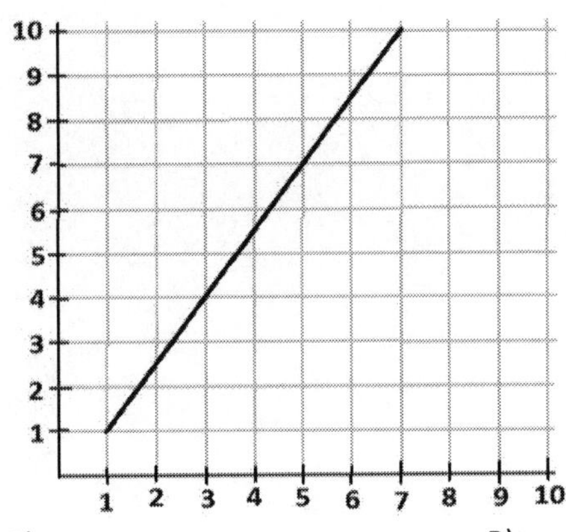

A)

X	1	3	5	7
Y	3	4	7	11

B)

X	1	3	5	7
Y	3	5	7	10

C)

X	1	3	5	7
Y	3	4	8	10

D)

X	1	3	5	7
Y	1	4	7	10

6.42) Which table blow represents the data presented in this graph

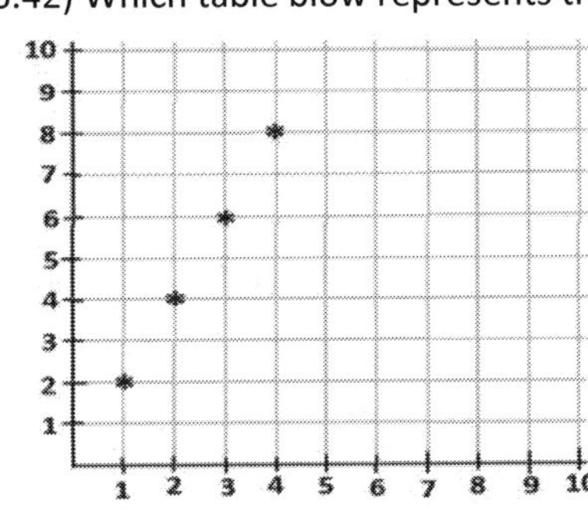

A)

X	Y
1	2
2	5
3	6
4	8

B)

X	Y
1	2
2	4
3	6
4	8

C)

X	Y
1	2
2	4
3	5
4	8

D)

X	Y
1	2
2	4
3	6
4	7

6.43) In the order pair (3,4) what is the value of X

Croquis of a Deliberate Crime

YouTube

6.44)Given the graph below

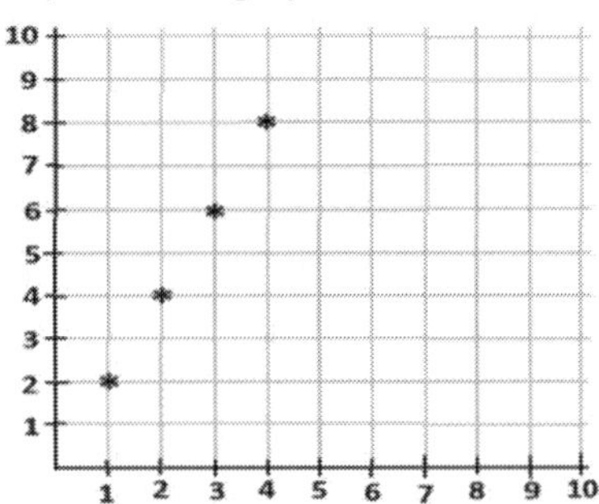

What is the relationship between each point?

A) Multiplication, each X is multiplied by 3 to get Y
B) Addition, each X is added to 1 to get Y
C) Multiplication each X is multiplied by 2 to get Y
D) Addition, each X is added to 1 to get Y

6.45) What are the coordinates of the vertices in the drawing below

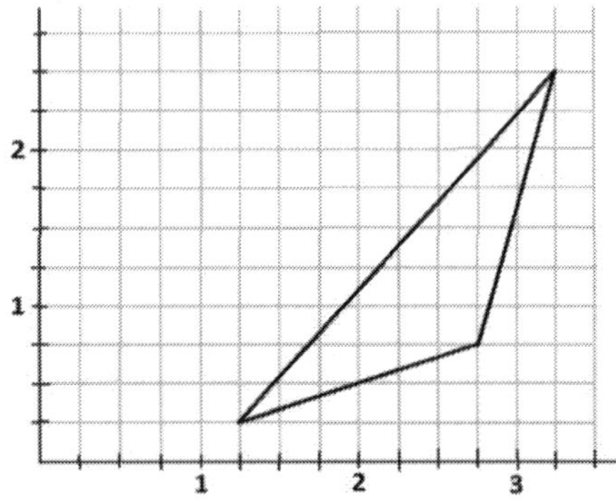

6.46) What are the coordinates of the two points shown below

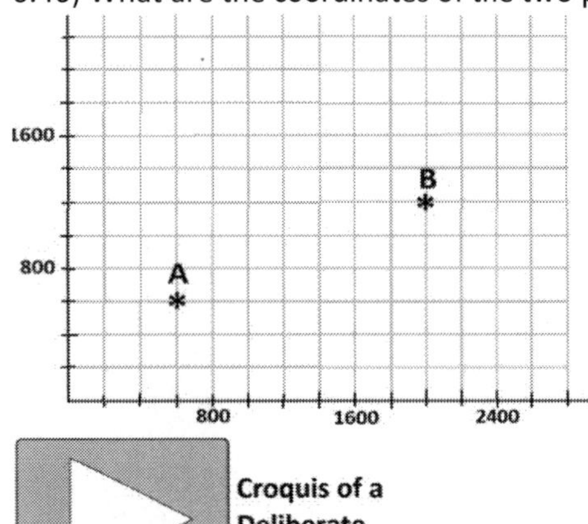

YouTube

Croquis of a Deliberate Crime

If you don't get the correct answer, and want an explanation on how to work the problem, go to YouTube and type in "MMT" then the problem number. An example would be, MMT 3.9.w12,. The video will show you how to work problem 3.9.w12.

For one on one tutoring via skype at $35.00/Hr.; contact me at marksmathtutoring@yahoo.com

6.47) Below is a graph of my brother and my weight as a function of our age.

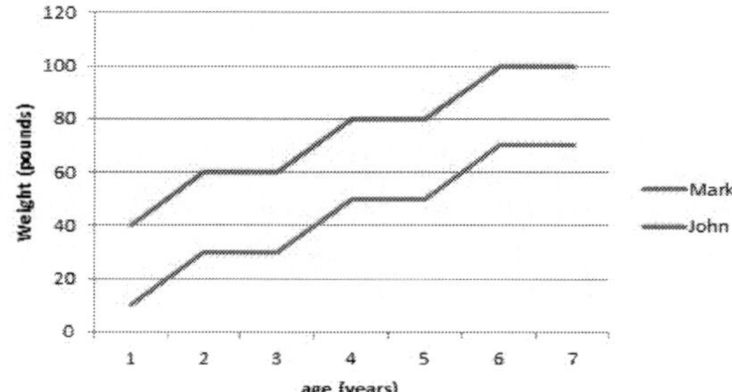

Given this information what will my heavier brother's weight be in his 9th year

6.48) what is the coordinates of the dot in the graph drawn below

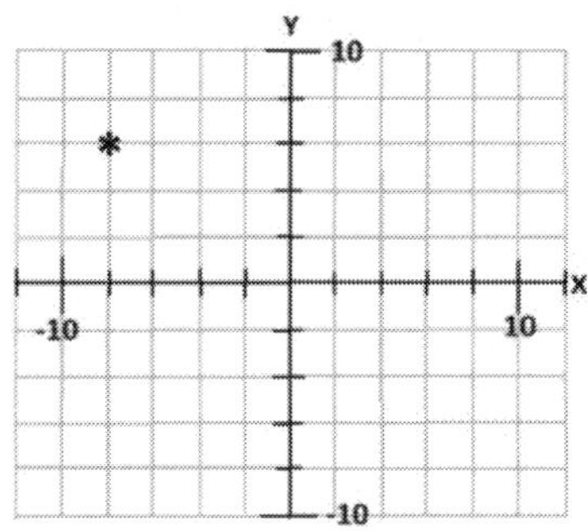

6.49) Given the graph below

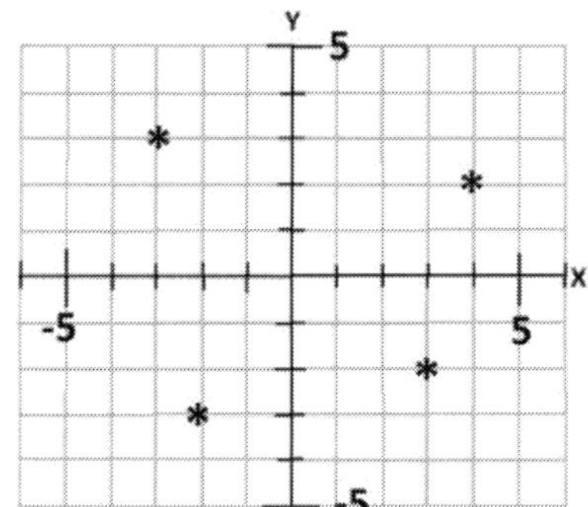

Which of the following coordinates are not on this graph

A) (-3,3)
B) (-2,-3)
C) (-2,3)
D) (4,2)

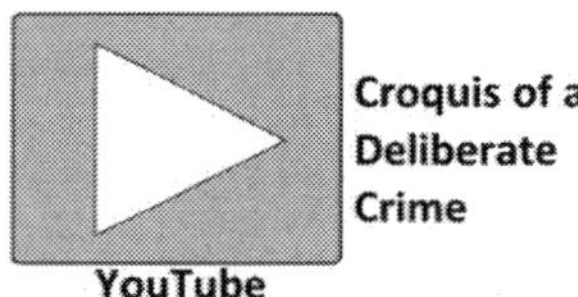

If you don't get the correct answer, and want an explanation on how to work the problem, go to YouTube and type in "MMT" then the problem number. An example would be, MMT 3.9.w12,. The video will show you how to work problem 3.9.w12.

6.50) Given the graph below

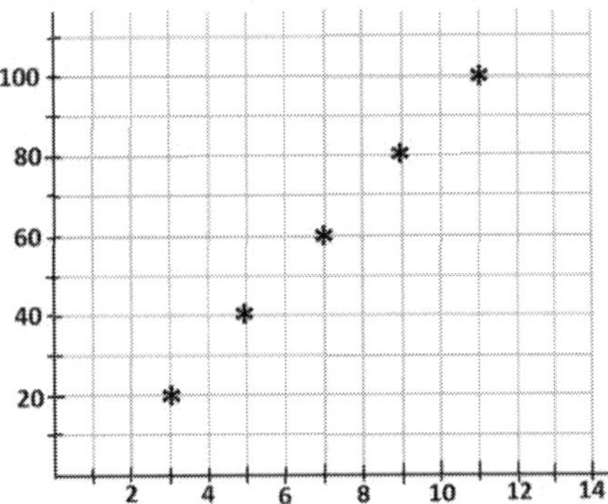

What are the independent variable values, and the dependent variable values

6.51) Given the graph below

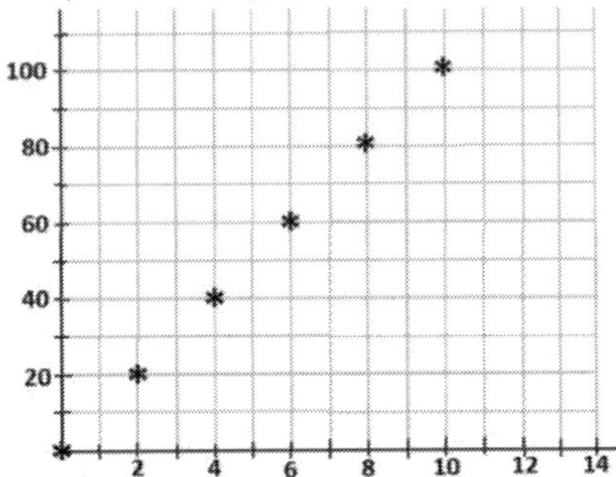

Which of the following equations shows the relationship between X and Y

A) Y = 20X

B) Y = X + 20

C) Y = 10X

D) Y = 10÷X

6.52) Which ordered pair is **NOT** shown in the graph below

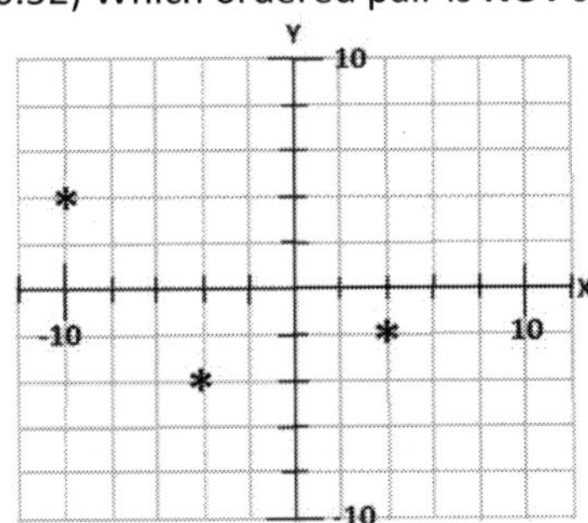

A) (-10,4)

B) (-4,-4)

C) (4,2)

D) (4,-2)

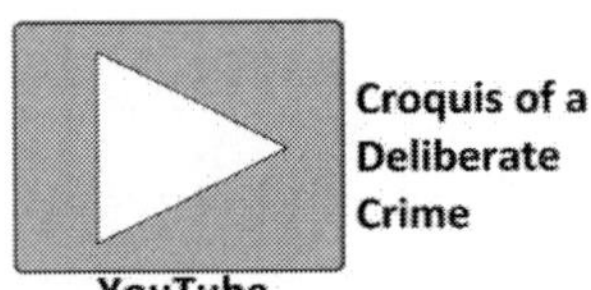

6.53) Given the graph below

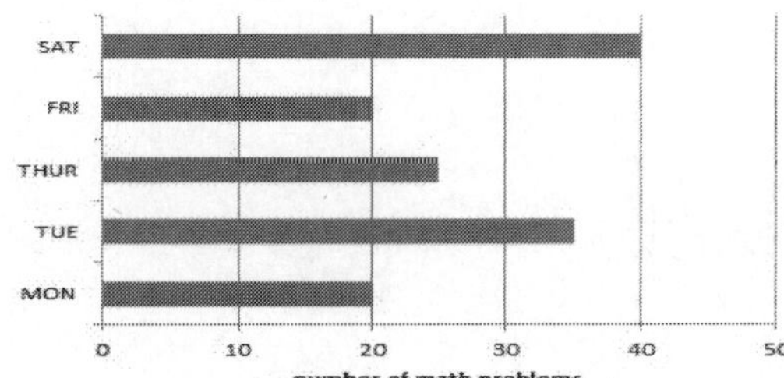

Which one of the following statements is true
A) The total number of math problems was 130
B) Monday had 10 more than Thursday
C) The total was 140
D) Wednesday had the most math problems

6.54) If I caught 10 fish with a total weight of 400 pounds and the weights of nine of them are shown in the graph below

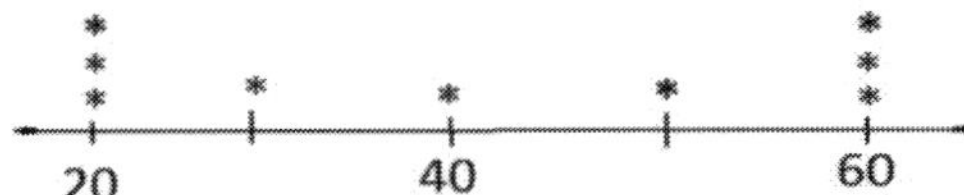

What was the weight of the tenth fish

6.55)I caught 40 fish. 15 Trout, 10 Bass. The remainder were Tuna and Salmon in a 2:3 ratio. Which pie graph best describes this relationship

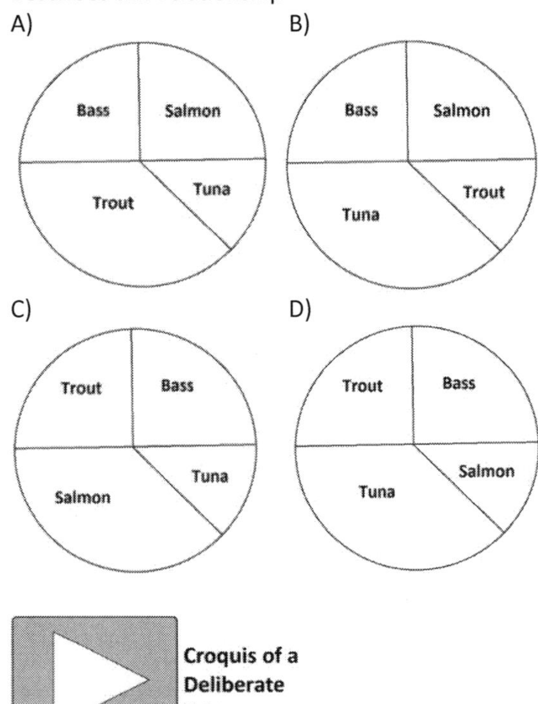

Croquis of a Deliberate Crime

YouTube

For one on one tutoring via skype at $35.00/Hr.; contact me at marksmathtutoring@yahoo.com

6.56) Given the graph below detailing the fish I caught

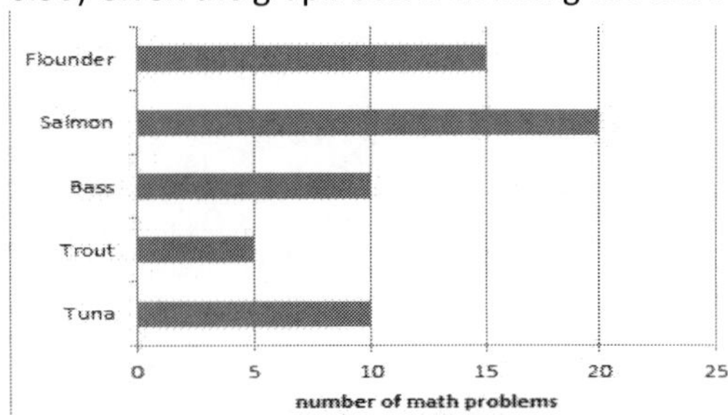

Which of the following statements is true

A) I caught five more trout than tuna

B) I caught twice as many salmon than tuna

C) I caught twice as many trout than bass

D) I caught five more flounder than trout

6.57) Given the data in the steam leaf diagram below

Length of Trout (inches)

STEAM	LEAF
12	25, 50, 50
13	25,75
14	50, 50, 75
15	25, 50, 75, 75

KEY
12|25 = 12 .25 INCHES

Which one of the graphs below shows this information

A)

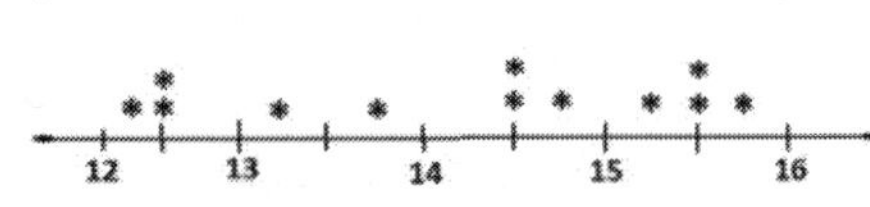

B)

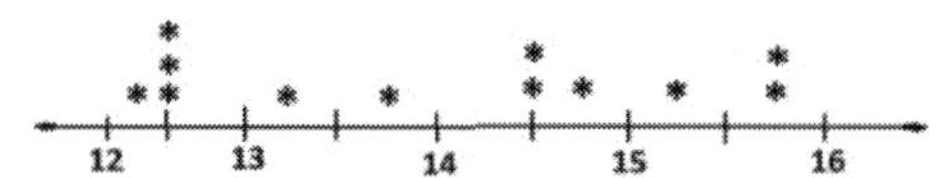

C)

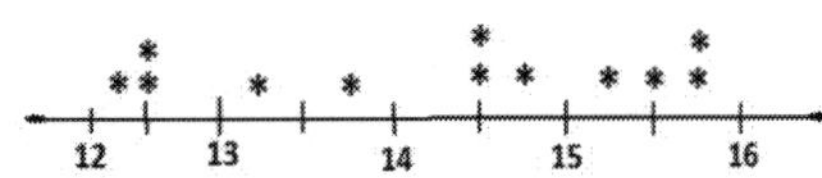

D)

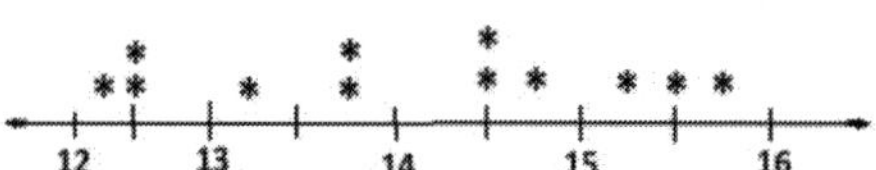

6.58) Given the graph below

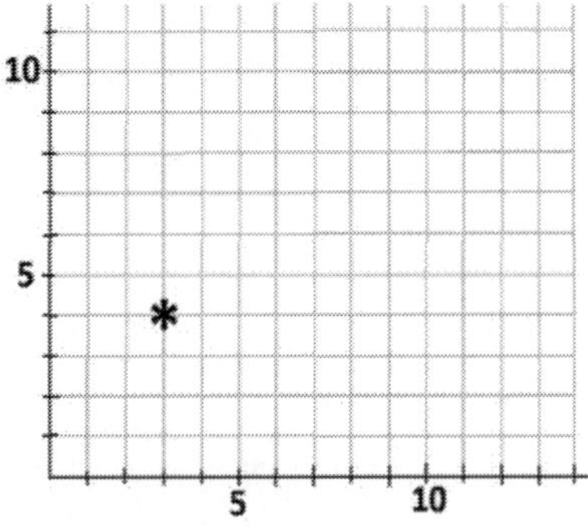

Which of the following points { (1,4), (2,3), (5,4)} is closest to the point shown

For one on one tutoring via skype at $35.00/Hr.; contact me at marksmathtutoring@yahoo.com

6.59) Given the graph below

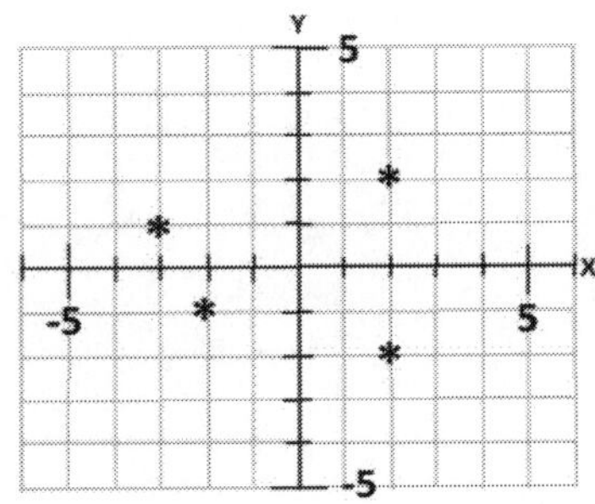

Which of the following coordinates is not on this a point on this graph
A) (-3,1)
B) (2,2)
C) (-1,-2)
D) ((2,-2)

6.60) Given the table below detailing the amount of money I earned last summer for different activities

ACTIVITY	AMOUNT EARNED
Baby Sitting	25
Washing cars	47
Mowing Lawns	35
Cleaning yards	33

Which of the following graphs best shows the amount I earned on a percentage bases

A)

BABY SITTING | WASHING CARS | MOWING LAWNS | CLEANING YARDS
0% 20% 40% 60% 80% 100%

B)

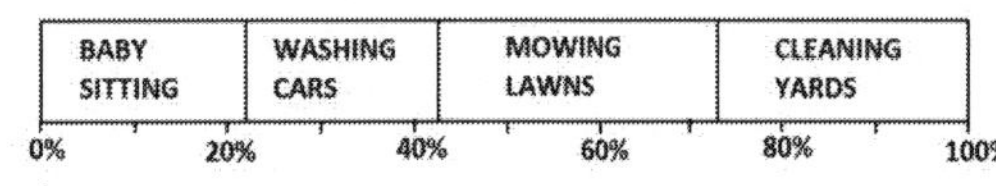

C)

BABY SITTING | WASHING CARS | MOWING LAWNS | CLEANING YARDS
0% 20% 40% 60% 80% 100%

D)

BABY SITTING | WASHING CARS | MOWING LAWNS | CLEANING LAWNS
0% 20% 40% 60% 80% 100%

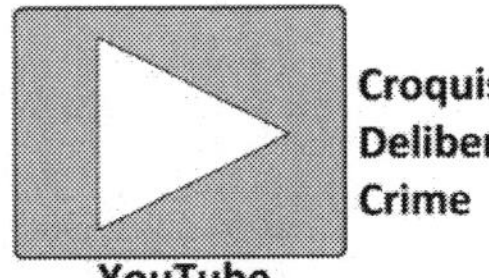

Croquis of a Deliberate Crime

YouTube

If you don't get the correct answer, and want an explanation on how to work the problem, go to YouTube and type in "MMT" then the problem number. An example would be, MMT 3.9.w12,. The video will show you how to work problem 3.9.w12.

For one on one tutoring via skype at $35.00/Hr.; contact me at marksmathtutoring@yahoo.com

6.61) Given the graph drawn below

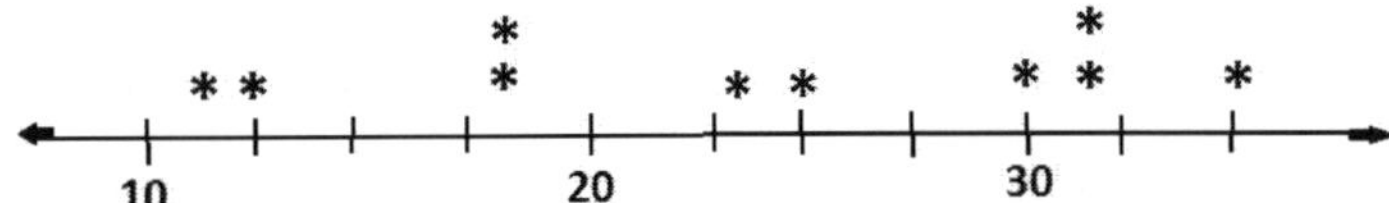

Which of the following steam and leaf diagrams best fit this data

A)

WEIGHT OF DOGS (POUNDS)

STEAM	LEAF
1	1, 2, 8, 8
2	3,5
3	0, 2, 2, 5

B)

WEIGHT OF DOGS (POUNDS)

STEAM	LEAF
1	1, 2, 8, 8
2	3,5
3	0, 2, 2, 9

C)

WEIGHT OF DOGS (POUNDS)

STEAM	LEAF
1	1, 2, 8, 8
2	5, 8
3	0, 2, 2, 5

D)

WEIGHT OF DOGS (POUNDS)

STEAM	LEAF
1	2, 8, 8
2	3, 5
3	0, 2, 2, 5

6.62) Given the graph below

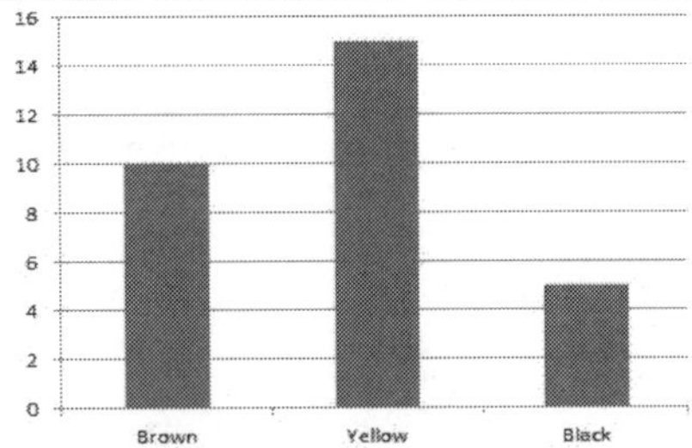

Out of 400 dogs how many will be yellow

6.63) Given the data outlined in the graph below, showing the weights of dogs

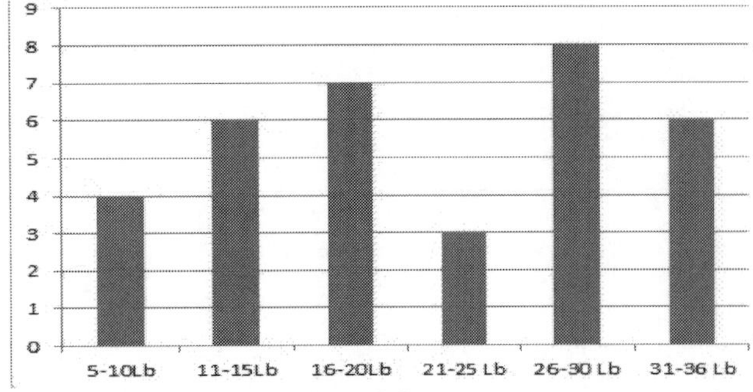

Given this data which of the following statements must be true

A) Half the dogs like to chase cars

B) A total of 34 dogs were weighted

C) Half the dogs weighted over 21 pounds

D) Less than half the dogs weighted more than 16 pounds

6.64)I interviewed 10 families to find out how many pets they had. The data is shown in the graph below

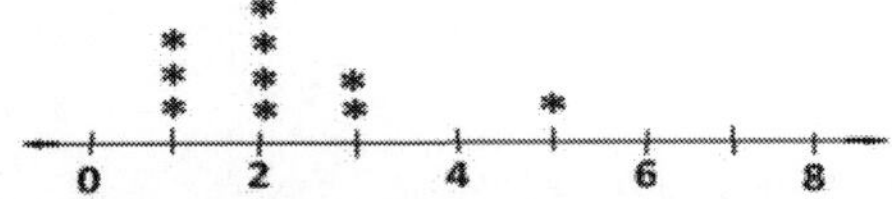

Based on this data what is the most common number of pets for a family

6.65)Based on the graph below

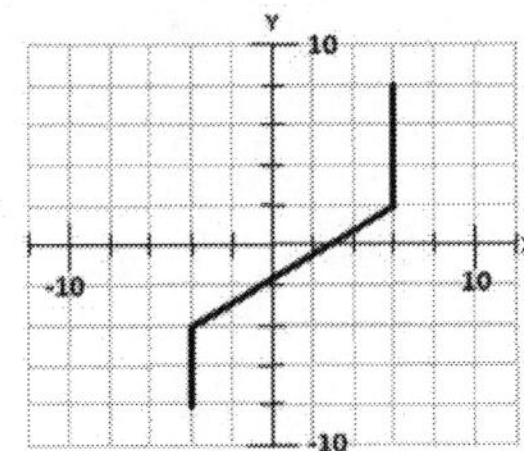

Which of the following coordinates is not on the line drawn
A) (6,8), B) (0,-2) C) (-4,-4) D) (-2,0)

6.66) Given the graph below

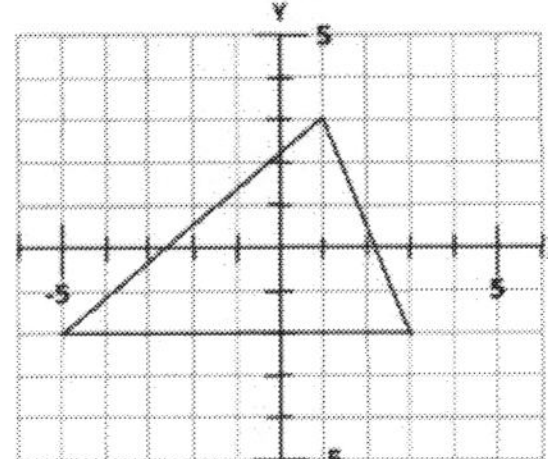

Which of the following coordinates is not a point on the triangle
A) (-5,-2) B) (3,-2) C) (1,3) D) (3,-1)

6.67) The vertices of the triangle are (-3,-4) (1,3) and (4,-2)

A)

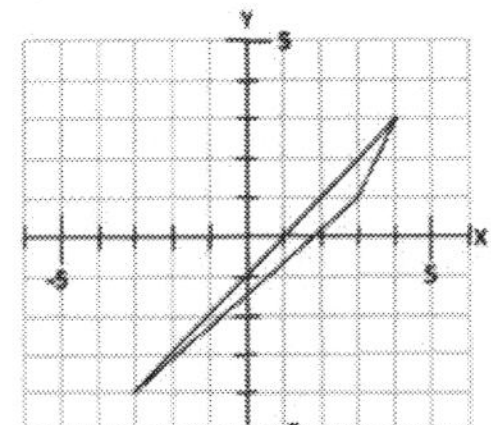

B)

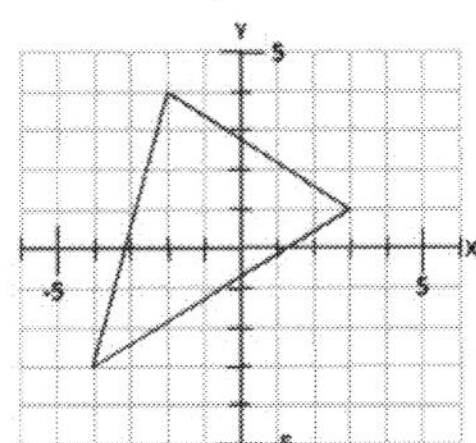

C)

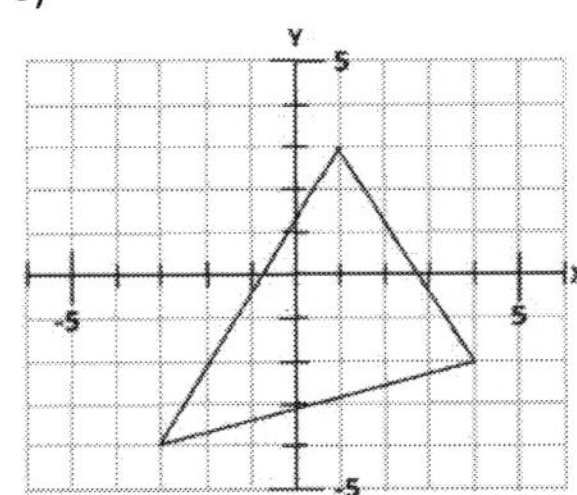

D)

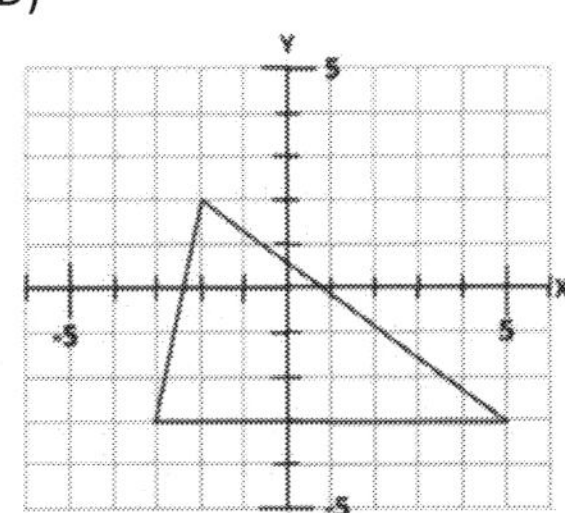

6.68)I compared my test score with a friends. The graph below illustrates the number of question we each missed on four different math test.

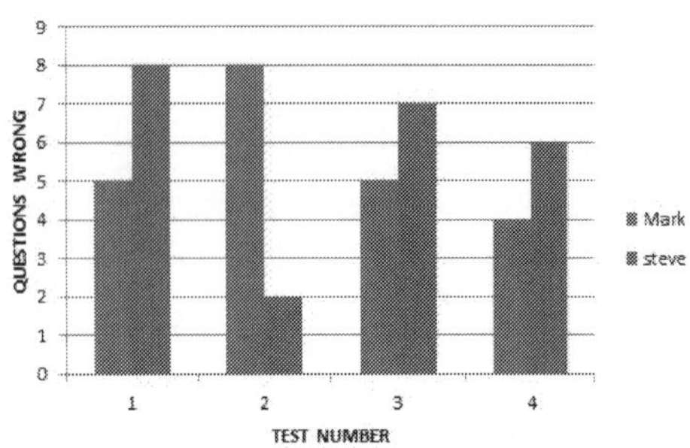

Which of the following statements is true.

A) On test one Steve missed 50% more questions than I did

B) I missed more questions in total than Steve did

C) On test three I missed three times as many as Steve did

D) On test four Steve missed 50% more than I did

6.69) The following graph details the number and types of fish I caught while on vacation

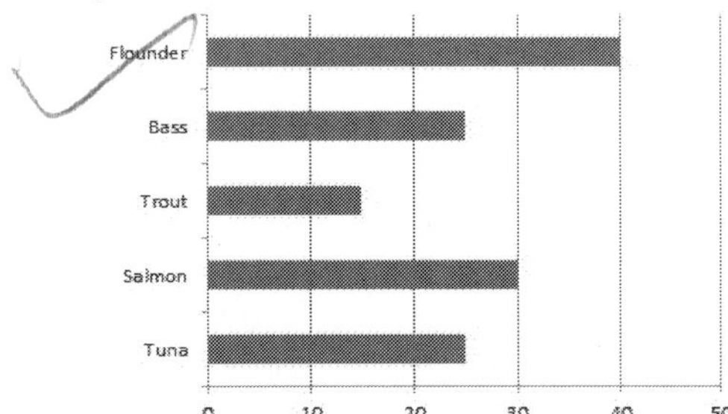

Given this data which of the following statements is true

A) I caught 3 times more Flounders than Trout

B) 50% more Bass than Trout

C) I caught 1/3 more Flounders than Salmon

D) Twice as many Flounder than Tunas

6.70) Given the data { 56, 58, 59,63,67,74,76,77,77, 84, 86, 89, 91, 94} Which of the following graphs this data correctly

A)

STEAM	LEAF
5	6, 8, 9
6	3, 7
7	4, 6, 7, 7
8	4, 6, 9
9	1, 4

B)

56 58 59 | 74 76 77 | 84 91 86 94 98 63 67

C)

STEAM	LEAF
5	6, 8, 9
6	3, 7
7	4, 6, 7
8	4, 6, 9
9	1, 4

D)

56 58 59 | 74 76 77 77 | 84 91 86 94 98 63 67

6.71) Given the graph below what is your best estimate of a value X=7

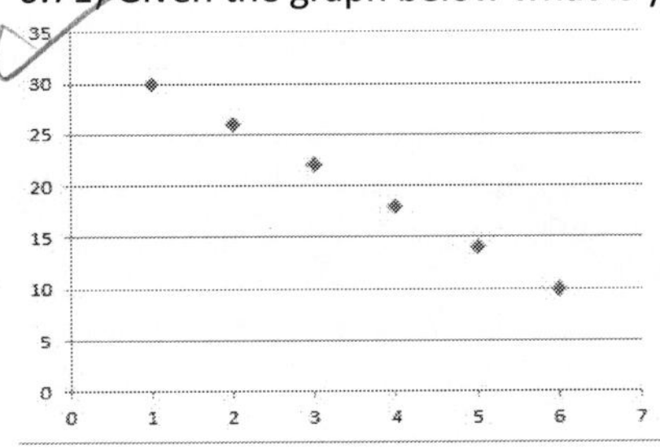

A) Y=10
B) Y=0
C) Y=6
D) Y=-2

6.72) The following graph show the balance in my savings account after I make a monthly payment

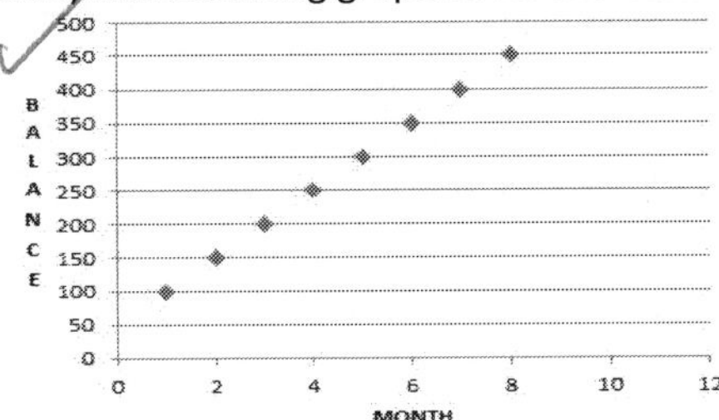

What is your best estimate for the balance after 12 months
A) 550
B) 650
C) 600
D) 500

6.73) Which letter corresponds to a point with a value X<1 and Y>1

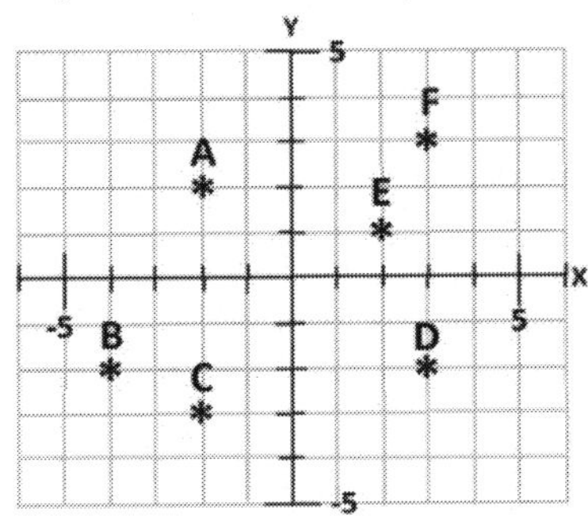

6.74) What would be a solution that satisfies both relationships

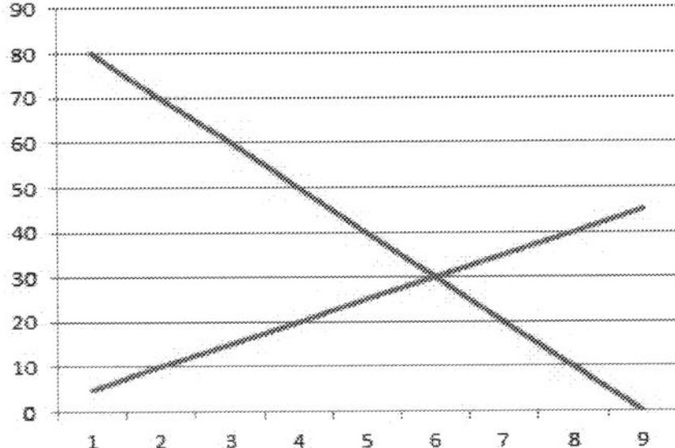

6.75) Given the graph below showing how many fish I catch per hour, what is your best estimate on how many fish I will catch if I fish for 12 hours

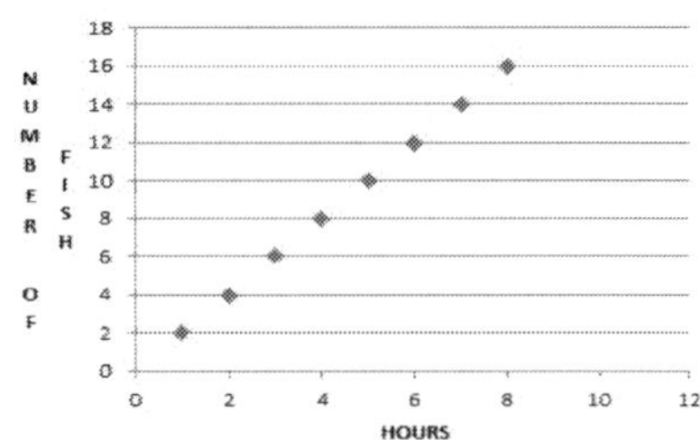

6.76) Which of the following graphs best described a positive linear relationship

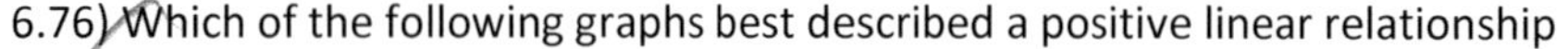

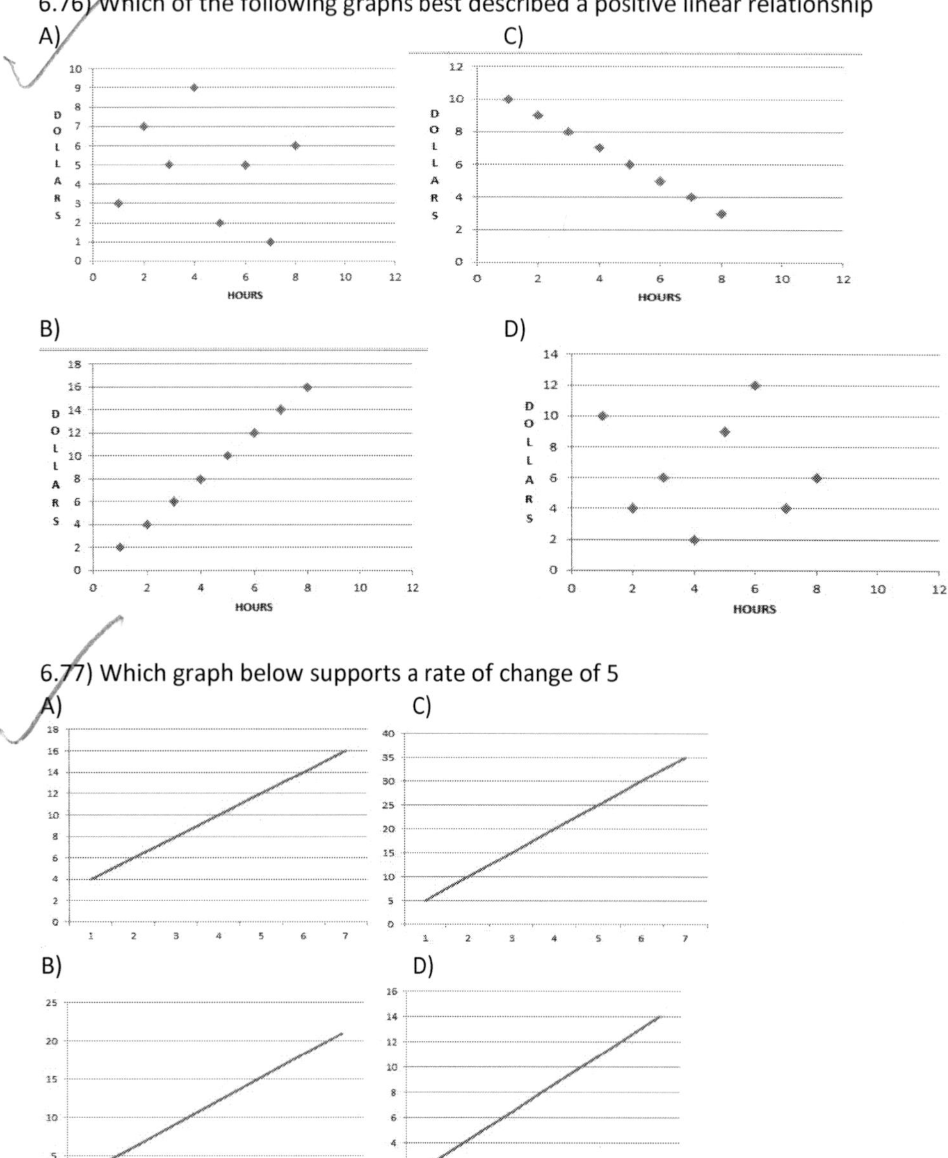

6.77) Which graph below supports a rate of change of 5

A)

C)

B)

D)

7.0 MEASURMENTS

7.1) Use a ruler to measure in centimeters the two arrows below. What is the difference in their heights

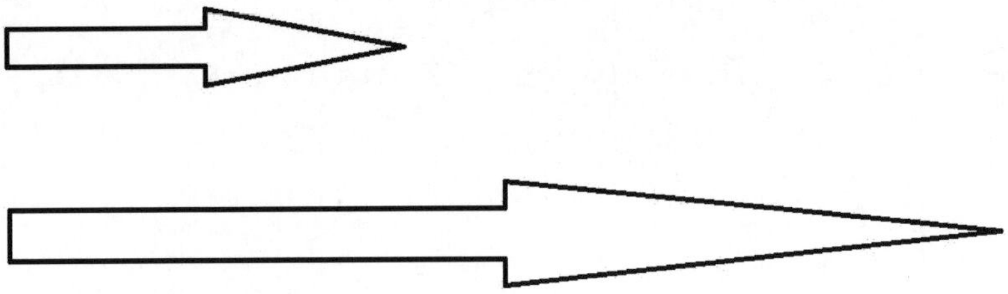

7.2) Use a ruler to measure and determine the perimeter, to 1/2 of an inch, of the following drawing

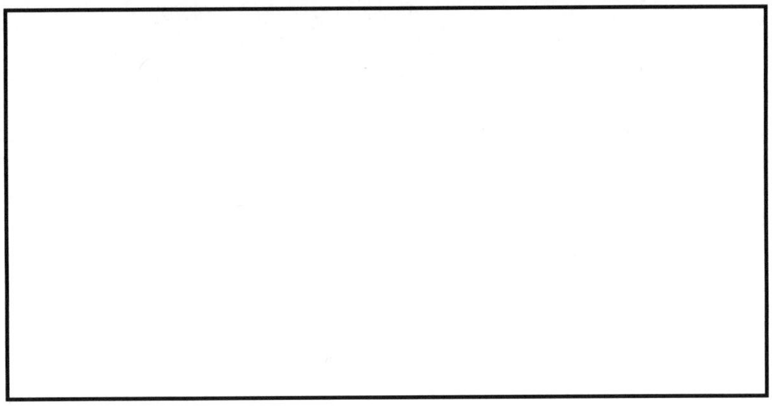

7.3) Use a ruler to determine the length to the nearest ½ inch of the following lines

A)

B)

C)

D)

7.4) If each square is 1 feet square what is the area following figure occupies?

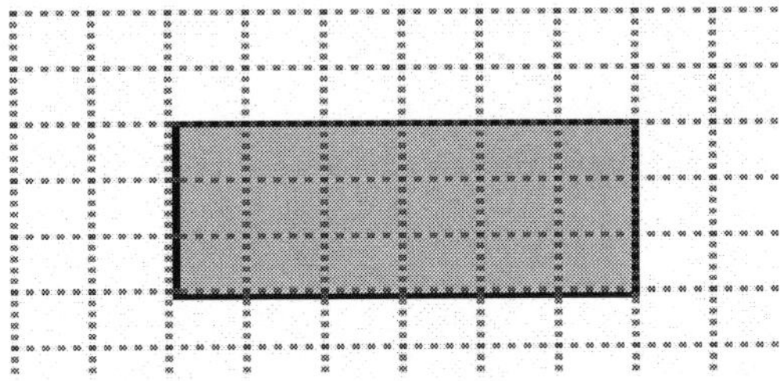

7.5) What is the difference in inches between the length of these two figures. Your answer should be to the ½ inch.

7.6) My mom placed a turkey in the oven at 1:45. 30 minutes later she put a pie in the same oven. She cooked both at the same time for 45 minutes. What time did she take both the turkey and pie from the oven?

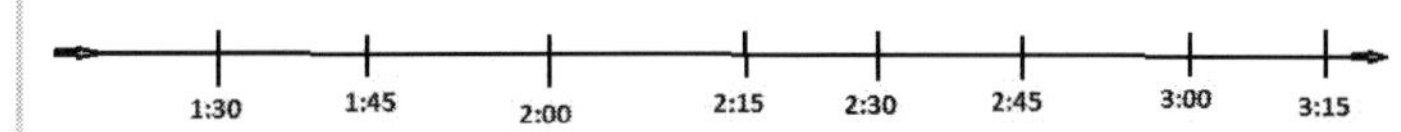

7.7) On a fishing trip your family catches 50 fish then throws 15 back. Which number lone would be best in determining the number of fish your family kept.

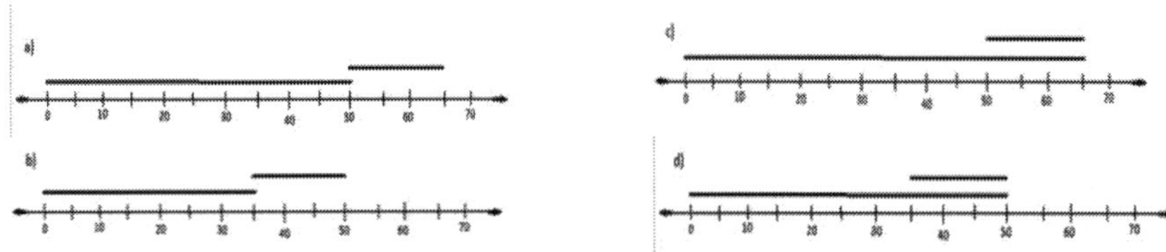

7.8) Michelle studies math from 3:15 p.m. to 6:45 p.m. Which clock shows a time that she would be studying.

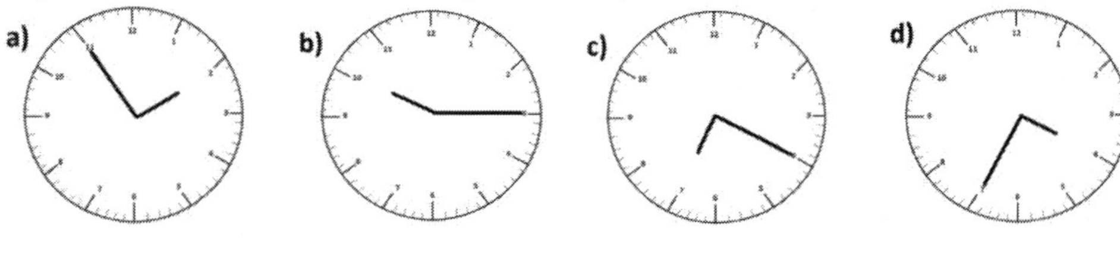

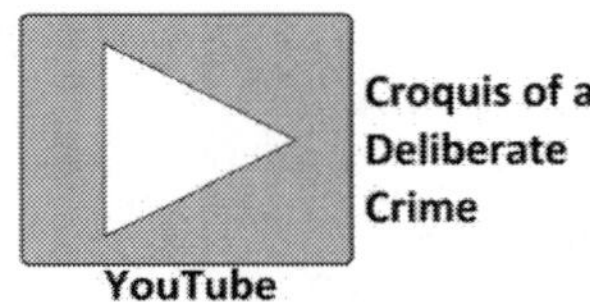

If you don't get the correct answer, and want an explanation on how to work the problem, go to YouTube and type in "MMT" then the problem number. An example would be, MMT 3.9.w12,. The video will show you how to work problem 3.9.w12.

For one on one tutoring via skype at $35.00/Hr.; contact me at marksmathtutoring@yahoo.com

7.9) The two clocks below show what time I started jogging and them stopped

Which digital clock below shows a time of day I would have been jogging

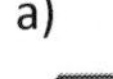

a)

b)

c)

d)

7.10) Mom put a turkey and a pie in the oven. They both went in at 4:15. The pie finished at 5:30. The turkey went an additional 45 minutes. Which clock below show the time the turkey was finished?

a)

b)

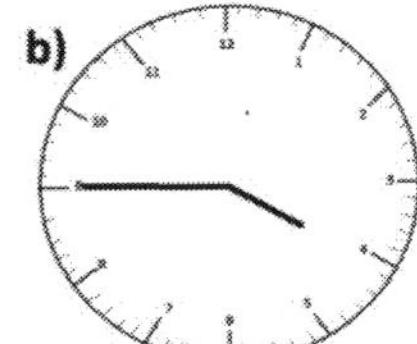

c)

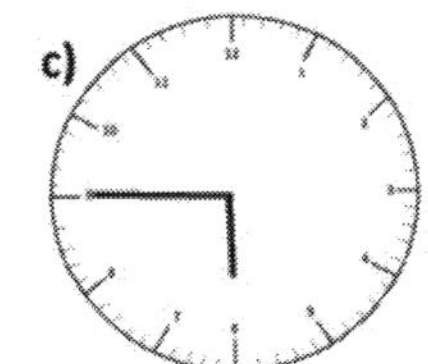

d)

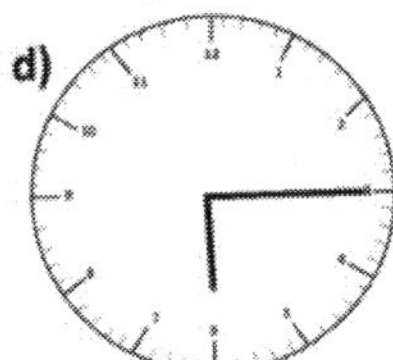

7.11) which letter best represents a point at 115?

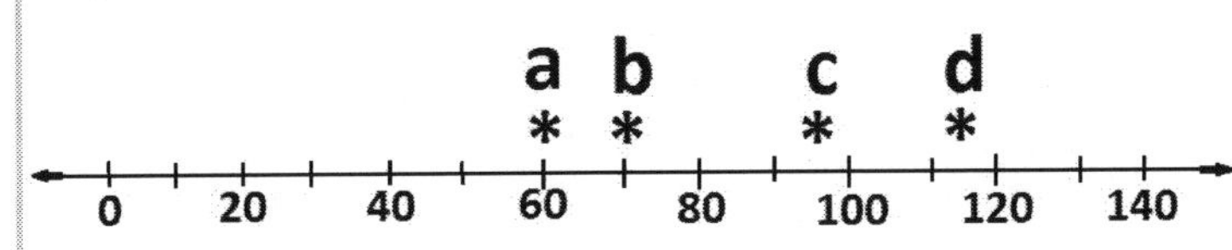

7.12) Which number best represents the dot in the plot below

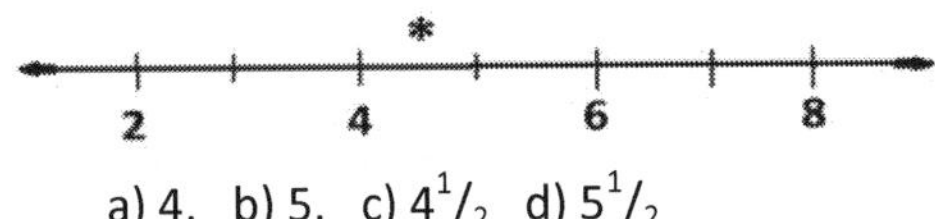

a) 4, b) 5, c) $4^1/_2$ d) $5^1/_2$

7.13) Which thermometer below show the temperature of 69°F

a)

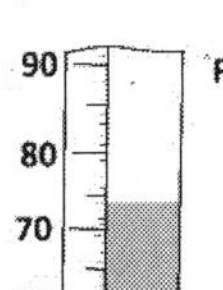

b)

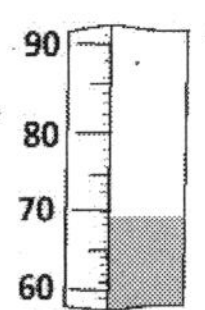

c)

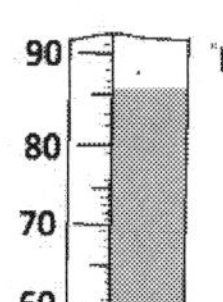

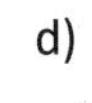

d)

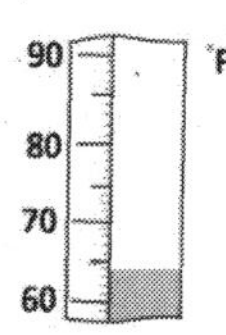

7.14) What Is the temperature shown below

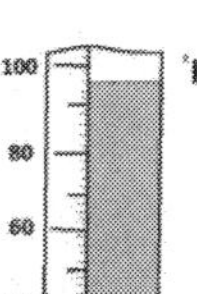

7.15) What is the temperature shown below

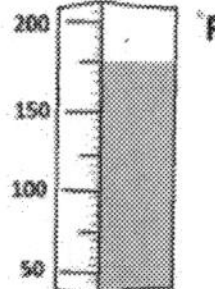

7.16) What is the temperature shown below

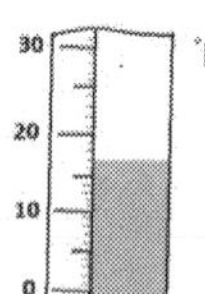

7.17) What is the temperature shown below

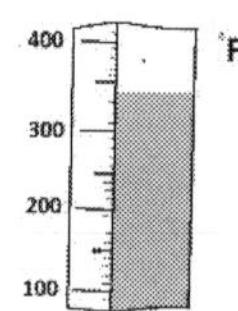

7.18) what is the value of the point in the diagram below

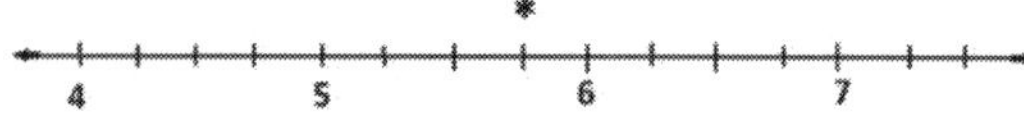

a) $6^1/_4$, b) $6^3/_4$, c) $5^3/_4$, d) $5^1/_4$

7.19) Given the number line below,

Which stament below is correct
a) The dot has a value is more than 300
b) The dot has a value of less than 200
c) The dot has a value closer to 300 than 200
d) The dot has a value closer to 200 than 300

7.20) Given the number line below

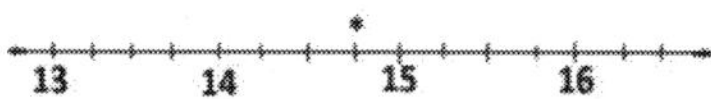

The is the correct value of the dot
a) $14^1/_4$, b) $15^3/_4$, c) $14^3/_4$, d) $15^1/_4$

7.21) Which number line best represents the value of ½ foot

a)

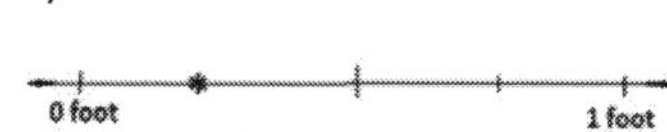

b)

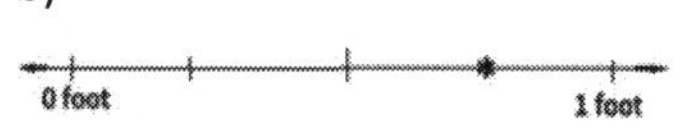

c)

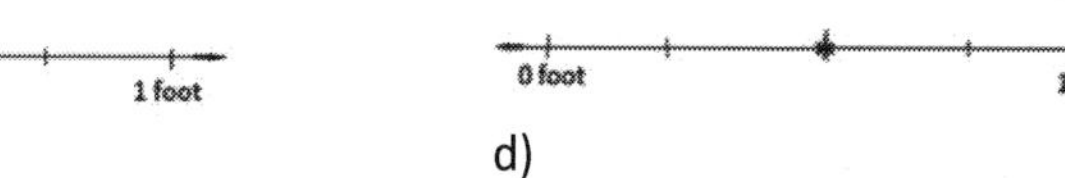

d)

7.22) What number best represents the dot on the following diagram

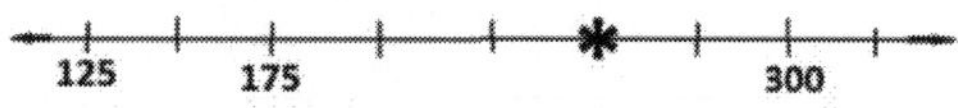

a) 275, b) 325, c) 225, d) 250

7.23) What are the vaues of the dots shown on the ruler below

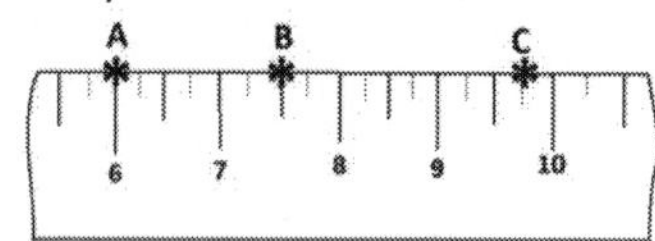

a) A=6, $B=7^1/_2$, $C=9^3/_4$
b) A=6, $B=7^1/_2$, $C=9^1/_4$
c) $A=6^1/_2$, $B=7^1/_2$, $C=9^3/_4$
d) A=6, $B=6^1/_2$, $C=9^1/_4$

7.24) The dot on the following number line represents a fraction

Which of the follwing number lines represents the same fraction

a)

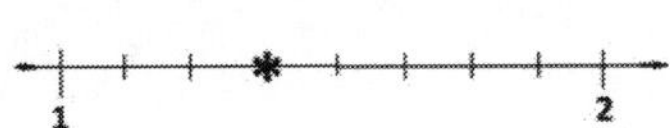

c)

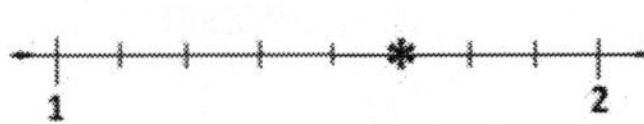

b)

d)

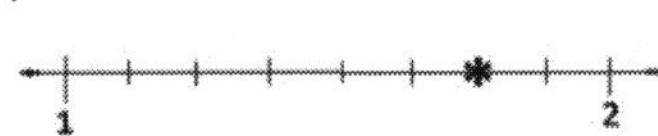

7.25) Which letter on the diagram below best represtents the number 243?

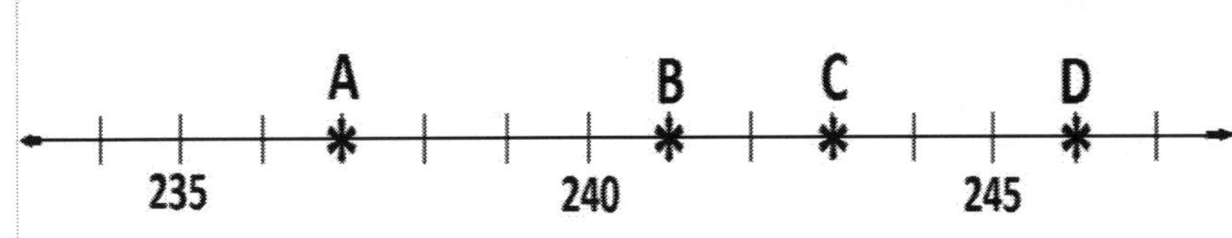

a) A
b) B
c) C
d) D

7.26) Which letter in the diagram below best represtnes the number 18 $^3/_4$

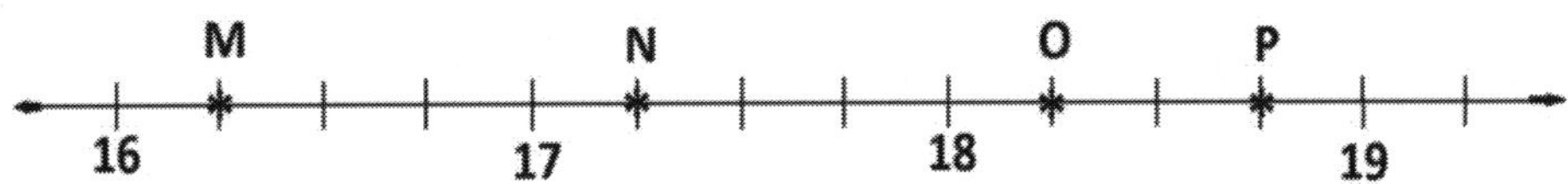

a) M
b) N
c) O
d) P

7.27) The R on the number line below is what value?

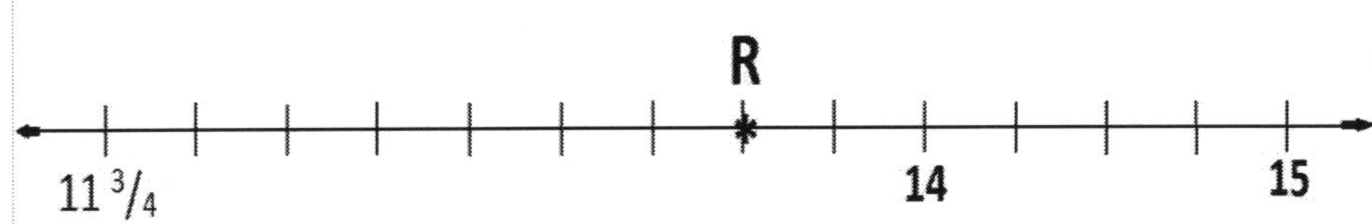

a) 13 ½
b) 12 ¾
c) 13 ¾
d) 12 ½

7.28) What iis the best value for the letter R in the number line below?

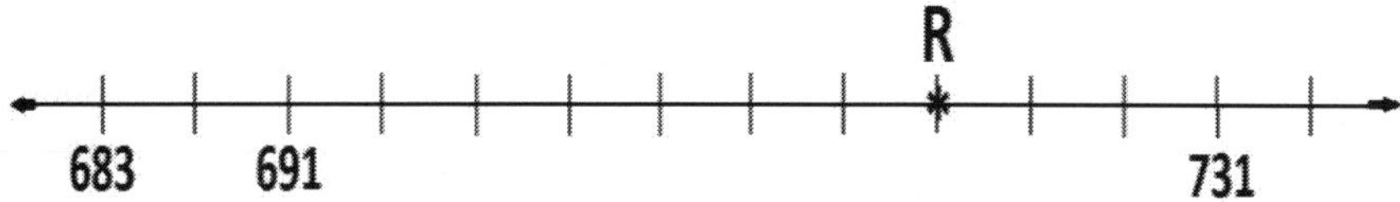

a) 719
b) 715
c) 723
d) 727

7.29) The letter U in the diagram below best representes what number?

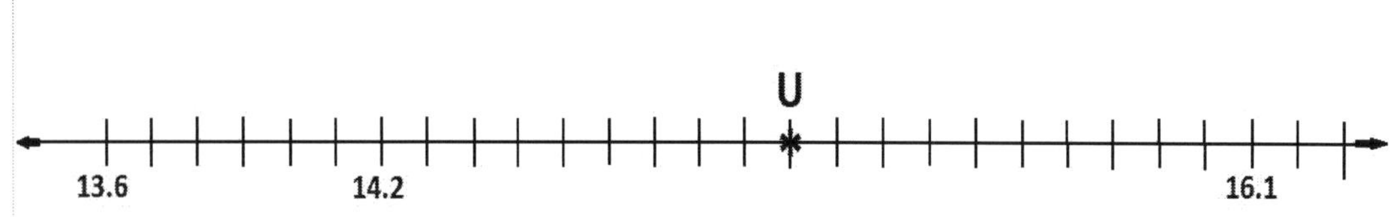

a)15.1
b) 14.9
c) 14.7
d) 15.2

7.30) The letter T in the number line below beast represents what number

a) 32
b) 32.1
c) 31.9
d) 31.8

7.31) What is the value of this angle?

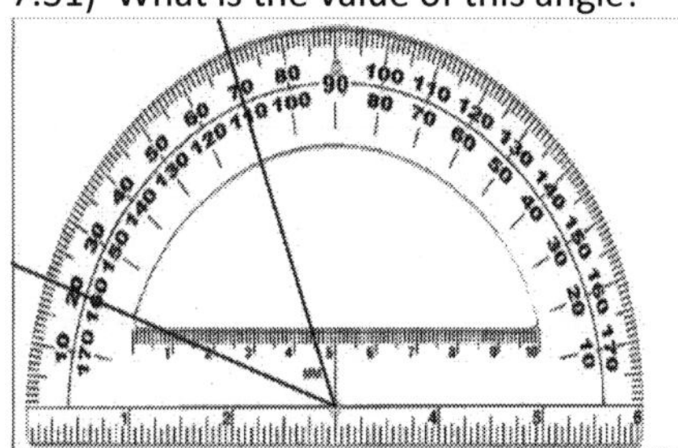

a) 70 degrees
b) 20 degrees
c) 50 degrees
d) 110 degress

7.32) What is the value of this angle?

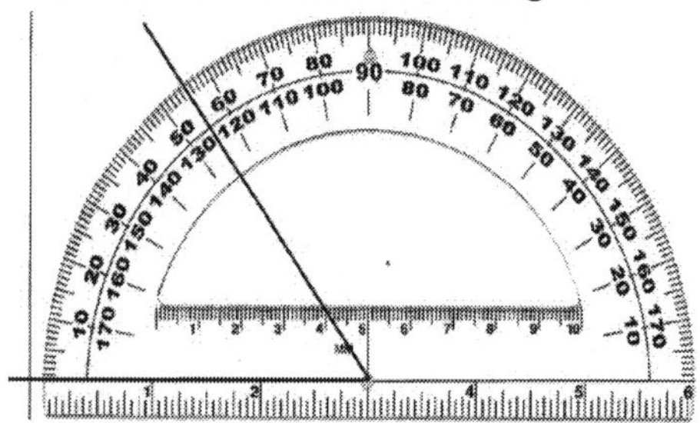

a) 55 degrees
b) 125 degrees
c) 135 degrees
d) 45 degrees

7.34) What is the value of this angle?

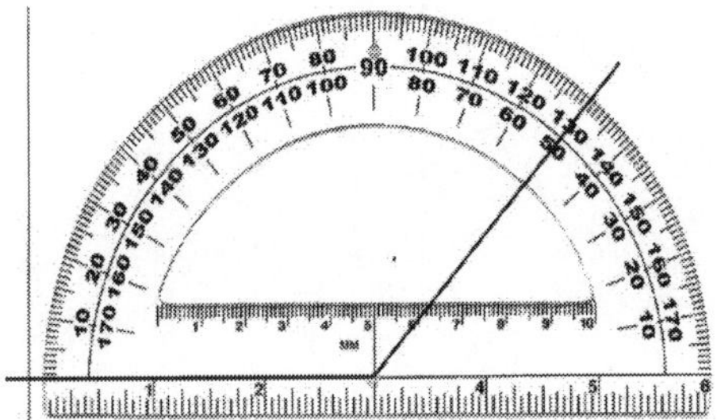

a) 50 degrees
b) 130 degrees
c) 45 degrees
d) 135 degress

7.35) What is the value of this angle?

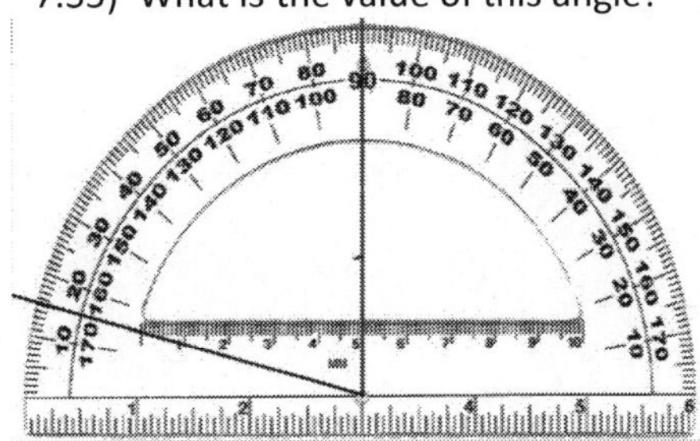

a) 75 degrees
b) 165 degrees
c) 95 degrees
d) 40 degrees

7.36) What is the value of this angle?

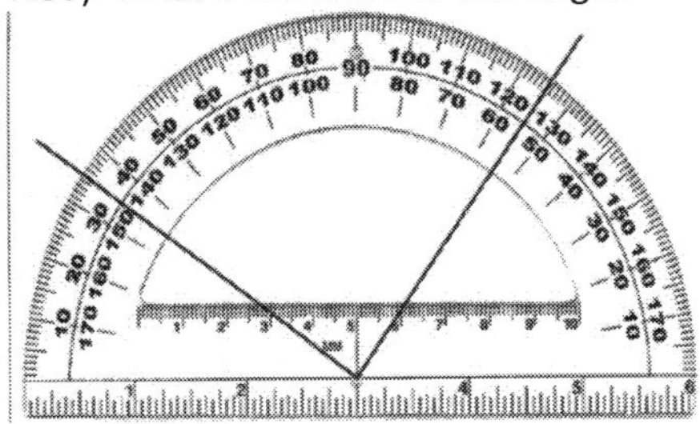

a) 90 degrees
b) 125 degrees
c) 135 degrees
d) 190 degress

7.37) What is the value of this angle?

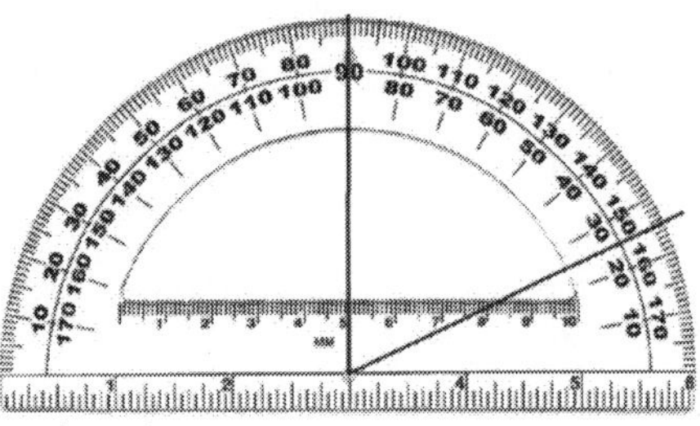

a) 65 degrees
b) 155 degrees
c) 90 degrees
d) 25 degrees

7.38) What is the value of this angle?

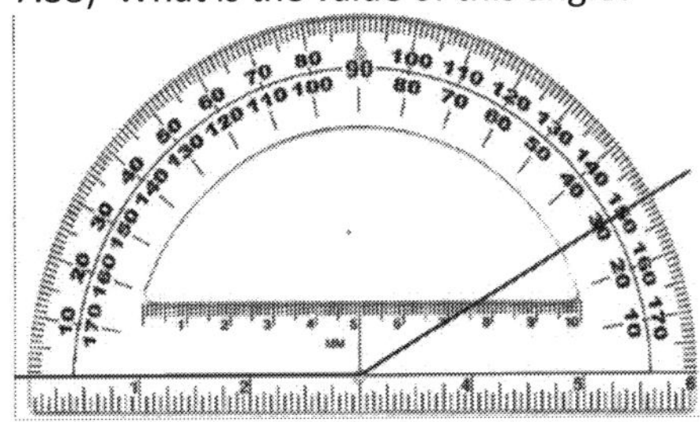

a) 0 degrees
b) 30 degrees
c) 130 degrees
d) 150 degress

7.39) What is the value of this angle?

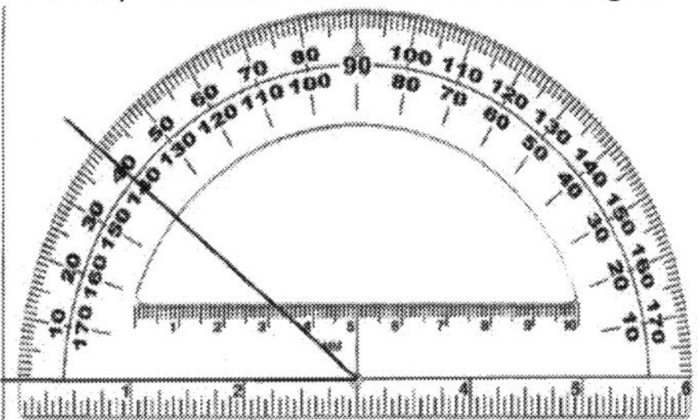

a) 65 degrees
b) 0 degrees
c) 40 degrees
d) 140 degrees

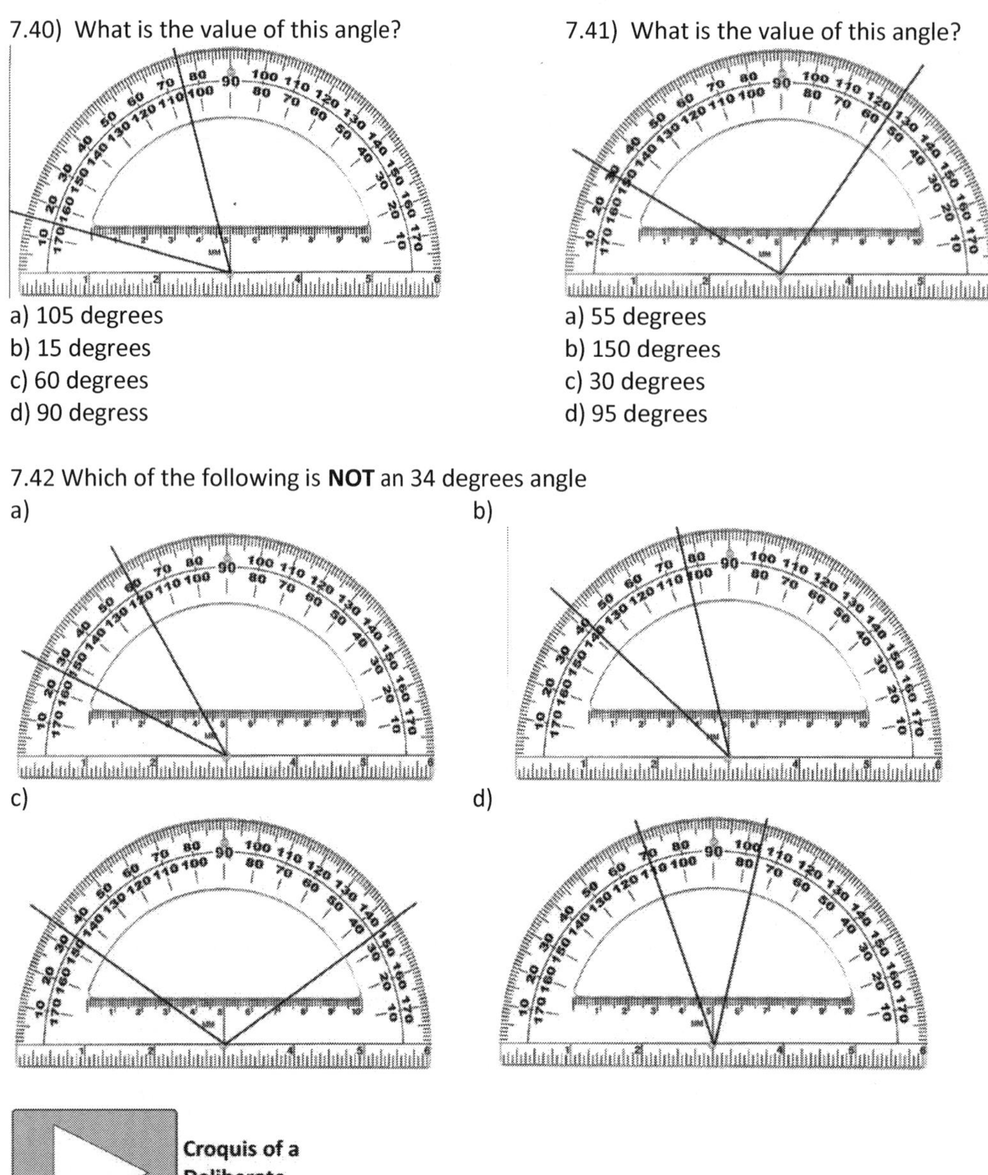

7.40) What is the value of this angle?

a) 105 degrees
b) 15 degrees
c) 60 degrees
d) 90 degress

7.41) What is the value of this angle?

a) 55 degrees
b) 150 degrees
c) 30 degrees
d) 95 degrees

7.42 Which of the following is **NOT** an 34 degrees angle

a)

b)

c)

d)

If you don't get the correct answer, and want an explanation on how to work the problem, go to YouTube and type in "MMT" then the problem number. An example would be, MMT 3.9.w12,. The video will show you how to work problem 3.9.w12.

For one on one tutoring via skype at $35.00/Hr.; contact me at marksmathtutoring@yahoo.com

7.43) 7.42 Which of the following is **NOT** an 67 degrees angle

a)

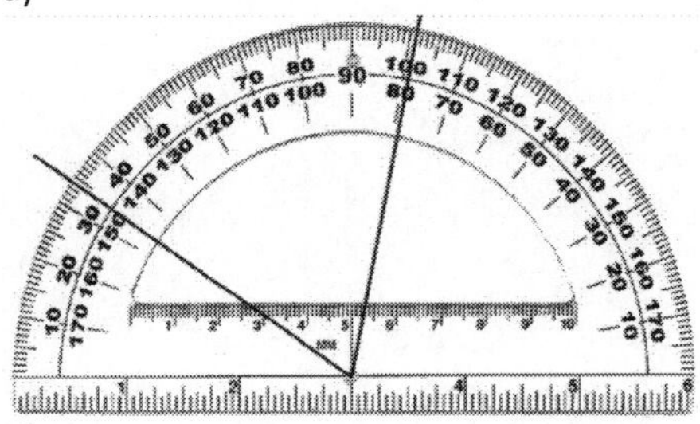

c)

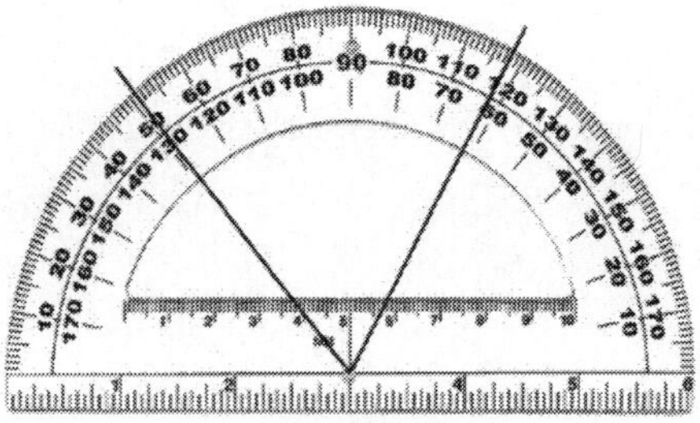

b)

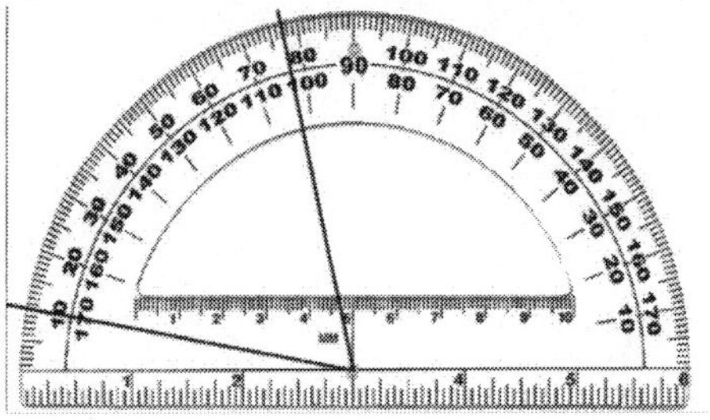

d)

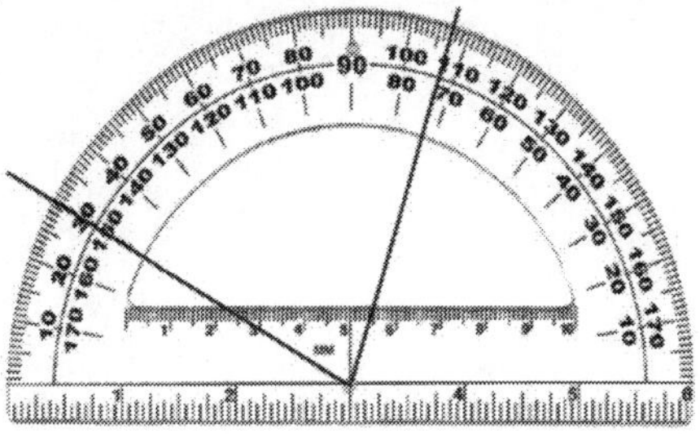

7.44) Use a ruler, what is the perimiter of this draqwing to ½ inch

7.45) Use a ruler to measure the perimiters of the two following shapes. What is the difference in their perimiters to ½ inch?

7.46) What is the temp shown below?

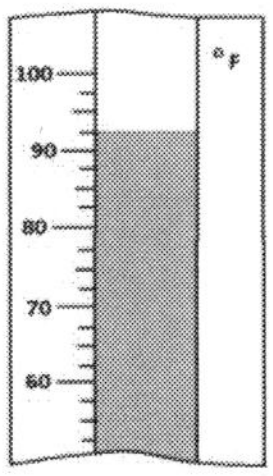

7.47) What is the temp shown below?

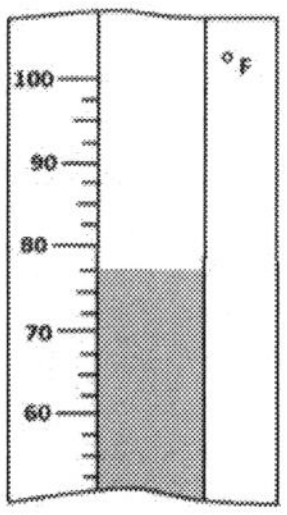

7.48) Use a ruler. What is the length on the line drawn below in centimeters to ½ centimeter?

7.49) Use a ruler. What is the length on the line drawn below in centimeters to ½ centimeter?

7.50) Use a ruler. What is the length on the line drawn below in centimeters to ½ centimeter?

7.51) If I start sleeping when the clock reads as below

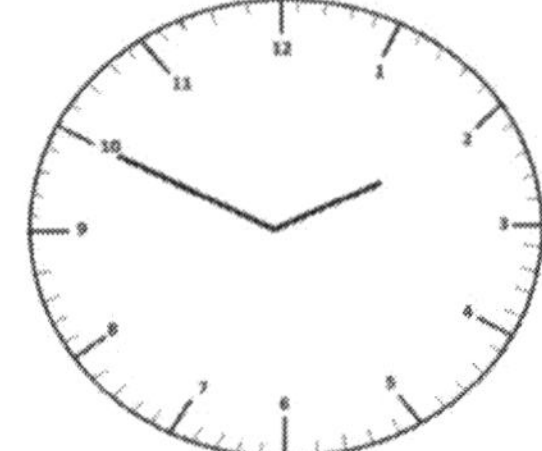

If I want to sleep for 1 hour and 45 minutes what time should I wake up

7.52) I I start walking at the following time

If I want to walk for 2 hours and 35 minutes what time will I stop.

7.53) If I want to stop reading that the time shown below

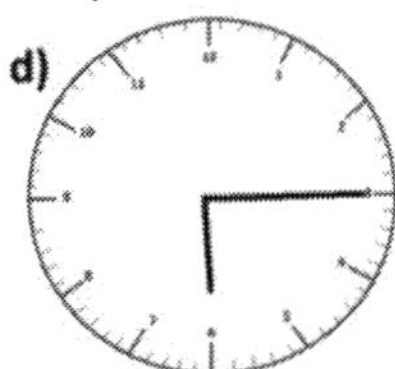

If I want to read for 1 hour and 50 minutes what time should I start

7.54) If I finish fishing at the time shown below

If I want to fish for 2 hours and 50 minutes what time should I start

7.55) If I start cleaning at the time shown below.

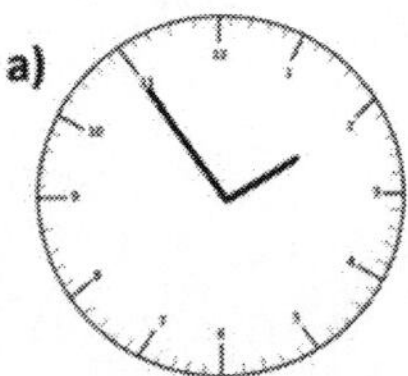

If I want to clean house for 3 hours and 30 minutes, what time will I fininsh

7.56) If I want to do something and start at the time shown below

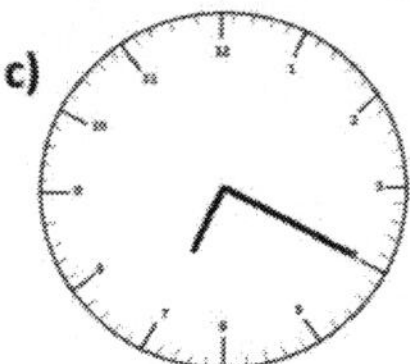

If I do it for 2 hours and 45 minutes what time will I finish

7.57) Given the drawing below what is the coordinates of the center

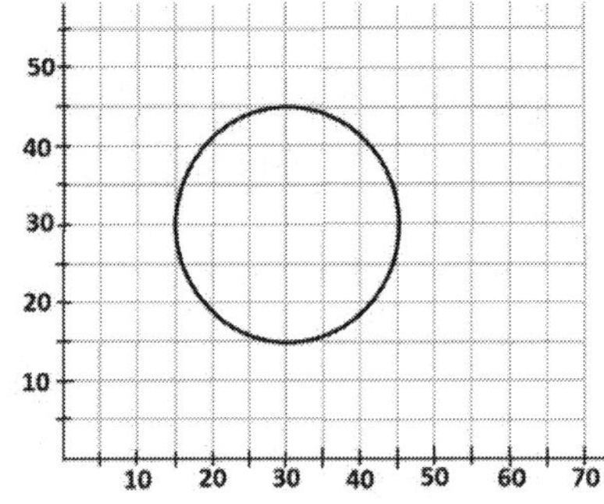

7.58) Given the graph below

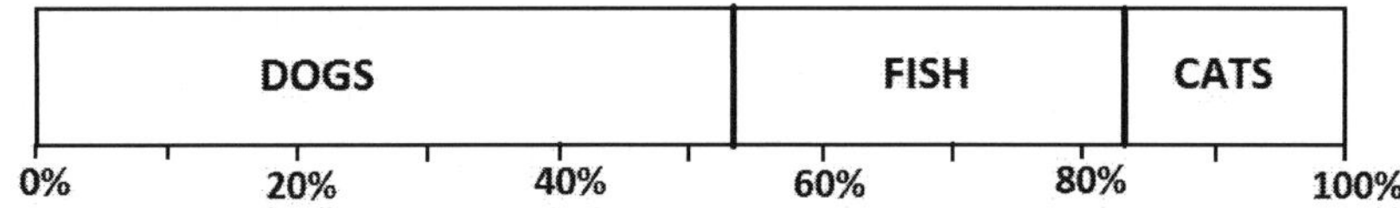

Which of ther folwwing table could detail the same data

A)

ANIMAL	NUMBER OF PETS
DOGS	27
FISH	30
CATS	8

B)

ANIMAL	NUMBER OF PETS
DOGS	17
FISH	15
CATS	28

C)

ANIMAL	NUMBER OF PETS
DOGS	27
FISH	15
CATS	8

D)

ANIMAL	NUMBER OF PETS
DOGS	37
FISH	15
CATS	8

7.59) If I plot the follwowing loints on the line graph below,

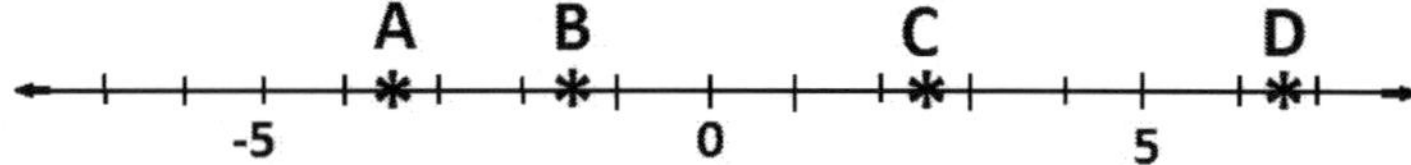

which points is not plotted corretly
A) A= -7/2
B) B= -6/4
C) C= 3/2
D) D= 26/4

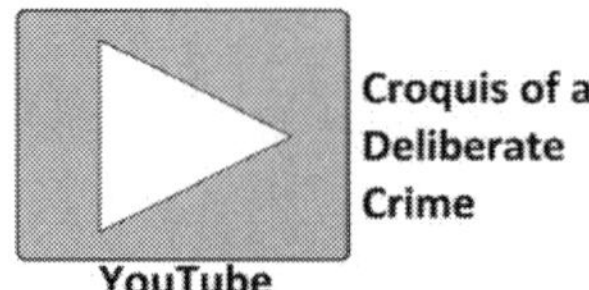

If you don't get the correct answer, and want an explanation on how to work the problem, go to YouTube and type in "MMT" then the problem number. An example would be, MMT 3.9.w12,. The video will show you how to work problem 3.9.w12.

For one on one tutoring via skype at $35.00/Hr.; contact me at marksmathtutoring@yahoo.com

8.0 STATS

8.1) Roger has marbles in a bag, with the following colors and quantities.

COLOR	QUANTITY
Red	10
Blue	15
Green	10
White	5
Brown	20

If Roger picks a marble at random what are the odds of it being a Red one
a) 10 in 60, b) 10 in 50, c) 50 in 60, d) 15 in 60

8.2) Given the diagram below

□ □ □ □ ○
□ □ □ □ ○

If I pick a shape at random without looking what are the odds it will be a square
a) 8 out of 10, b) 2 out of 10, c) 3 out of 5, d) 2 out of 5

8.3) Given the table below describing the types of cookies in a box

COOKIE TYPE	QUANTITY
Sugar	17
Oatmeal	15
Chocolate	20
Mint	17
Cinnamon	13

If I pick a cookie at random without looking what two types of cookies will have the same odds of being picked?

8.4) Pam has 18 brown marbles, 12 Green marbles, and 21 white marbles in a bag. If she chooses one at random without looking which statement below is true?
a) She will pick a brown one for sure
b) She is less likely to pick a Green one than a Brown
c) She is more likely to pick a Brown than a White
d) It is impossible to pick a Green marble

8.5) If I have 10 chocolate and 20 vanilla cupcakes in a box If I pick one at random what are the odds of it being chocolate

8.6) If I pick a day of the week at random, what are the odds it will be a weekend?

8.7)If I have 4 green, 6 brown, and 2 white marbles in a bag. I choose one without looking, what are the odds of it being a brown.

8.8) There are 56 girls and 49 boys in school. One has a secret. What are the odds it is a boy

8.9) There are 24 dogs in your neighborhood. One of them gets into the trash. What are the odds it is your dog.

8.10) If the lake has 112 bass, and 45 catfish what are the odds of catching a bass.

8.11) If there are 6 cokes and 8 sprits in the cooler. I pick one at random what are the odds of it being a coke.

8.12) If you made a 100% on a test with 12 questions, and your parents pick one problems to show them you can do it, what are the odds it will be one you got correct.

8.13) If your brother had two friends over to play baseball. One of them threw the ball and broke a window. What are the odds it was your brother

8.14) What are the odds the days you read this question is a weekday

8.15) Given the graph below what is the mean, median, and mode

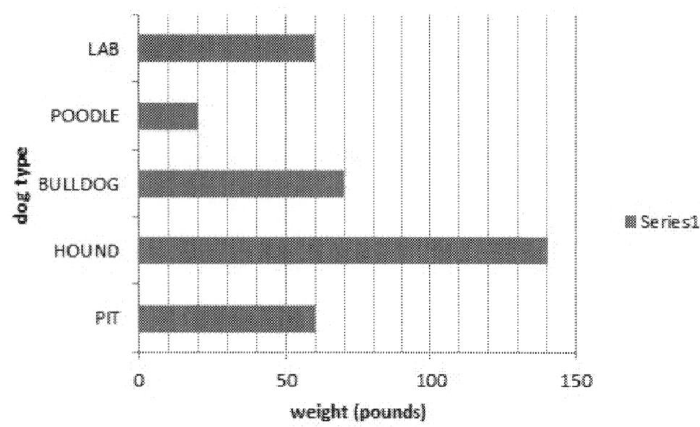

8.16) Given the table below what is the mean, median, and mode

SPORT	NUMBER
SOCCER	35
FOOTBALL	17
BASEBALL	176
BASKETBALL	125

8.17) Given the graph below what is the mean, median, mode

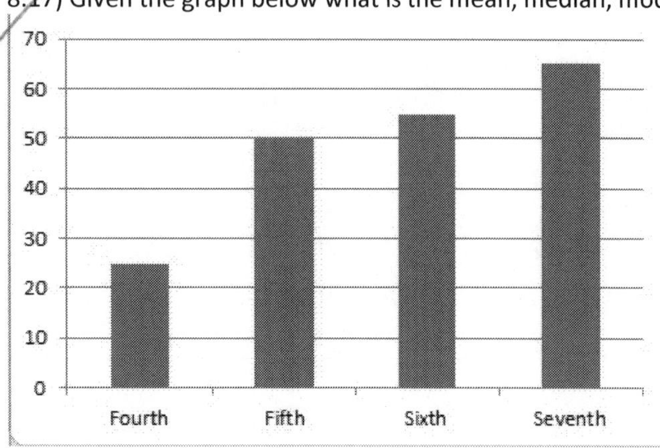

8.18) Given the table below what is the mean, median, and mode

NAMES	NUMBERS
Mike	35
James	25
John	15
Elmer	40

8.19) Given the graph below what is the mean, median, and mode

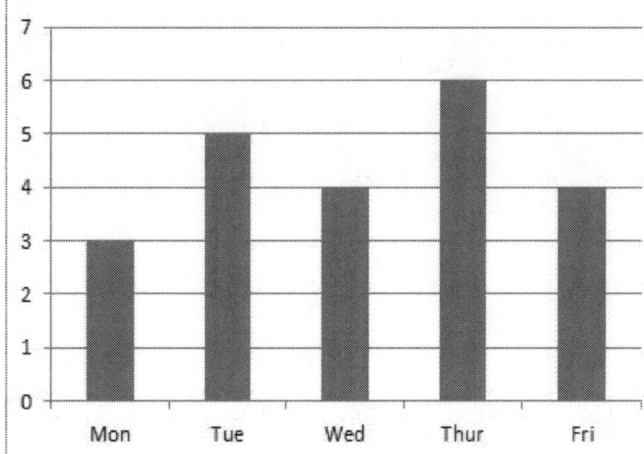

8.20) Given the graph below what is the mean, median, mode

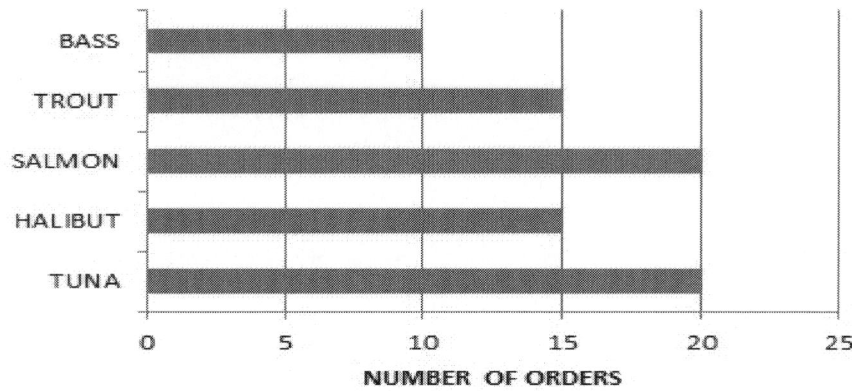

8.21) Given the graph below what is the mean, median, mode

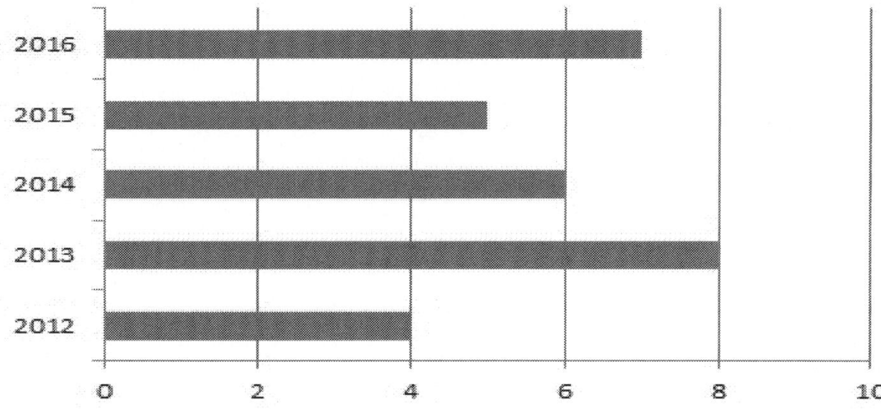

If you don't get the correct answer, and want an explanation on how to work the problem, go to YouTube and type in "MMT" then the problem number. An example would be, MMT 3.9.w12,. The video will show you how to work problem 3.9.w12.

8.22) Given the graph below what is the mean, median, mode

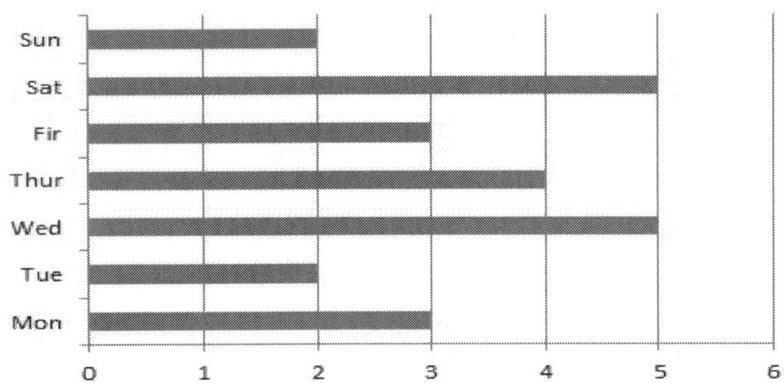

8.23) Given the graph below what is the mean, median, and mode of the dogs

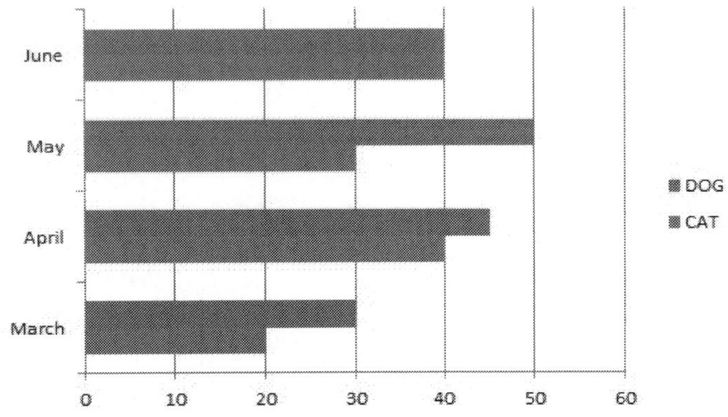

8.24) Given the graph below what is the mean, median, and mode of mowing

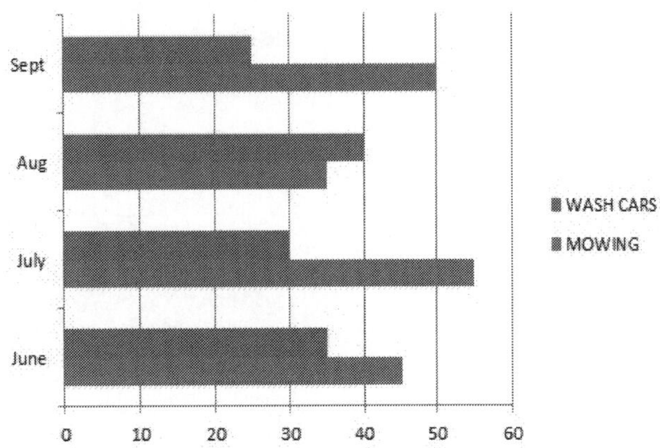

8.25)Given the following numbers

{ 12, 5, 8, 7, 10, 14, 8, 22}

What is the mean, median, and mode

8.26) Given the following numbers

{ 55, 89, 36, 47, 78, 45, 36, 67, 91, 23}

What is the mean, median, mode

8.27) Given the graph below

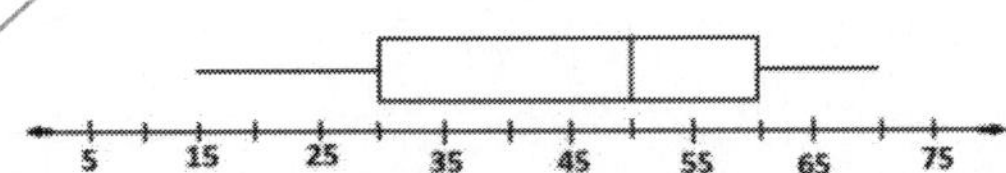

Which of the following statements is true
A) Half the numbers are above 50
B) All numbers are below 60
C) The mean is 50
D) The median is 50

8.28) Given the data below
{235, 356, 142, 568}
What is the range

8.29) Given the graph below

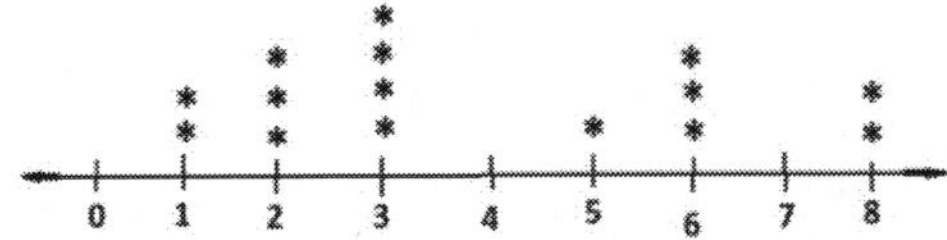

Which statement below is true
A)The median is 3 and the interquartile range is 4
B) The median is 4 and the interquartile range is 3
C) The median is 3 and the interquartile range is 7
D) The median is 4 and the interquartile range is 7

8.30) Given the graph below

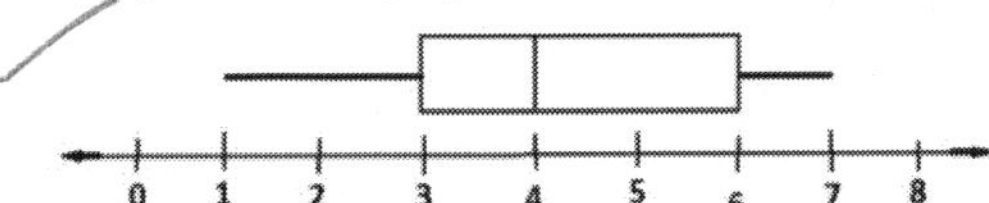

Which of the following is true
A) The mode is 4
B) The smallest number in the data is 3
C) The mean is 4
D) All numbers were less than 7

8.31) What is the range of the following numbers
{ 3,5,7,3,4,9,7,10}

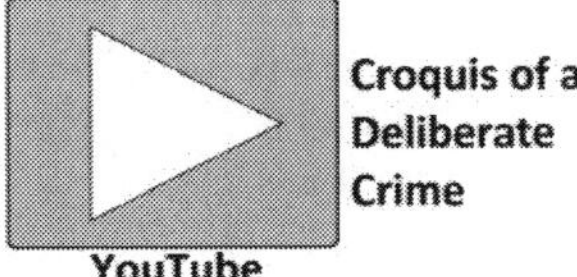

For one on one tutoring via skype at $35.00/Hr.; contact me at marksmathtutoring@yahoo.com

8.32) Given the diagram below

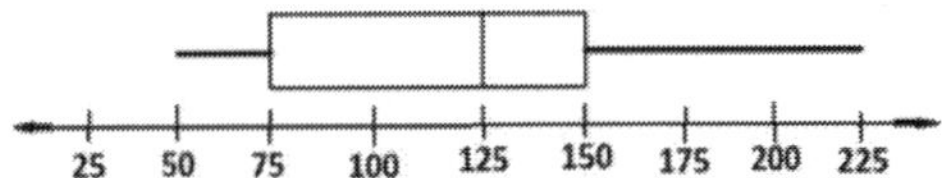

Which of the following statements is **NOT** true
A) The mean is 125
B) Largest value in the data was 225
C) Ranger is 200
D) Interquartile range is 75

8.33) Given the steam leaf diagram below

STEAM	LEAF
1	0, 1, 3, 4, 5
2	2, 4, 6
3	3, 5
4	1, 1, 7

2|5 MEANS 25

Which of the following statements is **NOT** true
A) The range is 37
B) The median is 24
C) The mean is 23.5
D) Interquartile range is 24.5

8.39) What is the range of the following data
{ 235, 117, 342, 431, 257, 489}

8.40) Which of the following is the best measure of the attendance during a performance
A) Mean and Mode
B) Median and Mode
C) Mean and Median
D) Ranger and Median

8.41) If I roll two dice, one white and the other red, what are the odds of white cube showing a odd number and the red showing a number greater than 3

8.42) Given a set of baseball score which of the following best describes the difference between the high and low
A) Mean
B)Median
C)Mode
D)Range

8.43)) If I roll two dice, one white and the other red, what are the odds of white cube showing a number greater than 4 and the red showing a number greater than 2

8.44) If I roll two dice, one white and the other red, what are the odds of white cube showing a number greater than 4 or the red showing a number greater than 2

8.45) If I flip penny and a nickel what are the odds that both coins will show heads

8.46) If I flip penny and a nickel what are the odds that one or the other coin will show heads

8.47) I recorded the number of fish I caught last summer in the table below

FISH	NUMBER
Bass	127
Tuna	35
Flounder	228
Trout	87
Salmon	69

What is the mean of these data points

8.48) I recorded the largest crowds at a baseball game for each month. If I report the most common of these numbers which one the following should I use.
A) Mean it is the average
B) Ranger it gives the differences
C) Mode it is the number that appears most often
D) Median it is the one data point in the middle

8.49) Given the following numbers {3,5,8,11,14,17,21,22,28} What is the difference between the median and the mean

8.50) If I record the attendance at a baseball game which of the following would be best to determine the attendance at the next game.
A) Mode
B)Median
C)Range
D)Mean

8.51) Given a list of number representing attendance at a game which set would best describe the attendance levels
A) Mean and Median
B) Mean and Range
C) Mode and Range
D) Mode and Median

8.52) If there are seven numbers in asset organized from smallest to largest. Which number is in the middle of this set.
A) Mean
B) Mode
C) Median
D) Range

8.53) Given the two graphs below

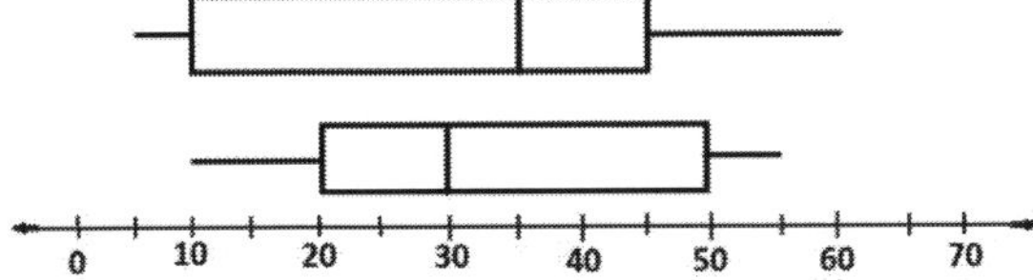

Which of the following is true
A) The difference in the Ranges is 10
B) The difference in the Medians is 5
C) The difference in the Mean is 5
D) They both have a Median between 30 and 35

8.54) I interview 2 classes of 35 kids each. In each class 3 said they don't like to fish. Given this information which of the following is a reasonable conclusion.
A) If I interview 5 classes a total of 6 kids will say they don't like to fish
B) The mean of kids that don't like to fish per class is 3
C) The Range of kids that don't like to fish is 3
D) There is no reasonable conclusion to be drawn from this data

8.55) If I have a bag of marble with the following numbers of each color.
3 brown
4 white
2 green
4 black
5 blue
2 red
If I randomly pull a marble 100 times, one at a time and replace it, how many times will I get a green or red marble.
A) 20
B) 30
C) 40
D) 50

8.56) If I spinner the arrow drawn below what are the odds of getting a odd number

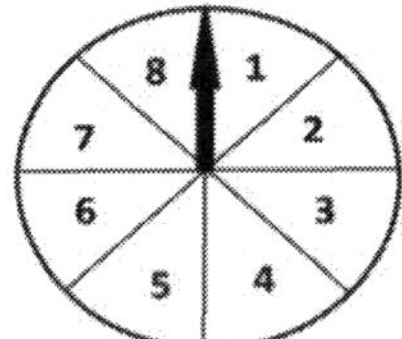

8.57)My local library has the following number of books in each category shown

CATEGORY	NUMBER
History	24
Fiction	16
Western	30
Mystery	26
Romance	4

If I choose one book at random what are the odds it will be a Western or a Mystery

8.58)Given the spinner drawn below

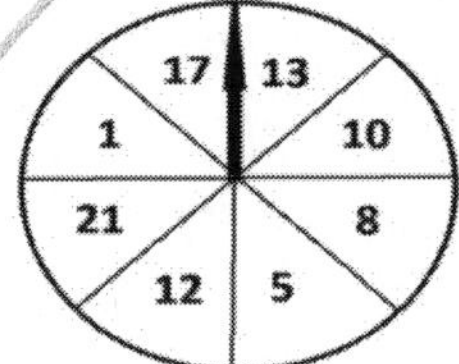

If I spin the arrow 16 times how many times will I get an even number

For one on one tutoring via skype at $35.00/Hr.; contact me at marksmathtutoring@yahoo.com

8.59) Given the graph below

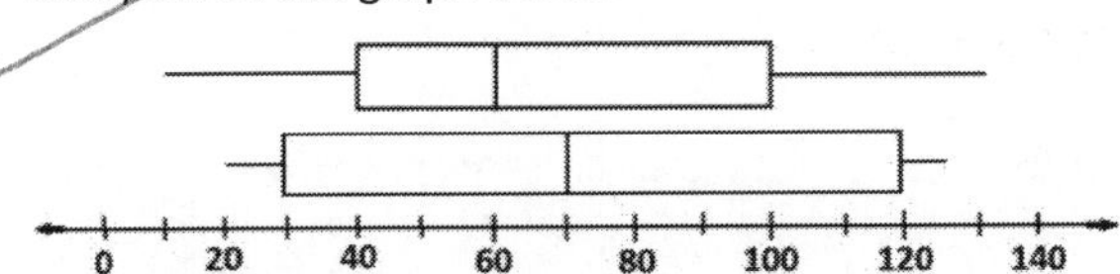

Which of the following statements is true
A) They both have about the same Range
B) They have different Medians
C) The difference in the Means is 10
D) The difference in the ranges is 40

8.60) I am having a party and will give each quest a cupcake. I have 6 red for every 9 white ones. If I have 165 quests how many will receive a white one

8.61) Given the graph below

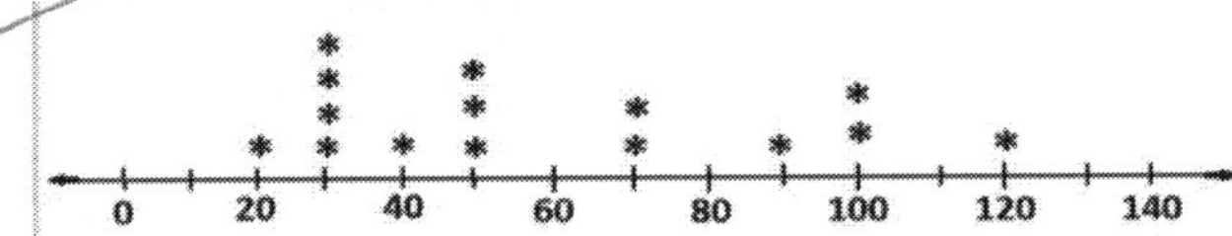

Which of the following statements is **NOT** true
A) The Range is 100
B) The mean is 58.7
C) The median is 40
D) The Mode is 30

8.62) If you throw a die numbered 1 thru 6 and flip a coin. What are the odds you will get a odd number on the die and a heads on the coin

8.63) If I have a bag of jellybeans. 6 are blue and 4 green. What are the odds of picking two blues in a row if I replace the first one after removing it.

8.64) If I have two bags of jellybeans. The first has 4 green and 5 whites. The second has 3 blacks and 4 reds. If I select one jellybean from each bag at random what are the odds of getting a green from the first and a red from the second.

8.65) If my bag of jellybeans has 2 red and 3 green, what are the odds of selecting a red twice in a row if I replace the bean after the first selection

8.66) Given the graphs below of grade two different classes made on a math test

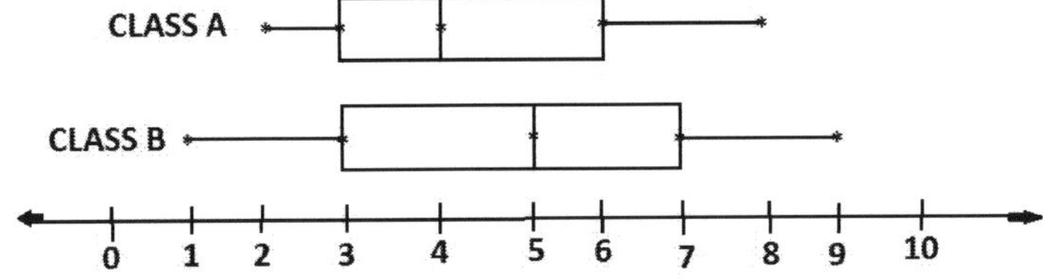

Which of the following conclusion is correct
A) They both have the same interquartile range
B) They both have the same median
C) They both have the same 1st interquartile
D) They both have the same mean

8.67) If the bag of jellybeans has 4 red and 6 green what are the odds of picking a green twice if I DON'T replace the bean after the first selection

8.68) If I use the spinner shown below and spin twice. What are the odds of getting a white section twice in a row

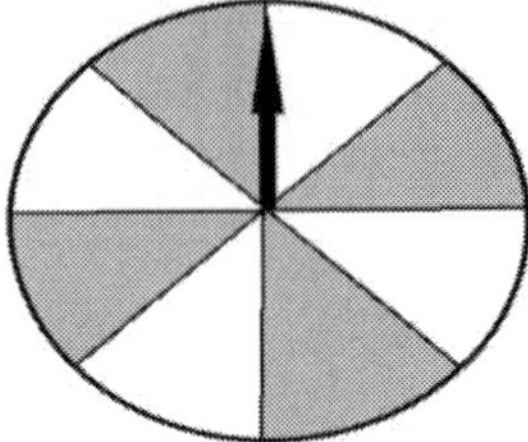

8.69) Given the following numbers { 3,5,7,4,6} what is the mean absolute deviation

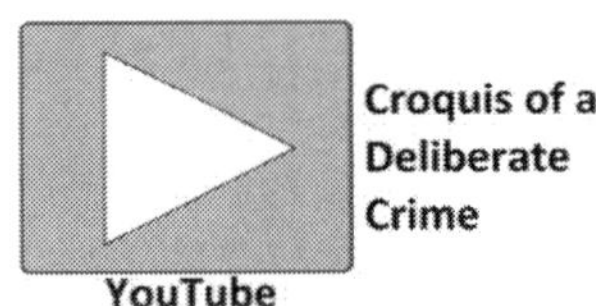

If you don't get the correct answer, and want an explanation on how to work the problem, go to YouTube and type in "MMT" then the problem number. An example would be, MMT 3.9.w12,. The video will show you how to work problem 3.9.w12.

For one on one tutoring via skype at $35.00/Hr.; contact me at marksmathtutoring@yahoo.com

9 ORDER OF OPERATIONS

9.1.1) 23x2+4
9.1.2) 16x3-6
9.1.3) 3x5x4
9.1.4) 3-6x7
9.1.5) 16+4÷2
9.1.6) 35÷7-2
9.1.7) 24x2-6
9.1.8) 13+6x2
9.1.9) 10÷4÷2
9.1.10) 12x3-6
9.1.11) 35-5÷5
9.1.12) 2+14÷7
9.1.13) 2-5x6
9.1.14) 3+4x3
9.1.15) 8÷2+6
9.1.16) 9÷3+3
9.1.17) 4+8÷4
9.1.18) 3x4÷2
9.1.19) 2x4x5
9.1.20) 21x3-6

9.1.21) 21+(4x6)
9.1.22) (2+3)x6
9.1.23) 5x(3+6)
9.1.24) 5÷(2+8)
9.1.25) (14x2)-6
9.1.26) (3+6)÷3
9.1.27) (12÷4)+4
9.1.28) (10x4)+6
9.1.29) 4+(2x4)
9.1.30) (3+6)x3
9.1.31) (10÷2)÷5
9.1.32) (12+3)÷5
9.1.33) (4x3)x2
9.1.34) (6÷2)÷3
9.1.35) (41-35)x2
9.1.36) (2x67)-4

9.1.37) 2(3)-3(1)
9.1.38) 3(4)+2(4)
9.1.39) 4(2)-3(5)
9.1.40) 5(2)-3(4)
9.1.41) 8(3)+3(5)
9.1.42) 2(7)-3(7)
9.1.43) 1(9)-0(6)
9.1.44) 2(5)+3(7)
9.1.45) 4(6)+5(2)
9.1.46) 5(1)-5(2)
9.1.47) 6(3)+2(4)
9.1.48) 5(2)-3(2)
9.1.49) 3x2+3x4
9.1.50) 6x2-4x5
9.1.51) 8÷2-6x3
9.1.52) 12÷3+3x4
9.1.53) 6x2+3x6
9.1.54) 2x5+4x7
9.1.55) 3x5-15÷3
9.1.56) 21÷3-4x2
9.1.57) 10x3-6x7
9.1.58) 35÷5+2x4
9.1.59) 12x3-2x6
9.1.60) 60÷6+2÷1

9.1.61)[2x(3+2)]-4
9.1.62) 4+[(5+2)x3]
9.1.63) 4-[(1x2)+3]
9.1.64) 15÷[(3x4)-7]
9.1.65) [3x(3+3)]+5
9.1.66) [3x(4+5)]-4
9.1.67) [(2+3)x2]÷5
9.1.68) [3x(7+3)]+3
9.1.69) [4x(3-2)]-11
9.1.70) 7÷[(2x3)+1]
9.1.71) [3x(3+6)]-5
9.1.72) [(4+4)x2]÷8
9.1.73) 10÷[(2x3)-1]
9.1.74) 2-[(3x2)+7]
9.1.75) 9-[(2x3)+3]
9.1.76) [2x(8+7)]-6
9.1.77) [10x(6+1)]-8
9.1.78) [3x(13+12)]-10
9.1.79) [2x(3-4)]-6
9.1.80) [(1+3)÷2]÷2

9.1.81) [2(4)-3(6)]+4
9.1.82) [4(1)+2(4)]-5
9.1.83) [4(1)-5(3)]+3
9.1.84) 3+[3(4)-2(6)]
9.1.85) [3(5)-2(8)]+10
9.1.86) [(4+1)x(2+3)]÷5
9.1.87) [(2+4)÷(2+1)]+3
9.1.88) [5(2)+3(4)]÷11
9.1.89) 5-[2(4)+3(5)]
9.1.90) [3(5)-4(4)]X5
9.1.91) 20÷[2(3)-1(1)]
9.1.92) 3X[2(3)-3(4)]
9.1.93) 5÷[5(4)÷2(2)]
9.1.94) 6X[4(5)-6(5)]
9.1.95) [2(3)+3(6)]+4
9.1.96) 10X2(3+5)

9.1.97) (1235-438+124÷2)X3
9.1.98) 15-(16+6÷3)
9.1.99) $\frac{12-(18X6)}{3}$
9.1.100) 180-4(18+7)-12
9.1.101) 3(120÷2+30)-10
9.1.102) 65-2X6+16÷4=
9.1.103) Which one of the following two equations are equal
A) (4+Y)X2, 4+(YX2)
B) (20÷Y)+10, 10+(20÷Y)
C) 5-(YX3), (YX3)-5
D) 10÷(Y+4), (10÷Y)+4

9.1.104) (-2)(8)+(-9÷3)

9.1.105) which two expressions are equivalent
A) 4(T+3), and 4T+12
B) Tx(8+9), and (Tx8)+9
C) T÷ (3+5), and (T÷3)+5
D) (2+4)xT, and 2+(4xT)

9.1.106) What is the value of the following expression
84-3X6+12÷4
9.1.107) Which two of the following expression are the same
A) 6+(2xY), and (6+2)xY
B) (12÷y)+4, and (y÷12)+4
C) 8-(yx2), and 8-(2xY)
D) 10-(2÷Y), and (10-2)÷Y

9.1.108) Which expression below is the same as (40+6)÷20
A) 46÷2x5x4
B) 46÷(5x4)
C) (46÷2)x5x4
D) 46÷2x(5x4)

9.1.109) Which expression is equivalent to 36xY
A) (30xY)+(6xY)
B) (30xY)+6
C) (30x6)+Y
D) Y+30x6

9.2.1) What is the result of the following expression
$32+2X3^2=$
9.2.2) What is the value of $9+(3+4)^2$

If you don't get the correct answer, and want an explanation on how to work the problem, go to YouTube and type in "MMT" then the problem number. An example would be, MMT 3.9.w12,. The video will show you how to work problem 3.9.w12.

For one on one tutoring via skype at $35.00/Hr.; contact me at marksmathtutoring@yahoo.com

10 ALGEBRA

10.1.1) X+5=3 10.1.2) X-6=4 10.1.3) X+4=8 10.1.4) X-6=12 10.1.5)X+4=-12
10.1.6)X-3=-8 10.1.7)X+6=5 10.1.8)X+9=-1 10.1.9)X+8=6 10.1.10)X+4=-8
10.1.11)X+11=5 10.1.12)X-7=-8 10.1.13)X-15=10 10.1.14)X-7=-4
10.1.15)X-9=-7 10.1.16)X-3=-12 10.1.17) X-3=10 10.1.18)X+13=3
10.1.19)X+4=5 10.1.20)X+8=-10 10.1.21)X-12=-4 10.1.22)X+6=-9
10.1.23)X-4=6 10.1.24)X+7=7

10.1.25)2X+2=1 10.1.26)5X+10=3 10.1.27)-7X-3=7 10.1.28)9X+6=-4
10.1.29)-4X-11=6 10.1.30)6X+12=10 10.1.31)4X-5=-7 10.1.32)-9X-13=2
10.1.33)3X+4=-15 10.1.34)10X+14=18 10.1.35)2X-7=-5 10.1.36)10X-8=-4
10.1.37)-8X-6=4 10.1.38)-15X+15=1 10.1.39)14X-20=-7 10.1.40)-4X-4=8
10.1.41)-9X+5=-2 10.1.42)-12X-2=11 10.1.43)3X-12=-3 10.1.44)-6X+9=4
10.1.45)-3X+8=1 10.1.46)-5X-9=-2 10.1.47)8X-10=4 10.1.48)-2X-14=5
10.1.49)-2X+7=2 10.1.50)7X+13=6 10.1.51)4X+3=-7 10.1.52)-3X+11=-6
10.1.53)9X-5=-3 10.1.54)12X+6=3 10.1.55)8X-3=5 10.1.56)-5X-6=11
10.1.57)18X+4=9 10.1.58) 3X-7=-2 10.1.59) 6X+7=-8 10.1.60) 2X-5=-3
10.1.61)-4X+2=9 10.1.62)-3X-6=-6 10.1.63)-12X-9=1 10.1.64) 14X+7=-9
10.1.65)-7X-12=0 10.1.66) 15X+9=-2

10.1.W1) What is X equal to in the following expression 3X+4=X-2

10.1.w2) Given the diagram below

What value of X makes this true

10.1.w3) If I fish with a friend and together we catch 5 fish per hour for 3 hours, he catches a total of 3 and I catch X, What is the value of X

10.1.w4) What is the value of T in the equation of 6T÷3=T-2

10.1.w5) I am spending $39.00 to buy pies and cakes. Each pie is $6.00 and the cakes are $7.00. If I buy 3 pies which equation below helps me determine how many cakes, X, I bought
A) 39 = 6x-7
B) 39 = 6X+7
C) 39 = 7X +18
D) 39 = 7X-18

10.1.W6) What is the value of X in the equation 6X+2=38

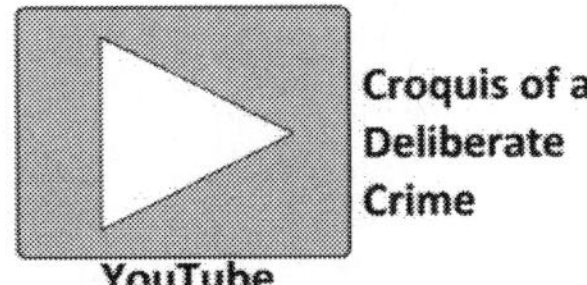

10.1.w7) Which table below shows the results of Y= 0.5X+13

A)

X	Y
1	13.5
2	14
4	15.5
6	16
7	16.5

B)

X	Y
1	13.5
2	14.5
4	15
6	16.5
7	17

C)

X	Y
1	13.5
2	14
4	15
6	16
7	16.5

D)

X	Y
1	13.5
2	14
4	15
6	16
7	17.5

10.1.w8) Which of the following equations can best model the data in the following table

X	Y
1	7.5
2	9
4	12
7	16.5

A) Y = 2X + 5.5
B) Y = 1.5X+6
C) Y = 2.5X+5
D) Y = 3X+4.5

10.1.w9) What is the solution to the equation 6.4 = 3.4X-4.7

10.1.w10) If a taxi charges $2.50 to pick you up and $0.50 per mile which of the following equations could be used to find the total cost, T, for X miles.
A) T = 0.50+2.50X
B) T = 0.50-2.50X
C) T = 2.50+0.50X
D) T = 2.50-0.50X

10.1.W11) Which of the following equations best describes the relationship shown in the graph below

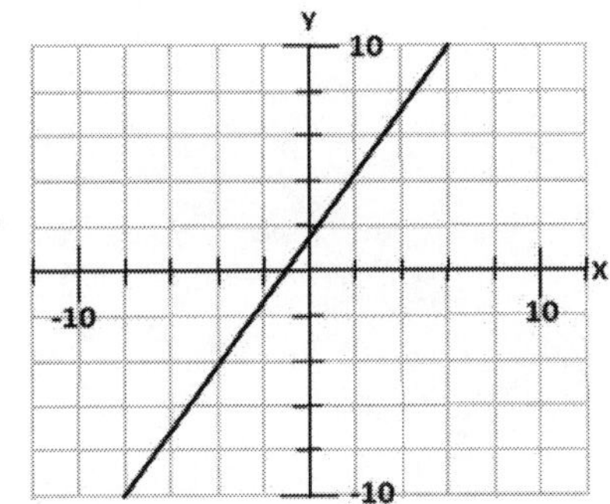

A) $Y={}^{14}/_{20}X+{}^{10}/_{7}$
B) $Y={}^{20}/_{14}X+{}^{10}/_{7}$
C) $Y={}^{20}/_{14}X+{}^{7}/_{10}$
D) $Y={}^{14}/_{20}X+{}^{7}/_{10}$

10.1.w12) A fish can eat 4 times an hours which graph below describes this relationship

A)

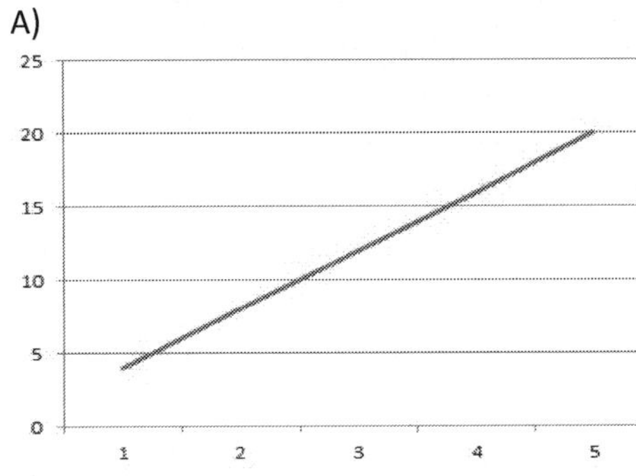

B)

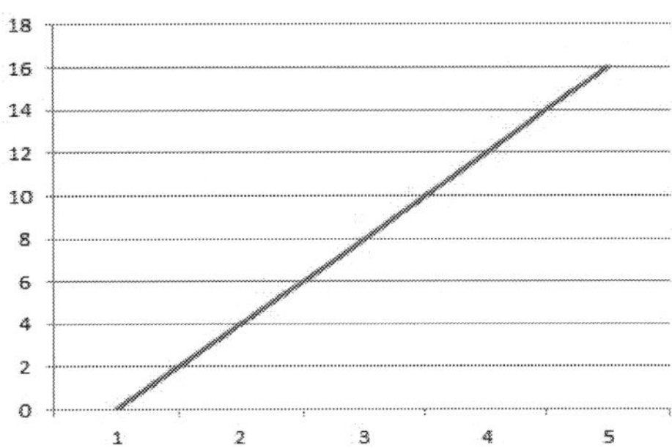

C)

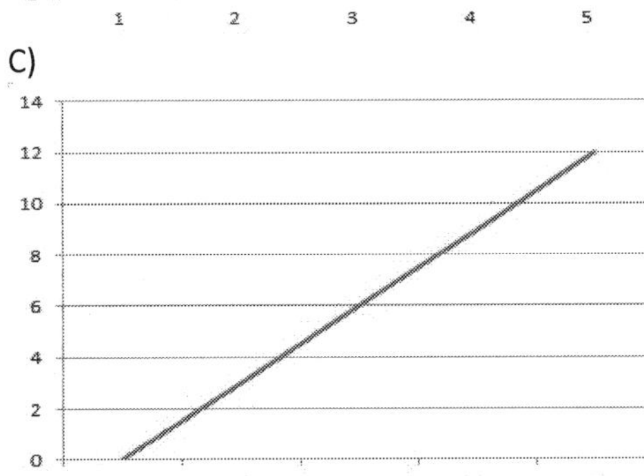

D)

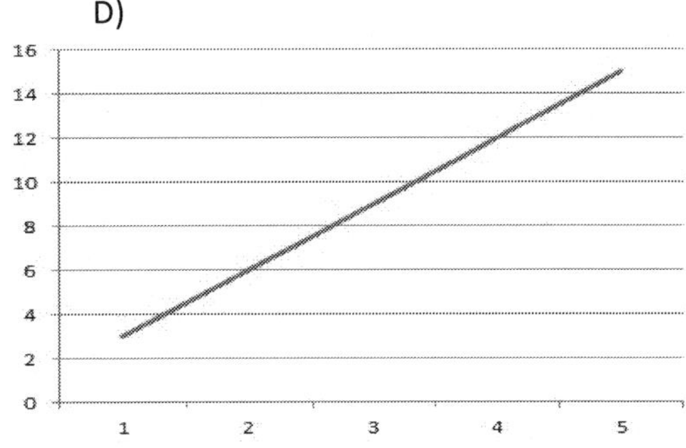

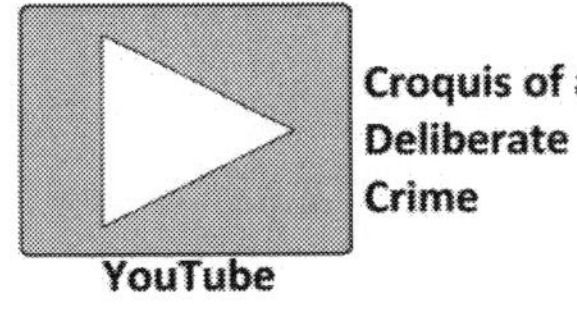

If you don't get the correct answer, and want an explanation on how to work the problem, go to YouTube and type in "MMT" then the problem number. An example would be, MMT 3.9.w12,. The video will show you how to work problem 3.9.w12.

For one on one tutoring via skype at $35.00/Hr.; contact me at marksmathtutoring@yahoo.com

10.1.W13) If I build a model of the Titanic and one inch is equal to ten meters which of the following graphs best shows this relationship

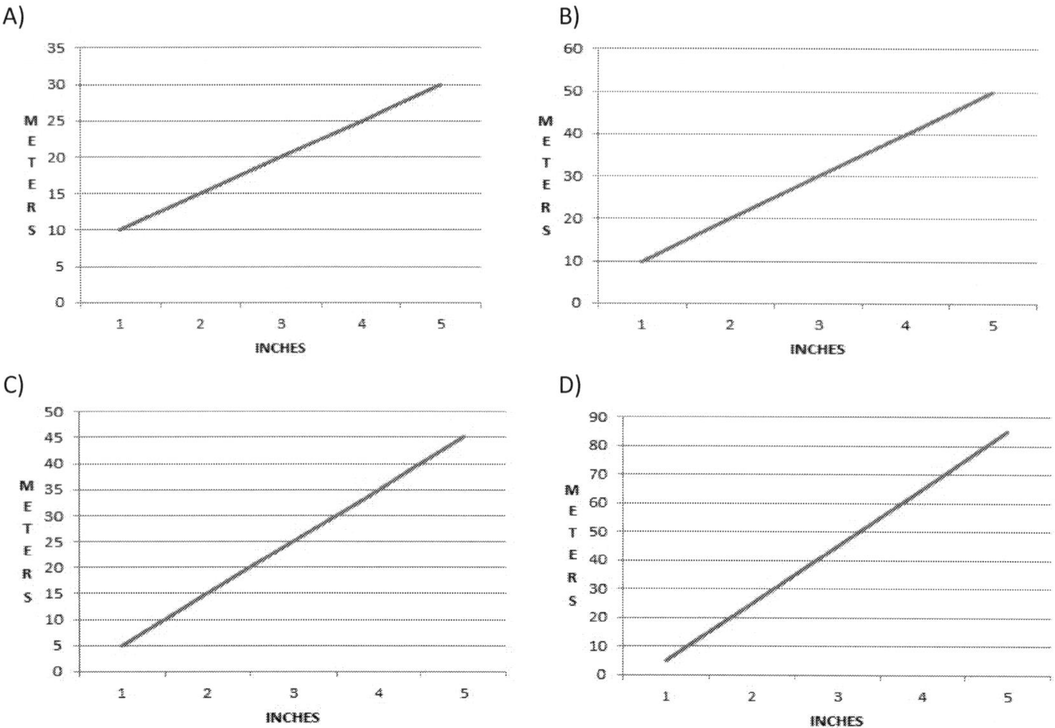

10.1.w14) If I have \$45.00 in my savings account and add another \$15.00 per month which equation below best determines the total,T, in my account for each month, M.

A) M= 45T+15
B) T=45M+15
C) T= 15M+45
D) M= 15T+45

10.1.W15) Given the following equation

Y=4X+5

Which of the following is the Y value of as sequence of x.

A) 5, 7, 9, 10
B) 9, 13, 17, 21
C) 7, 10, 13, 15
D) 8, 10, 13, 15

10.1.w16) What is the value of Y in the equation 0.086X + 3500, if X = 1500

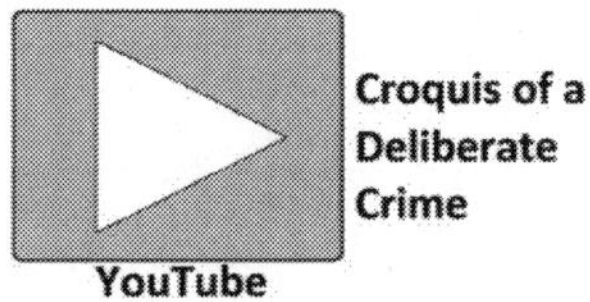

10.1.w17) Which of the following equation would satisfy the data given in the following table

X	Y
0	6
2	11
4	16
6	21

A) Y=X+6
B) Y=X-6
C) Y= 6X+2.5
D) Y=2.5X+6

10.1.w18) If I have $200 in my bank account and spend $12.00 day, which of the following equation shows the relationship between Y the amount in my account and X the number of days
A) Y=200X-12
B)Y=200-12X
C)Y=200X+12
D) Y=12X+200

10.1.w19) Which table below details the relationship of Y = 500-5X

A)

X	Y
0	500
2	510
4	520
8	540

C)

X	Y
0	500
2	490
4	480
8	460

B)

X	Y
0	500
2	495
4	490
8	485

D)

X	Y
0	500
2	505
4	510
8	515

10.1.W20) I HAVE $35.00 in my bank account, and I make $15.00 for every lawn I mow. What would ne the amount in y account if I mow 12 lawns.

Inequalities

10.2.1) -2X+3<-4 10.2.2) 5X+5≤-6 10.2.3) 4X+6>7 10.2.4)-12X+7≤10
10.2.5) 9X-10≤ 2 10.2.6) 10X+4> -3 10.2.7) 15X-8≥ -5 10.2.8)11X+15≤ 6
10.2.9) 3X-5< -8 10.2.10)8X-13< -6 10.2.11)9X+4≥8 10.2.12)-15X-11< -6
10.2.13)-5X-6≤ -7 10.2.14)-4X+3≥ 4 10.2.15) 2X-3< 7 10.2.16)13X-5≤ -2
10.2.17)-7X+4> -7 10.2.18)-8X-2≤ -11 10.2.19)-3X+10<-6 10.2.20)-6X-6≥ 3
10.2.21) -4X-3< -10 10.2.22)-10X+5≤ 5 10.2.23)-12X+20> -9 10.2.24)-3X+4≤ -5

10.2.w1) Which of the following equation will give the answer of x>3
A) 2X+3>4
B) 2X-3>4
C) 3X+2<5
D)2X-2>4

10.2.w2) Which of the following statements can describe the relationship shown below

125-3X>42

A) It cost me 125 to buy a lawn mower. I cut lawns for 3, and need to find out how many lawns, X, I need to cut to earn $42.

B) I have 125 in my savings account and deposit another 3 every day. How many days would I need to save to have $42

C) I have 125 dollars and I buy cakes for $3 each. How many cakes , X, can I buy and still have more than $42 left over

D) I have 42 in my account and save another 3 per week. What is the number of weeks, X, I need to save to get 125

Functions

10.3.1) f(2); X+2= 10.3.2) f(3); 4X+6= 10.3.3) f(4); 5X-7= 10.3.4) f(3); -3X-4=
10.3.5) f(-2);-2X+3= 10.3.6) f(-4);4X+5= 10.3.7) f(-3); 8X +4= 10.3.8) f(5); -6X+6=
10.3.9) f(6); -5X -2= 10.3.10) f(7);3X+7= 10.3.11) f(8);-4X-3= 10.3.12) f(-6); 5X+8=
10.3.13) f(-5); -10X= 10.3.14) f(9); 10X-5= 10.3.15) f(2);2X+10= 10.3.16) f(-8); 7X-7=
10.3.17) f(3); 6X +4= 10.3.18) f(-5);-5X+2= 10.3.19) f(-4); -7X-9= 10.3.20) f(-7);-3X-11=
10.3.21) f(4);-3X-3= 10.3.22) f(-6); 7X-6= 10.3.23) f(-2); 4X-4= 10.3.24) f(5); -8X-5=
10.3.25) f(-5);-4X+5= 10.3.26) f(-3); -6X-8= 10.3.27) f(-9);-2X-2= 10.3.28) f(4); 6X+3=

10.3.W1) If X = 6 which of the following expression is true

A) 2(4-X)=4

B) 2(X-4)=4

C) 4(X-2)=2

D) 4(X+2)=2

Pythagorean's Theorem

Diagram 1

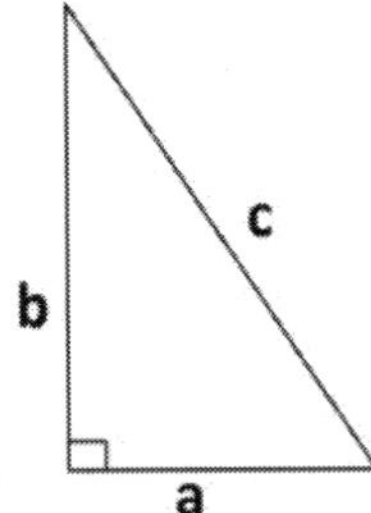

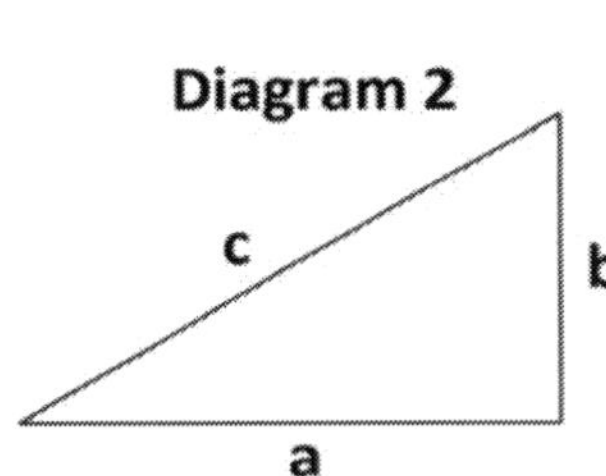

10.4.1 For diagram 1; if a=2, b=4, what does c=
10.4.2 For diagram 1; if a=3, b=5, what does c=
10.4.3 For diagram 1; if a=1, b=2, what does c=
10.4.4 For diagram 1; if a=2, b=6, what does c=
10.4.5 For diagram 1; if a=3, b=2, what does c=
10.4.6 For diagram 1; if a=1, b=5, what does c=

10.4.7 For diagram 1; if a=1, c=9, what does b=
10.4.8 For diagram 1; if b=2, c=6, what does a=
10.4.9 For diagram 1; if a=3, c=20, what does b=
10.4.10 For diagram 1; if b=1, c=15, what does a=

10.4.11 For diagram 2; if a=3, b=8, what does c=
10.4.12 For diagram 2; if a=4, b=6, what does c=
10.4.13 For diagram 2; if a=2, b=2, what does c=

10.4.14 For diagram 2; if a=6, b=7, what does c=

10.4.15 For diagram 2; if a=3, c=12, what does b=
10.4.16 For diagram 2; if a=1, c=15, what does b=
10.4.17 For diagram 2; if b=1, c=9, what does a=
10.4.18 For diagram 2; if b=3, c=8, what does a=
10.4.19 For diagram 2; if a=3, c=13, what does b=
10.4.20 For diagram 2; if b=4, c=12, what does a=

If you don't get the correct answer, and want an explanation on how to work the problem, go to YouTube and type in "MMT" then the problem number. An example would be, MMT 3.9.w12,. The video will show you how to work problem 3.9.w12.

For one on one tutoring via skype at $35.00/Hr.; contact me at marksmathtutoring@yahoo.com

100 ANSWER KEY

2.0 Logic

2.1) B 2.2) D 2.3) C 2.4) C 2.5) B 2.6) D 2.7) 1
2.8) 7 2.9) D 2.10) D 2.11) B 2.12) A 2.13) C 2.14)C
2.15) B 2.16) B 2.17) A 2.18) B 2.19) A 2.20) A 2.21) A
2.22) 16, 94, 32 2.23) 37 2.24) 18 2.25) 20 2.26) 60 2.27) C
2.28) A 2.29) D 2.30) C 2.31) 227 2.32) 373.8 2.33) 748 2.34)A
2.35)15 ½ YRS 2.36) 24.9 2.37) 45 Lbs 2.38) Company A 2.39) Company A
2.40) Company B 2.41) 270 2.42) 30 2.43) 24 2.44) 84 2.45) 200
2.46) 63 2.47) 108 2.48) 96 2.49) Yes 2.50)Yes 2.51) No
2.52) No 2.53) Yes 2.54) 6 Ft 2.55) 45 2.56) 455 2.57) 18 pounds
2.58) 56 2.59) 210 2.60) C 2.61) 11 2.62) A 2.63) 30 pounds
2.64) C 2.65)C 2.66)A 2.67) 480 2.68) 105 2.69) 240
2.70) 240 2.71) 26 2.72) B 2.73) 34 min 2.74) B 2.75) D
2.76) C 2.77) D 2.78)32 2.79) 4 2.80) 3 2.81) 17
2.82) 1200 2.83) 2.25 2.84) 5 IN 2.85) D 2.86) C 2.87) C
2.88) 32 2.89) 3 HRS 3.4 MIN 2.90) B 2.91) 67.5 2.92) 620
2.93) 48 2.94) D 2.95) D 2.96) B 2.97) C

2.1.1) 192 2.1.2) 34,000,000 2.1.3) 152 2.1.4) 1230 2.1.5) 254 2.1.6) D
2.1.7) 24 2.1.8) 101.2 2.1.9) 135

3.1 Addition Single Digit

3.1.1) 4 3.1.2) 2 3.1.3) 10 3.1.4) 13 3.1.5) 5 3.1.6) 10
3.1.7) 3 3.1.8) 16 3.1.9) 9 3.1.10) 10 3.1.11) 11 3.1.12) 8
3.1.13) 9 3.1.14) 14 3.1.15) 7 3.1.16) 15 3.1.17) 6 3.1.18) 11
3.1.19) 4 3.1.20)12 3.1.21) 10 3.1.22) 14 3.1.23) 10 3.1.24) 13
3.1.25) 11 3.1.26) 15 3.1.27) 18 3.1.28) 9 3.1.29) 12 3.1.30) 9
3.1.31) 3 3.1.32) 15 3.1.33) 8 3.1.34) 7 3.1.35) 13 3.1.36) 6
3.1.37) 13 3.1.38) 16 3.1.39) 15 3.1.40) 7 3.1.41) 11 3.1.42) 11
3.1.43) 10 3.1.44) 13 3.1.45) 9 3.1.46) 14 3.1.47) 13 3.1.48) 12
3.1.49) 16 3.1.50) 9 3.1.51) 10 3.1.52) 14 3.1.53) 5 3.1.54) 11

3.2 Addition Two Digit

3.2.1) 34 3.2.2) 42 3.2.3) 50 3.2.4) 133 3.2.5) 105 3.2.6) 93
3.2.7) 56 3.2.8) 129 3.2.9) 70 3.2.10) 111 3.2.11) 59 3.2.12) 124
3.2.13) 107 3.2.14) 65 3.2.15) 136 3.2.16) 104 3.2.17) 72 3.2.18) 60
3.2.19) 74 3.2.20) 90 3.2.21) 151 3.2.22) 125 3.2.23) 88 3.2.24) 59
3.2.25) 108 3.2.26) 73 3.2.27) 85 3.2.28) 88 3.2.29) 87 3.2.30) 133
3.2.31) 83 3.2.32) 106 3.2.33) 105 3.2.34) 87 3.2.35) 111 3.2.36) 71
3.2.37) 55 3.2.38) 113 3.2.39) 121 3.2.40) 132 3.2.41) 164 3.2.42) 68
3.2.43) 121 3.2.44) 143 3.2.45) 120 3.2.46) 136 3.2.47) 55 3.2.48) 129

3.3 Addition Multiple Digit Addition

3.3.1) 2476 3.3.2) 2428 3.3.3) 503 3.3.4) 6990 3.3.5) 8323 3.3.6) 933
3.3.7) 1814 3.3.8) 1294 3.3.9) 6628 3.3.10) 1118 3.3.11) 600 3.3.12) 1253

3.3.13) 1081	3.3.14) 1065	3.3.15) 236	3.3.16) 1048	3.3.17) 732	3.3.18) 416
3.3.19) 974	3.3.20) 590	3.3.21) 651	3.3.22) 1025	3.3.23) 2288	3.3.24) 528
3.3.25) 531	3.3.26) 737	3.3.27) 861	3.3.28) 897	3.3.29) 878	3.3.30) 1333
3.3.31) 836	3.3.32) 1070	3.3.33) 1058	3.3.34) 5925	3.3.35) 11215	3.3.36) 589
3.3.37) 914	3.3.38) 3455	3.3.39) 1980	3.3.40) 1460	3.3.41) 3380	3.3.42) 276
3.3.43) 221	3.3.44) 643	3.3.45) 1120	3.3.46) 536		

3.12.1) 13.3	3.12.2) 2.22	3.12.3) 19.4	3.12.4) 13.3	3.12.5) 3.03
3.12.6) 63.3	3.12.7) 5.6	3.12.8) 8.58	3.12.9) 1.15	3.12.10) 77.7
3.12.11) 5.9	3.12.12) 39.85	3.12.13) 35.72	3.12.14) 6.5	
3.12.15) 9.64	3.12.16) 21.2	3.12.17) 4.68	3.12.18) 6	3.12.19) 13.465
3.12.20) 4.2327	3.12.21) 50.3	3.12.22) 84.75	3.12.23) 85.21	
3.12.24) 63.51	3.12.25) 5.675	3.12.26) 85.93	3.12.27) 75.73	
3.12.28) 38.342	3.12.29) 60	3.12.30) 1.253		

3.3.w1) 1078	3.3.w2) 749	3.3.w3) 197	3.3.w4) 499	3.3.w5) 82	3.3.w6) 17
3.3.w7) 129	3.3.w8) 305	3.3.w9) 157	3.3.w10) 784	3.3.w11) 627	3.3.w12) 22, 26
3.3.w13) 44	3.3.w14) A	3.3.w15) $690	3.3.w16) $44.05	3.3.17) 1195	
3.3.w18) C	3.3.w19) A	3.3.w20) A	3.3.w21) D	3.3.w22) B	3.3.w23) B
3.3.w24) A	3.3.W25) D	3.3.w26) B	3.3.w27) D	3.3.w28) A	3.3.w29) 4:30
3.3.w30) 8:10	3.3.w31) 4:00	3.3.w32) 5:30	3.3.w33) D	3.3.w34) A	3.3.w35) 2
3.3.W36) c					

3.4 Subtraction Single Digits

3.4.1) 2	3.4.2) 2	3.4.3) 2	3.4.4) 1	3.4.5) 1	3.4.6) 4
3.4.7) 3	3.4.8) 3	3.4.9) 0	3.4.10) 1	3.4.11) 3	3.4.12) 1

3.4.55) -2	3.4.56) -8	3.4.57) -2	3.4.58) 1	3.4.59) 11	3.4.60) 1
3.4.61) 3	3.4.62) -2	3.4.63) -7	3.4.64) 0	3.4.65) 3	3.4.66) -4
3.4.67) -1	3.4.68) -4	3.4.69) -3	3.4.70) -3	3.4.71) 2	3.4.72) -5
3.4.73) 0	3.4.74) -4	3.4.75) 6	3.4.76) 4	3.4.77) 2	3.4.78) 3
3.4.79) -3	3.4.80) 1	3.4.81) 0	3.4.82) 9	3.4.83) 0	3.4.84) -5
3.4.85) -1	3.4.86) -1	3.4.87) 4	3.4.88) -1	3.4.89) 5	3.4.90) -4
3.4.91) 1	3.4.92) 0	3.4.93) 3	3.4.94) -5	3.4.95) 1	3.4.96) 7
3.4.97) -2	3.4.98) 5	3.4.99) -3	3.4.100) -4	3.4.101) 3	3.4.102) -2
3.4.103) 0	3.4.104) 5	3.4.105) 2	3.4.106) 0	3.4.107) 1	3.4.108) -7

3.5 Subtraction of Two Digits

3.5.1) 58	3.5.2) 2	3.5.3) 18	3.5.4) 37	3.5.5) 61	3.5.6) 13
3.5.7) 58	3.5.8) 33	3.5.9) 60	3.5.10) 13	3.5.11) 9	3.5.12) 46
3.5.13) 67	3.5.14) 7	3.5.15) 32	3.5.16) 90	3.5.17) 16	3.5.18) 56
3.5.19) 4	3.5.20) 32	3.5.21) 17	3.5.22) 71	3.5.23) 30	3.5.24) 39
3.5.25) 30	3.5.26) 51	3.5.27) 9	3.5.28) 74	3.5.29) 19	3.5.30) 25
3.5.31) 21	3.5.32) 9	3.5.33) 53	3.5.34) 25	3.5.35) 1	3.5.36) 9
3.5.37) 47	3.5.38) 51	3.5.39) 57	3.5.40) 18	3.5.41) 8	3.5.42) 44
3.5.43) 29	3.5.44) 61	3.5.45) 14	3.5.46) 62	3.5.47) 9	3.5.48) 29

3.5.49) -12	3.5.50) -8	3.5.51) 18	3.5.52) 17	3.5.53) -9	3.5.54) -27
3.5.55) -22	3.5.56) 33	3.5.57) -30	3.5.58) -37	3.5.59) -51	3.5.60) 46
3.5.61) 37	3.5.62) -33	3.5.63) -48	3.5.64) 80	3.5.65) 16	3.5.66) -4
3.5.67) -36	3.5.68) -18	3.5.69) 17	3.5.70) 71	3.5.71) -30	3.5.72) -21
3.5.73) -30	3.5.74) -51	3.5.75) 9	3.5.76) 64	3.5.77) -41	3.5.78) 25
3.5.79) -9	3.5.80) -70	3.5.81) 53	3.5.82) -25	3.5.83) -59	3.5.84) 9

3.5.85) -13 3.5.86) 1 3.5.87) 57 3.5.88) -2 3.5.89) -2 3.5.90) 34
3.5.91) 29 3.5.92) -9 3.5.93) -56 3.5.94) 62 3.5.95) -1 3.5.96) -67

3.6 Subtraction Multiple Digit

3.6.1) 746 3.6.2) 2026 3.6.3) 183 3.6.4) 140 3.6.5) 8279 3.6.6) 1029
3.6.7) 1736 3.6.8) 328 3.6.9) 6418 3.6.10) 234 3.6.11) 90 3.6.12) 755
3.6.13) 371 3.6.14) 67 3.6.15) 52 3.6.16) 792 3.6.17) 158 3.6.18) 272
3.6.19) 264 3.6.20) 82 3.6.21) 117 3.6.22) 71 3.6.23) 970 3.6.24) 110
3.6.25) 199 3.6.26) 483 3.6.27) 89 3.6.28) 639 3.6.29) 194 3.6.30) 247
3.6.31) 414 3.6.32) 594 3.6.33) 528 3.6.34) 4703 3.6.35) 1113 3.6.36) 53
3.6.37) 1038 3.6.38) 58 3.6.39) 138 3.6.40) 1034 3.6.41) 228 3.6.42) 2823
3.6.43) 1326 3.6.44) 102 3.6.45) 3132 3.6.46) 57 3.6.47) 214 3.6.48) 129
3.6.49) 191 3.6.50) 144 3.6.51) 2862 3.6.52) 38

3.6.53) -2254 3.6.54) -4974 3.6.55) -517 3.6.56) -6660
3.6.57) -1421 3.6.58) -271 3.6.59) -164 3.6.60) 328
3.6.61) 6418 3.6.62) -366 3.6.63) -910 3.6.64) -145
3.6.65) -129 3.6.66) -833 3.6.67) -148 3.6.68) -208
3.6.69) -2842 3.6.70) -7848 3.6.71) -736 3.6.72) -318
3.6.73) -83 3.6.74) -429 3.6.75) -2230 3.6.76) -290
3.6.77) 199 3.6.78) -517 3.6.79) 89 3.6.80) 639

3.13.1) 8.7 3.13.2) -1.78 3.13.3) -12.6 3.13.4) -0.3
3.13.5) -1.37 3.13.6) -56.7 3.13.7) -2.2 3.13.8) 7.62
3.13.9) 0.15 3.13.10) -70.3 3.13.11) 0.9 3.13.12) -38.15
3.13.13) -34.28 3.13.14) -3.3 3.13.15) -8.76 3.13.16) -2.8
3.13.17) 4.12 3.13.18) -0.4 3.13.19) 8.735 3.13.20) 0.2127
3.13.21) 18.3 3.13.22) -51.75 3.13.23) 80.81 3.13.24) -56.89
3.13.25) -2.125 3.13.26) 76.27 3.13.27) 54.73 3.13.28) 36.858
3.13.29) 9 3.13.30) 0.455

3.14.1) 25.3 3.14.2) 0.44 3.14.3) 54.4 3.14.4) 44.2 3.14.5) 1.826
3.14.6) 198 3.14.7) 6.63 3.14.8) 3.888 3.14.9) 0.325 3.14.10) 27.38
3.14.11) 8.5 3.14.12) 33.15 3.14.13) 25.2 3.14.14) 7.84
3.14.15) 4.048 3.14.16) 110.4 3.14.17) 1.232 3.14.18) 8.96
3.14.19) 26.2515 3.14.20) 4.47627 3.14.21) 548.8 3.14.22) 1126.125
3.14.23) 182.622 3.14.24) 199.262 3.14.25) 6.9225 3.14.26) 391.713
3.14.27) 684.915 3.14.28) 27.8992 3.14.29) 879.75 3.14.30) 0.340746

3.16.1) 1 3.16.2) -4 3.16.3) -2 3.16.4) 0
3.16.5) -6 3.16.6) -9 3.16.7) 2 3.16.8) -4
3.16.9) -11 3.16.10) 4 3.16.11) 5 3.16.12) -5
3.16.13) -10 3.16.14) -5 3.16.15) 5 3.16.16) 3
3.16.17) -2 3.16.18) 5 3.16.19) 1 3.16.20) -4
3.16.21) 13 3.16.22) 5 3.16.23) -10 3.16.24) 3
3.16.25) -4 3.16.26) -4 3.16.27) -7 3.16.28) -10
3.16.29) -1 3.16.30) -5

3.6.w1) A 3.6.w2) 99 3.6.w3) 29 3.6.w4) 44 3.6.w5) 1568 3.6.w6) A
3.6.w7) B 3.6.w8) 154 3.6.w9) A 3.6.w10) 474 3.6.w11) C 3.6.w12) 15
3.6.w13) 9353 3.6.w14) A 3.6.w15) 18850 3.6.w16) $4.50
3.6.w17) $10.76 3.6.w180 $7.88 3.6.w19) 88 3.6.w20) 7 Hrs. 25 Min

3.6.w21) 6 Hrs. 35 Min	3.6.w22) 6 Hrs. 20 Min	3.6.w23) 8 Hrs. 15 Min	
3.6.w24) 261	3.6.w25) 47.47	3.6.w26) 14.72	3.6.w27) 9.76
3.6.w28) 60,345	3.6.w29) 13,320	3.6.w30) C	3.6.w31) 404
3.6.W32) 1.95	3.6.w33) 5:45	3.6.w34) 12:45	3.6.w35) 12:40
3.6.w36) 10:05	3.6.w37) 12:45	3.6.w38) B	3.6.w39) $2.96
3.6.W40) 343.87			

3.7 Multiplication of Single Digits

3.7.1) 3	3.7.2) 0	3.7.3) 24	3.7.4) 40	3.7.5) 6	3.7.6) 21
3.7.7) 0	3.7.8) 63	3.7.9) 8	3.7.10) 25	3.7.11) 28	3.7.12) 12
3.7.13) 20	3.7.14) 45	3.7.15) 10	3.7.16) 54	3.7.17) 8	3.7.18) 24
3.7.19) 4	3.7.20) 32	3.7.21) 16	3.7.22) 45	3.7.23) 24	3.7.24) 40
3.7.25) 28	3.7.26) 56	3.7.27) 81	3.7.28) 0	3.7.29) 36	3.7.30) 14
3.7.31) 2	3.7.32) 56	3.7.33) 12	3.7.34) 12	3.7.35) 36	3.7.36) 5
3.7.37) 42	3.7.38) 64	3.7.39) 54	3.7.40) 6	3.7.41) 30	3.7.42) 18
3.7.43) 21	3.7.44) 36	3.7.45) 18	3.7.46) 45	3.7.47) 40	3.7.48) 35
3.7.49) 64	3.7.50) 14	3.7.51) 24	3.7.52) 49	3.7.53) 6	3.7.54) 18

3.8 Multiplication of Two Digit

3.8.1) 253	3.8.2) 440	3.8.3) 544	3.8.4) 4420	3.8.5) 1826	3.8.6) 1980
3.8.7) 663	3.8.8) 3888	3.8.9) 325	3.8.10) 2738	3.8.11) 850	3.8.12) 3315
3.8.13) 2520	3.8.14) 784	3.8.15) 4048	3.8.16) 1104	3.8.17) 1232	3.8.18) 896
3.8.19) 1045	3.8.20) 1944	3.8.21) 5628	3.8.22) 2646	3.8.23) 1711	3.8.24) 760
3.8.25) 2376	3.8.26) 682	3.8.27) 1786	3.8.28) 912	3.8.29) 1472	3.8.30) 4266
3.8.31) 1702	3.8.32) 1584	3.8.33) 2054	3.8.34) 1736	3.8.35) 2210	3.8.36) 1344
3.8.37) 714	3.8.38) 3192	3.8.39) 2848	3.8.40) 4355	3.8.41) 6723	3.8.42) 1431
3.8.43) 1395	3.8.44) 3450	3.8.45) 5092	3.8.46) 2812	3.8.47) 3663	3.8.48) 4368

3.9 Multiplication Multi Digit

3.9.1) 262,515	3.9.2) 447,627	3.9.3) 54,880	3.9.4) 1,126,125
3.9.5) 182,622	3.9.6) 199,262	3.9.7) 69,225	3.9.8) 391,713
3.9.9) 684,915	3.9.10) 278,992	3.9.11) 87,975	3.9.12) 340,746
3.9.13) 257,730	3.9.14) 110,084	3.9.15) 8448	3.9.16) 117,760
3.9.17) 127,715	3.9.18) 37,488	3.9.19) 101,745	3.9.20) 85,344
3.9.21) 104,228	3.9.22) 216,646	3.9.23) 65,511	3.9.24) 48,671
3.9.25) 60,590	3.9.26) 68,970	3.9.27) 183,350	3.9.28) 99,072
3.9.29) 151,512	3.9.30) 428,970	3.9.31) 172,875	3.9.32) 161,616
3.9.34) 210,145	3.9.35) 1,761,854	3.9.36) 22,779,864	3.9.37) 11,928
3.9.38) 195,853	3.9.39) 1,635,174	3.9.40) 540,531	3.9.41) 530,299
3.9.42) 403,744	3.9.43) 7595	3.9.44) 8050	3.9.45) 100,392
3.9.46) 130,416	3.9.47) 67,063		

3.9.w1) 24	3.9.w2) 42	3.9.w3) 6	3.9.w4) 24	3.9.w5) 42	3.9.w6) C
3.9.w7) 72	3.9.w8) 7	3.9.w9) 63	3.9.w10) 4	3.9.w11) B	3.9.w12) C
3.9.w13) D	3.9.w14)584	3.9.w15) 36	3.9.w16) 768	3.9.w17)315	3.9.w18) B
3.9.w19) B	3.9.w20) B	3.9.w21) 72	3.9.w22) 18	3.9.w23) 35	3.9.w24) 48
3.9.w25) B	3.9.w26) B	3.9.w27) A	3.9.w28) C	3.9.w29) C	3.9.w30) 56
3.9.w31) C	3.9.w32) 384	3.9.w33) 592	3.9.w34) 6900	3.9.w35) 4032	3.9.w36) B
3.9.w37) 900	3.9.w38) 4800	3.9.w39) D	3.9.w40) $10,850	3.9.w41) B	
3.9.w42) 1904	3.9.W43) $12,500		3.9.w44) 1176	3.9.w45) 48	
3.9.w46) C	3.9.w47) C	3.9.w48) B	3.9.w49) D	3.9.50) 364	
3.9.w51) 1264	3.9.w52) 125		3.9.w53) 837	3.9.w54) off season	

3.9.w55) 18.75 3.9.w56) 10,272 3.9.w57) 4.81 lbs 3.9.w58) C
3.9.w59) 811 3.9.w60) 5 hrs. 15 min 3.9.w61) 3 hrs. 45 min
3.9.w62) 5:45 3.9.w63) 8 HRS. 2 min 3.9.W64) B 3.9.w65) D
3.9.w66) A 3.9.w67) 173,280 3.9.w68) A 3.9.w69) B
3.9.w70) B 3.9.w71) A 3.9.w72)$14.60 3.9.w73)A 3.9.w74) 420
3.9.w75) D 3.9.w76) 3 3.9.w77) 29 3.9.w78) D 3.9.w79) 16
3.9.w80) A 3.9.w81) $37.05 3.9.w82) C 3.9.w83) $150
3.9.w84) 5 In

3.10 Division

3.10.1) 2 3.10.2) 1 3.10.3) 3 3.10.4) 1 3.10.5) 4 3.10.6) 2
3.10.7) 1 3.10.8) 5 3.10.9) 1 3.10.10) 6 3.10.11) 3 3.10.12) 2
3.10.13) 1 3.10.14) 7 3.10.15) 1 3.10.16) 8 3.10.17) 4 3.10.18) 2
3.10.19) 1 3.10.20) 9 3.10.21) 3 3.10.22) 1 3.10.23) 10 3.10.24) 5
3.10.25) 2 3.10.26) 1 3.10.27) 12 3.10.28) 6 3.10.29) 4 3.10.30) 3
3.10.31) 2 3.10.32) 1 3.10.33) 14 3.10.34) 7 3.10.35) 2 3.10.36) 1
3.10.37) 15 3.10.38) 5 3.10.39) 3 3.10.40) 1 3.10.41) 6 3.10.42)3
3.10.43) 10 3.10.44) 3 3.10.45) 3 3.10.46) 3 3.10.47) 2 3.10.48) 5
3.10.49) 1 3.10.50) 4 3.10.51) 2 3.10.52)1 3.10.53) 4 3.10.54) 1

3.10.55) 34 3.10.56) 36 3.10.57) 32 3.10.58) 28
3.10.59) 56 3.10.60) 52 3.10.61) 61 3.10.62) 47
3.10.63) 53 3.10.64) 58 3.10.65) 26 3.10.66) 89
3.10.67) 83 3.10.68) 91 3.10.69) 43 3.10.70) 52
3.10.71) 81 3.10.72) 64 3.10.73) 64 3.10.74) 67
3.10.75) 68 3.10.76) 368 3.10.77) 216 3.10.78) 24
3.10.79) 28 3.10.80) 19 3.10.81) 26 3.10.82) 45
3.10.83) 45 3.10.84) 57 3.10.85) 46 3.10.86) 216
3.10.87) 16 3.10.88) 93 3.10.89) 74 3.10.90) 52
3.10.91) 149 3.10.92) 26 3.10.93) 56 3.10.94) 35
3.10.95) 94 3.10.96) 84 3.10.97) 1112 3.10.98) 35
3.10.99) 93 3.10.100) 35 3.10.101) 18 3.10.102) 34
3.10.103) 32 3.10.104) 21 3.10.105) 94 3.10.106) 76
3.10.108) 36 3.10.109) 287 3.10.110) 35

3.10.113) 136 3.10.114) 64 3.10.115) 286 3.10.116) 127
3.10.117) 237 3.10.118) 17 3.10.119) 58 3.10.120) 194
3.10.121) 78 3.10.122) 61 3.10.123) 62 3.10.124) 47
3.10.125) 96 3.10.126) 283 3.10.127) 47 3.10.128) 36
3.10.129) 52 3.10.130) 85 3.10.131) 283 3.10.132) 47
3.10.133) 27 3.10.134) 99 3.10.135) 41 3.10.136) 148
3.10.137) 49 3.10.138) 32 3.10.139) 486 3.10.140) 194
3.10.141) 13 3.10.142) 84 3.10.143) 12 3.10.144)37

3.15.1) 4.8 3.15.2) 0.1 3.15.3) 0.2 3.15.4) 1.0
3.14.5) 0.4 3.15.6) 0.1 3.15.7) 0.4 3.15.8) 16.9
3.15.9) 1.3 3.15.10) 0.05 3.15.11) 1.36 3.15.12) 0.02
3.15.13) 0.02 3.15.14) 0.33 3.15.15) 0.05 3.15.16) 0.77
3.15.17) 15.71 3.15.18) 0.88

3.17.1) -63	3.17.2) 27	3.17.3) -26	3.17.4) 36
3.17.5) -166	3.17.6) 180	3.17.7) 3.9	3.17.8) -32
3.17.9) -30	3.17.10) 21	3.17.11) -6	3.17.12) -255
3.17.13) -216	3.17.14) 4	3.17.15) -36	3.17.16) -9
3.17.17) 2	3.17.18) -2	3.17.19) -1	3.17.20) 3
3.17.21) -1	3.17.22) 2	3.17.23) -1	3.17.24) 3
3.17.25) -2	3.17.26) 9	3.17.27) -13	

3.10.w1) 4 3.10.w2)4 3.10.w3) 0 3.10.w4) 3 3.10.w5) 7 3.10.w6) 5
3.10.w7) A 3.10.w8) 7 3.10.w9) A 3.10.w10) B 3.10.w11) A 3.10.w12) B
3.10.w13) C 3.10.w14) B 3.10.w15) A 3.10.w16) 108 3.10.w17) 23
3.10.w18) B 3.10.w19) B 3.10.w20) C 3.10.w21) B 3.10.w22) D 3.10.w23) D
3.10.w24) 27 3.10.w25) 24 3.10.w26) 180 3.10.w27) 34 3.10.w28) 170
3.10.w29) 43 3.10.w30) B 3.10.w31) 57 3.10.w32) 65 3.10.w33) 21 3.10.w34) C
3.10.w35) D 3.10.w36) C 3.10.w37) A 3.10.w38) 6.35 3.10.w39) 37.5
3.10.w40) 48 3.10.w41) C 3.10.W42) C 3.10.W43) 24
3.10.w44) C 3.10.w45) 0.31 3.10.w46) 133 3.10.w47) 7.32 in
3.10.w48) 33 3.10.w49) $137.51 3.10.w50) 127 3.10.w51) 55 min
3.10.w52) 35 min 3.10.w53) 1 hr. 45 min 3.10.w54) 1 ht. 5 min
3.10.w55) 6 3.10.w56) 6 3.10.w57) 7 3.10.w58) 7
3.10.w59) 2 3.10.w60) 6 3.10.w61) 2 3.10.w62) 16
3.10.w63) D 3.10.w64) B 3.10.w65) $12.51 3.10.w66) B
3.10.w67) C 3.10.w68) 6 3.10.w69) $0.78

3.11 Inequalities

3.11.1) F	3.11.2) F	3.11.3) T	3.11.4) F	3.11.5) T	3.11.6) F
3.11.7) F	3.11.8) T	3.11.9) T	3.11.10) F	3.11.11) T	3.11.12) F
3.11.13) T	3.11.14) T	3.11.15) F	3.11.16) F	3.11.17) F	3.11.18) T
3.11.19) T	3.11.20) F	3.11.21) T	3.11.22) F	3.11.23) F	3.11.24) F

3.11.25) F	3.11.26) T	3.11.27) F	3.11.28) T		
3.11.29) F	3.11.30) T	3.11.31) F	3.11.32) F	3.11.33) F	3.11.34) F
3.11.35) F	3.11.36) F	3.11.37) F	3.11.38) F	3.11.39) F	3.11.40) T
3.11.41) T	3.11.42) T	3.11.43) F	3.11.44) F	3.11.45) T	3.11.46) F
3.11.47) F	3.11.48) F				

3.11.49) T	3.11.50) F	3.11.51) F	3.11.52) T	3.11.53) T	3.11.54) F
3.11.55) T	3.11.56) F	3.11.57) F	3.11.58) T	3.11.59) F	3.11.60) F
3.11.61) F	3.11.62) F	3.11.63) T	3.11.64) F	3.11.65) T	3.11.66) F
3.11.67) F	3.11.68) F	3.11.69) T	3.11.70) F	3.11.71) T	3.11.72) F

3.11.w1) A	3.11.w2) D	3.11.w3) D	3.11.w4) D	3.11.w5) C	3.11.w6) B
3.11.w7) C	3.11.w8) C	3.11.w9) C	3.11.w10) C	3.11.w11) C	3.11.w12) C
3.11.w13) B	3.11.w14) A	3.11.W15) D	3.11.W16) A		

3.18.1) 2^2x7	3.18.2) 3^3x5	3.18.3)5^2x2	3.18.4) 7^2x2	3.18.5) 2^4x3	3.18.6)2^5x3
3.18.7) 5^3	3.18.8) 3^3	3.18.9) 3^4x2	3.18.10) 5^3x3	3.18.11) 2^5x5	3.18.12)3^4x5
3.18.13) 2^6x3	3.18.14) 2^3x3	3.18.15) 5^3x3	3.18.16) 5^2x3	3.18.17) 2^2x11	3.18.18) 3^2

3.18.19) 2	3.18.20) 3	3.18.21) 2	3.18.22) 3	3.18.23) 2	3.18.24) 2
3.18.25) NONE	3.18.26) 3	3.18.27) 2	3.18.28) 3	3.18.29) 2	3.18.30) 3

3.18.37) 2 3.18.38) 5 3.18.39) 5 3.18.40) 2 3.18.41) 3 3.18.42) 5
3.18.43) 3 3.18.44) 2 3.18.45) 3 3.18.46) 5 3.18.47) 5 3.18.48) 5

3.19.1) $6X10^{16}$ 3.19.2) $7X10^{9}$ 3.19.3) $7.5X10^{14}$ 3.19.4) $10X10^{10}$
3.19.5) $7X10^{11}$ 3.19.6)$7.5X10^{17}$ 3.19.7) $15X10^{6}$ 3.19.8) $9X10^{10}$
3.19.9) $6X10^{13}$ 3.19.10) $45X10^{12}$ 3.19.11) no 3.19.12)$21X10^{5}$
3.19.13) $10X10^{16}$ 3.19.14) $28X10^{9}$ 3.19.15) $10X10^{12}$ 3.19.16)$48X10^{13}$
3.19.17) $30X10^{-1}$ 3.19.18) $64X10^{-10}$ 3.19.19) $54X10^{5}$ 3.19.20) $10X10^{-3}$
3.19.21)$36X10^{-12}$ 3.19.22) $56X10^{-5}$ 3.19.23) $9X10^{-5}$ 3.19.24) $14X10^{-7}$
3.19.25) $24X10^{-5}$ 3.19.26) $40X10^{2}$ 3.19.27) $42X10^{-7}$ 3.19.28) $49X10^{-2}$
3.19.29) $7/9X10^{2}$ 3.19.30) $4/5X10^{-10}$ 3.19.31) $1/3x10^{-1}$ 3.19.32) $1x10^{-7}$
3.19.33) $1/2x10^{3}$ 3.19.34) $5/7x10^{10}$ 3.19.35) $1/2x10^{12}$ 3.19.36) $3/4x10^{1}$
3.19.37) $9/4x10^{1}$ 3.19.38) $1/7x10^{12}$ 3.19.39) $8/9x10^{-8}$ 3.19.40) $1x10^{2}$

4.0 Geometry

4.1) D 4.2) C 4.3) A, B, E, F, G 4.4) C 4.5) B
4.6) A 4.7) D 4.8) 9 4.9) 15 4.10) 18 4.11) 21
4.12) B 4.13) A 4.14) 6 4.15) 120 4.16) 76 4.17) No
4.18) C 4.19) A 4.20) YES 4.21) C 4.22) D 4.23) 4
4.24) 17 4.25) 22 4.26) 4 4.27) B 4.28) 28 4.29) 36M
4.30) B 4.31) 153 4.32) 69 4.33) B 4.34) A 4.35) B
4.36) A 4.37) D 4.38) D 4.39) C 4.40)B 4.41) 8
4.42) 10 4.43) 125 4.44) 27 4.45) 72 4.46) 216 4.47) 24
4.48) 64 4.49) 16 M^3 4.50) 240 ft^3 4.51) 64 ft^3 4.52) 125 m^3 4.53) 450
4.54) 225 4.55) 52 4.56) 156 4.57) B 4.58) A 4.59) C
4.60) C 4.61) D 4.62) D 4.63) A 4.64) B 4.65) D
4.66) C 4.67) C 4.68)A 4.69) A 4.70) D 4.71) C
4.72) A 4.73) B 4.74) B 4.75) C 4.76) 131 4.77) C
4.78) C 4.79) A 4.80) A 4.81) A 4.82) C 4.83) B
4.84) 260 4.85) 450 4.86) D 4.87)8 4.88) C 4.89)C
4.90) C 4.91) 21 4.92) A 4.93) 18.8 4.94) 25 4.95) 56
4.96) 9 4.97) 53 4.98) A 4.99) 100 4.100) 35
4.101) 500 4.102) 51 4.103) 67 meters square 4.104) 40 4.105) 20
4.106) 40 4.107) 20 4.108) 20 4.109) 10 4.110) C 4.111) A
4.112) A 4.113) C 4.114) D 4.115) D 4.116) 48 4.117) 93
4.118)B 4.119) A 4.120) B 4.121) B 4.122) 113.1 4.123) C
4.124) 4 FT 4.125) 1963 4.126) 300 IN^2 4.127) 40 4.128) C 4.129) 2309 FT^3
4.130) C 4.131) 38 4.132) 2356 CM^3 4.133) 1920 4.134) 24 FT^2
4.135) 2262 4.136) D 4.137) 1078.5 M^2 4.138) 102.16 FT^3 4.139) 11.2 IN^3
4.140) 131.4 4.141) 296 CM^2 4.142) 314.2 FT^3 4.143) 465 4.144) 47.1
4.145) 960 FT^3 4.146) 960 FT^3 4.147) 38.3 IN^2 4.148) 10 FT 4.149) 84
4.150) 15 in 4.151) 22 in 4.152)432 in^3 4.153) 25 in 4.154) 467.5 in^2
4.155) 78.5 ft^2 4.156) 21.5 BY 10 4.157) 4.2 BY 2 4.158) 3 4.159) ½
4.160) 9 4.161) 4 4.162) ¼ 4.163) 1/9 4.164) 3 4.165) 2
4.166) ½ 4.167) 1/3 4.168) 4 4.169) 1/3

4.170) 8 Ft 4.171) 4 4.172) 992 4.173) 1131 4.174) 108 4.175) C
4.176) 254.5 4.177) 452.4 in^3 4.178) Diameter = 25, Height=10
4.179) 523.6 4.180) 600 4.181) 9 4.182) 20.6 in^2

4.183)154.6 4.184) 42.5 4.185) C 4.186) C 4.187)D 4.188) D
4.189) A 4.190) 587 4.191) B 4.192) 381.7 4.193) 70 4.194) 500
4.195) 2094

5.0 Fractions

5.1 5.2) 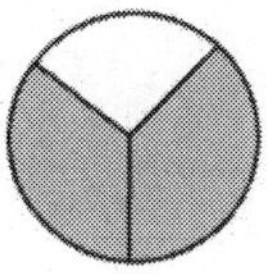 5.3) 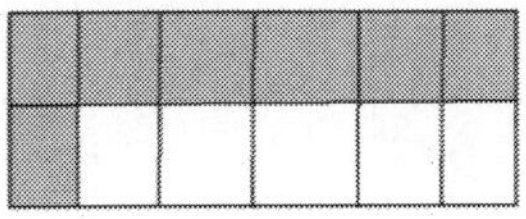 5.4)

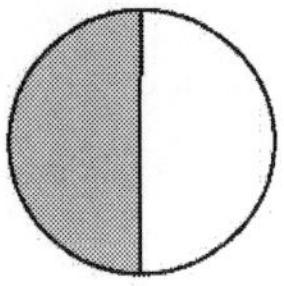

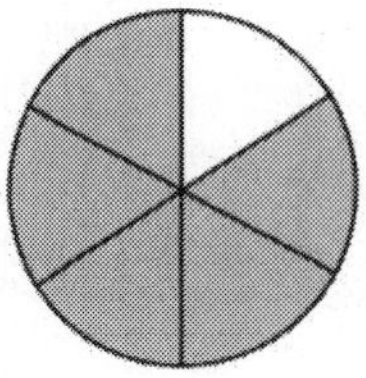

5.5) 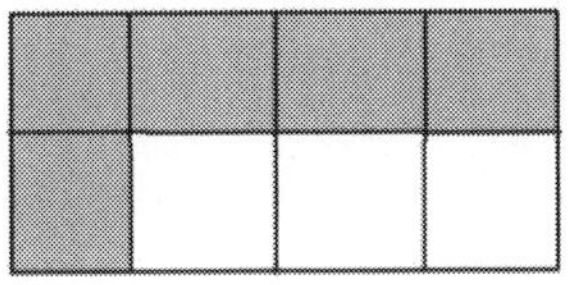 5.6)

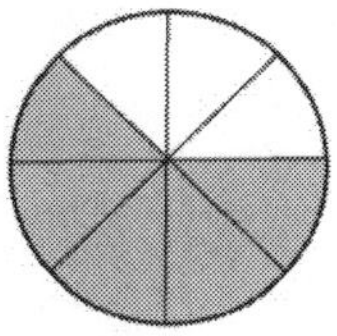

5.7) Y 5.8) Y 5.9) N 5.10) Y 5.11) N
5.12) N 5.13) Y 5.14) N, 2/4<3/8 5.15) N, 2/3>3/6 5.16) N, 3/8<3/4
5.17) N, 1/3<3/8 5.18) N, 3/4>1/2 5.19) Y 5.20) y 5.21) N, 2/12<2/6
5.22) N, 2/6<2/3 5.23) y 2/4=4/8 5.24) N, 4/6>4/8 5.25) y, 6/12=3/6
5.26) Y, 3/4=9/12 5.27) N, 2/12<2/6 5.28) Y, 1/3=2/6 5.29) N, 1/8<1/4
5.30) B,3/4 5.31) C, 2/3 5.32) A 1/8 5.33) b, 8/12
5.34) A, 4/6 5.35) A, 7/8 5.36) Sarah, 1/3 5.37) 3/4 Lb.
5.38) You, 2/3 Lb. 5.39) Al, 3/4 5.40) 1/3 `5.41) 2/3
5.42) 3/5 5.43) 5/9 5.44) 3/5 5.45) 2/3
5.46) 3/8 5.47) 3/6 5.48) D, 7/8>5/8 5.49) D, 1/4<3/4
5.50) A, 5/6>4/6 5.51) D, 8/12>3/12 5.52) B, 3/8<6/8 5.53) A, 2/3>1/3
5.54) A 5.55) B 5.56) B 5.57) A
5.58) B 5.59) B 5.60) N 5.61) N
5.62) D 5.63) B 5.64) C 5.65) C
5.6.66) < 5.6.67) <

5.6.68) < 5.6.69) < 5.6.70) > 5.6.71) > 5.6.72) <
5.6.73) > 5.6.74) > 5.6.75) < 5.6.76) < 5.6.77) <
5.6.78) < 5.6.79) < 5.6.80) > 5.6.81) < 5.6.82) >
5.6.83) < 5.6.84) < 5.6.85) <

Addition

5.2.1) 2/2 5.2.2) 5/3 5.2.3) 6/6 5.2.4) 5/4 5.2.5) 7/8 5.2.6) 10/9
5.2.7) 4/5 5.2.8) 6/6 5.2.9) 5/9 5.2.10) 6/7 5.2.11) 2/3 5.2.12) 5/6
5.2.13) 5/8 5.2.14) 5/7 5.2.15) 8/11 5.2.16) 9/16 5.2.17) 6/8 5.2.18) 5/7
5.2.19) 11/12 5.2.20) 12/13 5.2.21) 10/12 5.2.22) 12/15 5.2.23) 9/11 5.2.24) 11/10

5.2.25) 13/12 5.2.26) 15/18 5.2.27) 31/20 5.2.28) 11/14 5.2.29) 29/21 5.2.30) 20/21
5.2.31) 53/42 5.2.32) 11/10 5.2.33) 13/20 5.2.34) 73/56 5.2.35) 36/35 5.2.36) 15/28
5.2.37) 32/35 5.2.38) 11/24 5.2.39) 13/21 5.2.40) 26/48 5.2.41) 16/21 5.2.42) 23/21
5.2.43) 83/56 5.2.44) 45/28 5.2.45) 21/18 5.2.46) 5/6 5.2.47) 17/30 5.2.48) 38/24
5.2.49) 9/18 5.2.50) 10/24 5.2.51) 37/30 5.2.52) 43/25 5.2.53) 13/15 5.2.54) `17/12
5.2.55) 22/21 5.2.56) 70/48 5.2.57) 47/12 5.2.58) 118/24 5.2.59) 89/20 5.2.60) 302/56

5.2.61) 241/40 5.2.62) 233/42 5.2.63) 81/24 5.2.64) 159/40 5.2.65) 156/35 5.2.66) 31/12
5.2.67) 68/15 5.2.68) 202/35 5.2.69) 110/21 5.2.70) 235/56 5.2.71) 122/24 5.2.72) 87/12
5.2.73) 223/42 5.2.74) 145/24 5.2.75) 101/30 5.2.76)174/35 5.2.77) 77/30 5.2.78) 242/48
5.2.79) 211/40 5.2.80) 227/35 5.2.81) 110/21 5.2.82) 235/56 5.2.83) 156/32 5.2.84) 257/40
5.2.85) 101/20 5.2.86) 198/35 5.2.87) 213/56

5.2.88) 38/7 5.2.89) 61/8 5.2.90) 111/8 5.2.91) 67/6 5.2.92) 93/8 5.2.93) 125/9
5.2.94) 38/9 5.2.95) 66/7 5.2.96) 33/5 5.2.97) 60/7 5.2.98) 83/9 5.2.99) 78/9

5.2.100) 5/12 5.2.101) -11/15 5.2.102) -1/20 5.2.103) -4/32
5.2.104) -9/18 5.2.105) -26/21 5.2.106) -11/35 5.2.107) -13/20
5.2.108) -1/12 5.2.109) 2/24 5.2.110) 43/30 5.2.111) -2/12

5.2.112) -1/12 5.2.113) -22/15 5.2.114) -27/18 5.2.115) 23/15
5.2.116) -29/16 5.2.117) -47/12 5.2.118) -49/15 5.2.119) 7/12
5.2.120) -97/20 5.2.121) 22/16 5.2.122) -79/15 5.2.123) -6/8

5.2.124) 1/8 5.2.125) -13/3 5.2.126) -1/6 5.2.127) 1/5
5.2.128) -10/3 5.2.129) -21/4 5.2.130) -8/3 5.2.131) ¼

5.2.w1) 31/30 5.2.w2) 17/12 5.2.w3) 43/30
5.2.w4) 22/15 5.2.w5) 27/30 5.2.w6) 37/24
5.2.w7) 27/18 5.2.w8) 41/12 5.2.w9) 182/24
5.2.w10) 371/20 5.2.w11) 19/4

Subtraction

5.3.1) 0/2 5.3.2) 1/3 5.3.3) 4/6 5.3.4) 2/4 5.3.5) 2/8 5.3.6) 2/9
5.3.7) 1/5 5.3.8) 1/6 5.3.9) 1/9 3.3.10) 2/7 5.3.11) 0/3 5.3.12) 3/6
5.3.13) 1/8 5.3.14) 3/7 5.3.15) 1/11 5.3.16) 1/16 5.3.17) 8/8 5.3.18) 1/7
5.3.19) 1/12 5.3.20) 3/13 5.3.21) 1/12 5.3.22) 3/15 5.3.23) 3/11 5.3.24) 3/10

5.3.25) 5/12 5.3.26) 9/18 5.3.27) -1/20 5.3.28) -3/14 5.3.29) 1/21 5.3.30) 8/21
5.3.31) -17/42 5.3.32) 1/10 5.3.33) 3/20 5.3.34) -25/56 5.3.35) -6/35 5.3.36) 1/28
5.3.37) 18/35 5.3.38) -5/24 5.3.39) 1/72 5.3.40) -10/48 5.3.41) 2/21 5.3.42) -5/21
5.3.43) 13/56 5.3.44) 3/28 5.3.45) -9/18 5.3.46) -1/6 5.3.47) 7/30 5.3.48) -2/24
5.3.49) -3/18 5.3.50) 2/24 5.3.51) -13/30 5.3.52) 13/35 5.3.53) 7/15 5.3.54) 1/12
5.3.55) -8/21 5.3.56) -10/48 5.3.57) -7/12 5.3.58) -14/24 5.3.59) 39/20 5.3.60) 55/56
5.3.61) -31/40 5.3.62) -89/42 5.3.63) -17/14 5.3.64) -31/40 5.3.65) -44/35 5.3.66) -1/12
5.3.67) -28/15 5.3.68) -102/35 5.3.69) -44/21 5.3.70) -53/56
5.3.71) -14/24 5.3.72) -17/14 5.3.73) 41/42 5.3.74) -79/24
5.3.75) -31/30 5.3.76) -6/35 5.3.77) 7/30 5.3.78) 34/48
5.3.79) -99/40 5.3.80) -102/35 5.3.81) -34/21 5.3.82) -53/56
5.3.83) -3/8 5.3.84) -47/40 5.3.85) -11/40 5.3.86) -72/35
5.3.87) -59/56

5.3.100) 11/12 5.3.101) -1/15 5.3.102) 9/20 5.3.103) -12/32
5.3.104) -21/18 5.3.105) 2/21 5.3.106) 39/35 5.3.107) 3/10
5.3.108) -17/21 5.3.109) 34/24 5.3.110) 7/30 5.3.111) -10/12

5.3.112) 41/12 5.3.113) -22/15 5.3.114) -57/18 5.3.115) 77/15
5.3.116) 1/6 5.3.117) -31/12 5.3.118) -1/15 5.3.119) -49/12

5.3.120) 7/20 5.3.121) -68/16 5.3.122) -31/15 5.3.123) 46/8

5.3.124) 15/4 5.3.125) -5/3 5.3.126) -11/6 5.3.127) 19/5
5.3.128) -4/3 5.3.129) -5/4 5.3.130) -2/3 5.3.131) -15/4

5.3.w1) C 5.3.w2) 26 in 5.3.w4) A 5.3.w5) 1/20
5.3.w6) 1/10 5.3.w7) 1/36 5.3.w8) 7/18 5.3.w9) 13/45
5.3.w10) 37/35 5.3.w11) 41/20 5.3.w12) 57/20

Multiplication

5.4.1) 1/4 5.4.2) 2/9 5.4.3) 5/36 5.4.4) 3/16 5.4.5) 15/64 5.4.6) 24/81
5.4.7) 12/25 5.4.8) 20/36 5.4.9) 3/12 5.4.10) 2/12 5.4.11) 12/20 5.4.12) 2/14
5.4.13) 10/21 5.4.14) 4/21 5.4.15) 15/42 5.4.16) 3/10 5.4.17) 2/20 5.4.18) 21/56
5.4.19) 9/35 5.4.20) 2/14 5.4.21) 5/35 5.4.22) 1/24 5.4.23) 6/24 5.4.24) 3/48
5.4.25) 3/21 5.4.26) 6/21 5.4.27) 30/56 5.4.28) 18/28 5.4.29) 5/18 5.4.30) 1/6
5.4.31) 2/30 5.4.32) 15/24 5.4.33) 1/18 5.4.34) 1/24 5.4.35) 10/30 5.4.36) 12/35
5.4.37) 2/15 5.4.38) 6/12 5.4.39) 5/21 5.4.40) 25/48

5.4.41) 45/12 5.4.42) 195/24 5.4.43) 80/20 5.4.44) 135/56 5.4.45) 357/40 5.4.46) 84/24
5.4.47) 276/42 5.4.48) 112/14 5.4.49) 152/40 5.4.50) 160/35 5.4.51) 20/12 5.4.52) 64/15
5.4.53) 189/35 5.4.54) 121/21 5.4.55) 234/56 5.4.56) 153/24 5.4.57) 130/14 5.4.58) 286/42
5.4.59) 154/24 5.4.60) 77/30 5.4.61) 216/35 5.4.62) 49/30 5.4.63) 299/48 5.4.64) 217/40
5.4..65) 189/35 5.4.66) 121/21 5.4.67) 234/56 5.4.68) 189/32 5.4.69) 399/40 5.4.70) 126/20
5.4.71) 243/35 5.4.72) 187/56 5.4.73) 51`/7 5.4.74) 53/8 5.4.75) 355/8 5.4.76) 152/6
5.4.77) 189/8 5.4.78) 356/9 5.4.79) 33/9 5.4.80) 152/7 5.4.81) 52/5 5.4.82) 108/7
5.4.83) 74/9 5.4.84) 154/9

5.4.100) -2/12 5.4.101) 2/15 5.4.102) -1/28 5.4.103) -1/32
5.4.104) -5/18 5.4.105) 8/21 5.4.106) -10/35 5.4.107) 4/10
5.4.108) -6/12 5.4.109) -12/24 5.4.110) 15/30 5.4.111) -2/12

5.4.112) -35/12 5.4.113) 56/15 5.4.114) -35/18 5.4.115) -90/15
5.4.116) 35/6 5.4.117) 26/12 5.4.118) 40/15 5.4.119)-49/12
5.4.120) 117/20 5.4.121) -70/16 5.4.122) 88/15 5.4.123) -65/8

5.4.124) -14/4 5.4.125) 12/3 5.4.126) -5/6 5.4.127) -18/5
5.4.128) 7/3 5.4.129) 26/4 5.4.130) 5/3 5.4.131) -14/4

Division

5.5.1) 2/2 5.5.2) 6/3 5.5.3) 30/6 5.5.4) 12/4 5.5.5) 40/24
5.5.6) 54/36 5.5.7) 20/9 5.5.8) 30/24 5.5.9) 9/4 5.5.10) 12/3
5.5.11) 15/16 5.5.12) 4/7 5.5.13) 15/14 5.5.14) 14/6 5.5.15) 18/35
5.5.16) 6/5 5.5.17) 8/5 5.5.18) 24/49 5.5.19) 15/21 5.5.20) 8/7
5.5.21) 25/7 5.5.22) 3/8 5.5.23) 2/9 5.5.24) 8/18 5.5.25) 9/7
5.5.26) 9/14 5.5.27) 48/35 5.5.28) 24/21 5.5.29) 6/15 5.5.30) 2/3
5.5.31) 12/5 5.5.32) 18/20 5.5.33) 3/6 5.5.34) 6/4 5.5.35) 12/25
5.5.36) 15/28 5.5.37) 10/3 5.5.38) 9/8 5.5.39) 7/15 5.5.40) 30/40
5.5.41) 20/27 5.5.42) 52/90 5.5.43) 64/25 5.5.44) 119/64 5.5.45) 105/136
5.5.46) 63/32 5.5.47) 72/161 5.5.48) 32/49 5.5.49) 64/95 5.5.50) 56/100
5.5.51) 15/16 5.5.52) 20/48 5.5.53) 45/147 5.5.54) 33/77 5.5.55) 91/144
5.5.56) 54/68 5.5.57) 35/72 5.5.58) 132/91 5.5.59) 33/112 5.5.60) 35/66
5.5.61) 90/84 5.5.62) 42/35 5.5.63) 138/104 5.5.64) 56/155 5.5.65) 45/147
5.5.66) 33/77 5.5.67) 91/144 5.5.68) 72/84 5.5.69) 105/152

5.5.70) 45/56 5.5.71) 63/135 5.5.72) 77/136 5.5.73) 21/17
5.5.74) 8/53 5.5.75) 40/71 5.5.76) 48/19 5.5.77) 72/21
5.5.78) 89/36 5.5.79) 27/11 5.5.80) 38/28 5.5.81) 20/13
5.5.82) 18/42 5.5.83) 9/74 5.5.84) 22/63

5.5.100) -8/3 5.5.101) 6/5 5.5.102) -4/5 5.5.103) -4/8
5.5.104) -15/6 5.5.105) 12/14 5.5.106) -14/25 5.5.107) 5/8
5.5.108) -9/8 5.5.109) -18/16 5.5.110) 18/25 5.5.111) -6/4

5.5.112) -20/21 5.5.113) 42/20 5.5.114) -42/15 5.5.115) -50/27
5.5.116) 14/15 5.5.117) 39/8 5.5.118) 25/24 5.5.119) -21/28
5.5.120) 45/52 5.5.121) -28/40 5.5.122) 55/24 5.5.123) -20/26
5.5.124) -14/3 5.5.125) 9/4 5.5.126) -6/5 5.5.127) -10/9
5.5.128) 7/3 5.5.129) 26/4 5.5.130) 5/3 5.5.131) -14/4

5.5.132) $5^{1}/_{2}$ 5.5.133) $1^{1}/_{3}$ 5.5.134) $2^{1}/_{4}$ 5.5.135) 3
5.5.136) 5 5.5.137) $6^{1}/_{2}$ 5.5.138) 15 5.5.139) 3
5.5.140) $4^{3}/_{7}$ 5.5.141) 25 5.5.142) 7 5.5.143) 4
5.5.144) 7 5.5.145) $12\ ^{4}/_{6}$ 5.5.146) $10^{1}/_{4}$ 5.5.147) $9^{2}/_{7}$
5.5.148) $11\ ^{1}/_{5}$ 5.5.149) 19 ¾ 5.5.150) $12\ ^{2}/_{8}$ 5.5.151) $3\ ^{2}/_{5}$
5.5.152) $21\ ^{2}/_{3}$ 5.5.153) $21\ ^{2}/_{4}$ 5.5.154) $42\ ^{1}/_{3}$ 5.5.155) $11\ ^{1}/_{6}$
5.5.156) $25\ ^{3}/_{5}$ 5.5.157) $3\ ^{2}/_{4}$ 5.5.158) 11 5.5.159) 55
5.5.160) 27 5.5.161) 18 ¼

5.5.162) 5 5.5.163) 4 5.5.164) 5 5.5.165) 1/3
5.5.166) 1/5 5.5.167) ½ 5.5.168) 1/15 5.5.169) 1/3
5.5.170) 1/5 5.5.171) 1/15 5.5.172) 1/7 5.5.173) ¼
5,5,174) 1/7 5.5.175) 2/38 5.5.176) 1/11 5.5.177) 1/7
5.5.178) 25 5.5.179) 2/7 5.5.180) 3/2 5.5.181) 1/3
5.5.182) 2 5.5.183) 22 5.5.184) 1/42 5.5.185) 3/8
5.5.186) 16/3 5.5.187) 7/2 5.5.188) 11 5.5.189) 1/55
5.5.190) 1/27 5.5.191) 1/21

5.5.w1) 1/18 5.5.w2) 1/24 5.5.w3) 136 5.5.w4) 48/5 hrs
5.5.w5) 11/4 5.5.w6) 1 5.5.w7) 32/15 5.5.w8) 132
5.5.w9) 8 ¼ 5.5.w10) 7 ½ IN 5.5.W11) 10 5.5.W12) $7\ ^{1}/_{2}$

Inequalities

5.6.1) = 5.6.2) > 5.6.3) < 5.6.4) > 5.6.5) < 5.6.6) <
5.6.7) > 5.6.8) > 5.6.9) > 5.6.10) < 5.6.11) = 5.6.12) =
5.6.13) > 5.6.14) > 5.6.15) < 5.6.16) > 5.6.17) < 5.6.18) <
5.6.19) < 5.6.20) < 5.6.21) < 5.6.22) > 5.6.23) < 5.6.24) >

5.6.25) < 5.6.26) > 5.6.27) < 5.6.28) > 5.6.29) < 5.6.30) >
5.6.31) < 5.6.32) > 5.6.33) < 5.6.34) > 5.6.35) > 5.6.36) <
5.6.37) > 5.6.38) < 5.6.39) < 5.6.40) < 5.6.41) = 5.6.42) <
5.6.43) < 5.6.44) < 5.6.45) < 5.6.46) < 5.6.47) < 5.6.48) <

5.6.66) < 5.6.67) < 5.6.68) < 5.6.69) < 5.6.70) > 5.6.71) >
5.6.72) < 5.6.73) > 5.6.74) > 5.6.75) < 5.6.76) < 5.6.77) <
5.6.78) < 5.6.79) < 5.6.80) > 5.6.81) < 5.6.82) > 5.6.83) <
5.6.84) < 5.6.85) <

5.6.119)> 5.6.120) > 5.6121) < 5.6.122) < 5.6.123) > 5.6.124) >
5.6.125) < 5.6.126) > 5.6.127) > 5.6.128) < 5.6.129) < 5.6.130) >
5.6.131) > 5.6.132) < 5.6.133) < 5.6.134) < 5.6.135) > 5.6.136) <
5.6.137) > 5.6.138) > 5.6.139) < 5.6.140) < 5.6.141) > 5.6.142) <
5.6.143) < 5.6.144) > 5.6.145) < 5.6.146) < 5.6.147) > 5.6.148) >
5.6.149) < 5.6.150) <

5.6.251) < 5.6.252) < 5.6.253) > 5.6.254) > 5.6.255) < 5.6.256) >
5.6.257) < 5.6.258) < 5.6.259) < 5.6.260) < 5.6.261) < 5.6.262) <
5.6.263) < 5.6.264) < 5.6.265) < 5.6.266) < 5.6.267) < 5.6.268) >
5.6.269) < 5.6.270) < 5.6.271) < 5.6.272) > 5.6.273) > 5.6.274) <
5.6.275) < 5.6.276) < 5.6.277) < 5.6.278) < 5.6.279) < 5.6.280) <
5.6.281) < 5.6.282) < 5.6.283) > 5.6.284) < 5.6.285) < 5.6.286) >
5.6.287) > 5.6.288) > 5.6.289) > 5.6.290) > 5.6.291) > 5.6.292) <
5.6.293) < 5.6.294) <

5.6.w1) Mike 5.6.w2) C 5.6.w3) A 5.6.w4) C 5.6.w5) Guppy
5.6.w6) C 5.6.w7) C 5.6.w8) B 5.6.w9) B

5.7.1) $^{14}/_{10}$ or 1 $^{4}/_{10}$, 140% 5.7.2) $^{61}/_{10}$ or 6 $^{1}/_{10}$, 610% 5.7.3) $^{267}/_{100}$ or 2 $^{67}/_{100}$, 267%
5.7.4) $^{345}/_{100}$ or 3 $^{45}/_{100}$, 345% 5.7.5) $^{1878}/_{1000}$ or 1 $^{878}/_{1000}$, 187.8% 5.7.6) $^{935}/_{100}$ or 9 $^{35}/_{100}$, 935%
5.7.7) $^{14236}/_{100}$ or 142 $^{36}/_{100}$, 14236% 5.7.8) $^{225}/_{100}$ or 2 $^{25}/0_{10}$, 225%
5.7.9) $^{4325}/_{1000}$ or 4$^{325}/_{1000}$,432.5% 5.7.10) $^{1345/}{}_{100}$ or 13 $^{45}/_{100}$,1345% 5.7.11) $^{71}/_{100}$ or 71%
5.7.12) $^{766}/_{100}$ or 7 $^{66}/_{100}$, 766% 5.7.13) $^{3578}/_{1000}$ or3 $^{578}/_{1000}$, 357.8% 5.7.14) $^{55}/_{10000}$ or ,0.55%
5.7.15) $^{37}/_{100}$, 37% 5.7.16) $^{1235}/_{100}$ or 12 $^{35}/_{100}$,1235% 5.7.17) $^{32}/_{100,}$ 32%
5.7.18) $^{16}/_{1000,}$, 1.6% 5.7.19) $^{113}/_{10}$ or 11 $^{3}/_{10}$, 113% 5.7.20) $^{1}/_{10}$, 1000%
5.7.21) $^{27676}/_{10000}$ or 2 $^{7676}/_{10000}$, 276.76% 5.7.22) $^{6257}/_{1000}$ or 6 $^{256}/_{1000}$, 625.7%
5.7.23) $^{1735}/_{100}$ or 17 $^{35}/_{100}$, 1735% 5.7.24) $^{125}/_{1000}$, 12.5% 5.7.25) $^{91}/_{10}$ or 9 $^{1}/_{10}$, 910%
5.7.26) $^{346}/_{100}$ or 3 $^{46}/_{100}$,346% 5.7.27) $^{399}/_{100}$ or 3 $^{99}/_{1000}$, 399% 5.7.28) $^{101}/_{100}$ or 1 $^{1}/_{100}$, 101%
5.7.29) $^{341}/_{100}$ or 3 $^{41}/_{100}$, 341% 5.7.30) $^{125}/_{1000}$, 12.5%

5.8.1) 0.04, 4% 5.8.2) 0.27, 27% 5.8.3) 0.013, 1.3% 5.8.4) 0.3, 30%
5.8.5) 0.67, 67% 5.8.6) 0.012, 1.2% 5.8.7) 1.27, 127% 5.8.8) 0.03, 3%
5.8.9) 0.034, 3.4% 5.8.10) 1.7, 170% 5.8.11) 3.04, 304% 5.8.12) 1.002, 100.2%
5.8.13) 0.6,60% 5.8.14) 2.3, 230% 5.8.15) 3.5, 350% 5.8.16) 0.04, 4%
5.8.17) 4.01, 401% 5.8.18) 2.047, 204.7% 5.8.19) 2.137, 213.7% 5.8.20) 3.4, 340%
5.8.21) 16.7, 1670% 5.8.22) 3.003, 300.3% 5.8.23) 0.89, 89% 5.8.24) 1.27, 127%
5.8.25) 0.14, 14% 5.8.26) 0.006, 0.6% 5.8.27) 0.29, 29% 5.8.28) 0.009, 0.9%
5.8.29) 16.23, 1623% 5.8.30) 1.045, 104.5%

5.8.31) 0.7, 67% 5.8.32) 0.7, 67% 5.8.33) 0.7, 67% 5.8.34) 0.5, 50%
5.8.35) 1.1, 114% 5.8.36) 2.3, 233% 5.8.37) 0.8, 75% 5.8.38) 0.2, 20%
5.8.39) 0.3, 29% 5.8.40) 1.3, 133% 5.8.41) 0.2, 17% 5.8.42) 0.8, 80%
5.8.43) 0.6, 57% 5.8.44) 0.3, 33% 5.8.45) 0.2, 22% 5.8.46) 1, 100%
5.8.47) 1.3, 133% 5.8.48) 0.3, 33% 5.8.49) 1.4, 140% 5.8.50) 1.7, 167%
5.8.51) 0.5, 50% 5.8.52) 0.4, 40% 5.8.53) 1, 100% 5.8.54) 2.5, 250%
5.8.55) 1.5, 150% 5.8.56) 1.5, 150% 5.8.57) 0.4, 43% 5.8.58) 0.3, 33%
5.8.59) 1.2, 120% 5.8.60) 0.6, 60%

5.8.61) 36/100, 0.36 5.8.62) 1$^{28}/_{100}$, 1.28 5.8.63) 2/100, 0.02, 5.8.64) 65/100,0.65
5.8.65) 0.12, 12/100 5.8.66) 39/100, 0.39 5.8.67) 1$^{61}/_{100}$, 1.16 5.8.68) 23/100, 0.23
5.8.69) 51/100, 0.51 5.8.70) 1 $^{46}/_{100}$, 1.46 5.8.71) 4 $^{36}/_{100}$, 4.36 5.8.72) 2 $^{25}/_{100}$, 2.25
5.8.73) 87/100, 0.87 5.8.74) 1 $^{77}/_{100}$, 1.77 5.8.75) 2 $^{18}/_{100}$, 2.18 5.8.76) 4/100, 0.04

5.8.77) 1 $^{69}/_{100}$, 1.69 5.8.78) 47/100, 0.47 5.8.79) 3 $^{1}/_{100}$, 3.01 5.8.80) 2 $^{59}/_{100}$, 2.59
5.8.81) 3 $^{26}/_{100}$, 3.26 5.8.82) 2 $^{69}/_{100}$, 2.69 5.8.83) 2 $^{51}/_{100}$, 2.51 5.8.84) 78/100, 0.78

5.8.w1) C 5.8.W2) $199.26 5.8.W3) $3.26 5.8.W4) 165
5.8.W5) 45 5.8.W6) 0.17 5.8.W7) D 5.8.W8) 200
5.8.W9) $6.58 5.8.W10) $6,000 5.8.W11) Store A 5.8.w12) $15.60
5.8.w13) D 5.8.w14) 11% 5.8.w15) 22% 5.8.w16) C

5.10.w1) B 5.10.w2) B 5.10.w3) D 5.10.w4) C 5.10.w5) C 5.10.w6) C
5.10.w7) A 5.10.w8) A 5.10.w9) A 5.10.w10) A 5.10.w11) B 5.10.w12) C
5.10.w13) B 5.10.w14) D 5.10.w15) B 5.10.w16) B 5.10.w17) A 5.10.w18) D
5.10.w19) B 5.10.w20) B,C 5.10.w21) B 5.10.w22) B 5.10.w23) B 5.10.w24) C
5.10.w25) A 5.10.w26) D 5.10.w27) A 5.10.w28) 0.85 5.10.w29) C 5.10.w30) 67/6
5.10.w31) 29/50 5.10.w32) C 5.10.w33) B 5.10.w34) 20% 5.10.w35) 42%
5.10.w36) A 5.10.w37) 0.07 5.10.w38) C 5.10.w39) 11.25 Lbs 5.10.w40) C
5.10.w41) 62.5% 5.10.w42) 2 $^{1}\backslash_{4}$, 2 $^{3}/_{8}$, 2 $^{2}/_{3}$, 2 $^{5}/_{6}$ 5.10.w43) D 5.10.w44) B
5.10.w45) 25% 5.10.w46) $^{12}/_{20}$ or $^{3}/_{5}$ 5.10.w47) 2.05 5.10.w48) 22.2%
5.10.w49) C 5.10.W50) B 5.10.W51) 96% 5.10.W52) 20%
5.10.W53) C 5.10.W54) 10% 5.10.W55) 135 5.10.w56) 156%, 1 $^{3}/_{5}$, 1.70
5.10.w57) B 5.10.w58) 57/40 5.10.w59) 5 5.10.w60) 25
5.10.w61) $37 5.10.w62) 0.013, 1/9, 12%, $^{1}/_{6}$, 5.10.w63) 50
5.10.w64) 1.4, .36, .23, -0.57, -1.12) 5.10.w65) $25.30 5.10.w66) C
5.10.w67) Yes 5.10.w68) -0.086, 1/13, 0.13, 52% 5.10.w69) 18.6
5.10.w70) 126 5.10.w71) 40 5.10.w72) D 5.10.W73) -4.50, 350%, 3 $^{2}/_{3}$, 850/200
5.10.w74) 3/5, 55%, 0.5, 4/9 5.10.w75) $22, 800 5.10.w76) $50.00
5.10.w77) $1198.86 5.10.w78) $6083.26

6.0 GRAPHING

6.1) 4 6.2) 350 6.3)B 6.4)D 6.5) A 6.6) 500LBS
6.7) B 6.8) 20 MIN 6.9) A 6.10) C 6.11) D 6.12) B
6.13) C 6.14) C 6.15) A 6.16) C 6.17) D 6.18) C
6.19) B 6.20) 5 6.21) 5 6.22) 10 6.23) 55 6.24) 10
6.25) C 6.26) B 6.27) 1 6.28) 44 6.29) A 6.30) D
6.31) B 6.32) C 6.33) C 6.34) (5,5) 6.35) A 6.36) (2,2)
6.37) C 6.38) C 6.39) D 6.40) B 6.41) D 6.42) B
6.43) 3 6.44) C 6.45) (1 ¼, ¼), (2 ¾, $^{3}/_{4}$), (3 ¼,2 ½)
6.46) a=(600,600), AND b=(2000,1200) 6.47) 120 Lbs 6.48) (-8,6)
6.49) C 6.50) Independent {3, 5, 7, 9, 11}, dependent { 20, 40, 60, 80, 100}
6.51) C 6.52) C 6.53) C 6.54) 40 Lbs 6.55) A 6.56) B
6.57) C 6.58) (2,3) 6.59) C 6.60) C 6.61) A 6.62) 200
6.63) B 6.64) 2 6.65) D 6.66) D 6.67) C 6.68) D
6.69) C 6.70) A 6.71) C 6.72) B 6.73) A 6.74)(6,30)
6.75) 24 6.76) B 6.77) C

7.0 MEASURING

7.1) 3 CM 7.2) 6IN 7.3) A=1IN, B=2IN, C=2$^{1}/_{2}$IN, D=$^{1}/_{2}$ IN 7.4) 18
7.5) ½ IN7.6) 3:007.7) D 7.8) D 7.9) B 7.10) 30
7.11) D 7.12) C 7.13) B 7.14) 96 7.15) 175 7.16) 17
7.17) 340 7.18) C 7.19) C 7.20) C 7.21) C 7.22) D
7.23) A 7.24) B 7.25) C 7.26) D 7.27) C 7.28) A

7.29) A 7.30) C 7.31) C 7.32) C 7.33) A 7.34) B
7.35) A 7.36) A 7.37) A 7.38) D 7.39) C 7.40) C
7.41) D 7.42) C 7.43) D 7.45) 1 in 7.46) 92.5 7.47) 77.5
7.48) 1 7.49) 1 ½ 7.50) 3 ½

7.51) 4:35 7.52) 7:10 7.53) 4:25 7.54) 4:30 7.55) 6:25 7.56) 10:05
7.57) (30,30) 7.58) C 7.59) C

8.0 STATISTICS

8.1)A 8.2) A 8.3) Sugar and Mint 8.4) B 8.5) 10/30 or 1/3
8.6) 2/7 8.7) 6/12 or 1/2 8.8) 49/105 8.9) 1/24 8.10) 112/157
8.11) 6/14 8.12) 12/12 8.13) 1/3 8.14) 5/7
8.15) Mean = 56, median = 60, mode = 60
8.16) Mean = 88.25, Median = 80, Mode = no mode
8.17) Mean = 48.75, Median = 52.5, Mode = no mode
8.18) Mean = 28.75, Median = 30, Mode = no mode
8.19) Mean = 4.4, Median = 4, Mode = 4
8.20) Mean =16, Median = 15, Mode = 15
8.21) Mean = 6, Median = 6, Mode = no mode
8.22) Mean = 7.29, Median = 3, Mode = 2, 3, 5
8.23) Mean = 41.25, Median = 42.5, Mode = no mode
8.24) Mean = 46.25, Median = 47.5, Mode = no mode
8.25) Mean = 10.75, Median = 9, Mode = 8
8.26) Mean = 56.7, Median = 51, Mode = 36
8.27) D 8.28) 426 8.29) C 8.30) C 8.31) 7 8.32) C
8.33) C 8.34) 372 8.39) 372

8.40) A 8.41) ¼ 8.42) D 8.43) 8/36 8.44) 6/6 or 1 8.45) ¼
8.46) 1 8.47) 109.2 8.48) C 8.49) 0.38.50) D 8.51) A
8.52) C 8.53) A 8.54) B 8.55) A 8.56) ½ 8.57) 56/100
8.58) 6 8.59) B 8.60) 99 8.61) C 8.62) 3/12 or ¼
8.63) 36/100 or 9/25 8.64) 16/63 8.65) 4/25 8.66) C 8.67) 30/90 or 1/3
8.68) 16/64 or ¼ 8.69) 2

9.0 Order of Operations

9.1.1) 50 9.1.2) 42 9.1.3) 60 9.1.4) -39 9.1.5) 329.1.6) 3
9.1.7) 42 9.1.8) 25 9.1.9) 5 9.1.10) 30 9.1.11) 6 9.1.12) 4
9.1.13) -28 9.1.14) 15 9.1.15) 10 9.1.16) 6 9.1.17) 6 9.1.18) 6
9.1.19) 40 9.1.20) 57

9.1.21) 45 9.1.22) 30 9.1.23) 45 9.1.24) 5/10 or ½
9.1.25) 22 9.1.26) 3 9.1.27) 7 9.1.28) 46 9.1.29) 12 9.1.30) 27
9.1.31) 1 9.1.32) 3 9.1.33) 24 9.1.34) 1 9.1.35) 12 9.1.36) 130

9.1.37) 3 9.1.38) 20 9.1.39) -7 9.1.40) -2 9.1.41) 9 9.1.42) -7
9.1.43) 9 9.1.44) 31 9.1.45) 34 9.1.46) -5 9.1.47) 26 9.1.48) 4
9.1.49) 18 9.1.50) -8 9.1.51) -14 9.1.52) 16 9.1.53) 30 9.1.54) 38
9.1.55) 10 9.1.56) -1 9.1.57) -12 9.1.58) 15 9.1.59) 24 9.1.60) 12

9.1.61) 6 9.1.62) 25 9.1.63) -1 9.1.64) 3 9.1.65) 23 9.1.66) 23
9.1.67) 2 9.1.68) 33 9.1.69) -7 9.1.70) 1 9.1.71) 22 9.1.72) 2

9.1.73) 2 9.1.74) -11 9.1.75) 0 9.1.76) 24 9.1.77) 62 9.1.78) 65
9.1.79) -8 9.1.80) 1

9.1.81) 14 9.1.82) 7 9.1.83) -8 9.1.84) 3
9.1.85) 9 9.1.86) 5 9.1.87) 5 9.1.88) 2 9.1.89) -18 9.1.90) -5
9.1.91) 4 9.1.92) -18 9.1.93) 1 9.1.94) -60 9.1.95) 28 9.1.96) 160

9.1.97) 2577 9.1.98) -3 9.1.99) -32 9.1.100)68 9.1.101)260 9.1.102) 57
9.1.103) B 9.1.104) -19 9.1.105) A 9.1.106) 69 9.1.107) C 9.1.108)B
9.1.109) A

9.2.1) 50 9.2.2) 58

Algebra

10.1.1) -2 10.1.2) 10 10.1.3) 4 10.1.4) 18 10.1.5) -16 10.1.6) -5
10.1.7) -1 10.1.8) -10 10.1.9) -2 10.1.10) -12 10.1.11) -6 10.1.12) -1
10.1.13) 25 10.1.14) 11 10.1.15) 2 10.1.16) -9 10.1.17) 13 10.1.18) -10
10.1.19) 1 10.1.20) -18 10.1.21) 8 10.1.22) 8 10.1.23) 10 10.1.24) 0

10.1.25) -1/2 10.1.26) -7/5 10.1.27) -10/7 10.1.28) -10/9
10.1.29) -17/4 10.1.30) -2/6 10.1.31) -2/4 10.1.32) -15/9
10.1.33) -19/3 10.1.34) 4/10 10.1.35) 1 10.1.36) 4/10
10.1.37) -10/8 10.1.38) 14/15 10.1.39) 13/14 10.1.40) -12/4
10.1.41) 7/9 10.1.42) -13/12 10.1.43) 3 10.1.44) 5/6
10.1.45) 7/3 10.1.46) -7/5 10.1.47) 14/8 10.1.48) -19/2
10.1.49) 5/2 10.1.50) -1 10.1.51) -10/4 10.1.52) 17/3
10.1.53) 2/9 10.1.54) -3/12 10.1.55) 1 10.1.56) -17/5
10.1.57) 5/18 10.1.58) 5/3 10.1.59) -15/6 10.1.60) 1
10.1.61) -7/4 10.1.62) 0 10.1.63) -10/12 10.1.64) -16/14
10.1.65) -12/7 10.1.66) -11/15

10.1.w1) -3 10.1.w2) -2 10.1.w3) 12 10.1.w4) -6/5
10.1.w5) C 10.1.w6) 6 10.1.w7) C 10.1.w8) B
10.1.w9) 11.1/3.4 10.1.w10) C 10.1.w11) B 10.1.w12) A
10.1.w13) B 10.1.w14) C 10.1.w15) B 10.1.w16) 3629
10.1.w17) D 10.1.w18) B 10.1.w19) C 10.1.w20) 215

10.2.1) X>7/2 10.2.2) X≤-11/5 10.2.3) X>1/4 10.2.4) X≥-3/12
10.2.5) X≤9/12 10.2.6) X≥-7/10 10.2.7) X≥3/15 10.2.8) X<-9/11
10.2.9) X<-1 10.2.10) X<7/8 10.2.11) x≥4/9 10.2.12) X>-5/15
10.2.13) X≤1/5 10.2.14) X≤-1/4 10.2.15) X<5 10.2.16) X≤3/13
10.2.17) X<11/7 10.2.18) X≥9/8 10.2.19) X>16/3 10.2.20) X≤-9/16
10.2.21) X>7/4 10.2.22) X≥0 10.2.23) X<29/12 10.2.24) X≥9/3

10.2.w1) D 10.2.w2) C

10.3.1) 4 10.3.2) 18 10.3.3) 13 10.3.4) -13 10.3.5) 7 10.3.6) -11
10.3.7) -20 10.3.8) 24 10.3.9) -32 10.3.10) 28 10.3.11) -35 10.3.12) -22
10.3.13) 50 10.3.14) 85 10.3.15) 14 10.3.16) -63 10.3.17) 22 10.3.18) 27
10.3.19) 19 10.3.20) 10 10.3.21) -15 10.3.22) -48 10.3.23) -12 10.3.24) -45

10.3.w1) B

10.4.1) $2(5)^{1/2}$	10.4.2) $(34)^{1/2}$	10.4.3) $(5)^{1/2}$	10.4.4) $2(10)^{1/2}$
10.4.5) $(13)^{1/2}$	10.4.6) $(26)^{1/2}$	10.4.7) $4(5)^{1/2}$	10.4.8) $4(2)^{1/2}$
10.4.9) $(391)^{1/2}$	10.4.10) $4(14)^{1/2}$	10.4.11) $(73)^{1/2}$	10.4.12) $2(13)^{1/2}$
10.4.13) $2(2)^{1/2}$	10.4.14) $(85)^{1/2}$	10.4.15) $(135)^{1/2}$	10.4.16) $4(14)^{1/2}$
10.4.17) $4(5)^{1/2}$	10.4.18) $(55)^{1/2}$	10.4.19) $4(10)^{1/2}$	10.4.20) $8(2)^{1/2}$

10.4.w1) A	10.4.w2)D	10.4.w3)B	10.4.w4) \$10/Day
10.4.w5) A	10.4.w6) C	10.4.w7) \$55.00	10.4.w8) 2 Gal/Hr.

If you don't get the correct answer, and want an explanation on how to work the problem, go to YouTube and type in "MMT" then the problem number. An example would be, MMT 3.9.w12,. The video will show you how to work problem 3.9.w12.

For one on one tutoring via skype at $35.00/Hr.; contact me at marksmathtutoring@yahoo.com

Made in the USA
Middletown, DE
04 May 2021